D0070805

ALAN LOMAX

ALAN LOMAX

SELECTED WRITINGS 1934-1997

Edited by Ronald D. Cohen

With Introductory Essays by
Gage Averill, Matthew Barton, Ronald D. Cohen,
Ed Kahn, and Andrew L. Kaye

WITHDRAWN

Routledge
Taylor & Francis Group

NEW YORK AND LONDON

All writings and photographs by Alan Lomax are copyright © 2003 by Alan Lomax estate.

The material on "Sources and Permissions" on pp. 350–51 constitutes a continuation of this copyright page.

All of the writings by Alan Lomax in this book are reprinted as they originally appeared, without emendation, except for small changes to regularize spelling.

Paperback Edition first published in 2005.

Published in 2005 by
Routledge
Taylor & Francis Group
270 Madison Avenue
New York, NY 10016

Published in Great Britain by
Routledge
Taylor & Francis Group
2 Park Square
Milton Park, Abingdon
Oxon OX14 4RN

© 2005 by Taylor & Francis Group, LLC
Routledge is an imprint of Taylor & Francis Group

Printed in the United States of America on acid-free paper
10 9 8 7 6 5 4 3 2 1

International Standard Book Number-10: 0-415-93855-4 (Softcover)
International Standard Book Number-13: 978-0-415-93855-6 (Softcover)
Library of Congress Card Number 2002152034

No part of this book may be reprinted, reproduced, transmitted, or utilized in any form by any electronic, mechanical, or other means, now known or hereafter invented, including photocopying, microfilming, and recording, or in any information storage or retrieval system, without written permission from the publishers.

Trademark Notice: Product or corporate names may be trademarks or registered trademarks, and are used only for identification and explanation without intent to infringe.

Library of Congress Cataloging-in-Publication Data

Lomax, Alan, 1915–2002
[Selections]
    Alan Lomax : selected writings, 1934–1997 / edited by Ronald D. Cohen; with introductory essays by Gage Averill, Matthew Barton, Ronald D. Cohen, Ed Kahn, and Andrew Kaye.
        p. cm.
    Includes bibliographical references (p.) and index.
    ISBN 0-415-93854-6 (hardcover : alk. paper) 0-415-93855-4 (paperback : alk. paper)
    1. Folk music--United States--History and criticism. 2. Lomax, Alan, 1915–2002. I. Cohen, Ronald D., 1940– II. Title.

ML3551 .L65 2003
781.62'00973--dc21   2002152034

Taylor & Francis Group
is the Academic Division of T&F Informa plc.

Visit the Taylor & Francis Web site at
http://www.taylorandfrancis.com

and the Routledge Web site at
http://www.routledge-ny.com

Contents

V. Final Writings

General Introduction

by Ronald D. Cohen

Alan Lomax lived a long and exceptionally fruitful and influential life. Born on January 31, 1915, he survived until July 19, 2002, and for seven decades he substantially contributed to the collection, study, understanding, and promotion of "folk music," first in the United States, then throughout the world. As a teenager he accompanied his father on southern collecting trips, and even managed to publish his first article before turning twenty, the start of a most prolific career. Through his numerous articles and books, we are able to gain some understanding of his musical values, interests, and ideas as they continued to develop into his eighth decade. *Alan Lomax: Selected Writings 1934–1997* is an attempt to make available a judicious selection of his work covering his entire career, including the highly theoretical studies by the 1970s. We have not included book passages, since these should be read as part of the larger works, and are also more readily accessible. But many of these shorter writings—while most, but not all, were published—are difficult, if not impossible to obtain, and are presented here as originally printed or written. There has been virtually no attempt to edit, delete, update, or further elaborate, except in the introductory essays to each section or when absolutely/necessary.

Since there is currently no full biography of Alan Lomax, but only scattered brief studies and interpretations, we have tried to pull together enough information in the section introductions, by Ed Kahn, Andrew Kaye, Matthew Barton, Ronald Cohen, and Gage Averill, to give a general overview of his varied activities and contributions, as well as a nuanced explication of his actions and ideas. These essays are only the beginning, however, as considerably more work will have to be done before a "complete" picture will emerge of his rich and complex, as well as controversial, life. Thankfully, Nolan Porterfield has explored the careers of his father in *Last Cavalier: The Life and Times of John A. Lomax* (Urbana: University of Illinois Press, 1996), which includes substantial information on Alan's life through the mid–1940s. Otherwise, the story is far from complete, but we hope this volume will provide enough information to serve as a stimulus for future studies. In addition, there are the most helpful notes to the ongoing Rounder Records Lomax Collection reissue series, eventually scheduled to number 150 or so CDs, which extend our knowledge of his varied musical life. Alan Lomax was not only a collector, writer, and ethnomusicologist, but also a producer, performer, radio personality, promoter, filmmaker, and political activist, particularly in the United States and the British Isles. Indeed, his political life often consisted of behind-the-scenes activities, but he consistently held to a left-of-center agenda. Not all aspects of his life are touched on in his writings, but a lot can be discerned from other source materials, such as the Lomax Archives, the Lomax family collection in the Center for American History at the University of Texas, and the collections of the Archive of Folk Culture, American Folklife Center of the Library of Congress.

I wish to thank Richard Carlin, our most supportive and helpful editor at Routledge, for perceiving the wisdom of this book from its inception, and seeing it through to publication. Anna Lomax Chairetakis first recommended that Routledge might be interested, and she has been consistently helpful in providing her usual guidance, wisdom, and support as the project proceeded. Matt Barton has not only participated in writing two of the introductory essays, but he also selected the illustrations, with the assistance of Nathan Salsburg and the Lomax Archives staff, and the contents of the Rounder sampler CD, and in numerous other ways assisted in providing the requisite publications and bibliographic information, without which this volume could not have been published. Bill Nowlin at Rounder Records understood the value of a sampler CD and guaranteed its production and inclusion. Andrew Kaye and Gage Averill have been delightful to work with. Unfortunately, my good friend Ed Kahn died before he was able to relish his essay as a vital part of this book. His death is a great loss to folklore studies. I also want to personally thank the library staff at Indiana University Northwest, particularly Anne Koehler, for her assistance in locating rare publications.

Part I

1934–1950: The Early Collecting Years

Introduction by Ed Kahn

When Alan Lomax burst out of Texas onto the folklore scene, he came out with the force of a powerful Texas Norther. By the age of eighteen, he was a force to be reckoned with. In the years between 1933 and 1950, he established himself as a collector, popularizer, performer, writer, and folklore theoretician, as well as a behind-the-scenes political activist. Any of these avenues would have been sufficient for a fruitful career, but Lomax chose to pursue them all. In the years that followed, we can see the fruits of the seeds he sowed during these early years of his career. In his early work, we see his initial interest in folksong, folk music theory, dance, folk narrative and the relationship between these expressive materials and the broader cultural context.

Alan's story is amazing not only in that his interests and talents were so wide ranging, but for the fact that at the age of eighteen he virtually became an equal with his sixty-five-year-old father. John Lomax had made initial contributions to the study of American folksong, but that was far in his past. Now, in his golden years, he embarked on a second career in folklore and Alan unwittingly became his partner and then emerged as his own man.

In 1930, at the age of fifteen, Alan entered the University of Texas and before the school year was out, he applied for a scholarship to Harvard for the next year. Following his year at Harvard, he moved back to Austin and lived with his father while once more attending the University of Texas. In June 1933, he left Texas with his father to begin an extended field trip collecting folksongs that ultimately were deposited in the Library of Congress.[1]

This initial fieldwork was recorded on a Dictaphone machine, which eventually was replaced with a portable disc recording machine. By the time they reached Washington, D.C., in August of 1933, they had col-

1

lected some hundred songs on twenty-five aluminum and fifteen celluloid discs. Carl Engel, chief of the music division of the Library of
Congress, was so anxious to publicize any activity of the folksong
archives that he arranged an event in the Coolidge Auditorium of the
Library. Alan discussed their collecting activities and played discs from
the summer's activities. Alan's first publication was a broad discussion
of the 1933 field trip. This was published in the *Southwest Review* in the
winter of 1934. The focus of the article was on Negro folksongs as the
title, "Collecting Folk-Songs of the Southern Negro" suggests. From
1933 forward, Lomax's folklore career was in full swing. He did, however,
manage to complete a bachelor's degree from the University of Texas in
1936.[2]

As a collector, Alan took down interviews on a typewriter early on,
eventually using the most sophisticated tape recorders. He realized that
recording interviews allowed him to preserve not only the words that
were spoken or sung, but the context and style of a performance, too.
Eventually, he augmented his fieldwork to also include filming of some
of his collecting experiences. He elaborates on the advantages of recording fieldwork in the introduction to *Our Singing Country*. He points out
the limited scope of collecting without the use of the recorder. As he says,
the folk song " . . . collector with pen and notebook can capture only the
outline. . . ."[3]

After completing his degree from the University of Texas, he and his
wife, Elizabeth Lyttleton Harold, went to Haiti to do fieldwork. He published an article in the *Southwest Review* in January of 1938 detailing some
of this fieldwork. In this article, "Haitian Journey" we see for the first
time Lomax's interest in the broader context of folk song as well as his
emerging interest in dance and narrative. The year following the publication of this article on Haitian folklore, Lomax enrolled at Columbia
University for graduate work in anthropology. While he never completed
an advanced degree in anthropology, the rest of his career is clearly
marked by this experience as he increasingly worked as an ethnomusicologist with a strong anthropological bias.[4]

In 1937, Lomax was appointed director of the Archive of American
Folk-Song at the Library of Congress. This twenty-one-year-old kid was
a seasoned veteran, having done extensive fieldwork and published, with
his father, both *American Ballads and Folksongs (1934)* and *Negro Folk Songs
as Sung by Lead Belly* (1936). Lomax set out to record folksongs from
across America. The exact number of recordings in the Archives at that

time is unclear, but on various occasions Lomax cites the number of recordings. In the introduction to *Our Singing Country*, he says there are over four thousand aluminum and acetate discs in the Archive. In an interview in 1942, Lomax states that there are over 20,000 songs on records in the Archive. In the spring of that same year, under the direction of Lomax, a checklist of English language holdings of the Archive was published in mimeographed form as a *Check-list of recorded songs in the English Language in the Archive of American Folk Song to July, 1940*. In the introduction Alan makes reference to his historic recording expeditions of 1937–39, which took him to Kentucky, Indiana, Ohio, Michigan, and Vermont. These recordings are all included in the Check-list. This publication was important for it was organized by song title as well as geographically.[5]

Lomax had a way with informants. He knew how to put them at ease and gain their confidence so they felt comfortable offering their material to the stranger who came to value what they had perhaps never considered valuable. One of the things that set Lomax apart from many other fieldworkers of the time was his innate understanding of the dynamic quality of folksongs. He knew that folksongs were born, had a life, and then faded into obscurity. Lomax states his case succinctly in his 1942 interview with John T. Frederick on "Of Men and Books," a radio program from Northwestern University: "our folk stock is not stagnant, some songs are dying, some are on their last legs, but out of them and beyond them new songs are growing up better adapted to survive in our seas of restless and eternally unsatisfied people."[6] This statement underscores Lomax's approach to collecting. He wanted to collect what the informants had to offer. Many earlier collectors were rooted in antiquities and searched for survivals rather that repertoires of their informants. As a result, Lomax recorded much topical material that has not stood the test of time. In preparing for the publication of *Our Singing Country*, the Lomaxes sifted through hundreds of recordings in the Library of Congress archives that were made between 1933 and 1939 and selected a couple of hundred songs for inclusion. What is especially interesting about the volume is that many songs are introduced by a transcription of the informant's thoughts about the material. Also, many of the songs lacked pedigree, which to my mind is important as it underscores the willingness of Lomax to include folksongs that were new or not yet considered folksongs. It took guts for him to publish this material because it did not conform to the academic standards of the time.

Our Singing Country was a joint effort between the Lomaxes and Ruth Crawford Seeger, who was musical editor of the volume. Bess Lomax Hawes, Alan's sister, stated in a paper given at a commemoration of the 100th anniversary of Ruth Crawford's birth, that the collaboration on this volume opened Alan's eyes to musical analysis in a way that he had not previously focused. While Alan had concentrated on the context of the material, Ruth took the recording as a document that could not be questioned. Subsequently, in Alan's work, he, too, gained an added respect for the recorded document and rigorous musical analysis of the recorded material.[7]

On many of these early radio presentations, Lomax also emerges as a performer. By the late 1930s, Lomax was intimately involved in radio. He produced a series for CBS's School of the Air as well as a series called *Back Where I Come From*. These shows introduced a national audience to numerous artists who later received wide recognition. Among those showcased were Woody Guthrie, Josh White, Burl Ives, and Pete Seeger. Other established names like Leadbelly and the Golden Gate Quartet were also featured. Lomax, among other things, was a popularizer. He consistently worked to bring the voice of the folk to the masses.

While much of Lomax's early collecting centered around English language material, from the very beginning he was interested in other ethnic groups as well. *14 Traditional Spanish Songs from Texas* was taken from field recordings made between 1935 and 1939 by John Lomax, John's second wife, Ruby, and Alan.[8] In addition, early on he saw the importance of Cajun material from Louisiana.

Lomax always had a flair for the dramatic. In presentations, he often interwove pictures of the context of the material with the songs themselves. In this volume, we have Lomax's 1943 lecture/program of "Reels and Work Songs."[9] In this piece he sets the stage and context for every recording he presents. His language is almost literary as he draws a picture of the context for these selections, some recordings and some performed live by Willie Johnson and the Golden Gate Quartet. In some ways, this harks back to his father's presentation of cowboy songs in the lectures he gave earlier in the century. It was Alan's purpose in these lectures to change the way an audience listens to this material in the future.

Lomax's literary flair often bordered on the poetic. In his introduction to Woody Guthrie's "Roll on Columbia," published by the Bonneville Power Administration, Lomax tries to nail down the guitar style of Woody. He evokes pictures with his words, but if his intent was to accurately describe Woody's guitar style in anything other than poetic terms, he misses the mark. Here is how he describes Guthrie's, and by extension the Carter Family's, style of picking: "The vibrant underbelly is Woody's hard-driving Carter family lick on his guitar; the left hand constantly hammering on, pulling off and sliding to create all sorts of syncopation in the base runs and melody, the right hand frailing with a very flexible pick to make rhythmic rattles and rustles and bumps such as a hobo hears in a freight car or a hitch-hiker feels in the cabin of a big cross-country trailer."[10]

In 1941, Lomax had the opportunity to expand his radio prowess by producing a documentary made up of recordings he had made in the South in a valley about to be flooded by the Tennessee Valley Authority. This kind of program was something original and a direct result of the new recording techniques that allowed long narrative pieces to be recorded. In the end, Lomax edited the material into a coherent program. He weaved narrative and song together to tell a story, included in this volume as "Mister Ledford and the TVA."[11]

Lomax was in the center of the New Deal. He not only worked at the Library of Congress, but caught the attention of the Roosevelts. He performed at the White House and worked with Mrs. Roosevelt to plan programs at the White House and elsewhere that utilized American traditional music.[12]

As Lomax grew in stature, his writing was in great demand. In the December 1946 issue of *Vogue*, Alan reviewed a long series of recordings. We see the emergence of the commercialization of the folksong revival. While LP records were still several years away, 78 rpm albums were beginning to be marketed. His reviews are interesting in that they encompass traditional material captured on record as well as city artists performing traditional material. He pays special attention to the Library of Congress recordings that were making their way onto albums. Many of the early Library of Congress recordings are highlighted. In this set of reviews, Lomax differentiates between four kinds of presentations: 1) unsophisticated country singers, 2) commercial hillbillies, 3) city-billy ballad singers of the big towns, and 4) art singers. This is an important contribution to our later understanding of the folksong revival as each of these categories was well represented.[13]

By the 1940s, Lomax had really come into his own. He was busier than ever, with his work at the Archives and with various publications. Most apparent was his work with the media. He spent several years in the

Armed Forces, working primarily on radio shows. Then, after the war, he continued his research, and in 1945 received a Guggenheim Fellowship. Soon thereafter, he began working for Decca Records and produced several albums of historical significance. In 1947, he issued *Listen to Our Story* and *Mountain Frolic* on the Brunswick label, a subsidiary of Decca. These albums are important because they are two early examples of hillbilly records—originally marketed to a rural audience and repackaged and directed for a city audience. While Lomax's early work was focused on field recordings, early on he saw the value in some commercial discs. Despite his work in radio and the recording industry, he continued to publish and explore academic ideas. In 1942, he compiled a list of some 300 commercial recordings. This stands as one of the first discographies of commercial recordings of traditional material.[14]

While working at Decca, some obscure recordings from Africa came to his attention; nobody else at Decca had any idea about what to do with these discs. Lomax listened to one recording in particular and gave it to Pete Seeger. It was a song by Solomon Linde titled "Mbube." Pete listened to the recording and transcribed it as best as he could. The result was "Wimoweh."[15]

In his joint entry with Ben Botkin, for *Encyclopedia Brittanica*, Lomax surveys the development of folklore and folksong from 1937 through 1946. This is one of the first places where he clearly states the importance of sound recordings from cylinders on. He saw the impact on a wide range of workers—from the learned societies to the layman. He felt that these recordings both developed an interest in the real thing in folklore for audiences and brought about the popularization of authentic material. He develops the notion that old ballads were gradually being replaced by newer ballads and finally by lyric songs. This article has many important ideas that served as a foundation for later work by Lomax and others.[16]

In a 1947 article, "America Sings the Saga of America," Lomax states that American folklore had broken loose from its European roots and had begun to reflect American values. He also prints some of his earliest ideas about folklore being "healthily democratic" and "bridges across which men of all nations may stride to say, 'You are my brother.'"[17] It is likely that these thoughts, which were familiar to Lomax, were influenced by Charles Seeger, who talked about such ideas openly with the circle of folklorists in the Washington, D.C., area.

Lomax soon developed a serious interest in traditional jazz, and used his historic recordings of Jelly Roll Morton as the basis for his first book, which was not co-authored with his father. *Mister Jelly Roll* was published in 1950, just before Lomax left for Europe and began another chapter in his amazing career.[18]

I have not discussed Lomax's activist politics, beginning early, because he did not write about his beliefs and actions, but they were always present, overtly or covertly. He promoted the Almanac Singers in 1941–42, a loose group of activists that included Pete Seeger, Woody Guthrie, Josh White, and his sister Bess Lomax. Following World War II, he supported People's Songs, a national organization which promoted topical songs to support labor unions, civil rights, and a progressive political agenda. In 1948, during the culmination of his early political activism, Lomax became music director of Henry Wallace's Progressive Party presidential campaign. In 1950, he was listed in *Red Channels*, which promoted the blacklisting of numerous people in show business. He was described as "folk singer—composer—Author of book, 'Mister Jelly Roll.'" By then, however, partly motivated by his desire to escape the escalating Red Scare, he had moved to England.

NOTES

1. I wish to thank Nolan Porterfield, Bess Lomax Hawes, and Matt Barton for valuable help in the preparation of this article and especially for help in developing a chronology for these early years.

2. For a more detailed account of the 1933 trip see Nolan Porterfield, *Last Cavalier: The Life and Times of John A. Lomax, 1867–1948* (Urbana: University of Illinois Press, 1996), 295–304.

3. Lomax & Lomax, *Our Singing Country* (New York: The Macmillan Company, 1941), xiv.

4. Alan Lomax, "Haitian Journey—Search for Native Folklore," *Southwest Review*, January 1938, 125–147.

5. *Check-list of Recorded songs in the English language in the Archive of American Folk Songs to July, 1940.* (Washington, D.C.: The Library of Congress, 1942).

6. "Of Men and Books," *Northwestern University on the Air*, vol. 1, no. 18, January 31, 1942, 3.

7. Bess Lomax Hawes, "Ruth Crawford Seeger Talk," New York City, October, 2002.

8. Alan Lomax, *14 Traditional Spanish Songs from Texas* (Washington, D.C.: Music Division, Pan American Union, 1942).

9. Alan Lomax, "Reels and Work Songs," in *75 Years of Freedom: Commemoration of the 75th Anniversary of the Proclamation of the 13th Amendment to the Constitution of the United States* (Washington, D.C.: Library of Congress, 1943), 27–36.

10. Alan Lomax, "Foreword" in Woody Guthrie: *Roll on Columbia: The Columbia River Songs*, edited by William Murlin (Portland, Oregon: Bonneville Power Authority, 1988), iii. My thanks to Ed Cray for this citation.

11. Alan Lomax, in Eric Barnouw, ed., *Radio Drama in Action*. (New York: Rinehart & Co., 1945), 51–58.

12. Alan Lomax, "Folk Music in the Roosevelt Era," in *Folk Music in the Roosevelt White House: A Commorative Program* (Washington, D.C.: Office of Folklife Programs, Smithsonian Institution, 1982), 14–17.

13. Alan Lomax, "The Best of the Ballads," *Vogue*, December 1, 1946, 208.

14. Alan Lomax, "List of American Folk Songs on Commercial Records" (Washington, D.C.: 1942), originally published in "The Report of the Committee of the Conference on Inter-American Relations in the Field of Music, September 3, 1940"; manuscript copy in the Lomax Archives.

15. For a complete case study of this song, see Rian Malan, "Money, Greed and Mystery," *Rolling Stone*, May 25, 2000, 54–66, 84–85.

16. Alan Lomax and Benjamin A. Botkin, "Folklore, American" in *Ten Eventful Years, Encyclopedia Brittanica*, 1947, 359–367.

17. Alan Lomax, "America Sings the Saga of America," *New York Times Magazine*, January 26, 1947, 16.

18. Alan Lomax, *Mister Jelly Roll* (New York: Duell, Sloan and Pearce, 1950).

Chapter 1

"Sinful" Songs of the Southern Negro

I. THE PLANTATION, THE LUMBER CAMP, THE BARREL-HOUSE

This past summer I spent traveling through the South with my father* collecting the secular songs of the Negroes, work songs, "barrel-house" ditties, bad-man ballads, corn songs. Our singers classed all these songs, to distinguish them from recorded music and from written-out songs in general, as "made-up" songs. So it was that when we visited the Smithers Plantation in the Trinity River bottoms near Huntsville, Texas, and tried to explain our project to the plantation manager, we described the songs we wanted as "made-up." This genial person called in one of his renters, a stalwart fellow who went by the name of "One-Eye Charley." While One-Eye stood just inside the door, his body taut as if he were ready to run and could scarcely control himself, sweating in the extremity of his fear and embarrassment, the manager said:

"One-Eye, these gentlemen want to hear some real, old-time nigger singin', not hymns, but some of the songs that you've sort of made up out in the field, choppin' cotton or plowin' with the mules."

By this time One-Eye had strained his head up and away from us until it was impossible to catch his eye. Through his patched and tattered shirt, one could see the sweat bursting out and streaming down his hairy chest.

"I ain't no kind of a songster myself, boss. 'Cose I do hum dese here sancrified hymns sometimes, but I'se a member of de chu'ch an' I done clean forgot all de wor'ly songs I ever knowed. Now over on de Blanton plantation, 'bout fo' mile down de road, dey used to be an ole feller, name o' Patterin', what could sho'ly pick a geetar an' sing dem made-up, 'sinful' songs you talkin' 'bout. He de man you ought to see. 'Cose, he might be daid; I ain't been over dere for a year or two."

He turned and started out into the sun again.

"Wait a minute, you lyin' black rascal, you. You can sing an' you know it. These gentlemen have got a machine to make a record of your voice, if you can sing them one of your made-up songs."

"A recort like what you buy in de sto' in Huntsville?"

That evening, when darkness had come up out of the bottom and settled over the whole plantation, we lighted a little kerosene lamp inside the school-house and found that the room was full of Negroes—old men, peering at us out of dim eyes; young men, hats cocked at a rakish angle, red bandanas high about their throats, sitting off away from the women; women with babies; big-eyed children; young women, with their backs to the men, giggling. With the embarrassment that is usual to a ballad-hunter when he breaks the ice, I got up and asked if there was anyone present who could sing "Stagolee," the famous ballad of the Memphis bad man.

"Blue, Blue, sen' him Blue. Blue kin sing 'bout Stagolee. Blue knows mo' 'bout Stagolee dan ole Stag do hissef. Gwan up dere, Blue, white man ain' gwine hurt you. What you scai'd of? Dat horn too little fuh yuh to fall in it, too little fuh yuh to sing at wid yo' big mouf." So ran the murmurs of the crowd as they pushed forward out of the darkness in the rear of the room the Negro Blue. He deserved his nickname, for he was blue-black.

"Can you sing 'Stagolee'?"

"Yassah, I knows ole Stagolee, an' I'll sing it fuh yuh, ef you 'low me to sing 'nuther song fust."

"Is it a made-up song?" This from the plantation manager, who sat close by in the lamp-light. As he spoke and Blue replied, several women giggled in the darkness.

"Well, I reckon 'tis. Didn' I make it up dis aftahnoon in de fiel, spe-cial foh dese gen'lmuns? I reckon it's 'bout he madeupines' song dey is. Turn on yo' machine, young mistah, 'cause I ain' gwine sing it but one time an' I want to git on yo' recort."

And with his eye cocked at the manager, amid the giggling of the women that rose into a roar of nervous merriment, Blue sang of the tribulations of the Negro renter in the South, living and working under a system which is sometimes not far different from the peonage of Old Mexico:

Po' farmer, po' farmer, po' farmer,
Dey git all de farmer make.
His clothes is full of patches,

> His hat is full of holes,
> Stoopin' down pickin' cotton
> F'om off de bottom boll.
> Po' farmer, po' farmer, po' farmer,
> Dey git all de farmer make.
> At de commissary,
> His money in deir bags,
> His po' li'l wife an' chillun
> Sit at home in rags.
> Po' farmer, po' farmer, po' farmer,
> Dey git all de farmer make.

When the laughter of the Negroes had subsided, Bat stepped into the light of the lamp. Her skin was golden yellow. Her broad-brimmed straw hat sat far back on a kinky head, and from beneath it across her forehead stuck out two stiff, black pigtails. They weren't the result of a careless art, at all; for when I saw her again, the hat and the pigtails were the same.

"I kin sing some sperchil songs," she said.

"Sing your favorite, then."

In a beautiful soprano voice, she asked the Lord,

> When my mother's turned her back on me,
> Will you guide me?
> When I'm lef' as a motherless chile,
> Will you guide me?
> Lawd, teach me how to watch, fight and pray.

There was a long silence after she dropped her head and concluded the song. Then Bat went back into the darkness of the crowd and led out three other women.

"Dis is my quartet," she said.

This woman's quartet which she herself had organized and led, was by far superior to any other group we had heard. None of them, in all likelihood, could read, and certainly none of them had had the slightest training in music; but their harmonic and rhythmic scope and pattern, their improvisations, were unusual and beautiful. Their lower lips big with snuff, they swayed back and forth, eyes closed, to the beat of their own singing, a beat accentuated by the spatter of tobacco juice on the rough pine floor:

> Befo' dis time another year, I may be gone,
> An' in some lonesome graveyard, Oh, Lawd, how long?

Jes' so de tree fall, jes' so it lie,
Jes' so de sinner lib, jes' so he die.
My mother's broke de ice an' gone, Oh, Lawd, how long?
An' soon she'll sing dat heavenly song, Oh, Lawd, how long?

Burn-Down sat flat in the cool dust beneath the gnarled 'simmon tree, his legs sprawled out on the ground before him. He was picking his guitar and singing, half to himself, while about him, in various utterly comfortable and relaxed attitudes, were four or five other Negro boys. When we approached, lugging our little recording Dictaphone, he did not get up, but sent for a fruit box and a battered tub and in such a quiet and courteous fashion made us welcome to sit, that we forgot the usual awkwardness which besets the ballad-hunter. With Billy Williams of New Orleans, too, there had been no such awkwardness. I had told him that I was hunting for old-time Negro songs. He replied: "I knows what you wants. You wants to make records of my singin' an' play 'em over de radio en so nobody will ever wanter hear me play again 'cause den ev'-body'll know de songs dat I knows an' den where am I at? Des' like you says, dey ain' many of us folks what knows de ole songs lef', an' dat's what makes me my livin'. Dat's de way I sees it—a cole cash proposition, dat loses me money ef I makes any records fuh yuh. Every minute I picks de geetar, every note I sings, is wuth money to me. How much do I git?"

But Burn-Down was not so calculating. When he heard that we had driven twenty miles across the bottom to hear him sing, he was visibly pleased, and began to tune his guitar. He was, as are most "music physi-caners," a dreadful time in tuning it and twanging it and testing it out. "Know de Slim Riggins Blues? Well, den, I plays it for you." Very softly he sang at first; then, as the excitement of the music grew in him, he began to shout out the verses and his crazy old "box" began to jump and shake under the pounding rhythm; his muddied brown eyes took light and flashed in his sallow face as if there were rising up in him some fierce and consuming passion:

Oh——, you don' do me no good.
I don' blame you, do de same thing, ef I could.
I want all you women to treat me like I treats you;
Ef I treats you dirty, you treats me dirty too.
It's a low-down dirty shame;
She's a married woman, 'fraid to call her name.
Take me back, baby, take me back,
I won' do nothin' you don' lak.

I'll cut yo' wood, I'll make yo' fiah,
I'll tote yo' water from de Fresno bar.
I went to bed laughin', woke up hollin' an' cryin',
For a brown-skin woman come a-rollin' cross my min'.
De sun gonna shine in my back do' some day,
De win' gonna rise an' blow my blues away.

We went with Burn-Down and his three brothers that night twenty or thirty miles through the gloom of the bottom to a country supper, where there was to be dancing to Burn-Down's guitar, plenty to eat, and, Burn-Down had been assured, pretty girls. After many a precipitous ravine and teeth-rattling jolt, we drove up before a three-room cabin. Burn-Down introduced us to our hosts—a billowy Negro matron in a beautiful red turban and her husband, a toothless cotton-headed old fellow with a mouthful of snuff. We sat down on the front stoop under the shadow of the eaves and smoked and waited for the other guests to arrive. Out in front lay the yard, deep with dust, turned silver by a full moon. A white hound pup dragged his paralyzed hind-quarters painfully and slowly toward us and whined.

Presently the guests began to arrive, some on horseback, some appearing suddenly on foot out of the tall weeds; rattling up in flivvers, or driving their squeaking wagons. The babies were put at once to bed in a darkened room. The unmarried women, having dusted their shoes and plastered their faces again with paint, went on into the room where the dance was to be held, and walked about, giggling and chattering, while the young bucks outside smoked and spat, trying to seem unconcerned as to whether there was to be a dance or not. At last the hostess prevailed on Tom Moore, who had been invited to spell Burn-Down, to come in and begin the dance. He was a huge black man, more than six feet tall, tremendously powerful, with large, soft dark eyes, like a cow's. He began to pick the guitar and make it "talk" while he sang,

Reason I like, baby, ole Tom Moore so well,
Feed you jes' lak dey feeds in de Baker Hotel.

Two or three couples began to "slow-drag it" around the floor and the rest stood watching them, the men on one side of the little room and the women on the other. It was a small room, ten or twelve feet square, with an unpainted floor and walls covered with tattered comic sections in lieu of wallpaper; and as more and more couples swung into the dance and a swirling mass of Negro men and women, bodies pressed against their partners, shuffled about in a jerky one-step, the heat grew oppressive. At last I went among the crowd of the older Negro women at the doorway and looked on. When Tom Moore had sung as long as his throat could stand it, he gave over the "box" to Burn-Down. It was not long until Burn-Down, sitting in his corner, was ringed with a group of listeners who leaned over and encouraged him when he brought forth a particularly apt or lewd aphorism.

Two hours later I looked in again, and realized that the crowd I had thought thoroughly relaxed had, as a matter of fact, been somewhat nervous and constrained. For there was Burn-Down in the middle of the floor shouting a rhythm from which the melody had practically disappeared, beating his "box" until it seemed the thing would fly to pieces at the next stroke of his yellow hand, and literally held up by the bodies of the dancers around him, who were still shuffling with bent knees in the monotonous and heavily rhythmic one-step. Out in the moonlit yard again, away from the house, where the hound pup lay asleep in the dust, the separate sounds of feet and voice and strings disappeared, and in their place was a steady *wham-wham* that seemed to be the throbbing of the house itself; it was as if in the dark of the bottom down the slope some huge black man was pounding an enormous drum.

> Hey, black gal, yo' face shine like de sun,
> Rouge, lipstick, and powder, ain' gonna help you none.
> A dollar's round, goes from han' to han',
> Jes' de way dese wimmen goes from man to man.
> Better stop yo' woman fum smilin' in my face,
> Ef she don' stop smilin', I'll be rollin' in yo' place.
> Shake, shake, mama, I'll buy you a diamond ring,
> Ef you don' shake to suit me, won' give you a doggone thing.

The sun had just come up when the train pulled out for the woods. It carried the two-hundred-odd men who variously helped bring pine logs out of the woods for the Weir Lumber Company—the section gang, the sawyers, the track-laying gang, the men who served as nerves for the loader, most of them Negroes. I got off with the section gang. Under the urging of Henry Trevellian [Truvillion], their black foreman, the men set immediately to work straightening out the kinks in the track, for before many hours were gone, the heavy log trains would come, thundering and flying. Each of the men took up a long steel crow-bar and walked off down the track, while Henry knelt with his eye to the shining rail.

"Go down yonder to de first south-east johnny-head an' move it, jest ba'ly," he shouted.

"Run, men, run, you not too ole to run," sang one of the gang, a tall yellow man. The men walked leisurely to the point that Henry, in the technical language of the railroad, had indicated, jammed their bars down under the rail from the inner side, and waited for the yellow man, who evidently had the same position and prestige as the one-time shanty-man, to give them the beat for their heave against the rail.

I'm goin' tell you somethin' I ain' never tole you befo', he chanted.

> What de ole lady say when she come to die?
> Han' on her hip an' de odder on her thigh—
> Oh, Lawd,
> Have mercy,
> Oh, Lawd,
> Have mercy,

and these last phrases were repeated, the men heaving against the bars at each "Oh" and "mercy," until the rail had been moved "jest ba'ly." Then Henry interrupted with another set of directions about the next "johnny-head," and the scene was repeated farther off down the track.

> Cap'n got a Waterbury jes' lak mine,
> Keeps on a-tickin' but it don' keep time.
> Mary, Marthy, Luke an' John,
> All dem 'ciples daid an' gone.
> If I'd a knowed dat my cap'n was bad,
> Would'n 'a' sold dat special, dat I once did had.

While the men were breathing, I asked Henry if he knew any songs— "Brandy," "Casey Jones," "Stagolee."

"Tell yuh," he said. "Way back in de time when dey was buildin' de ole I. C. line th'oo Mississippi, I was section boss. I kin remember plenty times when I played cards settin' on de body of a daid man. Dey was a pow'ful lot o' killin' an' pow'ful lot o' rough men in dem days. Ole Isum Lorantz, de levee camp contractor, was 'bout de baddes' ob 'em all. Kill mo' men up an' down de Mississippi dan de influenzy. Long 'bout three, fo' clock in de mawnin', he'd be knockin' on de fo'-day gong wid his nigger-punchin' forty-fo'. De shack-rouster, he'd git up, an' 'gin to holler lak dis:

> 'Breakfas' on de table, coffee gittin' cole,
> Ef you don' come now, gonna th'ow it out do',
> Aincha gwine, aincha gwine, boys, aincha gwine?
> 'Li'l bell call yuh, big bell warn yuh,
> Ef you don' come now, gonna break in on yuh,
> Aincha gwine, aincha gwine, boys, aincha gwine?'

An' he go on lak dat, rhymin' tell it would wake you up laughin'. Yassah, I knows lots o' dem songs. Ef you come to see me when I gits home fum wuk, I'll sing all you want."

With that promise, I left Henry bawling at his men, went on through the woods to the "boss-camp," got the loan of a horse, and rode over to listen to the sawyers cutting timber. By this hour the July sun was blazing down through the pines, and when I came upon the loggers they were stripped to the waist; big and powerful, their bodies glistened as they threw cross-cut saws into the big trees. Presently, when the saw had bitten three-quarters through the trunk, when the pine had begun to quiver in every breath of wind, and when the men, having rested a moment, had started sawing again, furiously this time, so that the cut would be clean and the log wouldn't splinter as it went down, one would raise his head and send away through the woods a long, mournful, quavering cry, that ended with the *whoom!* of the tree as it crashed through the brush to the ground. My father called it the dirge of the dying tree, but I think that interpretation a bit romantic. The sawyers themselves told me that "jes' when we think our heart goin' fail an' we cain' saw another lick, we gives that call and it put our heart up so we kin finish our job clean; an' it warn anybody, too, dat de tree comin' down an' dey better look out."

With questioning, however, I found that "we is all 'ligious men an' don' sing anything but sperchils, except maybe a few hollers now an' den when we got 'bout forty rods o' de devil in us." But they promised to record their saw-holler when they came from work that evening, and I rode on over to the gang that was pushing a new spur of the little logging railroad out into the uncut timber. Little-Foot—that was my mount's name—carried me up the newly-laid spur. We had gone down into a creek bed and skirted a log bridge, and Little-Foot was stepping carefully along the ties that ran up the slope opposite, when I heard a man singing and looked up. The sun stood at noon; the thick growth of pines on either side of the track shone yellow, and the bed of the road was yellow before me. At the top of the hill, where behind a grey curtain of smoke bulged out the funnel-stack of an old-fashioned locomotive, a half-naked Negro man was singing as he spiked down the rails:

> . . . th'owin' ten pounds fum my hips on down,
> Jes' lissen to de cole steel ring,
> Lawd, Lawd, jes' lissen to de cole steel ring.
> Cap'n say to John Henry,
> "I b'leeve dis mountain's sinkin' in,"

John Henry say to his cap'n, "Suh,
Ain' nothin' but my hammer suckin' win',
Lawd, Lawd, ain' nothin' but my hammer suckin' win'."

The singing stopped. "Do you know any more to that song?" I asked.

"Nawsuh, dat's all I ever learnt. You fin' Henry Trevellian [Truvillion]. He taught me what I know. He de bes' songster in Weirgate, or anywhere else, foh dat matter."

But that night after work, Henry proved most disappointing. His memory, which had been prolific out on the job with his men, failed him time after time; his voice, which before had been rich and powerful, was somehow weak and thin; a defect in his speech, which had been scarcely noticeable, now made it almost impossible to understand him. And when his young wife brought a neighbor in to visit, he shut up completely. He was obviously afraid of something. At last it came out. It seems that up until a short time before, Henry had been a child of the devil, a sneering and unredeemable skeptic; but at last, under pressure, we suspected, from his wife, who was at least twenty years the younger, he had been converted and had joined the church, amid the rejoicings of the whole community. Thus Henry trembled, stuttered, and was unable to sing when his neighbor came in, afraid, perhaps, of the community's disapproval and of having his church membership annulled, for in Negro churches of the far South there is a stricter ban placed on the singing of non-sacred music than on stealing. We thought that if we could carry Henry off some Saturday night to a place where he could sit and talk out of sight of his wife or her callers, we should be able to get a marvelous store of songs and stories from him. This spring we intend to do just that.

After our experience with the section-gang foreman of Weirgate, we made straight for New Orleans, where we knew vice of all sorts flourishes, and where, accordingly, we hoped to record the songs and ballads that the country Negro was so reluctant to sing for us. On Friday night, with a brace of city detectives to serve as a card of admittance and a guaranty that we were all right, we went into the dives and joints of New Orleans. Our hopes ran high, until we noticed that shortly after our entrance into a beer-parlor, a constrained silence would fall on the assembled men and women; and not long after, we four, with the bartender, would be the only ones left in the silent hall.

The next morning I went back alone to one of the barrel-houses. There I was approached by an old peg-leg Negro man. "Was you de gem-mun huntin' foh songsters heah las' night? You know when I see you come in wid de law, I didn' know how to trus' you—I been arrested once befo' an' sent to de pen when I hadn' been doin' nothin'.—But, ef you reely wants old-time songs, I'm reely ole-time songster. Git me a li'l gin an' come on back in dis here booth. Now, I feel better, mo' lak singin' . . . Ever hear tell of de hoodoos dat dey used to have here in Lou'ana? Well, one Sain' John Eve me an' buddy decide we go out to one o' dem hoodoo shows, so we start out an' we go tell we come way out yander in de swamp to a sort of a hall. An' we go in an' set down wid some other niggers an' wait. After so long a time a yaller woman bust thoo' de black curtain at de back wid de bigges' rattlesnake wrop aroun' her neck I ever seen. Mus' been ten er fifteen foot long. Dey plays some music an' she an dat 'ere rattler an' some monst'ous black cats do a dance. Den pu'tty soon she disappear in de curtain. 'Bout dat time I ask my buddy didn' he think it 'bout time to be gittin' on home, but he say to wait a little, so we wait. After a while de bigges', blackes' nigger man mus' be in de worl', mus' been nine er ten er twelve foot tall, jump out o' dat curtain an' 'gin to dance. Dey beat on a little log drum an' sing while he dance an' dis what dey sing."

The old fellow then produced a mouth organ, wetted it with his lips and tongue, and played a gay little French folk-tune, quite different from any music we had so far heard. Then he sang the words which he remembered hearing sung on that night twenty years before, not understanding anything of their meaning—he did not speak French—but passing them on as accurately as he could recall. They were part French, part Creole, and, quite understandably, part poor memory.

"Well, dey keeps on playin' dat tune an' de big fellow keep on dancin', until he all lathered wid sweat an' he eye burn like a chunk o' fire. All de time he kep' growin' smaller an' smaller, an' littler, tell at las' he weren't no bigger dan a li'l baby. Den, bang, he disappeared. So I heads for home so fas' tell I fergot de river bridge an' had to swim de Mississippi dat night to git to New Orleans."

Beyond this story, however, the old man had little to offer me. His life had been and still was hard. At seventy-five he had risen to the position of cleaner of outhouses. And, after he had sung two spirituals—

Gwineter slip an' slide in de golden streams,
Till I shine lak de mawnin' star,

and

> God's gwinter give me dem eagle wings,
> For to carry me home,

and a ballad formerly popular on the Great Lakes, which he had confused with a very widespread hobo song,

> Ten thousand miles away from home,
> Jumpin' an' ole freight train,
> Ten thousand miles away from home
> My heart was filled with pain.
> Don' stop for water,
> Jes' take her on the fly.
> Won't we get holy Moses
> On the Pennsylvania line—

I left him.

Having so miserably failed in the New Orleans barrel-house region with
a police escort, I decided one Saturday night to visit it in the company of a
pimp whom I had met on one of my long walks through the city. (Father was
ill in the hospital with malaria, and I went alone, carrying my typewriter.) A
dollar and a few drinks would be pay enough for him, he said, especially
since the times were so hard. But in the first joint he left me to my own
devices and got into a pool game. He lost, of course, and I, the gull, had to
pay off. It was not long before friendly bartenders had him staggering drunk.
My patience entirely gone, I dropped him at his place of business. I wandered
on, then, by myself, and, although I saw one dead man—a fifteen-year-old
boy who had been stabbed with an ice-pick just before I came up—and one
rousing fight between a young boy, his girl friend, and an over-protective big
brother, the hours went on past midnight before I heard anything more than
Wayne King and his ilk, pouring out tea-room jazz from the radios that,
sadly for me, seemed to be fixtures of every barrel-house.

I heard a piano tinkling. In a dim-lit, dirty room, I saw a buck Negro
playing, around him in various drunken attitudes some ten or fifteen
Negro men and women. For the hundredth time I asked the question:
"Do you know the song about that bad man, Stagolee?"

"Wid a little mo' gin in me, I kin remember ev'ything that Stack did
and make up some mo'. But what you want to hear dat song fer?" He was
young and very tight.

"Oh, I'm just interested in old-timey songs. I'm collecting them. I
want to put you down on record." I showed him my typewriter.

"Well, dat's diffunt. You makes a recort and we splits de profit. O.K.,
Jake, bring me some mo' gin. Dis white frien' o' mine gonna pay de bill."

He drank and passed the bottle on to two of his favorite girl friends. Then he began:

> Stagolee he was a bad man, an' ev'ybody know
> He toted a stack-barreled blow-gun an' a blue-steel forty-fo'.
> Way down in New Orleans, dey call it de Lyon club,
> Ev'y step you walk in, you walkin' in Billy Lyon blood.
> He shot him three time in de forehead an' two time in de side,
> Say, "I'm gonna keep on shootin' 'till Billy Lyon die."
> Billy Lyon got glassy an' he gap an' hung he head,
> Stack say, "I know by expression on his face dat Billy Lyon dead."
> Stack tole Mrs. Billy, "Ef you don' believe yo' man is dead,
> Come up to de bar-room an' see de hole I shot in he head."

The above stanzas are only five out of twenty-odd that he sang me in his epic description of the quarrel between Stack Lee and Billy Lyon over a milk-white Stetson hat. While Stack was speaking to Mrs. Billy in the manner of a Homeric hero, my singer was pushed rudely by one of the drunken women. He arose in a great temper. "Goddam, let's git outta dis joint. Come on, white folks. I take you to a place where I got a friend that'll treat me right." Accompanied by another Negro man, who wanted a tip and so was helping me manage my temperamental singer, and by the two favored women, my singer and I swept out of the joint and got into my car. We drove bumping for miles through the back alleys of New Orleans, and found, at last, the "place where I got a friend." It was a narrow room, containing one battered piano, one feeble kerosene lamp high up on the wall, and a crowd of Negro men and women. We set at once to work, I sitting on a milk-crate with my typewriter on my knees, my singer thumping the piano. The lamp had been brought down so that I could see my machine. The patrons of the place were crowded in a tight semicircle around me, looking over my shoulders.

> Chief tol' his deputies, "Git yo' rifles an' come wid me.
> We got to arres' dat bad nigger, Stagolee."
> De deputies took dey shiny badges, an' dey laid 'em on de she'f.
> "Ef you wants dat nigger, go git him by yo' own damn se'f."
> Chief Maloney say to de bartender, "Who kin dat drunk man be?"
> "Speak sof'ly," say de bartender; "it's dat bad man Stagolee."
> Chief Maloney touch Stack on de shoulder, say "Stack, why don' you run?"
> "I don' run, white folks, when I got my forty-one."

At this point the group about me scattered. A little man rushed up, seized the lamp and put it back on its hook, took away my milk-crate, and asked my singer in the plainest of language to move along. Outside in the car I presently found my self-appointed assistant and the two women, and in a moment my singer appeared, rubbing his knuckles and smiling.

"Where have you been?" I asked.

"I had to see dat bartender who been rude to my white frien'. He say, 'You interruptin' my business.' I tell him, 'You think yo' business been interrupted already? Ain' nothin' to what it gonna be in minute.' An' I hand it to him."

By three-thirty I had written down all the boy knew about Stack Lee. We found a piano in a quiet house and sent po' Stack to hell, after he had been shot eight times and hanged, thus:

> He had a three-hundred-dollar fun'el an' a thousand-dollar hearse,
> Satisfaction undertaker put him six feet in the earth.
> De Devil's little children went sc'amblin' up de wall,
> Sayin', "Save us, papa, 'er Stack will kill us all."
> Stack he tole de Devil, "Come on', let's have a little fun;
> You stick me wid yo' pitchfork, I'll shoot you wid my forty-one."
> Stack he grab de pitchfork an' he laid it on de she'f.
> "Stan' back, you devils, gonna rule hell by myse'f."

All in all, I had written down forty-one stanzas, fine and strong.

After another week of search in New Orleans, however, I had not found another singer, besides the Billy Williams whom I mentioned above. Back and forth, up and down through the Creole-Negro section I walked, and heard not one word of French. "Dey ain' no style in it," I was told. I even went one night, unannounced and unwanted, into a nunnery, where I had heard that a little show was being given for the sisters by some good songsters, only to hear "Swanee River," "Old Black Joe," and the jazz "All of Me." We had found the educated Negro resentful of our attempt to collect his secular folk-music. We had found older Negroes afraid for religious reasons to sing for us, while the members of the younger generation were on the whole ignorant of the songs we wanted and interested only in the Blues (which are certainly Negro folk-songs, but of which we had already recorded a plenty) and in jazz. So it was that we decided to visit the Negro prison farms of the South. There, we thought, we should find that the Negro, away from the pressure of the churchly community, ignorant of the uplifting educational movement, having none but official contact with white men, dependent on the resources of his own group for amusement, and hearing no canned music, would have preserved and increased his heritage of secular folk-music. And we were right. In two months we recorded approximately a hundred new tunes from the singing of Negro convicts: work songs from the levee camp, the section gang, the workers in the woods and in the fields, and the chain gang—ballads, lyrics, reels, field calls. For this purpose we used a fine recording machine furnished us by the Library of Congress, where our records are to be deposited for the study of musicians. This machine draws its power from a set of batteries, and records electrically on aluminum or celluloid discs. Its play-back arm, which enables the singer to hear his song immediately after it has been sung, won us more songs than anything we said, more than all the cigarettes, tips, and compliments we distributed. It was often quite difficult to persuade the first man to record his song, but after he and his fellows had heard his voice, his mistakes, perhaps, coming back to him out of the loud-speaker, there was no longer any difficulty in getting what we wanted. At times our work was even held up by the eagerness of the men to "git on dat machine."

II. THE PRISON FARM

Of all the singers in the penitentiary, Mose Platt, "alis" Clear Rock, stands largest in my memory. According to his own telling, he is seventy-one years old and has spent forty-seven of those years in Texas prisons. He rather proudly calls himself a "habitual."

"What did they put you in here for, Clear Rock?" we asked him.

"I th'owed three. I got 'em wid rocks."

"Do you mean to say that you killed three people with rocks—bashed in their heads? Were they asleep?"

"Oh, nossuh, I got 'em when dey was comin' at me. I was a powful rock th'ower when I was a young man, could knock down a rabbit on the run. Well, dey gimme life fer dat, but I got pardoned out an' de nex' time I was jes' misfortunate, yassuh, jes' misfortunate. It mighta happened to anybody. I went back to Taylor when I got free an' took up wid a li'l yaller gal. I never ask her how ole she was, nor she me, fer matter o' dat. I had some enemies an' dey foun' out she were fourteen and sent de law atter me. So here I is fer de res' o' my life."

"Did you ever run away, Clear Rock?"

"I has dat, an' ef I don' want 'em to ketch me, dey cain'. Dey calls me 'Swif'-Foot Rock' 'cause de way I kin run. White man say one time he thought I mus' have philosophies in my feet. One time I took out down

one o' dem corn rows an' de men an' de dogs atter me. When I struck de
his-fault an' could see my road clear in front I lengthen my stride a little,
an' when I pass th'oo de li'l town dey call Houston, I was travelin'. De
win' was talkin' in my ears; say, 'Rock, whish way you gwine so fas'?' Well,
'bout an hour later de high sheriff ride inter Houston an' stop an' ask
lady did she see nigger pass dat way. An' she say, 'No, didn' see no nigger,
but a motorcycle pass here 'bout hour ago. By dis time it ought to be in
Mexico, 'cross de border.' Well, boss, my feet was splat-splattin' on de his-
fault so fas' it soun' like a motorcycle, my shirt-tail had caught on fire an'
made de tail-light, an' my two eyes was a-shinin' like de spylight on a
train . . . But I kin travel faster dan dat. One time ghos' or witch or
somepin' got atter me an' I jes' lean over. Well, when I look up I was in
Oklahoma. Befo' I could pertec' myse'f I had run clean fum Bastrop up
into Oklahoma. Dat's what you call runnin' yerse'f loose."

"Didn't they ever catch you?"

"Well, one time dey did. I was tired fum rollin' an' singin' all day in
de fiel'. It had been mighty hot dat day. An' dey put ole Rattler, de bes'
nigger dog on de Brazis, on my trail. I made up a li'l song 'bout dat time."

And he sang in a voice as clear and big and powerful as any we heard
all summer:

> B'lieve to my soul dere's a nigger gone,
> Heah, Rattler, heah,
> Run right down through dat corn,
> Heah, Rattler, heah.
> Go git de dog-man,
> Heah, Rattler, heah,
> Go an' ring de sergeant,
> Heah, Rattler, heah.
> Ole Rattler is a nigger dog,
> He run dat nigger right 'crost dat log.
> I'm on my way to de long-leaf pine,
> I b'lieve I'll run tell I go stone-blin'.
> Got a baby here, got a baby dere,
> Gonna take my baby to de worl'y fair,
> Ole Rattler's got no thimpathee,
> Got Big-Foot Rock settin' in a tree.

Clear Rock prolonged the chase over fifteen or twenty stanzas; and as
he grew more excited and the song moved more swiftly, one could see him
crashing through the brush toward the Brazos, torn by briar and thorn, his
clothes in tatters, and behind him the quick, sharp yelp of the hounds.

"I mus' be firs' cousin to Ole Riley an' Long John. Ole Riley walk de Brazos, was goin' so fas' he didn' have time to swim. An' Long John . . .

> Come on, honey, an' shet dat do',
> De dogs is a-comin', an' I got to go.
> Des hear ole sergeant, jes' a-huffin' an' a-blowin',
> Des hear ole Rattler, whinin' an' a-moanin'.
> He's Long John, he's long gone,
> Like a turkey th'oo de corn, wid his long clo's on.
> He's long gone, he's long gone.
> In two or three minutes, lemme catch my win',
> In two-three minutes, I'm gone agin',
> He's Long John, he's long gone . . .

"Old I'un Haid heah, he know de time when dem kind o' songs mean somepin' in de day when we was rollin' in de fiels fum can to cain't [sunup to sundown]. Sing 'em 'bout Ole Hannah,** buddy."

Iron Head, a short, grim-faced man of sixty-five, thirty years "off an' on" in the penitentiary, then sang "Old Hannah," a song as slow and weary as a day in the fields under the lash and the gun with the "hot boilin' sun" overhead.

This song describes the time when the state leased out its prisoners to private plantation-owners, and the men were driven unmercifully, fed miserably, and whipped, sometimes, until they lay dead under the "bull-whup an' de cow-hide."

> Go down, Ole Hannah, doncha rise no mo',
> Ef you rise in de mawnin', bring Judgment Day.
> You oughta been heah in nineteen fo',
> You could find a dead man at de en' of ev'y row.
> You oughta been heah in nineteen ten,
> Dey was rollin' de wimmen like dey was drivin' de men.
> Wake up, Lifetime, hol' up yo' head,
> You may git a pardon or you may drop dead.
> Rise up, dead man, an' he'p me drive my row,
> Wake up, dead man, an' he'p me turn my row.
> Go down, Ole Hannah, doncha rise no mo',
> Ef you rise in de mawnin', set de worl' on fire.

"Dat's a sho'-God song," one of the men remarked, and the others nodded assent. "Sing 'em 'Shorty George.' " But Iron Head refused emphatically. They kept at him, until at last he flamed out, "Goddam you big-mouth niggers, you know it wuk me all up to sing dat song."

Later he led us aside, over to the door of the trusty-shack, where he stood looking out into the July moonlight. "I'll sing dat song right easy foh you, ef you want me. You know it bad fer me to sing it. Make me want to run away. I'm a trusty, got an easy job. Ef I run away, dey sho' to catch me an' den dey put me in de line to roll in de fiel' an' I'm too ole fer dat kin' o' wuk. An' dat song make me want to see my woman so bad I cain' hardly stan' it here no longer." But he sang the song for us:

> Shorty George,*** you ain' no frien' o' mine,
> Taken all de women an' leave de men behin'.
> She was a brown-skin woman, mouth full o' gol',
> An' I wouldn' mistreat her, save nobody's soul.
> Dey brought me a letter I couldn't read foh cryin',
> My babe wasn't dead, she was slowly dyin'.
> Dey carried my baby to de buryin' groun',
> You oughter heard me holler when de coffin soun'.
> I went to de graveyard, peep in my mam's face,
> Ain' it hard to see you, mama, in dis lonesome place.

We looked closely at Iron Head. He was crying—"de roughes' nigger dat ever walk de streets of Dallas," crying. "But your woman isn't dead."

"She might as well be. I cain' go to her an' she scai'd to come to see me."

Clear Rock broke in: "Boss, did you ever hear dat song 'bout po' Bobby Allen? See ef you want to put it on yo' recort." And Clear Rock sang a version of the old English ballad, "Barbara Allen," that I think will create confusion in the ranks of scientific folk-lorists. He had combined "Barbara Allen" with "Sir Patrick Spens," "Little Lonnie," and "St. James Infirmary." He buried po' Bobby, who changed sex in almost every stanza, in the desert of Arizona with six cowgirls to act as her pallbearers; then, again with the true primitive's love for burial ceremony, he shipped her bier out of the depot in Dallas with her relatives "squallin' an' hollin'." No folk-lorist interested in versions A, B, C, D, E, and so forth of "Barbara Allen" among the Negroes, need go any farther afield than Clear Rock. He sang to Father Version A, and to me Version B, very much changed. When we wrote back for more, he sent us a new song, Version C. Only two weeks ago, when we visited him again, he sang us Version D. And every time he sang the song, no doubt, new stanzas would appear, and the wording would be vastly different. . . . We asked him whether he knew any cowboy songs.

"I know cowboy songs? Didn' I drive up de cattle on dis farm for nigh on ten years? I had to make me up some cowboy songs to move dem cattle on." He sang us twenty or thirty stanzas of his notion of "The Old Chisholm Trail," ending with the cowboy pitched off his pinto and lying hung in a mesquite tree.

"Clear Rock, you left that cowboy in a very uncomfortable position, sprawling along that limb."

"Lemme git him down, boss, lemme git him down," he said eagerly.

> Cowboy lyin' on a limb a-sprawlin',
> Come a little win' an' down he come a-fallin'.
> Wid a bum-ti-hiddle-um-a yeah, yum-a-yeah,
> Wid a bum-ti-yiddle-um-a-yeah.

We wrote down and recorded the songs of Clear Rock and Iron Head for a day and a night, and Clear Rock was still indefatigably improvising. Those two wore us out. We said to each other, "If we can discover so many songs in Texas, what won't we find in Mississippi and Louisiana!"

But we were in some measure disappointed. The officials of the Louisiana prison in their wisdom had decided, all history to the contrary, that Negroes work better when they are not singing. Lead Belly, however, was some consolation.

"I is de king of de twelve-string-guitar players of de worl'. When I was in Dallas, walkin' de streets an' makin' my livin' wid dis box o' mine, de songsters was makin' up dat song 'bout Ella Speed. Bill Martin had jes' shot her down an' lef' her lyin' in her blood up near de ole T. P. station. An' dis is de way dey would sing:

> Bill Martin he was long an' slender,
> Better known by bein' a bartender.
> Ella Speed was downtown a-havin' her lovin' fun,
> 'Long come Bill Martin, wid his Colt forty-one.
> De deed dat Bill Martin done,
> Jedge sentence, "You know you oughta be hung."
> Dey taken Bill Martin to de freight depot,
> An' de train come rollin' by,
> Wave his han' at de woman dat he love,
> An' he hung down his head an' he cry.

"De ballit I like bes', though, is de one 'bout po' Laz-us. Laz'us was a levee-camp roller. His job was to tend to de horses an' mules out to de lot. One Saturday it was cole an' rainy, an' Laz'us got mad, tired of job an' Cap'n cussin' an' bad food an' stinkin' horses an' manure on clo's, an' 'bout dinner time he went to he bunk an' got he blue-steel forty-fo' an' he Colt Special. Den he walk in de mess hall where all de mule-skinners was a-layin' in deir food an' he got up on de table an' went walkin' down de middle, trompin' inter all de food wid his muddy, manure shoes. When he git to odder en' table, he turn aroun' an' play wid he guns an' say, 'Ef any you boys think you got yo' feelin's hu't, come on up here an' I'll try to pacify yo' min'.' Co'se nobody make a move. Well, he see he weren't goin' git into no fight an' kill nobody dat way, so he go over to do' pay-car and ask for he pay. De clerk, he give him a li'l ole measly pay-check an' Laz'us say, 'What 'bout all dat back-pay you cheat me out of?' An he reach in de winder, knock de clerk in de head, an' take all de money an' lit out. Well, dat where de ballit take up.

> High sheriff tole de deputy,
> "Go out an' bring me Laz'us,
> Bring him dead or alive,
> Lawd, Lawd, bring him dead or alive."
> De deputy 'gin to wonder
> Where dey could fin' po' Laz'us.
> "Well, I don' know,
> Lawd, Lawd, I jes' don' know."
> Well, dey foun' po' Laz'us
> Way out between two mountains,
> An' dey blowed him down,
> Lawd, Lawd, an' dey blowed him down.
> Dey taken po' Laz'us
> An' dey laid him on de commissary gal'ry,
> An' dey walk away,
> Lawd, Lawd, an' dey walk away.
> Po' Laz'us' mother,
> She come a-screamin' an' a-cryin',
> "Dat's my onlies' son,
> Lawd, Lawd, dat's my onlies' son."

"Dat a mighty pitiful song, ain't it? De line sings it out at work some time right sof', when dey gits mad at de Cap'n. But de one de ole twelve-string box like bes' is de cocaine song—

> Chew my terbaccer an' spit my juice,
> Love my baby tell it ain' no use,
> Hi, hi, honey, take a whiff on me,
> Take a whiff on me, take a whiff on me,
> Hi, hi, baby, take a whiff on me,
> Hi, hi, honey, take a whiff on me.
> Yaller woman I do despise,
> But a jet black gal I cain' deny,

Hi, hi, honey, take a whiff on me, etc.
De blacker de berry, de sweeter de juice,
It takes a brown-skin woman for my pertikerler use.
Hi, hi, honey, etc.
Cocaine's foh hosses an' not foh men,
De doctors say it'll kill you but dey don' say when.
Hi, hi honey, etc.

Black Sampson, in for twenty years for murder, with only nine months of his sentence gone, had brought his religious scruples against sinful songs into prison with him. It seemed to him that his future in heaven remained perfectly secure while he sang,

Way down yonder in de hollow o' de fiel',
Angels a-wukin' on de chariot wheel,

and recorded the way he used to direct his men in song when he was the foreman of a steel-laying gang; but when we asked him to sing a levee-camp song, he refused. There was some reason in his objection, because the levee-camp holler, while it is innocent in most stanzas, comes out of a group life even harder, perhaps, than the life in a prison camp. The levee camp is out of touch with civilization, a refuge of outlaws and gamblers, and, at least in the old days, altogether lawless. Black Sampson, then, was adamant in his refusal to sing the levee-camp song. We argued in vain. The prison chaplain promised to make it all right with the Lord. "I got my own 'ligion," said Black Sampson. But the request of the warden was at last too much for his conscience. He capitulated, and stood up to sing before the microphone. When he had made sure that his words were being recorded, he said, "It's ha'd times when a po' man, member o' de chu'ch, has to sing a sinful song. But, oh, Lawd, de warden ask me to, an' he might turn me out, so, please Lawd, make it all right fo' me to sing dis." He had registered his protest on an aluminum plate. . . . Just as he was telling us good-bye, he turned to Father: "Will de big boys up in Washington hear dis song? I sho' hopes dey does. Maybe my singing he'p me git outa here—I jes' nachly don' like dis place."

With the same idea in mind, a Negro in the Tennessee penitentiary once drew us off to one side, far away from the crowd at the other end of the cell-block. There he made us comfortable, sat down himself, and produced a little tin bucket, which he placed between his knees, bottom side up. "Now I'm gonna beat de bucket foh you."

By squeezing it with his knees he produced two or three tones. His rhythmic variations were extraordinary. At last, he stopped and said, "Do you think my beatin' de bucket like dat'll he'p me git outa here?"

Late one August evening we sat on the front stoop of Camp Number One of the Prison Farm at Parchman, Mississippi, talking to the Superintendent. The men had come in from the fields, had eaten, and were bathing in the big dormitory in preparation for bed.

"You know, I've been in this prison system for over twenty years," said the Superintendent. "I still remember one night when I had a bunch of men out on the road, ten or fifteen years ago. I was sitting, fighting the mosquitoes and smoking. The night was too hot for sleep. Down below me where the men were I heard one convict singing, and for some reason I listened. A fellow gets so used to the men hollering and singing out in the fields that after a while you don't pay them any mind. But this time I listened. One of these goddam niggers can be funny when he takes a notion, and this one certainly was singing a funny song. It was something about a man getting ninety-nine years for killing his wife."

It had the feel to us of a new ballad. We pressed him. The Superintendent wouldn't sing it, but at last he sent a trusty with a shotgun into the dormitory to find somebody who knew the song. Presently the black guard came out, pushing a Negro man in stripes along at the point of his gun. The poor fellow, evidently afraid he was to be punished, was trembling and sweating in an extremity of fear. The guard shoved him up before our microphone.

"What's your name?" said the Superintendent.

"Joe Baker, alis Seldom Seen."

"What are you in here for?"

"Well, it was disaway. I never had been in no trouble wid de law, 'ceptin', co'se, I'd git drunk now an' den an' git ten days foh fightin' or disturbin' de peace. But one fellow kept messin' up wid my homely affairs, so I blowed him down. De jedge, he tole me dat he wouldn' sent me up foh life foh killin' dat man, but dat I oughtn' kep' on shootin' an' kill de man's frien' jes' standin' by. You know, suh, I didn' mean to kill dat odder man, but I jes' gits excited an' keeps on shootin'. Seem like I didn' stop in time, don' hit?"

"That's right, Joe. But Joe, do you know the song about the bad man who killed his wife?"

"Well, I don' rightly know. I used to sing it. Ef you give me a day or two to study it up, I might be able to sing it."

"Hell, you're going to sing it now. Turn on your machine, young fellow."

This is what we recorded:

> Late las' night I was a-makin' my roun's,
> Met my woman an' I blowed her down,
> Went on home an' went to bed,
> Put my hand-cannon right under my head.
> When dey arres' me, I was dress' in black,
> Put me on de train an' dey brought me back,
> Boun' me over in de county jail,
> Couldn' git a human fuh to go my bail.
> Early nex' mawnin' 'bout risin' o' de sun,
> Spied ole jedge a-drappin' down de line,
> Heared dat jailer clearin' his th'oat,
> "Nigger, git ready foh de deestreec' co't."
> Deestreec' co't is now begin;
> Twelve jurors, twelve big, hones' men;
> Lessen five minutes in step a man,
> He was holdin' my verdic' in his right hand.
> Seed ole jedge pick up his pen,
> "Guess you won' kill no women agin.
> Dis killin' o' women nachly got to stop.
> I don' know whether to hang you er not."
> Heah I is, bowed down wid shame;
> I got a number instead of a name.
> Ninety-nine years, in prison fuh life,
> All I ever done was to kill my wife.

Later, while a group of the men, hoes in hand, were grouped around the microphone, shouting out with all their voices a great work-song, one of the officials whispered to me: "Do you see that big, black, good-looking son-of-a——, leading that song? Here's what he done. His wife had been playing around with another man, see? And that fellow there told her that if he ever caught that man around he was going to kill every living thing on the place. Well, one day he caught them together in his bed and he pulled out his six-gun and shot them both dead there. Then he shot his little four-year-old son. His little feist dog came running around the house to see what the ruckus was, and he shot him. When the sheriff came after him, he was knocking the chickens off the fence, one after another."

And I looked up and heard the man who had killed "ev'y livin' thing," the leader of the thundering chorus of hoes and voices, sing:

> Oh, come an' git me an' take me home,
> Dese lifetime devils, dey won't leave me 'lone.

Here I am foh a hundred years,
Ef a tree fall on me, I don' bit mo' keer."

NOTES

* John A. Lomax, editor of *Cowboy Songs and Other Frontier Ballads*, etc.
** Old Hannah, the sun.
*** The prisoners have named the little gasoline-engine train that runs past the prison farm every day about sundown, "Shorty George." On Sunday it very literally does take away the women visitors and leave the men behind.

Chapter 2

Haitian Journey

I. THE CAMION

Through the cane field, across the irrigation ditches, and past the dissipated banana grove, a few strides this morning and then the white road whose tail coils over Morne Cabrite to the gray North runs under your feet toward Port-au-Prince. Let Monsieur Polinice limp along under the baggage! A fat black woman beats a little gray ass where his ears and raw tail peep out from her bulk, and this morning she must be properly greeted, *"Bonjour, Commère Bobo, ba' m' ti goute, s'il vous plaît."* You hope she will hurl mangoes at your head, but your pronunciation is bad, and on the road she speaks to no strangers. She has beaten her donkey fifty miles across the mountains with a load of mangoes for Port-au-Prince market, and she carries her shoes in her hand like a dignified woman on business.

You are setting out on a journey in Haiti, and you agree with Monsieur Polinice about the seriousness of journeying to the South. "To look at the Caribbean that rubs the shores of Yucatán and Colombia," you say. He responds solemnly, "Aux Cayes has strange gods; anywhere there may be a drop of green poison from the nostrils of a *mort* on your salt fish." Sweat ripples like silk across your breast, and the palms of your hands itch from the heat. To improve your diction you haggle with the taxi driver, who charges a nickel for a fifteen-mile ride if you consent to sit six to a seat in his well-worn Ford. But you look forward to one pleasant certainty—the camion will be painted yellow and trimmed in scarlet.

It was. It was like a great, square-cut, tropical fowl, a fantastic bird with an olive green beak and a black toupee, and it was named Fleur d'Innocence. In the wide front seat were Faine, the driver, a slender mulatto of Italian extraction; a fat French priest in tropical black; a pimply young

Cuban peddling the goods of his New York drug house through Haiti and Santo Domingo; and sometimes myself. Behind were six benches piled with bales of empty coffee sacks and then two crammed with Haitians.

A word should be added about the camion. In Haiti the rich and the tourists travel in private cars or in taxis. The peasants walk or beat their donkeys or occasionally, where the road permits, ride the Haitian bus, the camion. The driver makes no bones about crowding eight, ten, or even twelve people where there is barely room for six; but if anyone objects and becomes obnoxious, he and his luggage may be left unceremoniously by the roadside. The driver and his two or three porters will fall upon a helpless, squalling female, pull her out of the camion, hurl her parcels on the road, bully her fare out of her, and depart cursing the name of her mother. The drivers can steer their top-heavy charges for twelve or fourteen hours over roads that thread mangrove swamps and twist along the edge of precipitous mountains, and at the end of such a drive carefully, according to the nature of the passenger, extract every nickel of the fare that is owing. Their porters are even hardier. When the camion is crowded, they ride all day long in the dust, swinging from the tailboard, hanging on the running board or squatting on the top. Ragged, barefooted, profane, unscrupulous, protesting that their camions are bound to depart within the hour when they know that they can't possibly leave before the next day, these young monkeys, who carry all the burdens and are responsible for all the property of the camions, seem to lead charmed lives. And when the lordly drivers depart in the evening, the porters curl up on the narrow seats of the camions, wrap their heads in their straw mats and snore with the greatest pleasure.

When Faine had crammed his camion full, the great awkward bird took flight. The sun stretched taut the great palm and banana groves and cane fields. It scorched the stony hills brown and made the little dull-faced plants try to crawl back into their holes. It baked the white road until the blazing track coughed up huge clouds of choking dust, and focused on little towns with such clarity and ruthlessness that you closed your eyes, trembling. It puffed great blasts of the perfume of coffee blossoms into your face, and followed the coffee blossoms with the stink of pigsties. It plunged into the deep shade of the coffee groves and flashed across the hills, smiling wickedly at the goats. Then it hurtled over the last hill and smote the Caribbean with a brassy roar, and the blue sea resounded like ten thousand cymbals. Thereafter, as it fell westward, it grew calmer and was satisfied with making soft waves break into fierce smiles. Castles should have towered among the hills, and the narrow valleys along the sea-edge should have shone with armies. But there were only mud houses and poverty.

After night we lurched into Aux Cayes and sought the house of an old harridan who kept travelers. Under the pink canopy of a gigantic mahogany bed the sun still crackled in my veins and my fever soared.

II. AUX CAYES

The old harridan was howling at the servants for her coffee, and it was yet pitch dark. I tried to sleep, but her shrill voice penetrated and molded my dreams. And at last I in my turn began to shout for coffee. Revoli appeared with a cup of the same jet-black liquid with which Napoleon's armies had warmed their hearts in Italy, Austria, and Spain; and we cursed all the old women of the world while I drank behind the pink mosquito bar and felt the coffee wash away the dust of yesterday's ride.

As I dressed behind the door, the old madame asked after my health and then hurried on to matters that concerned her more nearly. She assured me that she was a respectable woman, that she had once been married to a marine, and that he had gone away to Les Etats-Unis and had left her enough money to bring up their children and keep three servants. Was I lonely? She could look around? No, she did not run a hotel. She took in only an occasional traveler who struck her fancy. Of course, her marine was coming back some day. He was now too busy making a fortune in my rich country to write to her. I agreed with her that Americans belong to a sadly undemonstrative race, but assured her that they have hearts of gold and are particularly fond of eggs and orangeade in the morning.

I breakfasted with a somber Revoli. When Revoli went traveling, his skin and his nose and his heart woke and told him that he was in a strange place. They kept asking questions and receiving the most curious answers. For the first two or three days in a strange town, he preferred to sit up all night and talk to anyone who would stay awake with him; and then after everyone had gone to bed, he would sit and smoke and watch the things of the night that came to visit him. This morning he referred enigmatically to tall red men without heads, to cars with wild blue lights and no drivers. He had never been to Aux Cayes before, but his night's watching with the spirits of the place had convinced him that it was a wicked city inhabited by legions of devils.

Yet I found Aux Cayes lovely in the early morning. The wide white road—the approach to the city—was flanked by rows of coconut palms. The greenery, still gleaming with dew, crowded in at their feet; and the walls of leaves were punctuated with bougainvillaea and trumpet vine. The merchants were leaning over their bolts of goods and barrels of salt and gossiping with the more elegant lawyers and doctors. Revoli and I approached diffidently and inquired of them about the state and condition of music in their city. It is strange how this question flabbergasts the businessman. "Songs," he says, "songs—what does one have to do with songs? They don't come by the pound or by the yard. Over the radio, yes, but here in my town there are no songs. We export and import here, but no songs."

Revoli understands. He knows that songs can be used to call the gods and dismiss those spirits that live in the sea and are fiercer than sharks. He knows that songs can heal sickness, break up homes and persuade men that they have turned into snakes so that they go wrapping themselves about the roof-trees. To these merchants and doctors, surprised at their business so early in the morning, he thereupon expounded our mission and in such a surprising mixture of French, Creole, English, and Spanish—in each of which he believes himself eloquent—that they sent us at once to M. Théomar François. It was like a Charlie Chaplin comedy. We blew the smoke of our fifty-cent cigars in their faces and then scuttled around the corner to hide the holes in our breeches.

This collecting job always carries one into places that don't exist except in dreams. Today it led Revoli and me across a court green with age and moss and stinking with refuse, up a stone stairway with hollows for the bare feet of the dead to step in, and into a room where a hundred cuckoo clocks were conversing with fiddles without necks, harps without strings. Revoli and I sat down on the edge of ancient French chairs and waited. The clocks pointed to various concert hours, and the ancient instruments sighed continually. Théomar François, the clock-maker, the maker of musical instruments, the composer of Aux Cayes, presently appeared, silent and broken like his old instruments. He talked about the songs in Aux Cayes as he might have discussed its half-demolished cathedral. On Saturday there would be Mardi Gras dancing in the streets, but it was not like the old days with their Banda, Policionelle, Minuet, Contredanse, and Cadre. "Vaudou," breathed Théomar François, "it is very rare in Aux Cayes, and the Rara, it is something new and practically unknown here."

That afternoon the old harridan's servant led us to four hounforts (as "Vaudou" cult houses are called) where we could see dancing, and then to a fifth in which we spent the evening at a fine and vigorous Danse Congo. The next day we stepped out of Théomar's front gate and down to the sea and spent the morning listening to the best singing I heard in Haiti. And all the songs were of the Rara.

Back of Aux Cayes are the hills. And in the hills are the real people of Haiti. Back of Aux Cayes are the hills, and in their tropic fashion they have a springtime full of the limpid odor of coffee blossoms. Their coffee comes down to Aux Cayes-on-the-sea by donkey-back or bullock-back and passes through the hands of Haitian middlemen into the sorting rooms of the German coffee-exporting houses. Haitian women squat on the green-gold carpet of coffee and sort it for maybe ten or twenty cents a day. A German steamer wallows in the rough water offshore. Then the coffee porters, who have been resting in the sun, wake up.

First comes the weighing. Revoli and I watch them. Before we begin, it is necessary to remember that in the tropics, where men sweat, they must drink. Here in Haiti, it is clarin, a raw, fiery-pure rum. When they work, they drink clarin. When they drink, they sing. When they sing, they dance. Burly, serious, calculating, kindly fellows, for them working well means singing, drinking, dancing, calling on the gods, and retailing scandal.

In the warehouse there is a mountain of coffee sacks, each one weighing nearly two hundred pounds. These are taken to the scales, given a final weighing, and then stacked again for their trip to the waiting coffee barge. In our country this would require hooks, barrows and seriousness. Here in Haiti it takes only bare hands and dancing Negro men. A sack of coffee flops off the stack and sends one porter shouting and spinning away under the impact. Sliding and whirling across the room, he stops against the far wall and runs to the scales, where his shoulders and neck toss off their burden. Another sack plops down beside his. Then the two stevedores leap into a corner, where one picks up a little iron pipe or vaxine and the other a pair of rocks. The first man blows his pipe and the other cracks his flints together, and presently ten men are capering together on the floor of the warehouse. As the weight of the coffee is taken, the dance loses man after man; the sacks leave the scales and are piled in a corner. At last the piper and his accompanist fling their instruments rattling into a corner and stagger away under their loads of coffee. The whole movement, a matter of four or five minutes, has come to an end. Ten sacks, two thousand pounds of coffee, have danced across the warehouse. Sweat soaks the rags of the men, and the clarin gurgles. The burly jig, the work dance, begins again. The men roar at each other like demons, and their backs creak under the awkward sacks. They dance and fling about like monkeys for an hour with never a pause, and suddenly you look up and the great stack of coffee has moved to the other side of the warehouse.

Out from the door of the warehouse the pier juts for a hundred yards into the shallow bay of Aux Cayes-under-the-sun. A quarter of a mile offshore the "Dutch" steamer shows its red belly above the chop and waits for the coffee barges. The thing to do now is to get the coffee from the warehouse and fill the barges. In America we should have a little railroad, some little trucks, or at least some barrows; but in Haiti men are cheaper than trucks or barrows, and so presently the human train emerges from the warehouse door. Legs bowed with strain, step a little unsteady, these men shuffle along under a burden so clumsy that their heads are almost hidden. The sacks rest along the nape of broad black necks, and when the shuffling, stooping line at last reaches the waiting bumboat, these powerful, sleek, gorilla necks, these square jaws, flip the sacks clear across the belly of the boat. *"Bon Dieu la po' nou' toute,"* they grunt, and wheel away like boxers, their chins almost touching their collarbones. When this gang of bullocks has shed its burdens, it gathers at the end of the pier; the vaxines begin to belch and grunt their earthy rhythm, the flints to click-click, and the porters dance down the quay toward the warehouse, their flat square feet stamping up the dust, their great throats roaring out one of their lewd songs.

> Koko m' pas lavé
> Woi, woi,
> Koko m' pas lavé
> M'enragé.

The backs begin to straighten, the eyes to lift their gaze from the earth. Back of the "vaxiniers," their long arms outstretched to catch the air in a gorilla clutch, huddled together, shambling, great black laborers shout their defiance of heavy coffee sacks and their love of the sun, shake their splendid loins and shoulders. Slap, slap, the great feet strike the dust. Another song, another deep and gusty roar rings across the bay to the Dutch steamer and the rosy young Dutch mate, leaning over the taffrail.

> Bobo enragé,
> Wy-o,
> Bobo enragé,
> Bobo campé sous terrace-là,
> Wo——.

III. ZOMBI

One morning in Aux Cayes I stepped into a bar and was cornered by the fat, middle-aged mulatto proprietress. She drew me aside and at the top of her voice shared with me the gossip of Haiti. The same thing had evidently happened to William Seabrook, for I recognized several of his *Magic Island* experiences in the series of stories she told me.

As a loyal Haitian she believed that the mysteries of the island should be talked about instead of covered up, as the upper class wished. Had I ever heard about the zombis of Haiti? She was scandalized at my ignorance. She was the one to tell me, and I must inform the world. She had grown up in the United States and knew a thing or two about public decency, and when she returned to Haiti after her marriage she was at first amazed, then frightened, and finally outraged by the things she saw her people suffering. The populace was afraid to walk abroad at night. Children and young girls were kidnaped and never seen again. Vaudou priests took these poor creatures off to the mountains, transformed them into zombis, and made them work on their plantations until they were dead. Graves were found empty the morning after burials. People were recognized on the streets who had been thought dead for several years. Taken to the police station for questioning, they shivered in the corner, shielded their faces from expected blows, did not recognize their next of kin. When these people were released at last, they died mysteriously or as mysteriously disappeared.

Did I know none of these things? When I confessed that I had heard stories of sorcerers who could induce a state of apparent death, wait until the night after burial, dig the "corpse" up, revive him, and then use him as a slave during life, the old lady nodded approvingly. But when I added that I held these stories only as so many old wives' tales, she waxed indignant.

Listen, then, and if I cared to investigate the truth of what she said, I had only to go to Port-au-Prince and ask so-and-so, a woman of unquestionable reliability, and then verify what she had said word-for-word with so-and-so and so-and-so. Listen.

Not fifteen years ago a beautiful young octoroon, one Margarite——, suddenly sickened and died. Her death had been the occasion of much sorrowful comment, but of course she had been forgotten before the year was out. Seven years later, the priest who had been sent to attend to the funeral of Monsieur——, a former Minister, made a tour of inspection of the premises and stumbled onto a locked door. He demanded the keys from the servant and was told that the master of the house carried the keys to that room on his person and that no one had ever been allowed to enter it. He found a key; and presently the door swung back on its well-oiled hinges. The priest saw a figure crouching against the wall. He called for a lamp, and saw a woman, hiding her face in her hands and trembling with fear. He approached her, raised her face up to the light. It was Margarite, whom he had taught, confessed, and given first communion. Instead of calling the police, he sent for the nuns, and together they hurried her to the convent. She had lost none of her beauty, but she seemed to have lost her wits. She responded to their kindest ministrations with tears of fright.

After some consultation the girl's family was sent for late at night. When her father and mother had examined the girl, they insisted that they had never seen her before and demanded politely why they had been disturbed at such an hour. Why, no, this wasn't their daughter. Had the holy father gone mad? Did he not remember that she had died seven years before? Surely he had officiated at the funeral? And now, if they might be excused, they would return to bed.

They bowed their way out and left the nuns open-mouthed. The grave must be opened. It was empty. Faced with the evidence, the girl's parents admitted that this might be their daughter but intimated that the less they heard about her the better they would like it. Later they made a belated and halfhearted offer to take charge of the girl, who was still unable to utter a syllable and who, so far as doctors could determine, was quite mad. This offer the priest gravely refused, and soon she was bundled aboard a liner and taken to France and hidden away in a French nunnery. All that can be heard from her to this day is that she has somewhat recovered from the effects of her enchantment, whatever it may have been, and that she stoutly refuses to return to Haiti.

This rather excitable lady provided me with material for leading questions that evening as I sat over my boiled fish and yams at the harridan's house. At the table I repeated some of the lady's conversation to Gran Moune, a nymphomaniac, and Revoli, and expressed my doubts as to her sanity. They pounced on me. They had seen this, they had known of such a one, their fathers had told them that. If I knew what they knew I would not walk out at night without a *garde* (protective amulet). At last the air cleared a little and Gran Moune emerged as the witness for the zombis.

"Es one time up north in Mirebalais. One day six peoples they run down street an' they so ugly till Mirebalais peoples think big devils have come from bush. All the police run but one captain. He brave. He stay and he take big gun and cocomacaque and he arrest those people and then he beat them, try to make 'em talk. An' they can't talk.

"Officer come look at them in prison. They know they dead peoples. Zombis. *Bocor* hid 'em in plantation hills an' servant give 'em salt so they can run away. They run, they run to town. *Bocor* took away their sense, but servant mix salt in their food an' they can run away. Pretty soon everyone come an' look at these dead people. An' they look like they ain't had nothin' to eat for fourteen years. Somebody been beat 'em plenty, too. They people finally come an' took 'em back home, but they all die in a year. *Bocor* kill 'em. This happened in one thousand nine hundred and twenty-eight in Mirebalais in North.

"Es another time a man had office in Port-au-Prince. Had one room was never opened. Full up with zombi. Do all his work for him. Write on machine. He ain't do no work but he get rich. Leave work at night. In morning all work finish. One day another man find keys, open door of room where zombi stay. Three zombi there. They 'es sit an' tremble. Man fell down he so fright. They took him to hospital an' he told police what he see. They come there an' carry zombi to hospital. Doctor work an' work but couldn't do nothin'. Priest leave 'em in church for one year, but those girl never talk. Dey go look for man who had office but he gone. Never see him again. He left his wife and little baby.

"These things I know. I seen 'em. This my papa told me. One time my mama was sick an' papa went to Sal Trou to find a houngan.* Houngan open door to hounfort, tell him, 'You lay down an' sleep until morning. Then I go with you. But if you hear the house fall down, don't be afraid. If it burn up, don't run.' My papa tell him, 'All right.' When he go in there he see a man hanging up on the wall on hook. He see a man's skull. In corner he see a pile of cadaver. My papa, he brave man an' he got good protection, too. He lay down but he not sleep. 'Bout midnight he hear some people come, hear houngan talkin', 'Got fresh meat.' Then, papa, he not wait for to put he clothes on. He pile 'em on he head an' he *sorti.* Run for fifteen mile. Sleep in cane field. He not go back to Sal Trou."

"What you say is a true thing," said Revoli, "an' now I gon' talk a story I heard when I *pitite-pitite* [small child]. Was fisherman. One day he go to fish an' on the edge of the sea he meet a man. He ask man if he want to go fishin'. Man said, '*Oui.*' Was zombi. Big devil. They git in de boat an' let

out sail an' pretty soon they begin to fish. That fisherman he ain't catch
nothin'. De zombi can't keep his hook wid bait, so many fish bite 'm. He
t'row hook over side of boat an' begin to pull it up an' he got t'ree, fo' fish
on she. In one minute de boat nearly sunk wid fish. De fisherman divide
'm wid one big fish to each pile an' one little fish to each pile. Zombi he
rake she hand t'roo pile an' mix 'em up. He say, 'Iguale, iguale' [equal,
equal]. Fisherman try to divide de fish again. Give all big fish to zombi.
Zombi mix pile, say, 'Iguale, iguale, iguale.' Man divide fish again. Ain't leave
but two, t'ree little fish for he own se'f. Zombi say, 'Iguale, iguale, iguale,' an'
he mix pile all up. Dat man he look at zombi fingernail. She one mile
long. He look at she hand. She two mile long. He look up at zombi. He
growed great big devil. Dat man he run to Cap-Haitien. When he start he
all de way down to de Port-au-Prince, one hundred an' fifty kilomet'. He
ask 'em when he get to Cap-Haitien when de nex' boat sail for Les Etats-
Unis. When nex' boat sail, he hide in a bunch of bananas an' he don't
come back no more. De man dat was captain of de boat t'row him over-
board 'cause he say he don' want no Haitian in he country. Man have to
swim to Guinea before he can land. He sho' tired too."

Even the old harridan, who had been sitting in the dark a few yards
away pretending not to listen, had to laugh. This was encouragement
enough for Revoli, for whom one "estory" means another as long as it is
night.

"I give you a true history," he said. "There was a vagabond in Port-au-
Prince. He find a hole in de back door of a meat shop. He can reach in an'
take all de meat he want. He been take meat every night. One time he
meet anudder vagabond an' ask him if he would go wid him to steal de
meat. De feller said, 'Yes.' So dey went to de place. De ol' woman own de
shop, she begin to miss her meat an' she think she catch de t'ief. She get
her machete an' sit by de door. De two vagabond come to de shop an' de
firs' one tell de odder one to stick she han' in de door an' reach all around
an' when he fin' de meat to pull it out de hole. De secon' vagabond, he
reach in wid she han' an' de ol' lady come down 'Whok' wid de knife. Cut
off he han'.

"De t'ief, he pull his arm out. De firs' t'ief ask him, 'What did you git?'

" 'I found me somepin' sweet,' de odder one say.

"De first t'ief stuck he hand in. De ol' lady cut he han' off, too.

"He say, 'Oh, oh, oh, it sho is a fine thing I get there. Why don' you
try again?'

" 'I got enough. I goin' home.'

" 'Well, let me see your hand, see what you got.'

" 'Let me see yours first.'

"They begin to cuss. They begin to fight.

"The second t'ief begin to holler, 'You brought me here into bad trouble.'

"The first t'ief say, 'Not more trouble than you let me fin'.'

"They fight until de police come an' fight both wid de cocomacaque an' take 'em off to de jail an' beat 'em until dey forget dey ain't got no hand. When I come up, I tell dem police not to beat de man so hard. So he quit beatin' him an' beat me. Beat me so hard that he knock me here to tell you dis tale."

The little boy of the house, the son of an American marine who had long ago left for the States, leaned forward and shrilled, "Cric!"

Revoli indulgently responded "Crac!" for this is the way that a proper Haitian begins a tale.

"Bouki have big argument with Ti Malice.** Bouki say, 'I can count better'n you. When I be in a hundred you probably be in ten.' Ti Malice make two pile of rocks, a hundred for he own se'f an' one hundred an' twenty-five for Bouki. He try to trick Bouki. But Bouki, he smart fellow. He make two pile wid fifty rock in each one. Dey give de word for 'm to start an' Bouki say, '*Un, deux, shinquante, shinquante, shent*' [one, two, fifty, fifty, a hundred]. He win. Dat be one time Bouki trick Ti Malice."

After this tale the evening turned to riddling, then to game songs, then to Mardi Gras songs; but when I crawled under my mosquito net I was still wondering about the zombis. The stories of the evening had begun with what the narrators believed were factual accounts, had run to hearsay and finally lapsed into straight medieval jest. It was now quite clear that for the illiterate Haitian, zombi might refer either to a malignant ghost or to the more gruesome exhumed mortals. That explained the frequency of the zombi stories one heard. But I had met no one in Haiti—and this included all the rich and educated Haitians of the upper class, the few Americans who remained on the island and the one anthropologist who was at work there at the time—who did not believe that there was something in some of these tales. I could not forget that the American psychiatrist at the Haitian insane asylum had told me that there was one patient under treatment who he believed was a genuine zombi. Dead so far as anyone could tell, buried, then found naked in the road fifteen years later, not twenty yards from the house where she had raised a family, she did not yet know who or where she was. He would try to find out what had happened to her. The houngans, he thought, must have some sort of drug which affects the brain.

IV. L'ASILE

The next day a young German merchant gave me a ride as far as Acquin. At dusk Revoli and I dropped off in the middle of the square and looked about for the caserne of the Garde d'Haiti, that efficient small army, trained and disciplined by the marines, which maintains its posts in every quarter of Haiti and polices it better than it has ever been policed before in its turbulent history. After the sergeant of the guard had inspected my letter from Colonel Calte, he thought somewhat better of me, and I was soon summoned to the lieutenant's house. He was in bed with *la fièvre* (malaria), the national malady. He apologized for his house and his lack of hospitality and cursed the luck that had sent him to this wretched and miasmic town. He gave me a delicious supper, however; and then Revoli, the sergeant and I went for a stroll about the town.

Acquin is a strange and ghostly place. Despite the malaria it throve once, until a hurricane came and blew the soul out of it. Now, around a littered square that no doubt once embraced a tidy little French park with a pavilion for a band, the empty white houses stand like slim, white hands raised in salute. The flag of decay floats in the darkness where at the upper end of the square the tower of a ruined Norman cathedral faces the sea.

Already at seven-thirty the town was deserted. All the doors and windows were tightly shut and light gleamed through only an occasional crevice. Saturday night in Mardi Gras season and asleep! Revoli nodded sagely. Didn't I see that he had been right? The people are afraid to venture out of their houses at night in this South that I liked so well. A wicked country where people are afraid of their own devils! The sooner we got back to Cul-de-Sac, the safer our souls.

At last, however, our search was rewarded. We found a *pandang*. Couples, the women in slippers, slid their feet a little, rubbed hips. In the corner of the bare room the malinoumbas (a box with five iron teeth, which, when plucked by an expert, outbasses a "bull fiddle") was growling beneath the delicate melody of a three-stringed guitar, and the skillful fingers of the drummer rippled across the faces of two "bongo" drums no wider than his hands. Presently Revoli, swearing that he could cheat at dice better than any man on the island, asked me to lend him a penny. I followed him to the rear, where four or five men, handling the most ancient pair of dice I have ever seen, soon took his money. Then we sat outdoors and had a drink of rum. Along the shore were black hummocks of campeche, a dyewood which is Acquin's chief export. (Fine mahogany is burned here for charcoal.) At their feet ran a little white road, along the dark edge of which the waves of the bay broke in the moonlight. Across the dim mirror the mountains loomed in the night. The wind from the sea, the noise of the waves, small waves; a melancholy town, malarial; but in the moonlight the old gray houses turned silver, and the blacks became gods or demons.

V. THE DANCE

Revoli had been calling me softly for a half-hour. I woke up and cursed him, for the gallery of the lieutenant's house was still swimming in the moonlight. It was half-past three. We were late. I listened to the infinite regrets of the lieutenant in his night cap. Then Revoli, the sergeant, who had been delegated to guide us as far as L'Asile, and I were riding through the locust thickets toward the black mountains. For an hour I lurched along with my yellow nag until the dawn showed the kids shivering beneath their mothers. In the soft light of morning, which is Haiti's rarest purple treasure, I smoked my first cigarette and, turning in my saddle, saw Revoli. He was riding a weary, female ass, on a sort of wooden sawbuck of a saddle that boasted no stirrups. Beneath his thighs were two great hampers of luggage, and in his lap he held my guitar. His feet dangled at that moment behind the ass's ears as he hauled away at the reins. We looked at each other and howled with laughter. The ghosts of Acquin dissolved in the morning air.

The mountains were green, the air was sweet with coffee blossom, and I liked the silent mountain women who strode downward past us with their market burdens on their heads. These Negro women of the mountains are as exotic and beautiful as the palms that rise up out of the crowding greenery. About the middle of the morning we heard drums to the left of us and turned into a clearing where a feast for the Vaudou gods was being concluded. We were gravely invited to get down and were given seats of honor beside the drums. Some nervousness was perceptible at our sudden arrival, but we were still welcome. They were mountaineers, first.

The *tonnelle* was bright with Mardi Gras decorations; the ground, wet and steaming with clarin. Libations had been poured to the gods and animals had been sacrificed. In a moment three women, their heads bright with gay handkerchiefs, came dancing into the enclosure. These women, for an hour or so, were the "horses of the gods." The ancient gods of Africa had "mounted" them, and, possessed of the gods, they were shown the deference owing to the ancient dead. These gods of Guinea danced up and saluted each of us after their fashion. A jolting right handshake and another with the left hands joined. Then three wet kisses on the mouth. The last of the gods was a slight yellow woman with cold gray demonic eyes who darted her little pointed tongue over her rotted teeth and rocked back on her heels shaking her belly before each kiss. The gods then invited us to dance and we all accepted. For my part, I danced badly. Everyone snickered, and I soon sat down to watch. It was intense, gay—yes, lovely. The people honored their gods and rejoiced that they were content with what had been offered; but law, money, practical people—the dull and inefficient weapons of the upper-class propriety— soon interfered. The sergeant began to growl about a fine, for the "manger loa" (feast for the gods) was being held without a permit.

Haiti, as a good Catholic country, officially outlaws Vaudou. The official attitude is outwardly supported by the upper class of mulattoes, although many, if not all, of them secretly participate in Vaudou rites. By and large, however, Vaudou is the peculiar property of the peasants, who make up over ninety per cent of the population. They understand the rites and know the secrets of the cult, and they guard these secrets jealously. The capitalist class feel, I believe, no little fear of Vaudou, especially since many Haitian revolutions have been led by Vaudou priests or by men thought to be especially favored by the gods of Vaudou. Besides this fear and besides the repulsion that the "cultured" Haitian feels or pretends to feel toward the primitive and superstitious Vaudouist, he has pretenses to keep up before all the world. As a Catholic, he is committed against Vaudou. As the European he feels himself to be, he scorns it. As a modern American businessman or practical government official, he feels himself superior to it.

The Constitution of Haiti, therefore, bans Vaudou, but it would be as difficult to abolish Vaudou in Haiti as to root out the habit of driving motor cars in America. The Haitian politician knows this, and, practically enough, exploits the peasant even as he pretends to be most friendly. The government levies a tax on all dances; indiscriminately demands a tax for all animals slaughtered at these dances, by head and by kind; but does not inquire too closely into the nature of the dance unless the taxes are not paid. This provides a sizable income for the government, and at the same time, an excellent opportunity for local police officials to line their own purses. I learned after months of mistakes that the best way to keep up with the Vaudou ceremonies is to make friends with the local sergeant. He always knows what is going on, and an introduction from him gives one carte blanche so far as the participants are concerned.

The sergeant was growling about the holding of a ceremony without a permit. Fine or no fine, however, the gods had come and the ceremony had to be carried through. The hands ceased to move on the drumheads. The crowd sifted out from beneath the *tonnelle* and gathered at the other end of the clearing. Gran Erzulie, malignant goddess of the bush, was being offered her food. At the foot of the little tree whose trunk was drenched with the vile clarin, a bougie, or handmade wax candle, was burning. Erzulie—that is, the little yellow woman possessed by Erzulie—broke up the big white yams and tore apart chunks of pork with her dirty hands and handed them around the circle. One old beggar on his thin legs received a bowl full of this food of the gods, while the possessed women danced about him singing,

> Alouba, 'louba, nous marré-o,
> Nous marré, Gran Alouba, n'a lagé-o,
> Alouba, 'louba, nous marré-o.

Their bare feet and ankles were splashed with the blood of the morning's sacrifice. We left them dancing.

NOTES

* Vaudou priest. A houngan is consulted first in any case of sickness. He tells the family whether the illness is from the Bon Dieu, from the "loa" (the African gods) or from an enemy. If the illness is from the Bon Dieu, a herb doctor is called or, in extreme cases, the person may be sent to the hospital. The houngans of Sal Trou are said to be very powerful. It is one of the most isolated towns in Haiti and, I am told, the most God-forsaken.

** Bouki and Ti Malice, the rich, blundering, greedy butt and the careful, cunning trickster, are the central characters of at least half the Haitian folk tales. They occupy the same positions as Br'er Fox and Br'er Rabbit in the folk tales of the Negroes of the Southern United States. Indeed, some of the tales are practically identical in plot. Bouki is regularly discomfited, oftentimes in a very gruesome fashion, while Ti Malice watches and laughs. Here is the only Bouki–Ti Malice tale that I heard in which Bouki triumphs. Bouki always talks with a lisp.

Chapter 3

Music in Your Own Back Yard

It's a cool summer evening and you're seated around the campfire, just talking lazily and singing songs. One of the girls has brought her guitar and she's strumming it softly. Then she starts to sing.

You've been out on the lake on a canoe trip all day, and hit some rough weather. One of the canoes tipped and it was a hard pull righting it and getting to shore. You still shiver a little from the wetting you got.

The singer takes a well-known tune—"Oh, Susannah," or "Pop Goes the Weasel"—and starts making up words, telling of the afternoon's adventure, strumming the accompaniment on her guitar. She changes the tune slightly to fit the new words. Soon all of you get the idea. It's fun, and you help with new verses and join in on the chorus.

It's just a pleasant way of passing the evening, the way of the cowpuncher on the Western plains, of the Kentucky mountaineers gathered around the smoky oil lamp. And when you sing a song about your own lives, you are doing the same thing they do—you are making folk music.

America, with its colorful background—cutting trails across vast, quiet wilderness, breaking new soil, building new cities—is rich in folk music. It has come straight from the hearts of people, from their loneliness and hunger and cold, from the rhythms of their daily jobs, from their lovemaking and their dancing, and often just from the joy of being alive and strong and healthy.

Since the beginning of the world, people have told their feelings in song. And they're still doing it. Doing it mostly in lonely spots where there are no radios and phonographs, no movies and concerts, where people have to entertain themselves.

Down in Texas, where I come from, there's a story told about Davy Crockett, the great hunter and scout of the Southwest, which shows how much the frontier folk needed song.

Davy was riding through the wilderness one day when he heard the sound of a shrill, high-pitched fiddle coming through the trees. He spurred his horse on and, stuck in the ford of a nearby stream, he discovered a parson in a dusty, black beaver hat, his fiddle tucked under his chin, his horse and buggy beside him.

Davy pulled the parson out, and when they were on dry land again, he asked curiously, "I kin see ye needed help, but why were ye *aplayin'* out there?"

"Well," said the parson, "I knew pint blank I could holler for help 'till I was hoarse and no one would come, but once my fiddle would get goin', 'twouldn't matter how wild the country—if there was a hunter or trapper within ten mile, the minute he heard it, he'd come runnin'."

The Forty-niners, bold, rough men who had left wives and sweethearts when the word spread that Sutter had found gold in California, loved music, too. They would pay a fiddler thirty-five dollars in gold, just to scrape away on a homemade fiddle for a couple of hours.

So did the cowboys. Their lives weren't as romantic as the movies would have you think. They rode all day long over the great dry plains of the Southwest, driving the herds before them, seeing that none of the weak little orphan calves—they call them "dogies"—strayed. And as they rode, they sang. Such songs as:

"Whoopee-ti-yi-yo, git along little dogies,
"It's your misfortune and none of my own,
"Whoopee-ti-yi-yo, git along you little dogies,
"For you know Wyoming will be your new home."

And as they worked, they would make up new verses to familiar songs, and out of their experience, compose whole new tunes. It's said that there was one song as long as the trail from Texas to Montana, and that there was a stanza for every cowboy who rode over the trail.

Back-breaking toil was mostly what these frontiersmen knew, and songs helped them at their work. Songs of Negro cotton pickers in the deep South, of sailors on the old fourmasted schooners, of lumberjacks and teamsters and railroad builders.

And of an evening, in isolated country districts, people would—and still do—gather together and clear the floor for square dancing and more songs. Men would woo the young country girls with courting songs. And there would be game songs for the children. These songs are our heritage as Americans. Woven in bright strands through the pattern of pioneer life, they are part of the American tradition of which we are so proud. To-day, almost too late, we realize that they are in danger of disappearing.

Yet these folk songs can easily be preserved. You, and all Americans, can find them right in your own back yards. Somewhere in your neighborhood there may be an old man, or woman—or perhaps a young one—who can sing you hundreds of love ballads and work songs. Your own grandmother may remember some.

I grew up in Austin, Texas knowing many of these tunes, for my father, John A. Lomax, is what is called a "folk song specialist," a rather frightening title which masks a job that is pure adventure. He travels around the country in his car—it used to be an old jalopy until a year or so ago—looking for people who can sing folk tunes. When he finds them, he gets out his portable recording equipment from the back of the car, and makes records—we call it "cutting" records—which are sent to the music archives of the Library of Congress in Washington. For the Government is eager to keep in permanent form the songs of its people.

Strangely enough, I was never much interested in folk music until my late teens. I went to the University of Texas, and then to Harvard, and I was planning to study philosophy—until one summer my father invited me to come along with him on one of his field trips.

That was in the summer of 1933, one of the most exciting summers I have ever spent. From then on, I've made it *my* job, too, to collect folk songs. I've traveled all over the country, thousands of miles, both with my father and alone—along the dusty roads of the South where you pass chain gangs at work, across the endless dry plains of the West, through the fishing villages of the New England coast, even down to the huts of the black natives of Haiti. The Library of Congress sent me to Haiti, and I was so fascinated by the music of the Haitians that my wife, Elizabeth Harold, and I spent our honeymoon there.

Our way of work is simple. From letters and books and word of mouth, we hear of someone, perhaps a Vermont woodsman or a Kentucky miner, who knows a store of old folk tunes. We get into our car and go to visit him.

But my father and I don't burst in like college professors in search of quaintness. We make friends. We live in the neighborhood. And before we even go to a place, we find out about the kind of work in that section so that we can talk about it. Only then do we go and ask for songs.

Mostly people are eager to sing for you, because they're proud of their own songs. And they should be, because many of them are talented artists. But occasionally they have to be coaxed a little.

I remember one occasion when my father and I were traveling down South, looking for Henry Trevelyan [Truvillion], part Indian but mostly Negro. Henry was foreman of a railroad section gang, and was supposed to know hundreds of old railroad songs. When we found him, we asked him to sing for us. He shook his head. "I don't sing, Mr. Lomax," he said.

We were puzzled, and then we understood. Trevelyan didn't sing in the sense we think of it. He would be lost on a concert stage, or with an orchestra. Singing was a part of his work, helping him to direct the men working under him in laying the ties for the railroad.

Understanding this, we got permission to accompany the work gang at three the following morning, when they went out into the woods to lay the tracks. We had our recording machine with us, and collected twenty songs—work chants, they really were—with Trevelyan singing the lead in his fine baritone, and the rest of the gang, working in rhythm, joining in on the chorus.

A few months later my father went back to see Trevelyan, in search of more songs. We were friends by then, and he was sure Trevelyan would be glad to sing this time. But there was more trouble. He had given up his railroad job and was studying to be a preacher. And for a preacher, singing was sin (many Negro preachers differ from this point of view). The only way my father could set his conscience at rest was by making him a present of a beautifully designed Bible cover, rich in color. That made the singing all right.

I've had other strange experiences in search of song. One, I remember, happened in New Orleans, where I'd discovered a Negro piano player who knew all the verses of "Stagolee," a song about a man who killed "Billy Lyons over a milk-white Stetson hat." I had heard several versions of the song, but I wanted the correct one.

This pianist was working in a dance hall in the evenings, and I went down there with my typewriter to get the words of all thirty verses correctly. For two hours he played and sang, while I sat at the typewriter and the dancers huddled around us, fascinated.

But the proprietor of the place became angry. He thought we were ruining his business. So he walked up to the piano, picked up the only lamp in the place, and without a word disappeared, leaving us in complete darkness.

The "Stagolee" man followed him, furious. In a few moments he was back, rubbing his knuckles, the lamp in his hand.

"I don't let no one treat my friends that-a-way," he remarked grimly. And the music continued. I never did see the proprietor of the place again.

Generally the reaction of people is friendly. They're proud you consider their music important, and they want to do the best job possible. I remember one Finnish singer in the Middle West, from whom we were recording a song about a Finnish Robin Hood. It took twenty minutes to sing. When we had cut the record, we played it back for him. His sharp ears discovered one tiny mistake, and he was so eager for perfection that he made us do the entire record over again.

Most people are fascinated to hear records of their voices. I once recorded a singing sermon delivered by a seventy-five-year-old Negro named "Sin Killer" Griffen. When I played the record back for the old preacher, he shook his head wonderingly.

"People been tellin' me I was a good preacher for nigh onto sixty years," he said, "but I never knew I was that good."

Our dusty car and our recording equipment have seen strange places in our travels. We have recorded songs in lumber camps, in the huts of share croppers, on ships smelling of tar and brine, among workers in cotton fields, and in automobile factories in crowded cities. Often in prisons (we find many fine songs in prisons where men are segregated and sing to pass the time) we cut our records in the hospital, because it is quiet there. And once I even remember being solemnly ushered into the execution chamber, because it was the only sound-proofed room in the prison. The only chair in the room—and somehow we all avoided it—was the execution chair. That setting didn't seem to bring out the best in song.

It was in a prison that my father and I met one of the greatest folk-song artists we have come across, Huddie Ledbetter—he was called Leadbelly. I would like to tell you a little about him.

Leadbelly called himself "de king of de twelve-string guitar players ob de world." He wasn't modest, but he was right. From him we got our richest store of folk songs, over a hundred new songs that Leadbelly had heard since his childhood in Morningsport, Louisiana, and had varied to fit his own singing and playing style.

Music was natural to Leadbelly. When he was a child, one of his uncles gave him an accordion. Here's how Leadbelly tells about it: "I was so glad I nachully jump an' shout. I played dat accordion *all* night long. Papa would raise up and say, 'Son, ain' cha fixin' to lie down?' But I was awhipping it down to de groun'."

Later Leadbelly got a guitar, which he loved even more, and he used to travel around Louisiana, singing for white folk and Negroes. He would sing songs he knew, and sometimes he would compose new ones. The songs came out of his daily experience, just as most folk songs do.

For example, Leadbelly used to hear his uncle, Bob Ledbetter, shout to his wife, Silvy, as he worked in the fields under the hot sun, "Bring me li'l water, Silvy." The words began to sound a chant in Leadbelly's mind, so he picked up his guitar, and started composing "Bring Me Li'l Water, Silvy," a song he still sings in concerts.

Leadbelly is a fine but erratic worker. He once told me that he was "de bes' cotton picker dat country (Texas) ever saw. Wouldn't wuck but five days a week, an' den pick mo' cotton dan any two niggers wuckin' six." But he had a terrible temper which was always getting him in trouble. And consequently, when we met him he was in the Louisiana State Penitentiary.

Leadbelly begged us to help him get out of prison, and said he had composed a song to Governor O. K. Allen of Louisiana that he would like the Governor to hear. So we recorded the song for him. It went like this:

"In nineteen hundred an' thirty-two,
"Honorable Guvner O. K. Allen,
"I'm 'pealin' to you.
"If I had you, Guvner O. K. Allen,
"Like you got me,
"I would wake up in de mornin',
"Let you out on reprieve."

We took the record to the Governor in Baton Rouge, and sure enough he let Leadbelly out of jail. I became ill about that time and had to go home, so my father took Leadbelly along with him on his trips through the South, to help him with the heavy recording machine.

Leadbelly sang for the convicts in many of the prisons. In one Alabama prison, the convicts had just been given their weekly tobacco allowance of twenty-five cents. After his songs, Leadbelly passed the hat among his four hundred listeners. They gave him a few nickels and over three hundred pennies—greater tribute to his talent than the applause of any wealthy audience.

When we went to New York, Leadbelly begged to accompany us. My father gave a talk and Leadbelly sang at a smoker given by a Philadelphia club. He was the hit of the evening. Seated at the speakers' table, dressed in his convict clothes which my father had kept, a red bandanna hiding a huge scar on his neck, Leadbelly sat quietly as my father explained his songs. And before he began each song, he was quiet again. We asked him why, later, and he said he was "thinking in his heart."

Leadbelly stayed in New York. He brought his girl, Martha Promise, up from Louisiana and they were married in Connecticut, with my father giving the bride away, me as best man, and the bridegroom dressed in a double-breasted cinnamon suit with red checks.

Leadbelly never got over his wonder that New York City was built on solid rock. He wrote a song about it. This is the last verse:

"I go down to Lou' siana
"An' I'll walk an' I'll talk,
"Tell ever' body 'bout City of New Yawk!
"An' I go down to Georgia
"An' I'll walk and tell
"Trains run over top o' town hyar
"And it's call-ed the El.
"An' have yo' heard about the mightee shock?
"They Tell Me New Yawk City
"Built on Solid Rock!"

Another unusual person we met in our travels was Aunt Molly Jackson, Kentucky backwoods nurse, one-quarter Indian, the rest American for generations back. Aunt Molly looks Indian. She must be nearly sixty, yet she stands tall and straight as a young girl. Her face is wrinkled, and yet her wrinkles are hard and firm, not soft, grandmotherly wrinkles.

Aunt Molly lived most of her life in Kentucky's bloody Harlan county, and from her childhood was taught old ballads by her grandmother, who, in turn, had learned them from *her* grandmother. They weren't easy to learn. Aunt Molly remembers, from the time she was three, sitting on her grandmother's knee and hearing the songs over and over again until she knew them. And then, when she was older, the young folk would get together for entertainment on a Saturday night—there were no movies for them to go to—and sing these ballads and love songs.

I once asked Aunt Molly if the young men ever courted the girls with these songs. "Certainly," she answered. "And it happened to me once. A young feller come from another State, and he would court me until I thought I would just have to marry him, and he'd sing me that song about 'East Virginia'—it goes like this:

"I was bowned and raised in old Virginia,
"To old Kentucky I did go,

"There I met a fair young lady
"Her name and age I did not know."

"Did you feel sorry for him?" I asked Aunt Molly.

"Yes, I guess I did. I was married to him for twenty years."

Aunt Molly raised her family in Kentucky, and watched her husband go down into the mines for a living. Conditions were so bad in the mining district in the twenties that she remembers men going down with nothing in their lunch baskets but a bottle of water.

So Aunt Molly started traveling around the country, singing and telling stories—she knew hundreds of them from her days of nursing—and raising money to help the miners. She came up to New York, where she has held people spellbound with her ballads.

There are hundreds more people like Leadbelly and Aunt Molly whom we've met in our travels—Captain William Applebye-Robinson, who has sailed on four-masters and steamboats, and was once a shantey-boy; Elmer George, a lumberjack from Vermont; Uncle Alec Dunford, who plays square dances in Galax, Virginia; Dominin Gallegher, a barge-man from Michigan.

And there are thousands more songs we haven't heard, although we've recorded twenty thousand for the Library of Congress. Only recently some more have turned up through the series of broadcasts on folk music I've been giving. The broadcasts are part of the *American School of the Air* series, and on them I've sung folk ballads and played the guitar, and invited as guest singers such people as Aunt Molly and Leadbelly.

Through the broadcasts alone, I've discovered many more songs. I asked the young people listening in to hunt in their own communities for songs, and some have had great success. One group from California went out to the oil fields, and uncovered several new tunes the oil workers sang.

One woman living in Cape May County, New Jersey, wrote in about some songs the pilots sang, off the New Jersey coast. Another sent me a song called "Little Colen Annie," which she'd spent thirty-five years trying to track down. Altogether about two hundred and fifty new songs have been sent in to me, in my six months of broadcasting. They've come from people who were interested enough in folk music to recall the songs they heard their mothers and grandmothers sing, and the songs specially known in their region of the country.

It's easy and it's fun and it's fascinating work—going around your own neighborhood looking for folk tunes. Some of you, perhaps, have heard unusual tunes all your life. And most of you know of some old character, living out your way, whose family has been in the district for generations. He is probably a mine of old songs and folk tales. Some of you live in neighborhoods where there are unique jobs—such as shrimp fishing down in Florida or whaling up in New England. They're good bets for songs.

These are the places to look, among the back roads in your own home town, and while you're out on camping trips. Ask around home, do a little detective work, and then go out looking for songs.

There's music in your own back yard.

Chapter 4

Songs of the American Folk

To the folksong enthusiast, *A Treasury of American Song* by Olin Downes and Elie Siegmeister (Howell, Soskin and Company, 1940) brings welcome and heart-warming recognition. For the past fifty years, the folksong collector, excitedly discovering the musical treasures of the back-country and the back-alleys, has called on the musician for help and for approbation. The help received has been part-time and largely amateurish—time taken from more important concerns. Approval and understanding have manifested themselves in occasional spurts of interest and in rather condescending and self-conscious arrangements or thematic use of American folksongs.

When the eminent musical team of Downes and Siegmeister, calling their volume *A Treasury of American Song* with no strings or conditions attached, include in it one hundred and twenty-two American folksongs out of a total of one hundred and fifty-two songs altogether, then the folksong enthusiast has reason to be pleased. And all the more because the songs have been selected with such good taste and such warm understanding. Few specialists could have chosen a group of one hundred and twenty-two with more discrimination than have these editors who are, comparatively speaking, newcomers in the field.

The volume "ranges magnificently" indeed from the starkly moving hymns of Puritan New England and the rather pedantically spirited songs of the American Revolution, through the early period of expansion West (the period of *O Susannah* and *Dan Tucker* and *Davy Crockett*), to the Civil War, which produced more great songs than any war in history. The great industrial and political growth of the next forty years was paralleled by a mushroom growth of American folksong. This is the period which produced *John Henry, The Jam on Gerry's Rocks, Jesse James, Frankie and Johnny,* the blues, the cowboy songs, ragtime, the Negro work songs, the hobo ballads, the mountain love song, the sentimental ballads of the nineties, jazz.

All these are remarkably documented with their introductory notes, in one hundred and fifty pages. Nor do the editors allow us to forget that the people have continued their song making since the turn of the century. The final section concludes with a group of "documentaries" in which one feels that the people have begun to examine their problems self-consciously and comment on them with an objective vigor and irony that reach deeper than a Robert Frost and are more honest and succinct than a T. S. Eliot. The last song in the book is the *Ballad of Tom Joad*, in which Woody Guthrie, Okie folk-balladist, has compressed the essence of the Steinbeck novel and movie for those of his people who couldn't afford the two dollars or even a thirty-five cent admission.

The commentary is only occasionally thin. It is usually illuminating and hardly ever precious; the introduction is, for my taste, the best single piece of writing that has been done about the American popular musical idiom. It begins nobly:

> "If ever there was a time in the history of our country that our people should know
> themselves and renew faith in the purposes and traditions which are part of us,
> that time is now. This faith and these accretions of national experience are
> expressed in the most characteristic of our songs. They come directly from the peo-
> ple, of whom Lincoln said so lovingly that 'God must have loved them since he
> made so many of them'."

The editors have understood the seemingly incoherent diversity of American folksong as an expression of its democratic, interracial, international character, as a function of its inchoate and turbulent many-sided development. Do the critics, the editors demand, "really believe that the folk music of any nation is the simon-pure product of its soil? Or of a single period? Folk music is created everywhere and its seeds are flung on the winds to uncounted destinations." Later, "But there are no more hard and fast classifications of the songs of the American people than there has been regularity in the development of our society or consistency in the program of our education" . . . Again "A landowner, let us say, had peasants whose dancing and singing he loved . . . But he never knew what it was to sing side by side with the peasant . . . In America the great majority of its citizens . . . worked with their hands, shared on unequivocal terms the common lot, the common tasks and vicissitudes." After pronouncing folksong, minstrel song and jazz the truest expression of democratic experience, the editors conclude by asking for "a genuinely modern, all inclusive and democratic culture."

This much for a brilliant and satisfying piece of literary editing. Turn the page to the musical introduction and one encounters the old snobbery, the same old romantic attitude. The composer, apologizing for his settings of the songs, maintains that they have to be heard in the native physical environment to be appreciated, that the melodies seem rather bare on the printed page, that the accompaniments are intended to supply the color of the original physical background. The fact is that Elie Siegmeister did not collect these songs in the field, as the fly-leaf hints; he collected from books in libraries or from a few singers encountered in New York City. He has not heard the songs in their original environment and his harmonizations supply him with false color and an unnecessary variety, which he would not need if he had known or understood the complexity and richness of the songs as they actually exist on the lips of folksingers.

Siegmeister can write eloquent words about the songs, but usually not such eloquent music. His harmonizations are certainly not so ponderous, pretentious and condescending as those that have preceded his, and where he handles something familiar, like a hymn tune or a song by Billings, he is occasionally eloquent. The settings of folksongs, however, only point up the more his lack of acquaintance with folksong itself; they are pretentious, quaint, funny, cute and, in the end, distracting.

I am also annoyed because the editors have failed to acknowledge their sources, the books from which their songs are taken and because they fail to give a nod to the collectors and editors who laboriously gathered together, preserved and fought for the recognition of the material these editors now somewhat cavalierly preempt. I am, however, seriously concerned that not all the arrangers, choral conductors, composers, and music editors can capture, reproduce or even imitate the honest and passionate utterance of American folksong. Not one of them can, even when armed with the genuine critical understanding of a Siegmeister, overcome rigidity of spirit, oversophistication of soul, desire for polite applause and write music as hot and sure and unashamed as our folksingers and "blues-blowers" have created in America.

The volume is lavishly and beautifully printed. It folds back in a friendly fashion on the piano and, from a hasty glance at the best-seller list, seems to be the best current introduction to a subject in which interest is rapidly growing.

Chapter 5

Preface: *Our Singing Country*

If, then, to meaness mariners, and renegades and castaways, I shall
hereafter ascribe high qualities, though dark; weave around them
tragic graces; if even the most mournful, perchance the most abased,
among them all, shall at times lift himself to the exalted mounts; if I
shall touch that workman's arm with some ethereal light; if I shall
spread a rainbow over his disastrous set of sun; then against all mor-
tal critics bear me out in it, . . . thou great democratic God! Who didst
not refuse to the swart convict, Bunyan, the pale, poetic pearl; Thou
who didst clothe with doubly hammered leaves of finest gold, the
stumped and paupered arm of old Cervantes; Thou who didst pick up
Andrew Jackson from the pebbles; who didst hurl him upon a war-
horse; who didst thunder him higher than a throne! Thou who, in all
thy mighty, earthly marchings, ever cullest Thy selectest champions
from the kingly commons; bear me out in it, O God!

—Moby Dick

At the crossings of many of the rivers on the cattle trails from Texas to
Montana, there are little wind-blown graveyards—the resting place of
cowboys drowned while swimming longhorn cattle across swollen
streams. Scratched on one leaning headstone is: "He done his damdest."

The function of this book [*Our Singing Country*] is to let American folk
singers have their say with the readers. Most of these singers are poor people, farmers, laborers, convicts, old-age pensioners, relief workers, house-
wives, wandering guitar pickers. These are the people who still sing the
work songs, the cowboy songs, the sea songs, the lumberjack songs, the
bad-man ballads, and other songs that have no occupation or special

group to keep them alive. These are the people who are making new songs today. These are the people who go courting with their guitars, who make the music for their own dances, who make their own songs for their own religion. These are the story-tellers, because they are the people who are watching when things happen. These are the great laughers and the great liars, because they know that life is so much more ridiculous than anyone can ever hope to tell. These are the people who understand death, because it has been close to them all their lives. They have looked at the faces of young men whose lives have been torn from them in industrial accidents. They have been acquainted personally with young girls who killed themselves when they were deserted by false-hearted lovers. They have sheltered the families of men who were sent to prison for murder. These people make deep, slow jokes while they are waiting for things to happen, and they know that what a man isn't willing to fight for must not be true for him. These people have a lot to say and a lot to remember, and that is why this book is mostly in quotation marks.

These people have been wanderers, walking and riding alone into the wilderness, past the mountains and the broad rivers, down the railroad lines, down the highways. Like all wanderers, they have been lonely and unencumbered by respect for the conventions of life behind them. Remembering the old songs in their loneliness, throwing up their voices against prairie and forest track, along new rivers, they followed the instincts of their new experience and the old songs were changed so as to belong to their life in the new country. New songs grew up inconspicuously out of the humus of the old, thrusting out in new directions in small, but permanent, fashion. There grew up a whole continent of people with their songs as much a part of their lives as their familiar ax, gun, or silver dollar. It took them long to recognize that new lives and new songs had been made here.

Yet, in mass, the songs are perhaps more unconventional than the new lives. The songs are the product of the mixing or extension of several peasant musical stocks—British, African, Spanish, French, and German. They are sung in styles which offend the cultivated ear; they are accompanied, if at all, in various unpredictable ways on a number of "limited," inexpensive, and portable instruments. They are often repetitious; they are frequently trite and sententious; but, taken all together, they reflect the life with more honest observation, more penetrating wit and humor, with more genuine sentiment, with more true, energetic passion than other forms of American art, cultivated or subsidized.

We have known country fiddlers who couldn't read or write, but could play two, three, or four hundred tunes. We have known white ballad singers who remembered one, two, three hundred ballads. We have known Negroes who could sing several hundred spirituals. We have shaken hands with a Mexican share-cropper who carried in his head the text, tunes, and stage directions for a Miracle play requiring four hours and twenty actors to perform. We have been in constant touch with people who felt that inability to improvise by ear unfamiliar tunes in three- or four-part harmony marked one as unmusical. Such artists with their audiences have created and preserved for America a heritage of folk song and folk music equal to any in the world. Such folk have made America a singing country.

Ms. Griffin, a "Georgy cracker" who "has done everything that an honest woman could do except lie and steal"—picked cotton, cleared land, danced in a minstrel show, raised twelve children, run her own sawmill; who came to northern Florida overland and on foot from southern Georgia; from whom seventy-five or more ballads and songs have been recovered, including one called "Lord Derwentwater."

Old Lize Page of Hyden, Kentucky, from whom Cecil Sharp collected some of his best songs.

Blind old Mrs. Dusenberry of the Ozarks, living in a little old log cabin in the hills, holding in her memory nearly two hundred songs and ballads.

Maggie Gant and her children, disposed east Texas share-croppers.

Mrs. Ward of the Wards of Galax, Virginia, a gentle-voiced and calm farmer's wife who has passed on a store of ballads and songs to a whole generation of her descendants.

Elida Hofpauir, fifteen, who knew a bookful of French and Cajun ballads, who worked in a tomato canning factory and wanted a dollar "store-bought" dress for a present.

Aunt Molly Jackson, who has filled seventy-five twelve-inch records for the Library of Congress with her songs and reminiscences about them, who was midwife to Clay County, the daughter of a coal miner and preacher, the wife of a miner, and a union organizer in her own right.

Johnny Green, cantankerous old Irish fisherman and lumberjack and lake sailor of Beaver Island, Michigan, who has "dug up" out of his own memory nearly three hundred come-all-ye ballads, the saga of his people in Ireland, in English wars, in American forests, and on the American lakes.

Elmer George, one-time lumberjack, now automobile salesman of North Montpelier, Vermont. Dick Maitland, seaman of Sailors' Snug

Harbor, eighty-odd, still as sturdy and foursquare as an oak ship, called by Joanna Colcord the best sea shanty singer she knows.

J. C. Kennison, scissors grinder, shacked up on the windy top of one of the Green Mountains in Vermont, holding proudly in his mind the memories of Young Beichan and his Turkish Lady and of Jim Fiske, "The kind of man would pat a dog on the head."

Captain Pearl R. Nye, rotund and apple-cheeked, who claims to know the name of "every canalboat and every skipper that sailed the 'silver ribbon' of the Ohio ship canal," who sent to us in the Library of Congress the texts of seven hundred songs and ballads once current on the canal, copied out on scrolls of cheap yellow paper—songs he said had "bobbed up" recently out of his memory. (Captain Nye remarked once, "My mind is a canal.")

Alec Moore, retired cowpuncher, who sings everything from "Bold Andrew Barton" to "The Bloody Sioux Indians," whose present occupation is riding herd on an ice-cream wagon on the streets of Austin, Texas.

The Sheriff of Hazard County, Kentucky, who gets re-elected each year partly by the speed, ferocity, and style of his banjo-picking at county meetings.

Woody Guthrie, dust-bowl ballad-maker, proud of being an Okie, familiar with microphones and typewriters, familiar, too, with jails and freight trains, "with relatives under every railroad bridge in California," who knows scores of the old songs, and makes up a new one whenever he feels that one is needed about the Vigilante Men or Pretty Boy Floyd or Tom Joad.

And now the names of some of the singers who have moved us beyond all others that we have heard between Maine and New Mexico, Florida and Michigan—the Negroes, who in our opinion have made the most important and original contributions to American folk song:

Aunt Harriet McClintock of Alabama, seventy-eight years old, who sat by the roadside and sang:

> Poor little Johnny, poor little feller,
> He can't make a hundred today;
>> Down in the bottom
>> Where the cotton is rotten,
> He can't make a hundred today.

Aunt Molly McDonald, who sat on the sunny porch of her shanty and swapped sixty little songs out of the slavery days with Uncle Joe, her husband, and laughed heartily between the stanzas.

Iron Head, grim-faced prison habitué, who always claimed that his choice, aristocratic repertoire of songs all came from one fellow prisoner.

Big John Davis, who was the best man, the biggest drinker, the most powerful argufier, and the best singer in Frederica, Georgia.

Allen Prothero, whose singing of "Jumping Judy" and "Pauline' is giving him posthumous fame, who "just nachully didn't like the place" where we found him, and died there in the Nashville Penitentiary of T.B.

Henry Truvillion, still leader of a railroad gang in the piney woods of No Man's Land between Texas and Louisiana, who each day sings and shouts his men into concerted activity by original and beautifully phrased songs, who owns a farm and a white cottage by the side of the road and yet has time to be the pastor of two country churches: "I collected $7.45 last Sunday, all mine; the Lord owns the whole world. He don't need no money."

Lightning, a dynamic black Apollo song-leader, called "Lightnin'" by his comrades because "he thinks so fast he can git around any of them white bosses," who sings "Ring, Old Hammer" so realistically that one can see the old blacksmith shop with swinging bellows and hear again the cheerful ring of the forgotten anvil.

Willie Williams, who could sing holler at his mules ("Don't 'low me to beat 'em, got to beg 'em along") or lead spirituals with equal power and fervor.

Dobie Red, Track Horse, Jim Cason, Big Nig, and many another Negro prisoner, from whom we have obtained our noblest songs.

Vera Hall and Dock Reed, cousins, who can sing all the unique spirituals that seem to have emerged from the countryside about Livingston, Alabama, the beauty of whose singing has been made known to the world through the interest and devotion of Mrs. Ruby Pickens Tartt.

Clear Rock (Texas), Kelly Page (Arkansas), and Roscoe McLean (Arkansas) are other unsurpassed song leaders.

Seldom does one discern in these folk a delicate concern "with the creation of an imaginary world peopled with characters quite as wonderful, in their way, as the elfin creations of Spenser."[1] Nor does one find in them an overwhelming desire to forget themselves and everything that reminds them of their everyday life. The American singer has been concerned with themes close to his everyday experience, with the emotions of ordinary men and women who were fighting for freedom and for a living in a violent new world. His songs have been strongly rooted in his life and have functioned there as enzymes to assist in the digestion of hardship, solitude, violence, hunger, and the honest comradeship of democracy.

The songs in this book, therefore, have been given a roughly "functional" arrangement—that is, according to the way they grew up and lived in the American community. The first half of the book contains those songs that have been sung in a normal community by or for or before men, women, and children—i.e., religious songs, dance songs, lullabies, love songs, and ballads. The last half contains those songs which grew up in circles mostly male, and were male in content and audience—the occupational songs and ballads, the work songs; and those songs which grew up in groups where the exceeding hardness and bitterness of existence tended to obliterate distinctions—the blues and songs of drink, gambling, and crime.

Only recently have artists and scientists seemed to care to know what the people thought and felt and believed, what and how they sang. With the development of the portable recording machine, however, one can do more than transcribe in written outline what they say. The needle writes on the disc with tireless accuracy the subtle inflections, the melodies, the pauses that comprise the emotional meaning of speech, spoken and sung. In this way folklore can truly be recorded. A piece of folklore is a living, growing, and changing thing, and a folk song printed, words and tune, only symbolizes in a very static fashion a myriad-voiced reality of individual songs. The collector with pen and notebook can capture only the outline of one song, while the recorder, having created an atmosphere of easy sociability, confines the living song, without distortion and in its fluid entirety, on a disc. Between songs, sometimes between stanzas, the singers annotate their own song. The whole process is brief and pleasurable. They are not confused by having to stop and wait for the pedestrian pen of the folklorist: they are able to forget themselves in their songs and to underline what they wish to underline. Singing in their homes, in their churches, at their dances, they leave on these records imperishable spirals of their personalities, their singing styles, and their cultural heritage. The field recording, as contrasted with the field notebook, shows the folk song in its three-dimensional entirety, that is, with whatever rhythmic accompaniment there may be (handclapping, foot-patting, and so on), with its instrumental background, and with its folk harmonization. A funeral service in the South, a voodoo ceremony in Haiti, a wedding in French southwestern Louisiana, or a square dance in the country may be recorded for future study; a "movie" would complete the picture.

It is always a dramatic moment for any one when his own voice comes back to him undistorted from the black mouth of a loud-speaker. He seems to feel the intense and absorbing pleasure that a child experiences when he first recognizes himself in a mirror. Our old hard-bitten Mexican vaquero in the mesquite country of southwest Texas, when the song was played to him unexpectedly, said with soft amazement, "Madre de Dios!" then after a time, "Muy hombre!" A Negro prisoner, wishing to communicate his extravagant and uncontrollable surprise, fell flat on his back and lay there till his buddies picked him up. A mountaineer, when asked if he would like to hear his record played back, said: "I reckon so. Anything I'll do oncet, I'll do hit twicet." "Ain't men sharp?" he added, when the record was finished. "A man can't stutter none talking into one of them things; got to stick to plain English. If he don't, it'll tell on him." On hearing his voice come back, an Alabama Negro exclaimed, "Dat's pure hit! Dat's hit directly!" Another decided: "That machine can sho beat me singin'." She didn't understand what was happening, but she pointed at the machine and said, "Stop dat ghost!"

Occasionally the singer's belief in the power of the recording he has made is pathetic beyond tears. In the Tennessee State Prison a young Negro convict came up to us shyly and asked to be allowed to make a record. When we asked what he wanted to record, he said, "Boss, I can beat on a bucket just as sweet as you please." All the prisoners present agreed that this was true. When the record was completed, he murmured, half to himself, "Well, I guess when they hear that up there in the White House, them big men sho goin' do something for this po' nigger."

There are now over four thousand aluminum and acetate discs by such singers in the Archive of American Folk Song, about two-thirds of them recorded in the field by ourselves. An order list of these records will be published shortly, containing over twelve thousand English titles, and foreign language supplements later on. A recent grant from the Carnegie Foundation for the installation of duplicating equipment will make these records available at cost to the public. We hope that the American people will learn from these records to know itself better, learn to sing its own folk songs in the rich and varied styles of our folk singers. It is possible to use some commercial records out of groups called "hillbilly" and "race" to the same ends.

This might seem to be the last book in the world which should owe its existence to the man who invented the L.C. card, Dr. Herbert Putnam. And yet, when one reflects that this same reserved and iron-willed Bostonian liberal also made the Library of Congress the only great democratic library in the world, it is not strange that he understood and wished to preserve—although he could seldom bear to listen to—the songs of the American people. Ruby Pickens Tartt and Genevieve Chandler, two intelligent and creative Southern women, explored the singing resources of their communities and welcomed us with our recording machine. Dr. W. P. Davis and his Bogtrotters of Galax, Virginia, introduced us to an unexplored and tune-packed section of the Virginia mountains, and it is with his kind permission that Galax songs are reproduced in this book. Dr. Harold Spivacke has been personally helpful and administratively generous throughout the making of this volume. Acknowledgment is hereby made to the Federal Writers Project and the Historical Records Project of the Works Progress Administration, under whose auspices a number of these songs were collected. Aunt Molly Jackson spoke the lines that make up much of the continuity of *Our Singing Country*.

Our Singing Country: A Second Volume of American Ballads and Folk Songs, with many regrets for all the songs we have to omit, stands only for work (as noted in the headnotes) we ourselves have done and our tastes and interests. It neither does justice to our collection, perhaps, nor, except in minor instances, draws upon work done, upon records made, or upon texts collected by any one else. We hope that the book is merely a foretaste of what may grow into a fairly complete collection of American folk tunes, and of the books, symphonies, plays, operas for which it should eventually provide material. Since the songs cannot be heard in all of their living quality, we have not hesitated to adopt certain means for conveying as much of their content as possible to the readers. We have in certain cases created composite versions of the texts of ballads or songs (as noted in the headnotes), so that the non-ballad-student among readers may quickly survey all the choicest lines that any group of song variants contains. We have not quibbled about the definition of folk song, but we have included whatever songs and ballads prove to have been current among the people and to have undergone change through oral transmission. To introduce the songs, we have generally used quotations from the records themselves. We have let the song-makers and the song-rememberers speak for themselves.

NOTE

1. *English Folk Songs of the Southern Appalachians*, by Cecil Sharp and Maude Karpeles, p. xxxvii.

Chapter 6

14 Traditional Spanish Songs from Texas

These songs come from the plain of South Texas. This plain stretches away from the country of live oaks and limestone hills near San Antonio, east to the swampy coastal plain of the Gulf and south through the arid flat-land of mesquite and cactus to the warm and sluggish Rio Grande. This country was the cradle of the Western cattle industry, the Texas cowboy, and the famous Texas longhorn. It has been a land of many wars and much violence. It has been, and still is to some extent, a wild country. In speech, in culture, in way of life and, most of all, in music, it is strongly Mexican.

San Antonio is the metropolis and cultural hub of this region. On the market square in little open-air stalls you may eat the best chile, tamales, enchiladas and tacos that money can buy and in the evening ten or fifteen bands of strolling singers are at your service. For a few pennies they will play for you brilliantly and sing in voices that are steel-hard and steel-clear, songs from all over Mexico, ballads of local murders, *historias* of the Villa revolution and *corridos* out of the cow country to the south. We have recorded numbers of songs from these singers of the market square, from school children, from private citizens like Rita and José Caballeros and from performers in "Los Pastores" and "Los Matachines," all in busy metropolitan San Antonio.

South and east, the singers are scattered through the country on ranches and farms. The López family belong to the blackland of sugar cane and cotton near Houston. Their home is the typical frame lean-to of the rural South. There are twelve children in the family. Every year the house of the Lópezes hums with the excitement of a theatrical rehearsal. Señor López is the director, producer, prompter and principal actor in the traditional Spanish religious drama, *The Good Thief*, whose cast is recruited almost entirely from among the twelve younger Lópezes.

Two hundred odd miles to the southwest in Cotulla, another Texas-Mexican farmer has kept alive a much older religious play, "Los

Pastores," which he presents each Christmas, for the pleasure of his friends and neighbors. I shall never forget my first sight of this man. We had driven over miles of red roads through mesquite and cactus thickets and suddenly came upon a field of newly turned red land which bore all the signs of a savage and bitter conflict between man and the wild earth. The field was dotted stumps. There in the center of this raw clearing, a powerfully built man, his tawny skin gleaming in the sun, was hacking at a tough mesquite. Our friend hailed him and he came striding across the furrows with his axe. His face was Indian in cast, his hair a black thicket over dark brows. Stripped to his belt, his heavy bare feet planted in the red soil, he greeted us with dignified words across the barbed wire. "This," my friend said, "is the director of 'Los Pastores.'"

This man had learned the full book of the mystery from his father, he from his father, and so it had come down from the past by word of mouth from one tough-handed Mexican farmer to the next—a whole libretto with all its songs, its cues, its costumes and stage business. That evening this rural man of the theatre and his troupe came with their ballad shepherd staves and sang for our recording machine.

In Brownsville, Manuela Longoria, principal of a Mexican school, sang for us songs which she had learned from her grandmother. In Brownsville, too, we recorded the ballads of blind José Suárez, the town minstrel. He has been blind since childhood, but his cane guides him everywhere through the city, to bars, to dances, to family parties, and everywhere his guitar and his ballads make him welcome. He says that he does not know how many songs he can sing, since new ones that he has not thought of in years come into his mind every day. He knows all the popular songs of the day, all the old border ballads, and, whenever anything of excitement and import occurs, he makes a new *historia* for the information of his people. His songs concern the bandits of the border country, the troubles of the migratory cotton pickers, the disasters of train wrecks, storms and wars and the pleasures of mescal.

These songs and these singers have deep roots in this country of South Texas, tough roots that run deep, straight down into the earth, like the roots of the mesquite and cactus. I once asked a huge laughing Mexican who played a small mandolin how he would explain to a foreigner his immense love for his hot, dusty, thin-soiled South Texas farm. My friend became serious. "I would tell him first," he said, "about the so poisonous rattlesnakes and moccasins. Then I would tell him about how many marvelous thorns we have, thorns on everything. Then . . ."

Chapter 7

Reels and Work Songs

You have already heard about the spirituals that came from the experiences of the Negro in slavery and the secular songs that told of his worldly problems under freedom. I want to present a group of songs that in point of time overlapped both the other groups: first, the reels or dancing songs made by rural Negroes and, second, the work songs sung in rhythmic labor activity in Africa, later under slavery, and, finally, on construction jobs all across the South.

The earliest accounts of Negroes in Africa and in this hemisphere spoke not so much of their pure singing, but of their singing in rhythm as they danced and as they worked. In the West Indies, where cultural intermixture has been less rapid than in the United States, all songs are essentially work songs or dance songs, even though they may at times have an intensely religious significance. The Negro singer generally does not sing without dancing; even if the singer is sitting in a chair his body swings and sways with the music—the arms, the hands, and the feet are alive; and what first astonished the whites about the Negro slaves was their love of the dance and their unbelievable facility for it. The whites noticed the rhythm of the banjo and the rattle of the bones (or else the rhythm of the African rattle and drum). Indeed, they first heard dance songs like this:

> Juba dis, Juba dat,
> Juba killed my yellow cat.
> Rabbit skip, rabbit hop,
> Rabbit et my turnip top.
> Rabbit hash, pole cat mash,
> Jay bird soup, raccoon mush,
> Rah rabbit, rabbit, rabbit!

It was this type of dance song that first moved the whites to emulation and imitation. Out of this imitation grew the blackface minstrel show, which was the principal amusement of the vaudeville theatres in the United States for nearly a century. These minstrel shows have been called the first contribution of the United States to the theatre.

The great minstrel tunes are those that are close to the Afro-American dance-song patters. "Old Dan Tucker," for example, is a tune which kept America laughing and dancing with its cheerful, itchy rhythms for scores of years. It persists because Dan Emmett, its composer, adhered closely to the Afro-American dance-song patterns.

> I came to town the other night,
> Just to hear the noise and see the fight,
> The watchmen a-runnin' all around
> Cryin', "Old Dan Tucker done come to town."

> So, git out the way old Dan Tucker,
> He's too late to git his supper,
> Supper's over and dinner's a-cooking
> Old Dan Tucker just standin' and lookin'.

In slavery, and out of a combination of European and African folk-tale patterns, the Negroes developed a whole cycle of animal tales whose heroes symbolized for him his problems as a slave. The principal figure in these tales was "Br'er Rabbit," born and bred in a briar-patch, who could always out-smart "Br'er Fox," his white master—out-think or, at least, out-run him. Many of the secular dance songs of the slaves concerned "Old Mr. Rabbit, whose ears was mighty long."

> Mr. Rabbit, Mr. Rabbit, your ears are mighty long,
> Yes, my lord, been put on wrong.

>> Every little soul must shine, shine
>> Every little soul must shine along.

> Mr. Rabbit, Mr. Rabbit, your tail's mighty white,
> Yes, my lord, I'm a-gittin' out of sight.

> Mr Rabbit, Mr. Rabbit, your coat's mighty grey,
> Yes, My Lord, 'twas made that way.

Negro folk-song is distinguished not alone for its dance, but for another type of rhythmic song, the work song. Work songs are not common, as many people suppose. They are confined to a few areas of world culture and to a few small groups in these areas. In North America the Anglo-American sea Shanties and the work songs of the Negroes are, I believe, the unique examples of this art and, curiously enough, they are

closely related. It is held on high authority, on the one hand, that some
Negro work-song melodies are derived from the tunes of the old
Shanties, and on the other, Joanna Colcord calls the Negro Shanty singer
of the nineteenth century "the best of all the leaders of Shanty singing."

The fact is that the custom of work-song singing is native to the
basic culture of the Negro people. Therefore, it is immaterial whether
they have adopted European melody or perpetuated their own African
heritage of melody or developed new Afro-American work-song melodies
of their own.

The stock of work songs that the Negro has created in the United
States can compare favorably with the spiritual tunes and the blues-rag-
time-jazz idioms that you already know. I want to play for you now a
group of typical work songs from across the South. These were recorded
phonographically in the only situation where work songs are still currently sung, on the great prison farms of the South. Most of the recordings were made under rather extraordinary difficulties by John A. Lomax,
Honorary Curator of the Archive of American Folk Song. These records
are not to be listened to for text or tune so much as for the wildness, freedom, and rhythmic beauty of their contents.

The first record is a typical mournful road-gang song called,
"Pauline." The singer, a young man of extraordinary vocal talent, died in
prison of tuberculosis some time after this record was made, but I believe
he left behind him as a melancholy monument an eternally tender and
lyric song. It is a work song from the road gang. He says, "I am going
back home to Pauline, going back to my shanty and lie down," and he
uses as punctuation, instead of commas and periods or semicolons, the
sound of his pick as it sinks into the road.

> Pauline, *hanh!*
> Pauline, *hanh!*
> I don't love, *hanh!*
> Nobody but you, *hanh!*
> Lawd, I'm goin', *hanh!*
> To my shanty and lie down, *hanh!*
> Lawd, I walked, *hanh!*
> And I cried, *hanh!*
> All night long, *hanh!*
> Well, it's oh, *hanh!*
> Lawdy, me, *hanh!*
> Well, it's trouble, *hanh!*
> I do see, *hanh!*

You been a long, *hanh!*
Long time 'bout makin' it up, *hanh!*
Lawd, in yo' mind, *hanh!*

In the next record you hear a group of men chopping together in the woodyard of the Texas Penitentiary. They tell the sun and the whole world how the blood is running warm in their veins. They tell the world how good they feel. Listening to this song you may understand why the work song has been called "the musical speed-up system of the South." Even under the hot sun, even with the mean boss-man and the long hours, the singers can shout their song because they feel the strength in their collective arms.

Old Hannah was a beaming,
Lawd, Lawd, Lawd, Lawd,
Old Hannah was a beaming,
God almighty knows.
'Bout to burn me down, suh!
Lawd, Lawd, Lawd, Lawd,
'Bout to burn me down, suh!
God almighty knows.

Down on the levee camp, in the dust behind the mules—down in the bottom, plowing in the fields, the lonely worker lifts up his head and tells the sun, the dust, and the mules all about his troubles. The song is primitive, African; you can hear the first echo of the blues, without any of the restricting 2/4 rhythms of accompaniment. This music cries like a mournful Southern hoot-owl in the black, lonesome bottoms.

Lawd, I looked all over the whole corral,
Couldn't find a mule with his shoulders well.
Down in the bottom, and up to my knees,
Working for my baby, she's so hard to please.

There you have the kind of free and untrammeled Negro singing that is behind the great Negro songs like "St. Louis Blues" and "Go Down, Moses." When you take a free, lilting melody like this, focus it in a particular environment and in the mouths of a group of men, a song like the great prison moan, "I ain't got no more cane on the Brazos," becomes unforgettable. The performer asks and answers his own questions.

You oughta come on the river in 1904,
Oh——
You could find a dead man in every turn row,

Oh——
You oughta been here in 1910,
Oh——
They were drivin' the women like they do the men,
Oh——

For the last song in this group of records, we come to the most intense, the angriest, the most passionate of the work songs in the South. Strangely enough, it is called "Rosie." "Rosie" is sung full-throated by fifty men, flat-weeding in an irrigation ditch in Mississippi. The hoes flash up together and all splash green. The leader says,

Little Rosie, your hair grow long,
    'Cause I'm goin' to see your daddy when I get home.
They ain't but the one thing that I done wrong.
    I stayed in Mississippi just one day too long.
Come and get me an'-a take me home,
These lifetime devils, they won't leave me 'lone.
Well, I come here wid a hundred years,
A tree fall on me, I don't bit mo' care.

Now I also want to show you a group of work songs in their functional context as they are actually used, and for that purpose Willie Johnson, The Golden Gate Quartet, and I have arranged a little dramatization of work song singing on a railroad. There is a special kind of song for every job in the South, and on the railroad there is a special kind of song for every job on the railroad. In the railroad songs one finds a sort of tenderness not to be found in other work songs, because these songs are all led by a tender-voiced tenor who is hired to do nothing else but sing, to soothe the men's feelings and keep them all working together so they won't get hurt on the job.

The Golden Gate Quartet will play the part of a Negro extra gang, building a new piece of railroad; Willie Johnson is going to be the foreman and Henry Owens the mellifluous tenor.

About four o'clock in the morning the camp cook goes around the bunk car, banging on a dishpan, and he wakes the men up with a song like this:

Raise up, boys, raise up!
Raise up, boys, raise up!
Breakfast on the table, the coffee's getting cold,
If you don't come git it, gonna throw it out doors!
Ain't you gwine,

Ain't you gwine, boys,
Ain't you gwine?
Raise up boys, raise up,
Ram, ham, chicken and mutton
If you don't come now you won't git nothing,
Ain't you gwine,
Ain't you gwine, boys,
Ain't you gwine?

When the men reach the stretch of roadbed they are going to lay track, they first have to unload the steel rails from the flat cars, and the foreman tells them just how this must be done.

Foreman.
Now look here, men, we got a carload of steel to unload here now and this is ninety-pound steel rail and it's thirty-foot long. We don't want to lose nary a finger. 'Course there's plenty more in the market down yonder where them come from, but they don't fit like these. Now, this here's a good way to get a leg broke. It's a good way to get somebody killed, an' every man lifting that rail got to lift together an' any man lift before I say, "Lift", we're gonna run him away from here. Now git around here, boys, and grab that rail like a cat grabbing a hot hoe-cake.

Leader.
Come on now, boys, gather round,
Bow down, put your glad hands on it,
Raise up! Throw it away!
That's good iron, I heard it ring.
Come on now, boys, come on back now, boys,
Get another one,
Bow down, put your glad hands on it now, boys,
Raise it high!
Throw it away!
That's good iron, I heard it ring.

After the rails have been placed on the ties, the next job of the gang is to spike the rails down with their spike-driving hammers and for this they have their own special song, "O Lulu":

O Lulu,
O Lawd gal,
I want to see you so bad,
Gonna see my long haired baby
Gonna see my long haired gal,
O well, I'm going across the country,
To see my long haired gal.*

After the rails have been spiked down temporarily, the next job is to

line the track up, to straighten it so the work train can move on down the
line. The song sung with this work is the most widespread of all railroad
work songs. The foreman straddles the rail, sights down it to find out
where the crooked part is:

> *Foreman.*
> Look here, fellows, this rail is as crooked as a slavery time fence rail. Now I want
> you to get this track lined up right now, so get your crow bars on your shoulders
> and run down about the fourth joint ahead and touch it just a little bit North.
> *Leader.*
> All I hate about lining track
> These old bars 'bout to break my back.
> *Group.*
> Ho boys! Can't you line 'em,
> Ho boys! Can't you line 'em,
> Ho boys! Can't you line em,
> See Eloise go lining track.
> *Leader.*
> July the red bug, July the fly,
> August ain't a hot month, pray to die.
> *Group.*
> Ho boys! Can't you line 'em,
> etc.

As the train passes over the new track, gravel is dumped out of the
cars and some of the men stay behind to tamp the gravel between the
ties—that is, to pack it in tight around the ties so the railroad will not go
crooked again—and the foreman hollers to his men to give him the tie-
tamping song about "T. P. and the Morgan":

> *Foreman.*
> Give us some gravel here, old man, and let's get to tamping these old loose ties
> down. All right, boys, gather round and get them tampers ready. Don't be afraid to
> bend your back. We'se railroad men! All right, caller, sing about the T. P. and the
> Morgan.
> *Leader.*
> T. P. and the Morgan,
> Standin' side by side,
> T. P. threw the water,
> Water in the Morgan's eye.
> *Group.*
> O tamp 'em solid, so dey won't come down,
> O tamp 'em solid, buddy, so dey won't come down.
> Well you can do it
> Well do it

Well you can do it.
God a'mighty made a monkey,
God a'mighty made a whale,
God a'mighty made a 'gater, 'gater,
Wid the hickies all over his tail.

I hope you may be ready now to listen to Negro songs with different ears. These songs are full of love for people, they are lonely for people and they are full of hunger for gentleness and kindness in this world. These songs rose up out of slavery, out of misery. They jumped up out of levee camps, they sprang from turpentine camps and back alleys. The people became happy and made them up in churches; the people "got high" and made them up at dances; they rose up out of tough people and good people. Some of these people were so mad that they could kill you as soon as look at you and, when some of these people had the quiet blues, they were so quiet you could hear them think for miles away. Some of these people could look past poverty and misery, they could look clear through the darkness and despair and ignorance and see something on the other side. The old folks said, "On the other side of Jordan." These songs rose up out of these people without their having to think about it, because they were lonesome for more kindness and goodness and richness than they could find in life right where they were.

So the last song in the program is going to be "Rock My Soul in the Bosom of Abraham."

Well the rich man lived
And he lived so well
And when he died
He got a home in hell.
Well, the poor man Laz'rus
Just as poor as I
An' when he died,
He had a home on high.
Well, you rock my soul in the bosom of Abraham.
You rock my soul in the bosom of Abraham
You rock my soul in the bosom of Abraham
Lawd, why don't you rock my soul!

NOTE

* From *Mules and Men*, by Zora Neale Hurston. Philadelphia: J. B. Lippincott, 1935.

Chapter 8

Mister Ledford and the TVA

Erik Barnouw

Alan Lomax, leading radio exponent of American folklore and folk music, was born in 1915 in Austin, Texas, where his father, John A. Lomax, had been associated most of his life with the University of Texas. Alan Lomax spent his early days around the university campus, except for some time on a West Texas ranch, periods of schooling in the East, and two years collaborating with his father on folk-song collection and in the editing of *American Ballads and Folk Songs* (1937 [*sic* 1934]) and *Negro Folk Songs as Sung by Leadbelly* (1939 [*sic* 1936]).

In 1936 he arrived in Washington looking for a job. The Library of Congress, for which he had already done folk-song recording in the field, sent him to Haiti to record *Vaudou* and other songs of the Haitian peasantry. His fiancée from Texas joined him at Port-au-Prince; they were married by a Haitian justice of the peace and spent their honeymoon recording songs of the Haitian Mardi Gras. She is Elizabeth Lomax, also a writer.

In 1937 Alan Lomax took charge of the Archive of American Folk Songs in the Library of Congress. For the next few years he was concerned with recording as much as possible of America's still-living folk music, as sung and performed by untrained and natural American folk singers and musicians.

In 1939 the Columbia Broadcasting System, largely through the enthusiasm of its Davidson Taylor, put Lomax to work on a folk music series for the *American School of the Air*—as writer, narrator, and singer. Lomax had never listened to radio, and was somewhat astonished to find himself in a huge studio holding a guitar, gazing at a microphone, and beyond it at the Columbia Symphony Orchestra conducted by Howard Barlow.

School audiences took to the shows. There was an astonishing informality about them that was refreshingly honest, and new in educa-

tional radio. Lomax brought to the microphone singers like Leadbelly
and the Golden Gate Quartet. Some of his guests were not very familiar
with the printed page, so that whole shows had to be planned verbally.
An entirely ad lib program from Galax, Virginia, with six mountain
musicians, won an award from the Institute for Education by Radio, as
the best music education show of the year. In 1941 Lomax's program
about the dust bowl, featuring the Okie ballad singer, Woodie Guthrie,
won a similar prize. As the series progressed, Lomax began to include
dramatic material, using his singers as cast. Thus he gradually evolved
into a dramatic writer.

In 1941 he turned to an important type of drama new to American
radio, which is represented by the following script. That year the
Rockefeller Foundation gave the Library of Congress a grant for an
Experimental Radio Project. The group was headed by Philip Cohen, and
included Joseph Liss, Charles Harold, Jerome Weisner, and as consultant,
Alan Lomax. They took the Library's portable recording equipment into
the field to gather material for a series of documentary programs about
life in the United States. Programs of this type, using *people*, not actors,
had been tried by the British Broadcasting Company, but were almost
unknown in America. Archibald MacLeish, Librarian of Congress, whose
own fine contributions to radio were later to include a series based on
early American "source" documents, saw in such programs an invaluable
living record of our own day and a natural extension of a library's function.

The following program is not, in the usual sense, "written." The creator of such a program—in this case Alan Lomax—uses as his material
not merely the voices, but the minds and emotions and impulses of the
people themselves. It was Lomax's job *not* to put words into their
mouths, but to draw the people out, to get "on the record" their currents
of thought, the feelings they had about their environment. In this case
the setting was of particular interest: a valley about to be flooded by the
TVA, and from which the people, old pioneer stock, were to be trans-
planted.

The program was built chiefly around one Paul Ledford, a farmer.
Lomax, who is natural and unassuming and puts people at ease, spent
many days with him, drawing him out on the story of his county and his
people. "For several days I let him do all the talking and make all the
decisions about where we were to go and whom we were to talk to.
Whenever he said anything that was particularly memorable, which I was

unable to record, I tried later on to reproduce the circumstances of the statement, and to record it with the same emotion as it had had originally. By the end of the first morning he was already completely at ease with the microphone and was interviewing his friends and neighbors with more ease than most of us ever accomplish."

Several hours of recorded material were brought back to the Library. Lomax, along with Jerome Weisner, in charge of the Library's Recording Laboratory, spent six weeks in cutting and splicing the material together, giving it a logical arrangement and structure.

The programs were broadcast by some sixty radio stations in 1941, and were very popular in the South. There is unfailing fascination in hearing, in a dramatic broadcast, one's own kind of talk. Paul Ledford and his neighbors, talking about the TVA, could not have been duplicated by any actors in the world. The quality of the dialogue is, of course, similarly difficult to suggest in print.

Wartime developments in recording equipment, which have made possible battle-front recordings of unusual dramatic impact, will undoubtedly stimulate the growth of recorded documentary drama during the coming years.

Lomax wrote and narrated programs for *Transatlantic Call: People to People* throughout most of 1943, then went into the army. He was assigned to the Armed Forces Radio Service, which put him to work, among other things, on a series on American folklore and folk music, for overseas troops.

SINGERS. It takes a worried man to sing a worried song,
It takes a worried man to sing a worried song,
It takes a worried man to sing a worried song,
I'm worried now, but I won't be worried long.
LOMAX. It takes a worried man to sing a worried song, and that's the way the folks in Young Harris County, Georgia, felt about things in the summer of 1941—they were worried.

The Tennessee Valley Administration was building a new dam to produce more electricity for national defense. The reservoir lake from this dam was going to flood their valley, and that meant that many farmers would have to move away from land that their families had held for generations. The Library of Congress had sent its sound-recording truck into the region to make recordings of the effect of the TVA program on the mountain people. The evacuation problem intrigued us, and we decided to pick one farmer, a good talker—and let him tell the story of the evacuation. Mr. Paul Ledford was the man we chose—the sort of fellow who asks questions and starts discussions at county meetings. This was what we recorded the first afternoon from Mr. Ledford . . .

LEDFORD [*Reflectively, looking out across the green farm that has been his family's for three generations . . . in the background you can hear the birds and the bees in the honeysuckle along the fence*]. Been here *all* my life; been here fifty years; *long* time . . . I know these mountains, and I know these good people in this—in this country. And we're right here in the foothills of the Blue Ridge [*Ledford spat and glanced up at the blue hills*] . . . along this little creek which is à tributary of the Hiawassie River, that goes into this dam that the TVA is abuildin' . . . I don't like this idee of buildin' a dam on a valley and floodin' a valley like this with water . . . practically *level* country to be in the mountains.

[*Music: Mountain fiddle tune, not gay or sad, behind this talk*]

LOMAX. As we sat talking with Mr. Ledford this fine August morning a neighbor came up the road. His name was Barrett and he was a renter, a man without land of his own. Ledford hailed him into the swing under the two great pine trees . . .

[*Music out*]

LEDFORD. Hello, Mr. Barrett!

BARRETT [*Off*]. How do.

LEDFORD. Come in . . . Set down in the swing under this pine tree here in the shade . . . Pleasant morning-sun shining beautiful, isn't it.

BARRETT [*Nearer*]. Certainly is.

[*Barrett speaks in a soft, almost diffident voice, a complete contrast to Ledford's positive, growling drawl*]

LEDFORD. Well, how you gettin' along?

BARRETT [*In*]. I'm gettin' along pretty well, except my leg—got a big risin' on my leg that's not doin' s' well.

LEDFORD. Well, that's bad—risin's bad. How long you had that risin'?

BARRETT. It's bin acomin' there about three days.

LEDFORD. Well, what do you know about the TVA and buildin' a dam this mornin'?

BARRETT. Well, I don't know much of anything and I just—that's my business out—I thought I'd come out and see when you was agoin' to try to locate your place—thought I'd go with ye.

LEDFORD. Well, I don't know what to tell you about that. You know there's not much use agoin' out to locate a farm until Uncle Sam comes along with the money to pay us off . . . 'Cause we couldn't tie a place down if we's to go without the money, you know. What do you think about it?

BARRETT. Well, I jest think I can't buy a place—I ain't able to buy; and I won't get no money out of it and I—I jest want to rent. . .

LEDFORD. Well then, the problem you have—you got to get out of here—and you're selling no land and got nothin' to git out on . . . Is that true?

BARRETT. That's true. . . . I ain't *able* to move, as fur as that goes—*anywhere* . . .

LEDFORD [*Pause*]. Well, have you talked to the TVA anything about gettin' any help?

BARRETT. No . . . I haven't—seen anyone to talk to . . . They never do stop—at my place. [*This last is spoken with a falling inflection of the voice, pathetic and defeated*].

LEDFORD [*After a considerable pause*]. Well, all the good times is past and gone, it looks like—in this country.

BARRETT. They certainly air.

LEDFORD. It's like the song . . . It went on to say: [*He sings*]
"All the good times is past and gone,
Don't cry, little Bonnie, don't cry. . . ."
That's pretty true in this country.

BARRETT. Yeah, it shore is.

[*Music: Banjo sneaks in during following*]

LOMAX. The morning passed in talks about the good old days in the neighborhood . . . Later Mrs. Ledford called us to dinner; and we ate chicken and dumplings, ham with good red gravy, turnip greens, potatoes and a deep apple pie. . . .

SINGER [*With banjo*].
Talk about your old cow meat,
Your mutton and your lamb—
If you want to please these people round yere
Bring on that country ham . . . [*Fade*]

LOMAX. When we finished our coffee, Ledford turned to us and said. . . .

LEDFORD. Come on, let's—let's go . . . I want to take you round to see some of m' neighbors. I want you to just see what we've got. I just want you to visit with them—want you to go in their homes—look around their houses—see what they've got to eat—eat with them—I want you to see what they've got to eat, how they're gettin' along . . . They're all out of *debt*—finest people on *earth*—never been none no better—best people I *know* of—best people you've ever been amongst in yore life, I'll bet you a purty, if you jest—if you jest open yore heart and *say* so . . . So let's go and see some of 'em.

SINGER [*With banjo*].

Away and away we're bound for the mountain,

Bound for the mountain, bound for the mountain.

Over the mountain, the wild steed's a-boundin',

Away to the chase, away, away. . . .

[*Fades, while banjo continues back of*]

LOMAX. We said, "Ledford, take us to see the man that you consider the most interesting person in the county." And so at his direction we headed off the main road up Partridge Creek to a vine-covered cabin set against the foot of the blue mountains . . . There we met Uncle Joe Kirby, the oldest resident of the county, still lively with all his eighty years. . . . Ledford did the interviewing. . . .

LEDFORD [*Fade in*]. How you gettin' along, Uncle Joe, now?

KIRBY [*A deep, old voice; it rumbles and rattles with age and power and conviction; each word is weighted and considered*]. Oh, purty well. I'm gittin' kinda come down to the feeble days, though; but I'm still purty *healthy* and *hearty*.

LEDFORD. Still able to *work* some?

KIRBY. Yes . . . Made a purty good little *crop* this *yur*. Of course, y' know, I'm jest a *boy* yit, jist goin' on eighty-one years old.

LEDFORD. Jest a boy yet!

KIRBY. Yes. [*He grins*]

LEDFORD. Well, that's *fine*. What do you think about the old days and the modern days of today—which do you *like* the best?

KIRBY [*After a pause and thinking it over*]. Well, that's sort of a *hard question* with me . . . I don't know whether I can *correctly* answer it or not. Now, *some* of the old times, I like 'em *pow'ful* well; but, some of 'em—I like the *modern* times mighty well, much *better*. [*He has his teeth into his idea now and he runs along swiftly*]. I couldn't see how I could *live* if my wife had to go back and make clothing and make everything with her *fangers* like my mother *did*—just *couldn't do* it—*never* could have done it . . .

LEDFORD [*Throwing it in*]. I guess not.

KIRBY. It don't look to me like . . . We raised a good crowd of children and she jest had her *hands* full and she had a good cook stove or a range. . . . When me an' my wife was *married*—I had bought this land *before* we's married, but that's been back about fifty-three or -fo' years ago—'Course money was pretty *hard* and *debts* was hard to pay; and me an' my wife, nary one, had no house stuff scarcely, just enough to sort of *do* with; and I had corn—I didn't *have* no wheat. The year before we was married, I didn't make much; I kinda *baffled about*—and I had enough on hand to pay for the land all except *seventy-five* dollars, but seventy-five dollars were hard to git. . . .

LEDFORD. UH-hunh.

KIRBY. And we lived *hard* and paid for our little home and got to whur, atter *bit*, we got to whur we could buy furniture and 'most anything and we've had a very plenty ever since—[*Rising feeling*] but we jest *starved* there and now for some—the *government* er somebody to come along and say, "You must jest get *out* of here and give us possession"—it sounds un*just* to me!

LEDFORD [*Pause*]. B'lieve in bein' free!

KIRBY. Yes, I *do*. . . . And I b'lieve in givin' 'em a chance to worship *God* accordin' to the dictates of his own *heart*, jest as our old Con-sti-tu-tion say . . .

LEDFORD. Yeah.

KIRBY. That's what I *b'lieve* in.

LEDFORD [*After pause*]. Well, I believe it's gettin' late, Uncle Joe, and I'm going to have to go on home now . . .

KIRBY [*Changing his tone and swinging into the mountain hospitality formula*]. Why not stay all night with me?—It's been s'long since you bin to see me and we're old friends and—

LEDFORD. I certainly would *enjoy* stayin' all night with yuh, but I can't stay tonight. . . . I'll come back, though, sometime, and I will stay all night and we'll talk more.

KIRBY. All right—I can jest—if I can't fill you on meat and bread, I sho can on hot air!

LEDFORD [*Chuckling*]. All right, that'll be fine.

SINGER [*With banjo*].

Away and away we're bound for the mountain,

Bound for the mountain, bound for the mountain . . .

[*Fade, continue banjo behind*]

LOMAX. As we drove away from Uncle Joe Kirby's house, Ledford saw two friends putting up their hay in a field near by the road . . . "Let's go down and see what they have to say about the TVA and building the dam," he said. And so we got the turntables rolling and carried our microphone down into the hayfield. . . .

FARMER [*Fade in, talking fast*]. . . . You can hear anything, Paul. And I've gotten so I won't *talk* for hearin' s' doggone many things . . . And then you come along and another fellow will tell you right the other way, and you don't know. . . . The best thing a man can do is to say nothing and listen to what he *hears*. . . .

LEDFORD. Yeah, that's about the best way . . . But then you turn around, on the other hand, I believe they're gonna treat us *right*—in the *end*. We're just drawed up at the idea—we were *scared*, I think, and—

FARMER. Well, I'll tell you, Paul, about the people in this country—they've never been outa here *nowhur*—

LEDFORD. That's hit.

FARMER.—and they don't know they's any other *place*—

LEDFORD. That's hit.

FARMER. That's the way I feel about it . . .

FARMER 2. They jest rushed hit on us s'fast that we—

FARMER. That's hit.

FARMER 2.—we jest got excited [*Chuckles*] and we talked pretty sassy sometimes to 'em.

LEDFORD. They give us too big a "Boo" fer sech a little calf—right on the dash.

FARMER 2 [*Still chuckling*]. Yeah.

LEDFORD. Like the man agoin' along the road and adrivin' a calf—met an *auto*mobile—he's right on the bridge—and he gives his automobile horn a toot and the calf jumps in the river. [*Chuckles*] He got out to apologize about it . . . "Oh," the fellow says, "that's all right. You jest give the calf a little too big a *toot*, that uz all." . . . They give us too big a toot, right on the spur of the moment. . . .

FARMER 2 [*Still laughing*]. Spur of the moment.

FARMER. Well, they say they're gonna try to place us back in as good a shape as they *found* us, Paul, and, if they *do*, why, of course—we'll not be at home any more . . . You know, satisfaction is what *you're* after and what I'm after. We don't keer anything, so much about prosperity and money—the age I've got on *me*, *I* don't—fer I don't feel as if I could *work* much more.

LOMAX. None of these men felt really resentful against the TVA . . . They were sick at heart and worried . . . They felt their roots being pulled at. But they knew the job had to be done—more power for more aluminum for national defense. Nevertheless, country-style, American-style, they had their fun at the expense of the TVA engineers. . . .

LEDFORD. Ever oncet in a while I see one of 'em around here with a load of poles—seems they git lost. [*This is very sarcastic and there's laughter behind every word*] They don't know whur this dam *is*!

FARMER. Yeah . . . There was one past my house the other day, had a John Deere tractor, huntin' the dam. And he was inquirin' of the Notteley Dam and wanted to know where it was at; and I said, "Why, the devil, you've done come through Nottelley Dam and gone to another'n!"

FARMER 2. They don't know where they're goin'. They's been s'many round here you couldn't turn yore team around 'thout steppin' on 'em!

FARMER. There's a while there we couldn't *plow* . . . Our mules just got scared, you know, and you just couldn't do nothin' with 'em. . . .

[*The three men go off into gales of high, cackling country laughter*]

[*Music: Mountain fiddle for bridge*]

LOMAX. The day was over and there was Ledford's house behind the two dark pine trees . . . We'd taken a look at the people of Young Harris County, Georgia, and we could open our hearts and agree with Ledford that they were some of the best people on earth. . . . As for Mr. Ledford, his heart was full of the rich and quiet peace of the countryside, and he knew now that he was not going to leave his county. Instead, he'd just move up out of the reach of the water. . . . With this resolve in every word, he told us good-bye and invited us to come down and spend a month with him.

LEDFORD. Now, you boys come back 'bout a year from now . . . I tell you the time to come—when I have my vacation off the farm is from the 15th of July till the 15th of August . . . If you'll come back here then, I'll really show you this country—take you into these mountains; I'll show you speckled trout; I'll show you virgin timber, that's been in these woods ever since I s'pose there's been an earth here, s'far as I know—I'll show you cold water runnin' out of the ground that will make your teeth hurt like drinkin' ice water when you drink it. . . . And some of the best people, the best type of people they is in the United States, in here. And they all, their desire and ambition is—is to—they're Americans—their ambition is to defend Ameriky. They'd fight for Ameriky, people in this country would . . . [*He spat*] both old and young. . . . You take these old mountain folks in here would even take up their old hog rifles if they'd git a chance to shoot old Hitler. . . . Genuine Americans—folks in here are. They's not a man in this country but what would fight—to the last drop of blood and the last ditch—to defend Ameriky. . . . That's the kind of people and type of folks we got in here—women and children. . . .

Chapter 9

America Sings the Saga of America

One of the most heartening things about America in 1947 is the spring freshet of enthusiasm for native balladry and folklore that is running through the country from coast to coast. Big, dulcet-voiced Burl Ives from Indiana, Josh White with his South Carolina blues, Woody Guthrie with his Okie songs, Susan Reed with her winsome Southern lyric songs have become nationally known. One folklore book, Ben Botkin's *Treasury of American Folklore,* has sold more than a half-million copies. The "Hootenanies" of People's Songs play to packed houses from Los Angeles to Manhattan. Walt Disney has three American folklore "cartoonies" in production.

There may be an element of escapism in this trend, but the causes, I believe, lie deeper in our national life: first, in our longing for artistic forms that reflect our democratic and equalitarian political beliefs; and, second, in our hankering after art that mirrors the unique life of this western continent—the life of the frontier, the great West, the big city.

We are looking for a people's culture, a culture of the common man. Like the little boll weevil of the ballad—

We're lookin' for a home,
Jest a-lookin' for a home.

American folklorists have been at work for more than a century and they have already accumulated a vast body of literature from oral sources. We can now assert that America's stock of folk song probably matches that of any other country in the world for size and variety. The problem that interests us, however, is: How has American folklore contributed to a democratic, people's culture?

Taken in rough, chronological order, the major finds of American folklore might be summarized as follows: (1) tall talk and tall tales; (2)

the Negro spiritual; (3) the survival of the British ballad; (4) the
American ballad; (5) the folklore of minority groups. Naturally, many
more folklore categories could be mentioned, but a discussion of these
will serve to indicate the main themes.

TALL TALK

From the beginning of the nineteenth century journalists were
recording the colorful speech of the American backwoods—tall talk that
reached out and easily embraced a big country:

"The boundaries of the United States sir?" replied the Kentuckian.
"Why, sir, on the north we are bounded by the aurora borealis, on the
east by the rising sun, on the south by the precession of the equinoxes
and on the west by the Day of Judgment."

Big talk about a big country brought into being a race of tall heroes
to match the vastness of the land and the prodigious jobs to be done.
Our tall-tale heroes, from Davy Crockett and Paul Bunyan to Kilroy—
have all exaggerated the achievements and capacities of the average
American of their time. They have all been, in the Hollywood sense,
supercolossal—this in contrast to the hero of the typical European fairy
tale, ordinarily a small fellow who managed to triumph over supernatural obstacles. This shift of emphasis and interest appears to reflect the
change in status of the *story-teller* from that of caste-ridden peasant of
Europe to freeborn working man of America.

THE NEGRO SPIRITUAL

This find in America came when radical Abolitionists heard for the
first time the songs of the freed Negroes, such as "Go Down, Moses," and
"No More Peck of Corn for Me." Here was proof that the Negro was not
a contented beast of burden, as so many Southern propagandists had
argued, but a primitive Christian, longing for freedom, if not in this
world, then in the next.

These songs still stand as evidence that an illiterate and enslaved
people can create music of compelling beauty and poetry of great power:

Didn't my Lord deliver Daniel!
And why not every man!
He delivered Daniel from the lion's den,
Jonah from the belly of the whale,
The Hebrew chillun from the fiery furnace—
And why not every man!

THE BRITISH BALLAD

Later in the century, it was discovered that this rich and ancient tradition was very much alive in the lonesome hollows of the Southern mountains, that the mountaineers still knew "Barbara Allen" and "Fair Ellender" and still sang

> *Come all ye fair and tender ladies,*
> *Be careful how you court young men*
> *They're like a star in a summer's morning,*
> *They'll first appear and then they're gone . . .*

The mildly Anglophile professors at first assumed that the mountaineers were a species of contemporary Elizabethans. Further study has shown, however, that such songs were once the property of the entire frontier.

It has shown, too, that the American singer, while he kept alive many of the lovely songs of his ancestors from across the seas, was no mere carrier of tradition. On the whole he has tended to purify his ballad heritage of its aristocratic and medieval overtone; to cling to "Barbara Allen" and forget "Sir Patrick Spens"; and to adapt the songs to American experience. Thus, for instance, in one American version of "The Gypsy Laddie," the injured husband, instead of calling for "a milk white steed," says:

> *Go saddle for me my buckskin hoss*
> *With a hundred-dollar saddle;*
> *Point out to me their wagon tracks*
> *And after them I'll travel,*
> *After them I'll ride.*
> *He had not rode till the midnight moon,*
> *Till he saw their campfire gleaming*
> *And he heard the voice of the big guitar*
> *With the voice of the lady singing*
> *The song of the Gypsie Dave.*

THE AMERICAN BALLAD

These American singers made new songs out of the old as their wagons rolled west. A new generation of folklorists found a new ballad literature. In the West they heard:

> *Come along, boys, and listen to my tale,*
> *I'll tell you of my troubles on the old Chisholm Trail.*

In the northern lumber-woods:

The shanty-boy's life is a weary, dreary life,
Though some say it's free from care,
Swinging our axes from morning till night
In the middle of the forest drear.

On the railroads:

Takes a mule,
Takes a track jack,
For to line
This old track back . . .

In the mines:

My sweetheart's a mule in the mines;
drive her without reins or lines,
On the bumper I sit and I chew and I spit
All over my sweetheart's behind.

On the Great Lakes:

The wind hauled round to the sou'-sou'west
It blew both stiff and strong;
You'd orter seen that schooner, Bigler,
As she plowed Lake Michigan. . . .

In the hobo "jungles":

O, why don't you work like other men do!
How the hell can I work when the sky is so blue!

They all sang, pouring the stuff of their workaday lives into thousands of stanzas, with plenty to say, too, about love, careless and otherwise. Here again, as in the American folktale, the central figure is the common man, taken at his own evaluation. And the idea implicit in this great rhymed history of the American pioneer worker can be summed up in the key lines of one of the noblest of the songs:

John Henry told his captain—A man ain't nothin' but a man.

MINORITY FOLKLORE

"A man ain't nothin' but a man!" In this sense America has reached out and welcomed the folklore of all the minority groups, racial and national. Jim Crow prejudice has been inoperative in folklore. In the nineteenth century the black-face minstrel show and, in the twentieth, the Negro jazz band, have lent a pleasant coffee color to our whole popular song and dance culture.

Louisiana speaks and sings with a heavy French accent; the Southwestern States are Spanish in color; and in the same way, our whole country is striped and streaked with the folk cultures of scores of minority groups. Here again folklore is a strong current in American life running counter to any authoritarian, Fascist tendency.

Further detail about many types of folklore could be added, but enough has been said to indicate that, so far, the impact of folklore on American thinking has been healthily democratic. Now that this vast underground stream of people's literature has begun to permeate our whole culture—through movies, plays, books, records, the radio and the schools—now that our once casual interest in American folklore is turning into a significant cultural movement, we must be prepared to guide it, for folklore movements can have dangerous potentialities.

Folklore can be used, fallaciously, to foster arbitrary notions of national or racial culture. In Italy, in Japan, and especially in Germany, Fascist leaders used folklore to whip up the enthusiasm of their people for aggressive war. The professional folklorist, Professor Naumann, working as Goebbels's assistant, helped to develop the Blud und Boden concept so important to the Nazis. Thus folklore, the literature of the people, has often been transformed into a weapon against the people.

The fact is, as every competent folklorist knows, that folklore has little, if any, connection with political boundaries or racist abstractions. The evidence of folklore shows that some folklore patterns are worldwide in their currency; that the human imagination is everywhere akin; that a charming story or melody skips blithely by political and linguistic boundaries and easily adapts itself to the cultural accent of its new home.

Rural folklore can be, falsely, opposed to city folklore, thus creating or widening the split between city and country populations. We are coming to find, however, that oral literature exists in the factories and slums, as another aspect of the rural folklore. But the Nazis, by emphasizing cultural differences and antagonisms, were able to use both groups to their own advantage.

Folklore can be petrified by improper use in education. A song is arranged and taught in the schools, for instance, as *the* correct version which all must sing if they are to sing properly. This strikes at the roots of the creative process of folklore, in which there may be many versions of a song, every one of which is as "correct" as every other.

Finally, tradition is opposed to fresh creation. While it is true that a folk community is to a degree artistically conservative, this is in the sense that democracy, itself, is conservative. Folklore change must wait upon the final approval of a human community.

One might say that every folklore item has been voted on by a broad electorate, an audience free to choose, reject or alter according to its lights. The teller of tales or the singer of songs often affects community taste by his own style of performance; he may stoutly defend his own version as the only correct one; but he is always conscious, as few cultivated artists can be, of the needs and preferences of his audience. He is *of* his audience.

Folklore, then, inherently rejects all authoritarian notions. It allows for the creative rights of the individual at the same time that it is flexible in its response to community sentiment. Perhaps here lie the reasons that folklore has a staying power unrivaled by even the very greatest of cultivated art.

It seems, then, that folklore is both democratic and international in its character—American folklore perhaps more strongly so than its African and European parent cultures. And it follows that folklore can play a great role in this century, since our big problem is to realize man's dream for democratic and peaceful plenty.

Folklore can show us that this dream is age-old and common to all mankind. It asks that we recognize the cultural rights of weaker peoples in sharing this dream, and it can make their adjustment to a world society an easier and more creative process. The stuff of folklore—the orally transmitted wisdom, art and music of the people—can provide ten thousand bridges across which men of all nations may stride to say, "You are my brother."

Chapter 10

Folk Music in the Roosevelt Era

This article is excerpted from an interview with Mr. Lomax conducted in December 1981 by Ralph Rinzler, Smithsonian Office of Folklife Programs.

My approach to my career as a folklorist began in 1933 in the Smithers plantation in a little country church with a dirt floor. A few ragged sharecroppers had been gathered together by the plantation manager to sing for us. They had sung some spirituals, and finally everybody said, "Let's have Old Blue sing." A big Black man stood up in front of the tiny Edison cylinder recorder. He said, "I want to sing my song right into it—I don't want to sing it in advance." We said, "Well, we would like to hear it first because we don't have very many unused cylinders." He said, "No sir, you are going to have to have this right straight from the beginning." We agreed, and so he sang:

Work all week
Don't make enough
To pay my board
And buy my snuff.
It's hard, it's hard
It's hard on we poor farmers,
It's hard.

After a few more stanzas, he spoke into the recorder horn as though it was a telephone. He said, "Now, Mr. President, you just don't know how bad they're treating us folks down here. I'm singing to you and I'm talking to you so I hope you will come down here and do something for us poor folks here in Texas."

When we played this back and looked around, we found that the plantation manager had tiptoed out. The crowd of Black people there was wild with excitement and happiness. For my part, I realized right then that the folklorist's job was to link the people who were voiceless and who had no way to tell their story, with the big mainstream of world culture. I realized then what my career was going to be, and when I came to Washington, there was a friendly atmosphere for that idea . . .

This period, the Roosevelt period, was not only one of political development, when for the first time America became conscious of its social responsibilities to the whole population. It was also a time when a rising interest in American culture flowered and bore fruit. Courses in American Literature, respect for American writers, search for American roots had been going on for well, let's say, since the Civil War. But America at that time, even at the advent of the Roosevelt era, still felt dependent on Europe for its cultural underpinnings. American music was still not felt to be equal to European music. American painting was still not thought to be equal to European painting. American writing—and this was a period in which Wolfe and Steinbeck and other American writers were beginning to be seen as major figures—not yet equal to the European tradition. The developing concern about what our own American culture was actually like, about who we were as people peaked at this time. And the search for American folk roots was a part of this.

WPA writers wrote about the people of their own cities or counties. They didn't just polish their own personal buttons. They had to get out and report America. America was being photographed, painted, even muralized. America as a multiple civilization was being recorded, studied and archived as never before. The White House sponsored and was delighted by the opening up of Washington and the country to further exploration: of what kind of place America was, of who Americans were in all their ethnic variety. The Roosevelts and the bright, young, intellectuals of the New Deal and Congress under Roosevelt's baton put their arms around the whole of American culture—minorities, ethnics, blacks, poor whites, Indians, coal miners, unemployed. Culturally, America had a whole 12 years to feel good about itself, to gather its strength, to become conscious of its power and potential. This country took a century-leap forward, culturally speaking, and we have been developing out of that ever since. America decided yes, we have good writers; yes, we have a theater; yes, we have our own music; yes, we have our dance and jazz; yes, we have a culture that's equal to anybody's in the world. And it was partially on the power of that discovery that we could fight World War II. That self-discovery poured energy right into the bloodstream of the people and helped us lick the fascists.

Carl Sandburg was the poet of the time. Artists, intellectuals, folk singers, industrialists, politicians, economists—everybody was together. Roosevelt's ability to enjoy everything, and his love and respect for his country and the American people were the magic ingredients. He was open and had the ability to be amused by the whole of life. In the end it was his smiling presence that had an enormous amount to do with the volte-face that the country made during this period: it was the fact that the White House was open to this cultural self-discovery.

Mrs. Roosevelt served, in a sense, as the President's contact with actual people, events, and communities. She went into the coal mines, saw the things that were going on, and had a strong interest in them. Mrs. Roosevelt began to hear enough of the people's music so that she developed a considerable taste for it. She had a critical discernment in the field, and when we discussed concerts at the White House she could pick and choose intelligently among the things that I proposed to her . . .

Adrian Dornbush and Charlie Seeger conferred with Mrs. Roosevelt on this particular concert in which they decided to show the King and Queen of England the kind of music we had in our country. I wasn't in Washington at that time. I was in Graduate School at Columbia University on a term's leave from the Library of Congress. I heard about the concert when they decided to have me because they couldn't lay their hands on a cowboy singer. They knew I sang the ballads that my father had collected, so they invited me to perform. My recollection of the concert is being in this dressing room downstairs where for the first time I met Lily May Ledford and her sister, who were among the Coon Creek Girls. I was anxiously trying to tune my guitar. I played my three chords, wondering where my voice was and sweating up a storm in my tuxedo. I was about 22 and felt like about 15. Finally we went up to perform. We were staggered on the stairs leading up to the East Ballroom from the downstairs dressingrooms so there would be no delay about getting us on and off the stage. I came on after Kate Smith, as I remember. She came on after the Black spiritual group sang. You can imagine how terrified I was with my three chords. And I walked out onto the stage and looked at this sea of Washington V.I.Ps. There was John Nance Garner, the Vice President, sitting close by the King, grinning because here was his state coming in to entertain. As I was singing I looked at the King and Queen. They were so much better groomed and so much more perfectly turned out than all the Americans, so perfectly polished, that you could really see an aura about them. I remember their toes were just barely touching the ground in the large, American chairs. They were right up close to the edge of the stage. I don't think I was ever more frightened in my whole life.

Roosevelt was on the front row with his head cocked over, smiling and swinging in time to the music. Oh yes, he loved that concert, he was having a ball. The Roosevelts towered over the King and Queen. They looked like little dolls compared to them. Even Roosevelt in his invalid's chair was a huge man. This presence and the vitality that poured out of him made that concert, I think, one of his peak moments.

Some time later Archie MacLeish, who was then the Librarian of Congress, and I were talking about what kind of music program we ought to have in the armed services. I felt that facilities for Americans who like to make their own music could be set up in the training camps. We would then get a literature of songs against fascism and songs about soldier experience, and marching songs, and so on. These would add enormously to the morale of America's struggle in World War II. He thought it was a good idea so he went to Mrs. Roosevelt with it. She decided to have a White House concert and a conference at the same time, including all the people in agencies in Washington concerned with morale. I was called down to the White House and spoke with Mrs. Roosevelt about this White House World War II concert. That was the first time I met her, and I was terribly impressed. She was so diffident and charming and at the same time very decisive and commanding. She was with you totally in what you were saying, picking out exactly what she wanted and needed. She had her own ideas about what should be done and had the money available to do it. In that half hour meeting, I think, we planned almost the whole thing. I suggested that we put on for that audience a range of American songs in English and then add per- formances by soldiers from nearby camps that would illustrate the kind of things the soldiers enjoyed doing. Since I knew that the President liked sea shanties, I felt we should get a sea shanty singer to begin.

Sailor Dad Hunt, who had settled down in the Virginia mountains after long years as a clipper ship sailor would do sea shanties. Burl Ives would represent middle American pioneer tradition, ballad tradition, lyrical tradition. Wade Mainer and his band would perform the Anglo-American Appalachian tradition. Josh White would do blues. And the Golden Gate Quartet would sing Black sacred music. I went out to the local boot camps and after a few days found two or three marvelous country and western groups who could really sing and play up a storm.

We designed a program booklet full of Davy Crockett mottoes and pictures from the era of the American frontier. We did this because at that point there was a problem about American morale. Many people wished we weren't in the War, and many people didn't understand fascism and how dangerous it was. I'd say perhaps the biggest thing that was accomplished by the people of this century was to defeat world fascism. The most urgent matter at that time was to stop fascism, and we were all part of that.

At the concert, much of the top brass from the Pentagon and their wives were in the front row. The first singer was Sailor Dad Hunt. He began with "When Jones's Ale was New." He got to the climax of the first verse and blocked—forgot the line. By that time the Golden Gate Quartet had fallen into rhythm with him, and Burl Ives and the rest of us were all tapping time; and we all kept tapping time until he came in with the missing line, and then the audience burst into applause. It was the whole show. He was obviously an old guy, and he was trying. That melted the hearts of the admirals and the colonels. For he was one of them. He was not a professional singer—he was an ordinary seaman who was trying to entertain them. That incident made the concert. It had become a human as well as a cultural event. Everybody stayed. When the young recruits came on with all their energy—most of the audience had never heard hillbilly music—it was a revelation to them. Fiddles, banjos, guitars and good country songs: all performed with enthusiasm by their trainees—they just couldn't get enough of that. They applauded and they stomped, and wanted to hear one more number and then one more. Everybody was loved. Everyone congratulated Mrs. Roosevelt, Archie and me, but we did not get our program of folk music into the camps. The Pentagon considered the morale of the armed forces a strictly military matter. I believe that's a mistaken idea. Morale, like culture, is everybody's creation. Both belong to all the people.

Part II

The 1950s: World Music

Introduction by Andrew L. Kaye and Matthew Barton

The writings chosen for this section span the period 1949–1960. Between 1950 and 1958, Alan Lomax lived in London, where he continued his multifaceted career as writer, broadcaster, performer, producer, and ethnomusicologist. One of his central occupations was the creation of a world survey of folk music on a series of long-playing discs for Columbia Records. For this project he completed four separate field-recording expeditions—to Ireland, Scotland, Spain, and Italy—between 1951 and 1955. Throughout his stay in England, he also made numerous recordings on excursions around the country, or even in his own London flat. His collecting labors resulted in thousands of recorded song performances, as well as scores of photographs, which remain of great importance to contemporary ethnomusicology. These recordings provided the basis for several volumes in the Columbia World Library series, as well as for other labels and numerous BBC programs. He also published several books during this time reflecting his continuing study of American music. *Mr. Jelly Roll,* an oral history of Jelly Roll Morton now considered to be a landmark publication in jazz history, was published in 1949. *Harriet and Her Harmonium*, a children's book about a young girl's musical journey across the United States in the 1850s, appeared in 1955, and *The Rainbow Sign*, an oral history of the African-American folk singer Vera Ward Hall and the preacher Reverend Ribbins, in 1959. The large and wide-ranging songbook *Folk Songs of North America*, which drew extensively on the fieldwork of Alan and his father John, was completed in England and published in 1960.

The writings included here reveal Lomax's increasing interests in world folk musics, their artistic qualities, their social utility, and the meanings they embody. These interests certainly developed early in Lomax's career as a song collector. During the 1930s, he worked with and sought out the counsel of specialists in comparative musicology, anthropology, and folklore. The Hungarian scholar and Erich Moritz Von Hornbostel student George Herzog contributed musical transcriptions to the Lomaxes' book on Leadbelly (1935), and taught in the anthropology department at Columbia, where Lomax did graduate work in 1939. At the Archive of American Folk Song during the Roosevelt era, Lomax worked with the socially engaged American musicologist and philosopher Charles Seeger (father of Pete Seeger). He consulted with anthropologist Melville Herskovitz, and worked closely with folklorist Zora Neale Hurston, in connection with his musical fieldwork in Haiti in 1937.[1] Lomax also audited courses offered at New York University by Curt Sachs, the German-born colleague of Von Hornbostel. Sachs and Von Hornbostel had pioneered the creation of a recorded archive embracing world musical traditions in the first decades of the twentieth century, and developed wide-ranging theories of the history and diffusion of world musical styles grounded in Kulturkreislehre and similar culture-geographical theories. Sachs's lectures made an enormous impression on Lomax, and he retained an enduring respect and admiration for the German-American scholar with a world-ranging musical vision.

Sachs emigrated to the United States in 1937, and was professor of music at New York University from 1937–1953. Von Hornbostel (1877–1935) belonged to the first generation of comparative musicologists working in Berlin in the 1890s and early twentieth century. He co-founded the Berlin Phonogramm Archive with Carl Stumpf in 1906. Sachs joined Von Hornbostel at the Archive during World War I. Lomax integrated what he had learned from his ethnomusicological mentors and from his own fieldwork in his popular work, such as the weekly show of folk music he produced for the Mutual Broadcasting System from 1946 to 1949. Billed as "Your Ballad Man," Lomax produced programs that frequently ventured into world music. A show entitled "Dancing Around the World" was typically eclectic, featuring (in order) recordings of Chicago blues, Appalachian and Cajun fiddling, Afro-Cuban music, West-African drumming, Django Reinhardt's "Djangology," an Irish jig, a Finnish polka, a Slavic kola, an Israeli hora, an Armenian dance tune, a Russian chorus, a Balinese xylophone orchestra, a Western Square Dance, klezmer wedding music, and a Dixieland revival recording featuring Sidney Bechet and Wild Bill Davison. A Carl Sandburg reading separated the two halves of the show. Lomax's commentary included observations about instrumental and vocal styles, calling attention to the Middle Eastern influences apparent in a klezmer clarinet solo, and the precise diction of a Finnish bandleader.

These interests in world folk music matched developing interests in the post–World War II musical community. In 1947, with the support of UNESCO (founded the previous year), the International Folk Music Council was formed with the goal of the "preservation, dissemination, and practice of the folk music of all countries."[2] In 1949, Moses Asch, a New Yorker and friend of Lomax, formed Folkways Records, a label "committed to preserving the entire range of the world's musical and oral traditions."[2] The term "ethnomusicology" itself was coined in 1950, and the Society for Ethnomusicology, an American organization, would be founded in 1955, the year that the first issues in Lomax's *Columbia World Library of Folk and Primitive Music* series were published.[4]

The first article included here, "Tribal Voices in Many Tongues," published in the *Saturday Review*, is a review of (then) recent recordings, and it reminds us of that exciting time when improved recording and playback technologies, along with increasing public interest was beginning to create, as Lomax predicts, "a 'Library of the Music of the World's Peoples,' something just dreamed about ten years ago." Lomax demonstrates his familiarity with the problems of notation, transcription, and comparison facing the emerging field of ethnomusicology, and explores the problem of the baffling diversity of world musical styles ("music is no universal language," he writes). In the questions and problems that Lomax raises we can see the seeds of an inquiry that would eventually lead to his development of Cantometrics in the 1960s.

In the summer of 1950, Lomax, a senior figure in the world of American folk music, participated in the historic "Midcentury International Folklore Conference" held at Indiana University. The next article is a transcript of Lomax's opening remarks for a symposium on the topic "Making Folklore Available." In his presentation, he emphasized the importance of modern communications media, including radio and film, as a means for disseminating folk music and the vital meanings that it embodies. He cited, in particular, the *American School of the Air* series he produced for CBS Radio in 1939 and 1940 and the VD awareness programs that he and Erik Barnouw created for the Armed Forces Radio Service in 1949. These and other programs by Lomax employed a wide range of folk, blues, country, and gospel performers. During the conference, Lomax consistently argued that the folklore scholar should also take on the roles of activist and popularizer to ensure that regional styles of folk music (and other folk expressions) continued to have an important role in society, and not be drowned out by the often centralized, commercially driven media. Recalling his vision for a "Library of the Music of the World's Peoples" of the previous year, he made the following proposal to the conference participants:

> What more people need are just good sets of examples from most of the culture areas. Every folklore center would like to have such samples. If we could agree on some kind of plan for the use of either tape or long-playing records—probably long-playing records—we could make a beginning at this meeting of an international exchange of folksongs between countries. I know that it is possible to get about fifty minutes of music from one record at the cost of about three dollars and a half. With two or three records you could get a very great deal of music from Turkey or Pakistan or any particular part of the world. And it could be quite within the realm of possibilities to establish an international exchange on this basis.[5]

Lomax later recalled, in an article published in *HiFi/Stereo Review* (May 1960), that he did not succeed in stirring his colleagues to take action on this project. He was nonetheless personally committed, and secured the agreement of Goddard Lieberson, president of Columbia Records, to issue a series of LP records surveying world folk music. Thus it was that in September 1950 he set sail for Europe with "a new Magnecord tape machine in my cabin and the folk music of the world as my destination." He envisioned a sojourn of a year "collaborating with the folk music experts of Europe and drawing upon their archives," but for reasons both personal and professional, he stayed on in Europe for some eight years, returning to New York City in July 1958.[6]

The ability to sell such a project to a man of Lieberson's stature is evidence of Lomax's powers of persuasion as well as his considerable national reputation. Before leaving for England, however, he was also busily circulating book, radio, television and other recording proposals. On January 28, 1950, he produced a memorial concert for Leadbelly at New York's Town Hall, featuring such jazz and folk luminaries as Count Basie, Sidney Bechet, Eubie Blake, Woody Guthrie, W. C. Handy, Lord Invader, Jean Ritchie, and Pete Seeger with the Weavers. In August of that year, the Weavers's rendition of "Goodnight Irene," whose copyright Lomax and his father shared with Leadbelly, went to the top of the pop charts (and the proceeds helped finance his overseas collecting). He was also being sought after by the BBC to broadcast programs on American folk music.[7]

Recent developments in recording technology also made his collect-

ing trip possible. The magnetic tape recorder, invented in Germany in
the mid-1930s, was only introduced in America after World War II. This
technology allowed for recordings of much higher fidelity than previously possible. Lomax first used the portable magnetic tape recorder,
recording on paper-backed tape, for his 1947 recordings of African
American folk songs sung by prisoners at Parchman Penitentiary in
Mississippi. In 1948, Columbia introduced the 33rpm long-playing disc,
which was to revolutionize the recording industry (especially after the
arrival of stereo in the late 1950s). The new format was far more "user
friendly" than the heavy and fragile 78rpm record, and it could hold over
50 minutes of music, compared to a total of about 6 minutes for the
standard 78. In a frank and impassioned letter to Woody Guthrie, written in Pontevedra in Spanish Galicia and dated December 5, 1952,
Lomax described both his homesickness and his determination to
remain in Europe until he achieved two central goals. "When I left the
states," he wrote, "I'd decided to do two things: publish the folk music of
the world all together in a big handsome set of thirty or forty long playing records, and to do my big book on the Negro singers like Vera Hall
and Doc [Reese] and Big Bill [Broonzy] which has been half finished."[8]
By the time of his return to the United States, Lomax had partially
achieved both goals. Materials for the envisioned "big book" (called *Salt
of the Earth* in one early proposal) would find their way into other books,
including *The Rainbow Sign*, a book of oral history based in part on his
interviews with folksinger Vera Ward Hall, published in 1959. Columbia
Records published the first volumes of The Columbia World Library of
Folk and Primitive Music in 1955. In all, seventeen volumes were released
before the project was discontinued in the early 1960s.

Beyond producing many recordings of high artistic quality, Lomax
sometimes was the first researcher to create a serious recorded document
of a region's rural folk music, which occurred in Spain and Italy. Like so
many times before in his life, Lomax found himself to be the right person at the right time in the right place. In Italy, for example, working
both on his own and in cooperation with Italian ethnomusicologist
Diego Carpitella, he created a pioneering collection of over 3,000 samples of Italian folk music, at the historical moment when many of these
styles were fading into disuse.[9] In a review of the recent re-edition of
Lomax's Italian recordings by Rounder Records (1999), ethnomusicologist Roberto Catalano observes, "Lomax and Carpitella set off to record
the scarcely known music of peasants, fishermen, shepherds, street ven-

dors, dockworkers, mountaineers, and suburban dwellers. They managed to accomplish their task shortly before everything in Italian society drastically changed following the developments of the economic boom of the second half of the 1950s."[10]

In addition to his collaboration with Carpitella, Lomax formed many other friendships and collegial associations while in Europe that were extremely productive and long lasting. In Great Britain and Ireland, for example, he worked closely with, among others, A. L. Lloyd, Peter Kennedy, Ewan MacColl, Hamish Henderson, and Seamus Ennis. MacColl credited Alan with bringing him together with A. L. Lloyd and encouraging their efforts to create a folksong revival in Britain similar to the one that Lomax had helped earlier spur in the United States. He was actively involved as a radio broadcaster in London, and introduced listeners of the BBC's Third Programme to American folk music as well as to materials he recorded in England, Ireland, Scotland, Spain, and Italy. All the while, he carried on a massive campaign of meetings and letter-writing to secure recorded materials and writings from ethnomusicological scholars and archivists from around the world for inclusion in the Columbia World Library series.[11]

The remaining articles in this section deal with Lomax's activities in Europe during the 1950s, his experiences as a field recorder and researcher, and his developing ethnomusicological theories on world folk music. A portion of a larger typewritten manuscript with the heading written in Lomax's hand "SPAIN: December 1952, Galicia," is part of an unfinished book project about his seven-month Spanish field recording trip of 1952–1953. He seems to have been working on this in 1960 with Jeanette Bell, his assistant on that trip, but the project was left uncompleted. Nonetheless, in this short excerpt we can appreciate Lomax's flair for combining an ethnographic eye, a musicological ear, and a novelist's pen. He used his Spanish field recordings as the basis for a radio series on the BBC in 1953. The popularity of these broadcasts led directly to his Italian field recording expedition of 1954–1955. We have also included the introduction to the two Italian volumes of the Columbia World Library series, co-authored with Diego Carpitella, as well as a proposal he circulated for a touring multimedia exhibition that he hoped would spark an Italian folk music revival.

In the mid-1950s, Lomax turned to theorizing the materials of world music he had been grappling with for some quarter century. In a brief, three-page article, "Folk Song Style: Notes on a Systematic

Approach to the Study of Folk Song, New York," which appeared in the *Journal of the International Folk Music Council, Geneva,* in 1956, Lomax offered a first attempt at articulating a synthesis of world music that would satisfy his own personal desire to make sense of the complex whole of world musical diversity, which was shared by his colleagues in the growing academic disciplines of folklore, anthropology, and ethnomusicology. In the article, Lomax singles out the problem of musical notation as a central one for the fields of "musical ethnography," and he uses the term which had only recently become established for this emerging field, "ethnomusicology," and proposes that a "fresh approach" needs to be considered, one that would consider "the musical event as a whole." The article also proposes a provisional culture–geographic map describing five world "song-style families," the Eurasian, the Old Eurasian, the African Negro, the Pygmoid, and the Amerindian. As brief as it is, this article, with its call for a revised notational/analytical system for ethnomusical analysis, and its concern for culture–geography, marks the beginning of Lomax's Cantometrics project. A significantly expanded version of this article, similarly titled "Folk Song Style: Musical Style and Social Context," was published in the distinguished journal *American Anthropologist* three years later, and is also included in this section. Here Lomax identifies a still provisional list of eight "main musical style areas."[12]

Lomax was also active as a performer while in England, giving occasional concerts and staging his ballad opera, "The Big Rock Candy Mountain," which premiered in December 1955 at Joan Littlewood's Theatre Workshop and featured the American folksinger Ramblin' Jack Elliott. At about the same time, he formed a skiffle group called Alan Lomax and the Ramblers that featured Ewan MacColl, Peggy Seeger, and Shirley Collins, among others. They recorded for English Decca and made several appearances on Granada Television. In his two commentaries on the English skiffle craze, Lomax omits mention of his own involvement in the scene. Although he prefaces the articles with an affirmation of his neutrality, as a folklorist interested in broad historical trends rather than preservation, his articles leave no doubt that he has strong points of view on folk music and the forms it should take. In particular, he advises skiffle musicians to avoid the "danger" of introducing "sophisticated chord progressions from the jazz boys," and he suggests, in the last paragraph of the second article, that British musicians should more actively seek to cultivate materials from local sources: "the wonderful traditional playing and singing that still live in out-of-the-way places in the British Isles." The ultimate goal would be the creation of "their own national amalgam of regional folk-song styles."

The final selection, "Saga of a Folksong Hunter," is a fascinating and eloquent account of the author's "twenty-year odyssey with cylinder, disc and tape." Here Lomax expresses his great passion for and love of the "field recording habit," which he believes holds the key to unlocking the deepest feelings of the singer and through this understanding "the character of his whole community." Lomax affirmed that true ethnomusicology was realized only through intimate contact between the researcher and the folk community, and that with contact came a responsibility on the part of the researcher to become a communicator and an advocate for the art and humanity of that community to the rest of the world. The original article was accompanied by more than a dozen of Lomax's photographs that he had taken in the field. These photographs are imbued with the same vitality and magic that we find in many of his original field recordings, and the almost one hundred records that Lomax had produced by that time. He opened the article with a startling observation that may yet prove correct: "our epoch may not be known by the name of a school of composers or of a musical style" but rather "the period of the phonograph or the age of the golden ear, when, for a time, a passionate aural curiosity overshadowed the ability to create music." It is clear that Lomax saw modern media as a double-edged sword. On the one hand, the recording device was a tool enabling cross-cultural communications on a scale previously unknown, and, on the other, it had the potential to stifle creativity. In the closing paragraphs of this article, Lomax reiterates his doubts, and warns of the possibility of a future world numbed by "automated mass-distributed video-music." The solution, he suggests, is "for us to learn how we can put our magnificent mass communication technology at the service of each and every branch of the human family."

"Saga of a Folksong Hunter" was written in New York following Lomax's field trip with Shirley Collins in the southern United States from August to October 1959, and it brings him and this section of the book full circle, both geographically and ideologically. In it he echoes the themes of preservation and advocacy that he took up at the conference in Indiana in 1950. The passionate writing style he displays here and elsewhere (as well as his intense emotional involvement with the people and the music that he documented) has often seemed at odds with the scientific bent of his later endeavors, although both tendencies were present early in his work. As he told his colleagues in 1950, he saw no contradiction in being both an activist and a scientist: "It seems to me, then, that the term 'advocate' isn't so dangerous. We say that we believe that the people who don't read and write also have a way of life, a way of expressing themselves that's very important. They, too, should have their place in the sun. This way of expressing this oral tradition is just as important and just as necessary to the health of civilization as the literary way. We really believe that. We are going to have to fight passionately for that." In July of 1958, Alan Lomax took that fight back to the United States, where his activities of the next several years would be undertaken against the backdrop of an urban folk revival built on foundations he, his father, and others had initiated a generation earlier.[13]

NOTES

1. Gage Averill, *The Alan and Elizabeth Lomax Haitian Recordings, 1936–7*, paper presented at the biannual meeting of the International Council for Traditional Music (ICTM), Rio de Janeiro, July 2001.

2. Maud Karpeles, "The International Folk Music Council: Twenty-One Years," *Yearbook of the IFMC*, vol. 1 (1969), 16.

3. Asch ran other labels prior to Folkways, and was instrumental in recording and publishing music by folk musicians who were also associated with Lomax, including Woody Guthrie, Leadbelly, and Pete Seeger; see Peter Goldsmith, *Making People's Music: Moe Asch and Folkways Records* (Washington, D.C.: Smithsonian Institution Press, 1998). The quotation is from Smithsonian/Folkways site, quoted on March 31, 2002 (http://www.folkways.si.edu/moe-book.htm).

4. Carole Pegg et al., "Ethnomusicology," in Stanley Sadie, ed., *The New Grove Dictionary of Music and Musicians*, 2nd edition. (New York: Grove's Dictionaries, 2001). The *Columbia World Library*'s seventeen volumes included: Scotland, Ireland, England, France, Spain, Northern and Central Italy, Southern Italy, Romania, Bulgaria, Yugoslavia, India, East Asia, Indonesia, Australia and New Guinea, British East Africa, French West and Equatorial Africa, and Venezuela.

5. Stith Thompson, ed., *Four Symposia on Folklore* (Bloomington: Indiana University Press, 1953), 141.

6. Alan Lomax, "Saga of a Folk Song Hunter," *HiFi/Stereo Review*, vol. 4, no. 5 (May 1960), 43. Lomax also found it prudent to remain outside of the country at a time when several of his friends and colleagues, including Pete Seeger, were being called to testify before Congress and were even blacklisted.

7. See E. David Gregory, "A. L. Lloyd and the Search for a New Folk Music, 1945–49," *Canadian Journal for Traditional Music*, vol. 27, no. 1 (1999/2000). According to Gregory, in 1949 Herman Grisewood, controller of the BBC's Third Programme, "had hoped that Alan Lomax could be persuaded to do a program on [folk music], but Lomax postponed his arrival in Britain for a year." According to a sporadic journal he kept at the time, Lomax spent several weeks in Europe in the summer of 1949, but does not appear to have had any plans to relocate at that point.

8. Alan Lomax to Woody Guthrie, December 5, 1952, courtesy of Lomax Archives. His projected "big book on Negro singers" formed part of his lifelong commitment to the recording, study, and promotion of African–American music. Lomax complained, in both his letter to

Woody and his later *HiFi/Stereo Review* article, of the difficulties he encountered on the Columbia World Library project in Europe. To his disappointment, he found that many European archival holdings were restricted in scope and quality, and to his chagrin he did not find the kind of cooperation he had expected from some European institutions and colleagues. He nonetheless was able to secure the friendship and assistance of a number of influential musical figures in Europe, as well as some degree of institutional support (for example, from the BBC).

9. See Tullia Magrini, "Italy, II. Traditional Music," Sadie, ed., *New Grove Dictionary of Music and Musicians*. Magrini writes, of Italy, "It was only after World War II that comprehensive documentation of the oral musical tradition got under way. Fieldwork initiated in 1954 by Alan Lomax and Diego Carpitella and carried out throughout the entire country by several scholars during the following decades has led to the production of about 200 LPs and CDs since 1954." Also, see Joseph Matii Perez, "Spain, II. Traditional and Popular Music and Musicians," ibid. Here the author notes that in the period prior to the 1960s, researchers in Spain did not make ample use of recordings: "phonograms . . . are unfortunately rare."

10. Roberto Catalano, "Review: Italian Treasury: The Alan Lomax Collection," *Music and Anthropology: Journal of Musical Anthropology of the Mediterranean*, no. 4 (1999).

11. Robin Denselow, *When the Music's Over: The Story of Political Pop* (London: Faber and Faber, 1989), 22–23; E. David Gregory, "Lomax in London: Alan Lomax, the BBC and the Folk-Song Revival in England, 1950–1958," *Folk Music Journal*, vol. 8, no. 2 (2002), 136–237.

12. "Folk Song Style: Musical Style and Social Context," *American Anthropologist*, vol. 61, no. 6, December 1959, 927–954. See the essay by Gage Averill in this volume for more details on this article.

13. Thompson, ed., *Four Symposia on Folklore*, 172.

Chapter 11

Tribal Voices in Many Tongues

I suspect it was on a tourist's visit to Naples in the nineteenth century that some sentimental literary gentleman opined, "Music is a universal language." This absurd notion has bedeviled collectors of folk and primitive music ever since. I only wish I could hold the author's head firmly against the bell of my loudspeaker while I played him a series of albums. Soft-headed as he was, he would be forced to say, "Music may be a universal language, but what a devilish lot of dialects!" As is so frequently the case, there is a perverse mite of truth in this apothegm. Of course there is no quicker way to establish a primary emotional contact with an exotic culture than through its music. Yet in all exotic music there lies a hard core of meaning and unfamiliar technique which must be absorbed slowly, and often suffered with, before the intent of the musical language comes clear to the listener.

I have never compared notes with my colleagues on the first impression an unfamiliar musical language makes upon their prejudiced collector's ears. I can recall my first six weeks of suffering in Haiti, while I sat next to the ear-shattering battery of vodun drums, blacking out aurally whenever I could endure no more of the highpitched, hard voices of the female choruses. Then I remember an extended period of suffering with backwoods fiddlers here in the States. I would prefer not to recall certain other experiences. In every case, however, once I got the hang of the music, once I began to hear the nuances of feeling and humanity amid the blare of strange sounds, there began an interest that turned into liking, thence veering wildly to the state of enthusiasm at which every collector arrives, determined to traduce his friends' musical tastes. At such times, we folklorists share the passion that must have fired Sir Walter Raleigh when he introduced tobacco to the court of Elizabeth.

Music is no universal language, gentle listeners, but if you will study certain recordings of African and Indian music, you will come to appreciate the artistry of songmakers who represent millions of human beings, hundreds of years of history. The portable electric recording machine, transported with no end of difficulty to various corners of the earth, has made your education relatively painless. Beauty lies within these unfamiliar continents of music, beauty which can carry you beyond, if not above, the horizons of the three B's, and of bebop, too.

Until the early thirties musicologists struggled with a system of notation unsuited to exotic musical systems or else endured the nerve-shattering surface of the cylindrical record. Nevertheless, Hornbostel, Sachs, and others gathered material that was suitable for study, if not for listening. The appearance in the early thirties of the portable electric recorder, which engraved with a diamond point on an aluminum disc, greatly stimulated field recording. Surface scratch was still present, but at least the amplifiers produced a realistic musical sound, sufficient to convince the layman (who financed these voyages) that the results were worth the money.

The continuing improvement of inexpensive recording devices has further increased the pace of musical documentation. One constantly hears of new batches of records—here a GI back from Micronesia with records, there a linguist with records of the ancient melodies of the Ethiopian Jews. The archives in Washington and, one hears, in Paris, London, and elsewhere, are growing rapidly. A Library of the Music of the World's Peoples—something just dreamed about ten years ago—may soon be a living reality.

Meanwhile many handsome albums of acoustically good records of African and Indian music have begun to modify our provincial aural preferences. The collection, editing, and annotation were done, in most cases, by real experts. Several of the albums are the lavish product of the Archive of Folk Lore in the Library of Congress (catalogue available on request) and the remainder mostly the issue of indefatigable Moe Asch, former owner of the Asch and Disc labels, now releasing an "ethnic series" labeled Folkways.

To begin with, here are some albums of African and Afro-American music:

"*Music of Equatorial Africa*," four 10" unbrk., $7.33, Folkways, recorded by André Didier on a mission to French Equatorial Africa. This is the best album of African music I know, aside from the now unavailable Belgian Congo records. A wide range of instruments—the drum, the antelope horn, the zither, the xylophone, the musical bow, and the sansa (a sort of abbreviated piano)—and an even broader range of song styles remind one again that Africa may be the most musical continent, a land where all life activities are part of an unbroken stream of rhythmic activity. In a note describing the xylophone record M. Didier says, " . . . two teams work in relays from sunset to daybreak; not one moment does the music stop while the men and women dance in circles around the xylophones . . . "

"Not one moment does the music stop"—this phrase explains much of the uncanny ease and rightness of African phrasing, whether it occurs in a hot jazz band, in a Brazilian Caboclo ceremony, or in a Babinga pigmy chorus (record three) where each singer produces only *one* note in the caracol-like melody. It is a prodigious amount of "practice" that produces the prodigies of polyrhythm, improvisation, and choral polish for which African music is notable. Absorption into the cultural patterns of this hemisphere added color to this music, but did not change its basic design—an impression clearly confirmed by the following albums.

"*Afro-Bahian Religious Songs*," five 12" vinylites, Library of Congress, $8.25, recorded by Melville and Francis Herskovits in Bahia, Brazil, the "Rome of the Africanos." These records and the fascinating ethnological essay accompanying them document the cult music of the Brazilian Negro of the North. The language is largely African; the melodies with their typically descending cadences are African; but, again, it is the precision of the choral responses, the dominance and virtuosity of the drummers that finally stamp the music.

Dr. Herskovits's Brazilian drummers do not strike me as quite so accomplished as those I recorded in Haiti. Of course, the brilliance of the folk music of this tiny island republic is altogether hard to explain. Perhaps it is a reflection of the revolutionary and independent spirit of the Haitian peasant, who feels comfortably superior to all "foreigners." A number of Haitian albums have been published, including the following:

"*Voodoo*," four 10" shellacs, General Records, recorded in New York and now out of print.

"*Haiti Dances*," two 10" shellacs, $2.89 (two singles also available at $1.05), Wax Record Co., New York. Mistakes in labeling and confusion in the explanatory notes detract little from the technical excellence and the musical interest of these records. The choral performances, taken in the neighborhood of Port-au-Prince, show city influence, but point to the probable direction of Haitian folk music as it gains acceptance by the elite and is "refined."

"Folk Music of Haiti," four 10" unbrk., $7.33, Folkways, an early reissue of a valuable Disc album which exhibited much of the variety of Haitian music—Mardi Gras drumming, mosquito drumming, and work songs, as well as vodun music. A product of Harold Courlander.

"Drums of Haiti," four 10" vinylites $7.33, Folkways, recorded and edited by Courlander, who is a novelist and one of the best and most active field recordists. It contains a wide range of drum rhythms, with especially brilliant examples of the social dances. On these records the drummers "break away" in superb style. Courlander's best album so far, *"Cult Music of Cuba,"* Disc, will also be reissued this year in improved pressings by Folkways. In Cuba, Courlander had to "bootleg" his recording sessions, for there the vodun cults are underground. This must have been an annoying problem for him, but we are the beneficiaries. There is not a careless or unimpassioned groove in the album.

"Trinidad Steel Band," two 10" shellacs, Disc, out of print, but worth a search if you want to hear where present-day sophisticated calypso came from. Contrary to the impression of the editor, the steel bands—composed of washtubs, tire rims, biscuit pans, and oil drums (each article chosen so that it is in tune with the others)—were the forerunners of the modern calypsonian orchestra. For the folk music of rural Trinidad we will have to wait until the Library of Congress issues some of the records Herskovits made on his expedition there.

"Bake the Johnny Cake," *"Cé la Rage,"* one 12", Murray Music Co., New York, is the only record I know of Bahamian folk music. A sophisticated performance by a Cuban style orchestra, but nonetheless genuine Bahamian and a record that will frighten no one.

Negro folk music prepared all of us to some degree to accept African music. The story is quite different so far as Indian music is concerned. Since the days when the voyageurs and other frontiersmen lived (and doubtless sang) with the Indians, few Americans have had more than a tourist's acquaintance with Indian singing. The sentimentalized scores of Cadman, MacDowell, and other long-hairs, the romantic tomfoolery of popular songs served only to increase our ignorance. Serious musicologists struggled with exotic scales and intervals they could not represent in conventional notation. Now, at last, we can soak in the strident and soaring singing of the first Americans—a style which, to my ear, is surprisingly consistent for all the regions which these records represent.

"Songs from the Iroquois Longhouse," five 12" shellacs, $8.25, Library of Congress, with a thirty-four-page illustrated booklet by the collector,

William Fenton of the Smithsonian Institution. Burly Bill Fenton has spent so much time ethnologizing on the reservation of the Five Nations at Allegheny, New York, that the people accept him as an Indian. As relaxation from the hard tasks of anthropology he learned to sing with such an Indian Caruso as Chancey Johnny John, who "knows a thousand verses of two score ceremonies and social dances." Later, with one of the Library's recorders, he captured the chanting of the old men, thanking the creator in voices that "carried over the fields and echoed from the hills." His records confirm his statement that this music, which ante-dates the coming of the white man, is still important to Indians who now "dance in rubber boots, chew snuff, and dress as other workers." The evenly spaced beats of the water drum, the growling antiphony of the old men, the liquid flow of the poetry, broken by occasional grunts or sharp cries, form a consistent pattern throughout the war dances, the squaw dances, and the ceremonies of this and the following album.

"*Seneca Songs from Coldspring Longhouse*," five 12" vinylites, Library of Congress, $8.25, recorded by William Fenton, with booklet.

"*Music of the Sioux and the Navaho*," four 10" unbrk., Folkways, $7.33. These songs from the Middle and South West, recorded and edited by Professor Willard Rhodes for the U. S. Indian Service, confirm John Collier's thesis that the Indian has made a cultural comeback. The youthful, vigorous voices express great confidence and joy and none of the "race weariness" we have been prepared to expect. Throughout the "Sioux Sun Dance," the "Rabbit Dance," the "Peyote Cult Song," throughout the "Navaho Riding Song," the "Corn Grinding Song," and the "Night Chant," these present-day Indian farmers and sheepmen leave no doubt of their preference for their own music. Modern influences appear in some of the texts, in the use of a harmonica on one strip, and in somewhat more vocal blending than one expects, but these are slight matters in relation to the "Indianness," the powerful vitality of these records. I commend this as everybody's Number One Indian album.

"*Folk Music of Mexico*," five 12" vinylites, Library of Congress, $8.25, recorded and edited by Henrietta Yurchenko, should be titled "Primitive Music of Mexico" because it's all Indian. It represents a Herculean achievement by Madame Yurchenko (whom we can also thank for the origination of the annual WNYC festival of music). Her patience and charm won the support of Mexican officials for her recording project; her courage and stamina took her into the wildest and least accessible corners of that country; and the music she recorded may well antedate the conquest of Mexico. Some of the groups she visited were refugees from the Aztec empire who have lived in unbelievable poverty and isolation for centuries. Theirs is "pure" music, if there is any such, and, to my ear, some of it is also "starved" music—fragmentary and almost without life. There are beautiful sounds, however, especially the Chiapan trumpet and flute which announce the coming of a day of fiesta. The only other records of Mexican Indian music I know about were made by John Green among the Yaquis, the Tarascans, and the Chicimecans. This General album is now, unfortunately, out of print.

"*Folk Music of Venezuela*," five 12" vinylites, $8.25, Library of Congress, recorded by Juan Liscano and edited by him with Charles Seeger. I have saved the "best for the last" in this album, which combines African, Indian, and Spanish influences. In Juan Liscano, Venezuelan poet and folklorist, one encounters the truly great field recordist. His records not only represent the folk music of his country at its best, but also captured the music alive, when it was "happening." They somehow transport one straight to Venezuela. The strange flutes and drums of the Caribbean Indians, the hot drumming of the Venezuelan Negroes, the Spanish ballads, the native songs gripped me and involved me in the life of the people which Liscano so well explains in his notes.

And more, these records offer the most convincing evidence that it is cultural exchange and competition, not isolation and purity, which are essential to the vitality of folk and primitive music. This is precisely the reason that this hemisphere has produced so many new and vital musical forms in recent centuries. Here the many peoples met, and swapped songs in an atmosphere of peace and relative democracy.

Chapter 12

Making Folklore Available

The question of making folklore available seems to me always raises uncomfortable points which we can avoid so long as we stick to strictly laboratory folklore. Because when we begin to make folklore available, we come into contact with all sorts of other fields, with other cultural workers. And these cultural workers begin to ask questions about us and about our material. They say, "Well, why concern yourself with folklore and why bother us with your material?" As long as we just collect and classify nobody bothers with us very much. The sociologist and anthropologist look in upon us, and feel that we are somehow their brothers, and they sometimes shrug in amazement at what we are doing and go on away about their business. But when folklorists appear as benefactors of the public and provers of public taste, etc., then folks ask why, and I think they are fair in raising that question.

First of all, in terms of the history of our craft, there is no question about why it has been supported, why national folklore institutes have been sponsored. One of the first acts of the submerged peoples of northeastern Europe, for instance, was to start a folklore movement, and as we all know many nationalities actually coalesced around the collection and the use of the folklore of the region and of the people concerned. Folklore then has been used to prove that a certain group of people formed a national entity, and it is quite understandable why in this area and in situations of this kind folklore has been encouraged, fostered, and used extensively.

We think of Sibelius in Finland, and we think of the tremendous work of the Swedes, and we think with a little less friendliness of the almost unbelievable researches of the Germans. Folklore has been national propaganda.

It is interesting to note that the great burst of interest in folklore in America came in World War II when for the first time America began to feel cut off from Western Europe and felt thrown back upon its own folks' national cultural resources. And, it was at this time, and I think it's no coincidence, that there began to be a great national interest in folklore for the first time in America.

I think we are all agreed that folklore in its nationalistic or even its regionalistic form is assuming its less pleasant, less scientific and really less valuable function. It is not our object to prove any longer that a nation is an entity because it sings a certain group of songs which we know have their kindred variants across the next national border. We know that the use of folklore in this fashion can be not only ugly but downright dangerous. All we have to do is think of the Hitler youth movement [in Germany] or the Solid South in America with its folk attitudes toward the Negro. So we have to look around for another set of values.

We must think about the value problem. Now, it seems to me, that the very act of preserving and presenting folklore is a way of saying that the material is valuable. We rush in ahead of, and sometimes way behind, the process of cultural and social change and rescue material from oblivion and at this point we can ask ourselves why. Why shouldn't culture be allowed to cast off its skin in its own sweet way? Why do we interfere with the process and preserve all of the skins that culture is constantly casting aside? Is this only in order to understand texts? I doubt that.

Rather it seems to me that in one way or another we all feel, we folklorists, that we are making a better present and preparing for some sort of juster future for all people. So, let us begin right where we are, where we folklorists stand with the simplest value notion. We are folklorists because we like folklore, or we like the people from whom it comes. We like the way folklore makes us feel and we like the way many people make us feel. I thought that the paper last night about the Lapps made this point very clearly and very frankly. Mr. [R. N.] Pehrson said that he liked the Lapps. They reminded him that there were certain values that were just missing from our present society. In some ways he felt more comfortable with the Lapps than he did in Chicago. And I think this is true, in one way or another, for all of us folklorists as we work in the field, or as we work in our libraries with our various kinds of folk literature or patterns of folk life. I think when we smile at the declaration of values that is as clear, naive, frank, and truthful as the one last night, we have forgotten our own motives in being folklorists.

Underneath we are all morally, emotionally, and esthetically involved with our material, and so all of us are artists and cultural workers, and there is no escape from that. You discover that very vividly when a radio executive says that Barbara Allen or some ballad that seems to you very beautiful "is just draggy. Please bring on a peppier tune," he says. Or when a child psychologist attacks you for bringing traumatic, cannibalistic *fantasies* into the lives of her little charges.

Malinowski in his last, posthumously published monograph, speaking for the ethnologists, said that the role of the ethnologist is that of the advocate of primitive man. And it is my feeling that the role of the folklorists is that of the advocate of the folk. (I am going to skip definition here because I think that belongs to another session, but we may all assume for a moment, since we are having an international folklore symposium, that we agree who the folk are.) We have seen the profit-motivated society smashing and devouring and destroying complex cultural systems which have taken almost the entire effort of mankind over many thousands of years to create. We have watched the disappearance of languages, musical languages, the sign languages, and we've watched whole ways of thinking and feeling in relating to nature and relating to other people disappear. We've watched systems of cookery (and if you are a lover of food, it hurts you right where you live) disappear from the face of the earth, and I think we have all been revolted by this spectacle and in one way or another have taken up our cudgels in the defense of the weaker parties.

Whether we classify folk tales, or sing ballads, I think it is all pretty much the same. We have become in this way the champions of the ordinary people of the world who aren't backed up by printing presses, radio chains, and B29's. We believe in the oral tradition, we believe in the small cultural situation, we think that some of these folk of the world have something worthwhile culturally, morally, etc. I don't propose to define a value system for folklorists because it seems to me that this set of values must emerge from actual work with material, but there are some general notions inherent in the whole process of collecting folklore and making it available which seem to me all one process in the end. So I'll just give some very off-hand things that you find right in the folklore itself. We all have found them, it seems to me, in one way or another, there.

We find that folklore is international in its main implications rather than regional or national. On the other hand we see that culture produced and consumed in the neighborhood or village situation seems to be a very healthy way for culture to grow. Things, cultural material of this kind, seem to have vitality and strength, a lasting power, and a staying power, which is equivalent to the very greatest of "serious arts" produced by the very greatest artists. We find that in folklore—in the folk tales, in the proverbs, in the songs—you get a kind of general ethical tone, a kind of rudimentary humanistic approach to life. It is not the same from culture to culture of course, but in every culture you find a very deep sense of values expressed in folklore and something that deserves to have its place in the sun, deserves to have its hearing.

We sometimes find that people who are loaded with superstitions live more honorably than people who fly airplanes. We begin to speak of the intelligence and the creativity of everybody, of every people and of every human being. I think it is a common experience of folklorists to realize that a charcoal burner, as we heard yesterday, may have a tremendously rich vocabulary. And a farmer has eighty thousand words that he knows, when it is possible that we may pick him off for not knowing more than three thousand of our vocabulary. We find intelligence, honor, character, and so on with the people.

In this way I think that we will arrive at values in our quest, but it's in working with the material itself. The values will grow as we work. Now, I propose that we should be two-way bridges and form a two-way inter-communication system. We, who speak for the folk in the market place here, have obligations to the people whom we represent. If our activity is solely to enrich a city, urban, middle-class culture, the suspicion that some of the folk have of us might actually be justified, that we are folklorists basically because we are enriching ourselves, either with prestige or actual money. So, I think, that we have to work in behalf of the folk, the people. We have to defend them, to interpret them, to interpret to them what is going on in the world which they do not make, but which begins to move in upon them and to crush their culture.

Now all of this, I feel, is a necessary introduction to any discussion of presenting folklore, and I am sure there will be many more emotions than rationalizations in these preliminary notes but these ideas have come from a long experience of presenting folklore here in America. Perhaps you would like to hear a little about that.

My main activity, although not the only one, has been in radio. As you know, we have four national radio chains, each with some hundreds of stations. Besides that there are hundreds of independent stations, unconnected. The reason for the existence of almost all of these stations is to present advertising and to make money. So any use by them of folklore has to be for that reason, or else to serve as their excuse to the Federal Communications Commission for owning the public air around

them and using it for profit. They are required by law to present a certain
number of public service programs. This is the sense in which folklore
has been presented on networks, as educational radio. It was supposed to
be good for school children to hear American ballads, to remind them of
an American past and make them feel the quality of the people building
and working and singing at the same time.

During the first years of these programs they attempted to put symphony music on right with the folk ballads. I was presented together
with a Columbia Symphony Orchestra. I sang "Buffalo Skinners" and
then the Columbia Symphony Orchestra played that. This was supposed
to show that you could use folk music for symphony, and it was because
of this natural nationalistic desire for us to have, at once, a symphonic
music based on our folk music. Well, of course, it didn't work. You can't
make that direct kind of jump. The people who write the symphonies
have to live the folklore to a certain extent. And so we still don't have folk
symphonies and folk operas, although we have been wishing for nothing
so hard at the upper levels of administration of our culture.

In the last ten years, however, the ballad has become part of the big
entertainment industry in America. There are now usually one or two programs on the air where ballads are sung, and out of this has come one
other thing which has been very, very important. A number of commercial record albums have been published and these have taken the songs to
the people who really wanted them, and were active consumers and learn-
ers of ballads. This has been a much more slow, solid, and healthy sort of
growth. Another kind of radio that has come along is local presentation
of local, regional music. This has also been commercial. It had to be or it
wouldn't go, and so there has always been the advertising and then
manipulating the programs and helping to decide what was going to be
sung, and the taste has not been the very best. So it has been a mixed
blessing. But, at least these local radio stations have been an outlet for the
local boys who wanted to make music and who didn't read, but just
wanted to get up and start to sing, and they have come by the thousands.
We have on that account an extremely lively, sometimes extremely annoy-
ing, a very much growing kind of local radio folk music, folkish music, or
I don't know what to call it—country music, come to town.

That is pretty much the picture in radio, so far. Of course, the ideal
in radio is for the people to talk back to the city, because radio can be a
two-way medium. We haven't come to this yet in America. I think that
will probably happen when television begins to take the commercial

starch out of the radio boys. They are going to have to fall back for pro-
gramming and for interest on their local audiences, and then the folk are
going to have their innings in American radio. I gather that they have
had that already in Sweden.

One other use of radio which I think you might think about is the
other side of the folklorist's job, which is to tell the folk, or to help the
folk to tell themselves, things that they need to know and that they can't
find out through ordinary channels of communication. The department
of health has been for the last five years carrying on a program, a campaign for blood tests for venereal disease. You can imagine the number
and kinds of prejudices there are against getting blood tests and even
opening up this subject in our puritan country, and radio has been the
principal medium for reaching the carriers of syphilis. They started with
the usual kind of American radio program involving Hollywood stars,
and big bands, and big names, and so on, but they invited me to write
one show for them. It was written for Roy Acuff who (as you probably
don't know) is, or was, the champion of all the hillbilly singers, that is the
country boys come to town making commercial music. Well this program was really written by Roy Acuff, because I went to see him. I didn't
know what he thought about syphilis. First of all he told me that he
couldn't say the word on the air, because he would lose his entire audience forever. And we had a long talk about it. He told me how he felt
about syphilis and in the process told me how his whole southern rural
folk audience felt about the subject. So it was very easy for me to go back
and write a little story using Roy's principal hillbilly songs and when this
program was broadcast, the people came into those southern syphilis
centers by the hundreds. They were saying everything from, "Roy said it
was all right, so I guess we should come in," or—this program was called
"Looking for Lester"; Roy was supposed to be looking for a friend who
was lost with the disease germ and was going to die—they would come
and say, "Wonder what's happened to poor old Lester," and offer their
arm for a blood test. This was so successful in relation to the other types
of program that they pretty much dropped the other techniques, and
since then there have been about fifteen of these ballad approaches to
the problem of syphilis. The last one that I did was a message directed to
the midwives of Georgia, the Negro midwives of Georgia. Well, you can
imagine that I could use many kinds of folklore in such a program: birth
superstitions, and midwife lore, Negro spirituals, and work songs. They
tell me that midwives approve it.

Well, this is one way it seems to me, in which the folklorist can know his function. I have felt for the last two years that I have really been a folklorist for the first time, a functioning folklorist, using folklore for the benefit of the people. Actually I have mostly let them do the talking because I am no great shakes as a writer, but I'm a good putter-together of ballads and folk sayings.

This same approach that is taking folklore for its own value and letting it do the work for you applies in other cultural situations about which I don't go into detail but which I want to suggest. If you have a folk festival, and if the people really make the folk festival in their own place, deciding themselves what they want in the festival, it's really going to have a dynamic growing. But if you split it up into little pieces and make your own potpourri in the city, or else if you go to your country people and tell them that they can't play a guitar because the tunes are modal, you are taking upon yourself an interfering role that is going to kill your folk festival in one way or another. In the same sense in public schools, it's not so important that every child in the nation sing "Skip-to-my-Lou" at nine o'clock in the morning. What is important is that the teachers in their own communities know that everywhere the children and their families are carriers of important literature and music and ways of living. And it is the job of the school to bring this material into the open and permit it to express itself, let the chips fall where they will. If the people have a chance not to be ashamed of their own material, if we stand just a little between them and the big powerful onslaught of commercial, heavily weighted culture, they will do their own job. The culture will work its own problems out, and so the thing that's important for the teacher is to let the children and their people come into the schools through the avenue of folk culture, whatever there is in the neighborhood. It doesn't matter—doesn't matter at all—what it is. And this is the way to international understanding, neighborhood understanding, and all these other values that I have briefly touched on that we all believe in. Now it seems to me that these are the important questions rather than the precise how. It is the way and the belief in the material and in its own content.

Chapter 13

Galician Music

The next morning we recorded the song which the director of the museum in Pontevedra had told us about. The traditional song of the Easter procession in Finisterre sung by the church choir, the usual collection of twelve girls and three men; nice folks, but they sang in a completely conventional style, giving us two songs of the Finisterre romeria as well as the Easter procession. Just as they were finishing, three burly boys came bursting into the doctor's kitchen and demanded to be heard. They demanded why we had recorded all of this nonsense and swung into one of their fishermen's ballads (Eres Una, Eres Dos).* It was easily the best thing we took in Finisterre, and we would have recorded more of these ballads if we had not been so frighteningly short of tape.

The doctor and I set out later in the morning for Corcubion, a port situated inland along the bay. It is a hungry town like Finisterre, but not quite so hungry, for there is a small chemical works that manufactures some essential component for the arms trade and little tramp steamers call in for the stuff, and so poverty isn't universal. The doctor was determined that I should record music traditional to the Fiesta of San Adrian, June 26th. As we got out of the car in the plaza of Corcubion he went over to talk to a wizened, wrinkled and ragged old lady of the market about this matter, and I looked around on the misery of the place and wished I was miles away. A little boy, half naked with bare feet red with the cold wet pavement came running up to me to beg a penny. I gave him some pesetas as his mother came along and picked him up in embarrassment. She might have been a pretty girl, but she was dirty, and her skin was sallow and her hair was lank; in fact she reminded you of any young woman you might see on tobacco road in the hookworm belt.

Something about her attracted me and I thought to myself, "Now this is the kind of person I would like to get to know instead of forever chasing the women with their old worn out songs."

I chatted with her a minute, gave her child some more money and then was called away by the doctor. For two hours we walked up and down the town trying to find the old women who had once been the leaders in the fiesta singing. One was sick, another was dead, another one hadn't sung in 25 years, another one wouldn't come out of her house to sing, another one wasn't at home; another one welcomed us in but hooted at the idea of remembering that old stuff. It was one of those discouraging tramps that are so familiar to folk song collectors and that turn the most interesting towns into little miserable, narrow hells of rejection and frustration. The doctor, however, had the courage of his antiquarian convictions, and I think we would have gone on tramping the rest of the day if I hadn't called a halt.

"Perhaps," I said "this old music is important for you in Galicia, but for my World Collection it's not worth a day of hunting."

The good doctor, always the agreeable Spanish gentleman, and with that strange glacial calm of his immediately agreed, and we went into the county clerk's office to warm our feet and ask if he know[s] a town where we might find some music. We sat with the local provincial officials and discussed various possibilities. One town here where a sword dance was still preserved, another town where they played a certain musical instrument . . . and then one man said, "Two of the best singers of the province have just moved here from across the mountains."

"To Corcubion—to this town?" I said.

"Yes," he said. "They are young women, and they know all the best songs."

"When can I see them?"

"Oh, perhaps this evening. They work you know."

"But perhaps they are home for lunch," I said.

"Oh well, if you are in a hurry—"

"Yes, I am in a hurry," I said. "Come along, let's go and at least try."

All of a sudden this cold morning of discouraging old hags had turned into a fine morning of young women from over the mountains. We went back through the narrow streets, up a rocky, manure spattered lane to a dark doorway, where the young man called out "Manuela, come down and talk to the stranger."

We heard feet on the stairs, the rickety old barn door swing open. There in the filthy barn stood the young woman I had met on the square.

"This," said the young man, "is the best singer in the region."

I couldn't help but feel triumphant, and I could see in her charming snaggle toothed smile that she was pleased too. Manuela's house was as miserable a place as I have ever seen, actually a sort of open loft over the stable below. There was no fire on this bitterly cold day. There was a ragged pile of cloth in one corner for a bed. There were a couple of broken chairs. Her mother was there, bent and querulous and filthy; toasted almost walnut coloured in the smoke. A couple of children were whimpering because dinner wasn't ready, and there was obviously no man in the house, or even attached to it.

Manuela, however, had that amazing temperament of the folk singer, and why should anyone suppose that it is different from the artistic temperament wherever it occurs? The only objection she could find to singing in the midst of this permanently poverty striken and crisis-ridden life of hers was that her two sisters weren't there to help her. Poor girl, she didn't know that lunch time means nothing to an American. Soon we were scrambling up another filthy lane on the edge of town and there with a gesture she said, "This is where Marucha lives—Come out Marucha, there is someone here who wishes to record you for the American Broadcasting System."

The house was hardly more than a tumble of stones with a black hole for a door, just a step better than a cave. Out of this black hole came a young woman holding a toddler by the hand and with a baby slung in the other arm; her thin cotton dress hitched up on one side, big heavy men's brogan shoes on her feet and a freckled pale face, with a twist of carrot gold hair on [her] head.

"This is the one who sings the high parts," said Manuela.

Her hand was small and strong and cold. She was shy too, in exactly the way all those southern mountain girls were shy.

"Where are you all from?" I asked. "Across the mountains?"

"Oh no," they said, "we were born and raised right here in Corcubion, but we are away much of the time working in the fields."

"You don't work in the fields." I said.

"Oh yes we do. Planting potatoes, reaping wheat—there is nothing in the way of hard work that we cannot do," Marucha, the red-headed one, said.

"I can plough all day if the men are away."

She didn't weigh more than 100 pounds, but she could handle two big oxen and ram a wooden plough into the rocky earth.

My friend from the city hall came up with the third of the sisters then. She was the black-haired one, the oldest, the most dragged out and starved looking. She had four children; Manuela the blond, three; the red-headed one, two—all by different men. Their father was a day laborer, he is dead now, "but he was an honorable man," said Manuela. "We are poor, but we are honorable."

The strange thing was that neither the little clerk from city hall, nor anyone else that day snubbed these girls, winked behind their backs or in any way implied that because of their foibles and illegitimate flocks they weren't as good as anyone else. They were poor, they were ragged and dirty, but they were honorable indeed.

"How much do you make in the fields" I asked them.

"Oh, ten pesetas with parvas," said Marucha "twelve pesetas secco."

"What do you mean by parvas?" I asked.

"Oh, a little bread and a drop of anise to warm you up in the middle of the day," laughed Manuela.

"And secco?"

"That means twelve pesetas and you go hungry if your children need everything you make," said the dark sister.

I took pictures of them standing among the grey granite 'orios' at the edge of town, like three poor little sparrows in a graveyard, they looked.

That night we didn't record in Manuela's house because one of their aunts had died recently and the family was officially in mourning and so it wasn't proper to make music in their house. The old bent lady in her one dirty black dress was too honorable to permit that, so the three sisters stood up in a stranger's house and alongside of them was a figure even more touching, even smaller and slighter than they, Juana Luna Sanchez. Some rough blow of life here at world's end had knocked out one of her eyes.

Manuela began.

Juana closed her one soft eye and began to sing in a high sweet trembling voice. Marucha let them go on for a line or two, the three harsh voices clanging like tenor horns while the panderetta and the castanets rang out the clashing rhythm. Then she raised her head and out of her little girl's throat came a high falsetto crying voice that put the white heat into the music. Short, starved, dirty and ragged, these four girls sounded their music like the strings of a guitar stroked by an expert hand.

In the next song they were joined by one of the old ladies. A market woman who had been out selling in the streets so many years that she was almost gone except for a huge drink-nobbled nose round which peered little sad sheep's eyes. Together the voices clanged and crashed with the careless precision of the jingles on a tambourine. The tunes were old, usually the songs began with a slow part . . . then with a long wailing cadence of alala's they suddenly rushed into a dance rhythm. Before the young girls began their song, however, we recorded the old ladies who had limped, been lifted and pushed up the stairs by various helpers to record the songs of the Fiesta of San Adrian. They were temperamental and touchy these old ladies, and as different to look at as if they had been born in four different countries. The head woman was big and heavy and dark with a great bust and tremendous vitality. There was one who was toothless and pouchy mouthed, withered and sorrow stricken with a look as if she had never had a night's pleasure in her life. The third was a market woman who is to be seen every morning in Corcubion with her box of sardines on her head, her wind nibbled face, her drink nobbled nose and her body gnarled and shrunken by poverty.

The fourth was white as a death shroud, except for her sunken dark-ringed eyes. She had a bad heart and had got out of her bed to come to the microphone.

When we explained again that we wanted the old fiesta songs just as they had been sung, these old ladies exchanged glances and cackled and slapped their whithered thighs, remembering the summer fiestas of years past at the time of the summer solstice.

On the 23rd of June in the evening the Mozos and Mozas gathered in the little plaza in the lower part of Corcubion and a big bonfire was built and there was singing of the ancient song "El Pan" with its references to pagan Agrerian rituals. For the night of San Juan there was another song for the folk who live near the plaza in the upper end of Corcubion. This one was accompanied on a big bass tambourine. Then on the next day, the real fiesta day of Corcubion, the day of San Adrian, 26th June, groups of singers formed in the two plazas and marched to the center of town, one singing "El Pan" and the other the song of San Juan and San Pedro and met and exchanged *desafios* in the center of the town. All this the old ladies re-created for us, the big busty one commanding and leading the others, the little warty-nosed one with her high falsetto part, and the one with the white face and the bad heart giving the soul to the tune. They were supposed to go home when the song was done; they had protested that they had no time even to meet us; but they stayed all evening, the circles growing darker and darker around the eyes of the sick woman and little nobbly-nosed straightening up her hunched back as she began to realize that she was the carrier of something important. Meanwhile in the other room in the dark in front of the recording machine another drama was being enacted.

Manuela took her child from Pip's lap then, and sang us a Galician lullabye—harsh voiced, a strange hypnotic tune, which by the time the recording was done had put the child to sleep. In many ways this had been the best evening of recording in Spain. This group of terribly poor women who might be passed on the street like a bundle of old rags, these cast-offs of this hungry coast had filled a hidious cold bare room with beauty for three hours, and had made recordings which scholars will study and listeners will enjoy for ever.

Dr. Recamen then did the only embarrassing thing I saw him do during our acquaintance. He took charge of the paying and instead of permitting me to divide my pesetas up in public, he stationed me on the stairs and solemnly called each poor creature from the bedroom and took the ten peseta note from my hand and thrust it into the trembling fingers of the old lady with such a gesture that it might have been a $100 bill, or a decoration personally presented by El Cordillo himself.

Then I ceremoniously escorted the lady with the weak heart to the car and drove her across the square 200 feet to her front door, the way I had fetched her. Then there was the machine to get down, then there were goodbyes. The three sisters with their no husbands and their many little blond children, barefoot, lost and sorrowful on the cold square of Corcubion, and we were driving home to the doctor's house to a supper of great pink spider crabs, and the doctor at last was friendly.

From now on there were to be no problems in Galicia. The songs that the chorus of old ladies of Corcubion recorded were opening every door for us, declaring us members of the clan. It is always the same with the Celts, whether in Galicia or Galway; there is the hostility, the complexity, the thousand reservations, the distrust of strangers, the duplicity even, and then the music begins . . . They are suddenly lifted up and they sail away, airborn, the strange Celts whose tunes are so close to bird song. But before – ah!, they are sitting eagles, awkward, solemn, mistrustful, to be in flight transformed, beautiful and without problems.

NOTE

* This song and others recorded by Alan Lomax in Galicia can be heard on *The Spanish Recordings: Galicia* (Rounder CD 1761).

Chapter 14

Italian Folk Music

With Diego Carpitella, 1955

Italy has preserved a folk-song pattern that is at once extraordinarily old and extremely varied, exhibiting, in many variations, the principle that the musical habits of an area—the way songs are sung there—resist change, perhaps more strongly than any other culture trait. Change seems to come about only when invasion alters the ethnic character of a region, or a social and psychological revolution completely upsets the structure of the old society.

Italy, of all the countries of the West, has the most complete folk-song history. In Sardinia the triple oboe brought by the Phoenicians from Egypt a thousand years before Christ is still in use, and keening for the dead, which is pre-Christian and pagan, is still a living custom in all the provinces south of Rome. The *tarantella*, the dance of the South, and the *saltarello*, the dance of Central Italy, seems to have been established in classical times. Field songs of the most antique style are everywhere in use. And from the early Middle Ages on, more or less precisely datable songs from almost every period of Italian history are recoverable from contemporary singers. Perhaps the most interesting recordings of this year's field work is that of the *Maggio* in the mountains north of Florence; these primitive folk operas date from the time before modern opera took its rise in Florence; and, almost certainly, show what opera was like at its beginnings.

The archaic character of Italian rural music is further evidenced in the instruments which are most commonly found. In order of frequency they are: the tambourine, which was the most popular instrument of the Greeks; the wooden or cane flute, also Greek in origin; the bagpipe; the jaw's harp and friction drum (most probably influenced by the Moors); the guitar; the violin; and, of recent introduction, but today eliminating all other instruments, the small accordion. In the last century, brass-band music has become standard at almost all Italian fiestas.

Many people have invaded this beautiful land since Roman times and everywhere there are pockets of folk song in which these invasions are evident. There are Moorish musical communities near Naples, relics of the eighth-century invasion of the Moors. In Apulia and Sicily one finds folk songs in Byzantine Greek dialect, imported about the thirteenth century. The Spanish left traces all through the South, especially in Sardinia. And one of the discoveries of this expedition was that there are enclaves of Slavic singers from the northeastern border to the very tip of Calabria, testimony to a slow popular migration from across the Adriatic that has gone on for centuries. Finally, throughout the Italian Alps, where populations are mixed, there are also decisive musical influences from the countries to the North.

All of these recent affects, however, have blended into an Italian pattern that is far older. As far north as the plain of the Po, Italy is a land of solo song and strident voices. From the Apennines through the Alps, singing and dancing are normally performed in groups; voices are liquid and blend easily in harmony. In central Sardinia, among a people who have retained a Neolithic hunting culture into modern times, one finds a polyphonic vocal style which is probably pre-Christian and may be the oldest type of European polyphony.

The same generalized pattern applies also in the case of Spain, which is a land of monody as far as the Pyrenees and, beyond, a land of group song and open voices. Apparently southern Italy and Spain belong to the Near Eastern and Oriental song family and the northern parts of both countries to an older European stock. Where these patterns are broken, a recent historical cause may nearly always be found, as in the case of the polyphonic Albanian settlements in southern Italy; but for the tendencies themselves an explanation must be sought in the character of the societies which have been dominant since antique times.

Since the period of the Renaissance this Italian peasant music, documented for the first time in these records, has lived almost without contact with the great streams of Italian fine-art music. It has followed its own course, unknown and neglected, like a great underground river. Indeed, this complete hiatus between folk art and fine art is one of the distinctive features of Italian cultural history. For many centuries until the period of the Risorgimento there was little national circulation of culture, and Italy remained split up into a great number of provinces and regions, each of which developed its own dialect and its own songs. The causes were various—a complex geography, lack of political unity, the

conquest of various parts of Italy by foreign powers, and the early flowering of urban culture.

The brilliant Italian cities developed a high culture the roots of
which were in the civilization of the classical past rather than in local
folk culture; and the peasants in the hills and villages were left to their
old ways. This split between city and country, which still persists, also
gave rise to an urban folk song, made by and for the popular artisan
class. It is these artisan songs that were heretofore thought of as Italian
folk song. Actually, they represent only that part of Italian folk music
which has been most influenced by Italy's cosmopolitan fine-art music.

Now that this great underground musical stream emerges for the
first time into the light, fresh from its antique sources, perhaps it can
play an important part in the growth of a new Italian culture.

Chapter 15

The Folk Song of Italy

Strange as it may seem, the true folk music of Italy is hardly known to people of Italy, much less to the outside world. Living in isolation in villages cut off by mountains, by the sea, by poverty, by outlandish dialects, the folk music of Italy has come down to our time as the most varied, the most antique and very possibly the richest oral tradition in western Europe.

The Folk Song archive at the Academia Santa Cecilia now contains 100 hours of folk songs recorded on tape in every province of Italy. It is the best folk song archive in the west, the only one capable of adequately and fully presenting its nation in terms of their songs, dances, lullabies, workchants, etc.

The Archive and its splendid activity need to be made known to the Italian people, especially to the artists and intellectuals. Because of the political and cultural history of the country, Italians have been cut off from their folk roots for centuries. The realization of the wonder and variety and richness of their living folk song tradition will, I believe, [bring about] a veritable cultural revolution.

What is needed? A grand, gala exhibition of these songs, done on a lavish scale in the biggest hall in Rome, something that every person in Rome will have to come to, that no foreign visitor can afford to miss.

The visitor will enter and buy his ticket to a blare of music. Then he will follow a prescribed route. From hidden microphones in the wall the people of Italy will sing their songs to him as he strolls past a montage of maps, photographs, paintings, diagrams, labels, cartoons, which describe the songs and their singers. He will wander from province to province, hearing worksongs, lullabies, serenades, fragments of the marriage ceremonies, funeral laments, pilgrimages, dances, etc., which make up the rich pattern of Italian popular music. He will hear the strains of

Italian opera from the mountain of Reggio Emilia—the still surviving Commedia delle Arte from the hills near Avellino—the Saracen dances of Positano—the sea shanties of Sicily—the wondrous music of the launedas (the Greek aulos) which have been played on the Island of Sardinia for 3,000 years—the pile driving song that built Venice—the May songs that inspired Lorenzo Magnificio—the music of the dance that pleased the Etruscans—the strange bass voice polyphony of the Ligurian mountains—the incredible falsetto songs of the Gargano shepherds—and so meet the Italian people as they literally expose their hearts and the things closest to their hearts in song.

After an hour's stroll the visitor will have heard all the most important elements of Italian popular music. He will have seen and studied the faces of the singers in photographs. He will have learned of the ancient folk migrations that formed the present face of rural Italy. He will know much of the lives and emotions of the Italian people that he could never discover in another way or by himself. Naturally, such an exhibit will demand the collaboration of RAI [Radio Italiana], to furnish technical advice and sound reproducing equipment. It will need the help of the best exhibit designers in Italy, men like Architecto Ponti. It will need money. But since this exhibition would serve to attract tourists and teach the important lessons of Italian culture, money should, it seems, be forthcoming from ENIT Tourismo and Belles Artes. Since such an exhibition could easily be toured from country to country, it should have the support of the appropriate agency there. Undoubtedly this exhibit will be imitated everywhere, for there will never have been another like it. Indeed there never has been a like opportunity. For there never has been before such a complete and fascinating collection of folk music from any one area so well recorded.

The Academia Santa Cecilia has promised full support and sponsorship. The participation of RAI is assured. Since I have had a considerable hand in building this archive and since the exhibit is my idea, the interest of the Embassy will be necessary to forward the matter with the Italian government.

Chapter 16

Folk Song Style: Notes on a Systematic Approach to the Study of Folk Song

During the past five years, as I have sifted through a vast number of recordings of primitive and folk music from many parts of the world, it has struck me more and more that a fresh approach was necessary in order to classify and understand this material. Our present system of musical notation, adequate for European fine-art music, is often unable to convey the most characteristic aspects of primitive and folk music. The more refined the scores, the more certainly the essence of the exotic music escapes through the lines and spaces.

On the other hand, when one considers the musical event as a whole, including the mannerisms of the singers, the social organization of the music, the timbre of the voice and the technique of vocalizing, the function of the music, its evident emotional content, along with the main points of musical emphasis (as opposed to musical details which strike the trained European musician), there seem to emerge certain generalized patterns which occur again and again. These patterns of musical behavior, which may be likened to a set of habits, I group together under the term *musical style*. I propose that the science of musical ethnography be based on the study of musical style or musical habits of mankind.

It has been my experience that the traditional singer acquires his musical style as a whole very early in his life. It forms all of his patterns of response to and performance of music. He is unconscious of it until some element of the pattern is absent or distorted. On the other hand, when the musical experience conforms to the dictates of the stylistic tradition, the individual experiences a rush of pleasure. He feels secure. He feels rooted again in the familiar emotions of his community and the patterns of his growing up.

It is by now a well-known fact that melodies, rhythms, scales, systems of harmony and song texts can be absorbed by a culture without changing fundamentally the over-all musical effect. Africans have taken up our folk song and fine art styles in many ways but still remain musically African, and innumerable other examples of the same kind can be enumerated. Therefore one must look to other qualities of musical style as the diagnostic or stabilizing elements of the style. I have come to believe that the social organization of the music, the characteristic timbre of the voice and its method of production, the motor activity connected with the music, and the inner emotional intent of the music are more basic than the formal musical material which is the normal subject of musicological analysis. These patterns can be linked to other aspects of the culture. They can be studied with the techniques of modern psychology and physiology; and they can form a basis for field observation on the part of any competent ethnologist.

Using this set of cues, I have arrived at a preliminary, though incomplete, classification of world folk song style by families. These families, although they have given rise to countless species and sub-species, appear to have persisted through many centuries and spread over whole continents. Briefly, I give below a painfully incomplete set of descriptions of these song-style families.

(1) *Eurasian*—This area of monody, usually associated with the spread of the high cultures of antiquity, spreads right around the world from Japan through the Far East, the Moslem World, the Mediterranean World, into France, the British Isles, and Colonial America. The voices are ordinarily high-pitched, often harsh and strident, delivered from a tight throat, with great vocal tension, body position rigid, facial expressions sad to agonized, prevailing mood of the music tragic, melancholy and nostalgic. Melodies long and highly ornamented. Control and individuality are the keynotes here.

(2) *Old Eurasian*—This area of group song, often harmonized, begins in the Hebrides and Wales, is found in the north of Spain and in Italy, in the Alps, Central Europe, parts of the Slavic World, the Caucasus, Tibet, Tribal India and possibly further East. Singing and dancing, choral and co-operative, voices deeper pitched and often liquid, throat relaxed, facial expression lively, melodies simple and less ornamented than in (1), mood from gay to grave.

(3) *African Negro*—With some noted exceptions, the area includes Africa, south of Moslem influence, and the Negro colonies of the New World. Song is largely a group product, often polyphonic and polyrhythmic. The individual voice plays through many pitches. The accent is on

the dance and rhythmic variety. Sensual motor activity, facial expression animated, music characteristically composed of short phrases which wander easily from song to song, mood often frankly orgiastic.

(4) *Pygmoid*—Small tribal groups in Central Africa, South West Africa and possibly also in India, Formosa, etc. This is communal musical style at its most extreme. Melodies often broken up between different members of the singing group. Polyphony and polyrhythm. Voices often high, clear, rather childlike, with much use of the yodel.

(5) *Amerindian*—Aside from the area of high culture in the Andes, Indian song can be viewed as a whole. The voices throaty, often harsh, conform to the normal speaking tone. Much group song in unison, connected with ceremonial dances. Singers tend to remain in one pitch range, often punctuating their songs with yells; texts, composed of nonsense syllables. A frequent function of the music is to aid in curing ceremonies. This song style seems to be muscularly oriented and connected with tests of endurance, with extremely long religious chants, that often produce a semi-cataleptic state.

From the still limited material available in the various museums where I have studied, I would judge that there are three (Australian, Melanesian, and Polynesian), other stylistic families. Additional material, especially from Asia, may show that there are others.

Working with this system of classification here so briefly summarized, I have made careful surveys of Italy, Spain and the Anglo-American folk song and am presently studying the folk song of the British Isles. In these areas it appears possible to connect the presence and the persistence of some sub-species of one of these great musical families with certain broad social and psychological patterns, such as the prevailing sexual *mores* of the community, the position of women, the treatment of children and the degree of social co-operation which the social structure of the community permits.

Viewed in this way, for instance, Italy and Spain, excluding the islands, may be divided into three main zones: the South, which is an area of Eurasian monody and of high-pitched strident singing; the Center, which is a modified Eurasian area of harsh-voiced singing with the main interest in the words rather than the tune; and the North, which in both Italy and Spain are areas of choral song and dance, bassy voices and liquid-voiced, blended singing. The folk song map of the United States from this perspective may, apart from its non-English-speaking enclaves, be regarded as an Eurasian continent with a large modified African enclave in the South.

Today it may be possible, with modern scientific measuring instruments such as the visible speech machine, the electro-myograph and other instruments, to describe the various types of vocalizing in precise scientific terms. Since there seems to be evidence that these unconscious but culturally transmitted vocal patterns are direct evidence of deepening emotional conditions, the study of folk music may then turn out to be a precise mode of analysis of the prevailing emotional temper of entire cultures. Thus, ethnomusicology may bring us close to deep-lying aesthetic forces which have been dynamic in all human history.

Alan Lomax broadcasting for
Mutual, c. 1946–48.
Photographer: Unknown

Americana on Records

When Alan Lomax came to Decca as an adviser on folk music about a year ago, he began playing records to find out just what Decca had in its files. Last week, he was still spinning disks, and the end was far from in sight.

There were Decca labels recorded under the direction of Jack Kapp, president of the firm, and his brother Dave. There were old Brunswicks, Vocalions, Gennetts, and Generals—many of them by long forgotten names like Doc Boggs, Furry Lewis, and the Rev. Edward Clayburn.

As Lomax progressed with his research (he is also working on a book under a Guggenheim fellowship), he became convinced that Decca possessed a collection of recorded folk music second only to the Archive of American Folk Song at the Library of Congress—which he and his father, John Lomax, began to build in 1933. Thereupon he and Kapp worked out an American Folk Music Series.

For catalogue purposes the series, now in its first year, has included such current modern folk singers as Burl Ives and Josh White. But last June, the first batch of the real old-timers appeared in an album titled "Listen to Our Story—A Panorama

of American Ballads." And last week, "Mountain Frolic," a collection of square dances and hoedowns, was on its way to dealers. In all, some 75 albums are planned.

The two old-time albums are the real McCoy, for here, on disks, is a permanent record of the music pioneer America grew up with. And in the "Sing-Along" book accompanying each album, Lomax has written the story of the people and their songs—plus words and music for those who want to try the songs at home or at school.

Lomax (right) with Carl Sandburg

Reprinted from September 22, 1947 issue.

"Americana on Records" article from *Newsweek*, September 22, 1947.

Alan Lomax recording in Mallorca, Spain, June 1952.
Photographer: Unknown

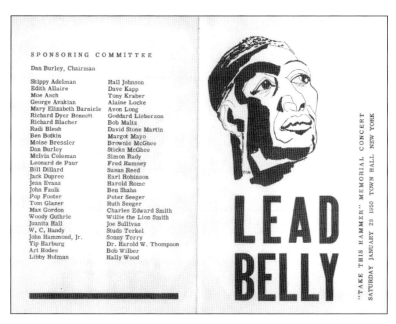

Leadbelly Memorial Concert Program,
New York, January 28, 1950.

Alan Lomax recording in La Conejera,
Granada, Andalucia, Spain, September 1952.
Photographer: Unknown

Maria Ribas, Ibiza, Spain, July 1952. Photographer: Alan Lomax

Alan Lomax (holding microphone) with Hamish Henderson Edinburgh, Scotland, 1958. Written on the back in Lomax's handwriting "Justice for Folklorists! A souvenir of Edinburgh University Rectional, 1958." Photographer: Unknown

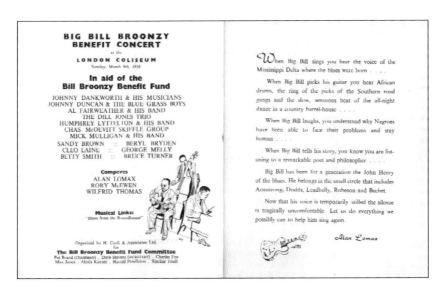

Big Bill Broonzy Memorial Concert Program,
London, March 9, 1958.

Alan Lomax in Galax, Virginia, August 31, 1959.
Photographer: Shirley Collins

Alan Lomax listening to playback with
Wade Ward, Galax, Virginia, August 31, 1959.
Photographer: Shirley Collins

Almeda Riddle (ballad singer), Miller,
Arkansas, October 1959.
Photographer: Alan Lomax

Stick fight, Plaisance (Mayaro), Trinidad, May 1, 1962.
Photographer: Alan Lomax

David Phillip (fiddle player), Toco (St. David),
Trinidad, May 3, 1962.
Photographer: Alan Lomax

Alan Lomax recording in La Plaine,
Dominica, June 26, 1962.
Photographer: Antoinette Marchand

Alan Lomax, New York, c. 1986.
Photographer: Peter Figlestahler

Chapter 17

Skiffle: Why Is It So Popular?
and Where Is It Going?

WHY IS IT SO POPULAR?

I believe the reasons for the popularity of skiffle and other types of American folk music in Britain are not hard to find. Nor do they reflect adversely on the creativeness of British singers and musicians.

A folklorist like myself, interested in broad trends in the history of his subject rather than the preservation of any special set of tunes or ways of singing, sees the skiffle story in this way.

The folk songs of Britain have a regional basis and are sung with regional accents. As the folk life of the regions disappeared the songs have tended, on the whole, to disappear.

They have largely been scorned by city folk, though there is no reason why this should be true of the future once the "city-billies"—the skifflers in particular—realize that the potentialities of British folk songs are the same as those of the American songs they now favor.

In the melting pot of the American frontier all these British regional song styles fused and combined, producing in the Appalachians, the Ozarks and other isolated areas, songs and ways of singing that were an Irish-Scots-English-Welsh amalgam—with an American twang, perhaps.

CITIFIED

Strange as it seems, this was the first *British* folk song tradition that had ever existed, and it took shape in America.

Is it any wonder that these Scots-Irish-English songs (that can still be found today in regional accents in rural Britain) should have pleased British audiences when they were sung in a citified fashion by Burl Ives, Josh White, and others?

In the mountains and backwoods of the Southern U.S. the Scots-

Irish-English Americans figured out ways to accompany these songs on guitar and banjo. Meanwhile they simplified the material somewhat, so that it became easier for unsophisticated city people to learn.

Into this American meld of British song came the influence of the Americanized Negro, with his great rhythmic gifts, his joyous sensuality, his irony and his feeling for the tragedies and contradictions of modern life.

These Negroes took over a lot of British songs and tunes and remade them in a wonderful way.

AFRICAN

It was natural that the resultant Afro-British products should become popular with the youngsters of skiffle—they had already succeeded in pleasing the racially prejudiced people of British descent in the South.

They have the driving African beat that has made jazz and South American dance music internationally popular in the last twenty years.

The music of all the world is being Africanized in our century. There is nothing wrong with this, so far as I can see, since the Africans have the richest and most joy-filled folk music of any people on earth. Certainly the skifflers should not be reproached for liking to play a part in this.

This American-amalgamated, British-derived Africanized music has already filled a large vacuum in the musical life of urban Britain.

Before skiffle, even three or four years ago, relatively few people in London made their own music. Singing and playing was a thing for show-offs or professionals.

Pub singers mulled over and over the dry bones of the Cockney music-hall songs which had little meaning for the younger generation.

Nowadays the young people of this country have songs they like to sing. They have the confidence to sing them. They are not ashamed of making music, but enjoy it.

Singing appears to be on the road to becoming again the national pastime it was two or three centuries ago, before the industrial revolution forcibly muzzled the naturally emotional, expansive and musical peoples of these islands.

WHERE IS IT GOING?

The first songs to become popular among the young skifflers were the American Negro prison songs. There they showed fine taste, because these are the best and most powerful of our folk songs.

At first it seemed very strange to me to hear these songs, which I had recorded from convicts in the prisons of the South, coming out of the mouths of young men who had suffered, comparatively speaking, so little.

But I soon realized that these young people *felt* themselves to be in a prison—composed of class-and-caste lines, the shrinking British Empire, the dull job, the lack of money—things like these. They were shouting at these prison walls, like so many Joshuas at the walls of Jericho.

HEALTHY SIGN

Now it is noticeable that the skifflers are beginning to show interest in other songs than jailhouse ditties and bad man ballads.

They have begun to make a world for themselves, in which other emotions than anger and rebellion can live—though their anger is very understandable and their rebellion is a healthy sign.

Most important, they are learning to make their own music.

I have the greatest confidence in the world that their mastery of their instruments will increase, that they will get tired after a while of their monotonous two-beat imitation of Negro rhythm and that, in looking around, they will discover the song-tradition of Great Britain. This tradition, in melodic terms, is probably the richest in Western Europe.

HOME-GROWN

Then they will produce something a bit more home-grown. To my mind, the skifflers have already considerably Anglicized our American versions of British songs. And I suspect that this process will go on, and that soon more regional British songs will be skiffled.

Then, the people of this island may—with the stimulus of skiffle music—go on to create their own national amalgam of regional folk-song styles.

Meantime the skifflers are learning to play and sing together, and they are establishing a nation-wide audience for what is to come—and this is more than Cecil Sharp, Vaughan Williams and the British school system have been able to do.

PRACTICE

In these early stages the noise is sometimes pretty awful, and the endless repetition of flattened-out tunes can be frightening. A lot of people cannot stand it. I'll admit I can listen only so long myself.

But I will say this: many of the groups, after a year or two or even less than that are playing as well as the first of our hillbilly bands and Negro country orchestras used to do.

All they need is practice—and they are practicing, mostly in public! There is no reason why anyone who doesn't enjoy listening to these rehearsals in public should stay. The kids who do stay are all watching and learning and planning to buy guitars.

DANGER

The principal danger, I am sure, is that the skifflers will learn too much too fast. If they take over a lot of sophisticated chord progressions from the jazz boys, they'll be lost.

They must find their own way, and inevitably they will stumble on to the right road, if they remain sincere in their wish to sing good, hard-hitting songs.

ENDLESS

An endless supply of material is available in the recordings of their hillbilly and Negro friends overseas. A much more important source, I believe, is the wonderful traditional playing and singing that still live in out-of-the-way places in the British Isles.

Chapter 18

Folk Song Style

The data for a fresh approach to the study of folk and primitive song have been piling up during the last decade. Previously the student had to depend upon acoustically poor recordings or upon musical transcriptions which were admittedly skeletal. Today the tape machine gives us a high-fidelity record of the folk performance in all of its tonal nuances, with none of its color lost or distorted. Long-playing records make this new world of musical color available to students everywhere. Soon vision on tape machines will produce archives of the musical act itself, but it is already possible to listen to people singing and making music in every part of the world by the simple act of putting a few records on the turntable.

The first impact of this experience is revolutionary. Mankind's range of inventiveness at the tonal level seems well-nigh limitless. Old musical horizons are swept away forever, and a confusing host of musical languages and dialects are exposed to view. As students of man's culture we have at hand the keys to many human mysteries, for if music is the language of feeling, the age-old traditions of folk and primitive music may stand for formative emotional patterns that have persisted and affected human behavior during all history. As citizens of one world and as social scientists, we must help to find avenues of growth for all mankind's musical languages. Let anyone who slights this latter problem think of the role that our Afro-American rock-and-roll has played in the lives of his children during the past decade.

It is quite apparent, even from a cursory look, that a Western musical education does not prepare us to understand, much less to classify and analyze, the varied musical interests of mankind. Western European musical notation and thinking are not adequate for the description of folk and primitive music. Melodic ornamentation and systems of rhythm occur which make the notation of a simple primitive chant into a formidable score, from which the transcriber himself is often unable to reproduce the music. Charles Seeger explains the difficulty as follows:

> The Occidental notation system . . . is a set of directions for the reproduction of products so as to conform to the peculiar traditions of the Occidental fine art. When, therefore, we notate in it a product of the traditions of the folk art . . . the act is one of translation from one idiom into another. The notated folk song is then, not a primary but a secondary datum of study. Employment of special symbols to indicate deviations . . . not traditional in fine art, may increase the accuracy of the translation. But it may lull the student into an illusion that it is not a translation. . . . (Seeger 1949: 828)

So much for the musical scores of the past, in which the features that give folk and primitive musics their special charm disappear in a confusion of symbols. Comparative musicology, based on study of these distorted skeletons, has not lived up to its promise, either in exposing the patterns of mankind's musical thought or in showing how these patterns may co-exist in the future. A new approach is called for.

An important step toward more precise musical analysis has been the recent invention of the melody writing machine. This device, for which Seeger is responsible (Seeger 1958: 2), draws a melody as a continuous line on a piece of graph paper on which a semi-tonal staff is indicated by ruled lines and seconds are marked by a timer. Thus the slides, attacks, releases, wavers, and so on, that distinguish a singing style are faithfully reproduced as a part of the melody. The perfection of this machine will make it possible to transcribe folk and primitive tunes quickly and easily, and thus build up precise, composite pictures of the melodic patterns of a given culture. Yet in my view, this undoubted technological advance cannot provide a broad enough base for a true musical ethnography. Seeger recognizes this (1958:1).

A song is a complex human action—music plus speech, relating performers to a larger group in a special situation by means of certain behavior patterns, and giving rise to a common emotional experience. At the risk of going over elementary ground, I ask the reader to consider a series of familiar musical situations: The symphony hall, where the audience sits motionless and withdrawn into a rapture of inner contemplation, while on stage a man with a little stick directs the cooperative activity of a hundred musicians, each one with his attention riveted on a page of type; the bedding-ground of a Texas trail-herd, where two weary cowboys rode around the cattle singing, crooning, talking, keeping up a steady stream of familiar sounds to reassure their nervous charges against the sudden noises and unknown terrors of the night; an African village dance, led by a battery of drums, where a dancing throng dramatizes erotic, hostile, and playful impulses, and one or two choirs sing well-rehearsed polyphony; a Near-Eastern bard, his eyes closed, his face contorted with his inner vision, reciting a traditional epic for his village, while a small orchestra provides a repetitious musical ground for the thread of his solo voice. .

Other examples would only further emphasize the point that musical reality is three-quarters composed of such materials, and it is therefore unscientific to focus our interest on formal musical patterns torn out of their context (as if music was intrinsically different from other human activities), or upon the precise measurement of particles of sound (as if musicology were a branch of physics).

I propose that the new science of musical ethnography be based on the study of the musical styles or musical habits of mankind. I prefer the term "style" to "habit," because the former gives the sense of a dynamic current in culture, while the latter puts the accent on noncreative, mechanical activity. Fine art has no corner on fantasy or creation (Rouget 1954). Moreover, a style is the result of a certain group of practices; it is the qualitative end-product of a certain set of actions. At the same time, it is the goal the culture aims for; it represents the intention of a culture. Nonetheless, since a style is the end-product of a pattern of behavior, it can be broken down into its separate elements and described.

The study of musical style should embrace the total human situation which produces the music:

(1) The number of people habitually involved in a musical act, and the way in which they cooperate.
(2) The relation between the music makers and the audience.
(3) The physical behavior of the music makers—their bodily stance, gestures, facial expressions, muscular tensions, especially those of the throat.
(4) The vocal timbres and pitch favored by the culture, and their relationship to the factors under 3.
(5) The social function of the music and the occasion of its production.
(6) Its psychological and emotional content as expressed in the song texts and the culture's interpretation of this traditional poetry.

(7) How songs are learned and transmitted.

(8) Finally, we come to the formal elements in the situation: the scales, the interval systems, the rhythmic patterns, the melodic contours, the techniques of harmony used; the metric patterns of the verse, the structure of the poetry, and the complex interplay between poetic and musical patterns (here see Seeger 1958), the instruments and instrumental techniques. Only when the behavioral patterns covered by points 1–7 are taken into account can the formal elements under 8 be properly understood, for they are symbols which stand for the whole.

A musical style is learned as a whole and responded to as a whole by a member of any culture. If some familiar element is absent in a performance, the music gives far less satisfaction. Conversely, the very magic of music lies in the fact that its formal elements can conjure up the total musical experience. An Andalucian gypsy finds it difficult to sing well in his flamenco style unless he is in a bar with wine on the table, money promised, women to clap and dance the rhythms, and fans to shout encouragement. Yet a melody hummed at work in an olive grove conjures up this experience to his imagination.

The child begins to learn the musical style of his culture as he acquires the language and the emotional patterns of his people. This style is thus an important link between an individual and his culture, and later in life brings back to the adult unconscious the emotional texture of the world which formed his personality.

Thus from the point of view of its social function, the primary effect of music is to give the listener a feeling of security, for it symbolizes the place where he was born, his earliest childhood satisfactions, his religious experience, his pleasure in community doings, his courtship and his work—any or all of these personality-shaping experiences. As soon as the familiar sound pattern is established, he is prepared to laugh, to weep, to dance, to fight, to worship. His heart is opened. The amount or kind of rhythmic, melodic, or harmonic material then offered him depends upon the musical inventiveness of his culture, but the quantity or excellence of all this does not affect his basic response, so long as it conforms to the musical style that formed him. I have been in villages (1)* where one or two tunes brought forth the satisfaction that dozens of melodies did in another place, or that a symphony produced in a city audience. Apparently the character and the variety of the music matters less than its conformity to tradition, which produces a sensation of security. The work of composers in the folk world is, so far as I have observed, limited by this stylistic security-bringing framework.

An art so deeply rooted in the security patterns of the community should not, in theory, be subject to rapid change, and in fact this seems to be the case. Musical style appears to be one of the most conservative of culture traits. Religion, language, even many aspects of social structure may change; an entirely new set of tunes or rhythms or harmonic patterns may be introduced; but, in its overall character, a musical style will remain intact. Only the most profound social upheavals—the coming of a new population, the acceptance of a new set of mores—or migration to a new territory, involving complete acculturation, will profoundly transform a musical style, and even then the process takes place very slowly.

Here it might be useful to examine a comparative trait list of two styles, with which most of my readers will be familiar, and between which cross-culturation has taken place. The backwoods white folk culture in the Southern United States has been swapping tunes and texts with its neighboring Negro folk culture for almost two centuries and both sing in English, yet it is still possible to differentiate them as follows (2):

American White Folk	*American Negro Folk*
Solo voiced. The group sits and listens in silence, sometimes sings in poor unison on refrains, has to be taught harmony by a teacher (2a).	Mainly choral. The group needs an expert leader to cue them into various points of a song, when they take over with blending voices, improvised harmony, hand and foot rhythm, dancing, etc.
The body is held tensely, as the singer sits or stands stiffly erect. The head is often thrown far back.	The body of the singer moves sinuously or in relaxed easy response to the beat. He dances his song.
The singing expression is mask-like and withdrawn, normally, and agonized on high notes.	The singer's expression changes with the mood of the song, line by line; there is a great deal of smiling and even laughing in many performances.

American White Folk	*American Negro Folk*
The voice is rigidly pitched, somewhat higher than the normal speaking tone, confined to a limited range of vocal color; it is often harsh, hard, nasal—the ideal being a pure violin-like tone with which the singer can make ornaments on the melody.	The voice is based in the singer's normal speaking pitch, is markedly relaxed and resonant. It plays through the entire vocal range, introducing falsetto passages and bass grunts with no self-consciousness.
Social functions: to tell a story, point a moral, establish a mood, amuse, instruct.	Social functions: to co-ordinate and enliven group activity in work, dance, worship, with other functions secondary.
Occasion: much private singing in a mood of reverie or for close friends or relatives; public performances the source of tension and embarrassment.	Occasion: in almost all folk group activities, one good songster after another takes the lead and directs the group. Little shyness in public. Reverie singing recreates the pleasure of group activities.
Emotional content: strong sexual and aggressive feelings well masked in impersonal stories, in moralizing or melancholy songs, or in "funny" rhymes. Dominant mood in important songs is melancholy, nostalgic, factual, or comic. Strong death-wish expressed.	Emotional content: sexual and aggressive content openly expressed. Strong satiric impulse. Many songs obliquely protest against racial injustice. The music conveys the mood of the singer, however veiled the text may be. Romantic love absent. Love of fellow-man a main theme. Death-wish present but weak.
Learning process: the careful memorizing of all details of the song from an authoritative source. Singers pride themselves on acquiring a ballad intact on one hearing. The words are learned first.	Group singing from babyhood on enables a singer to "catch" a tune and at once be able to improvise something similar or join the chorus. The tune is learned first.
Tunes are extended, ornamented, considered as units; fragmentation and excessive variation are disapproved of. Simple rhythms, which sometimes wander in conformity to the demands of the text.	Tunes are composed of short phrases which tend to wander from song to song. Improvisation is prized. Polyrhythms and a hard driving beat which normally dominates tune and text.

American White Folk	*American Negro Folk*
Texts normally dominate the song. Strict stanzaic structures. Memory slips source of embarrassment. Precise repetition the desired trait.	The texts are often fragmentary, consisting of one new line per stanza with extensive refrains. Both verses and refrains wander from song to song. Each singer recreates the song and re-orders the words with each performance. No premium on memory; improvisation prized.
In primitive state, no accompaniment. Early use of dulcimer and fiddle. Gradual adoption of banjo, guitar, and other stringed instruments for a full-fledged accompaniment style, and playing of dance-tunes—like a Near-Eastern orchestra (3).	Hands and feet, then other rhythm-makers, used from beginning; early adoption of all European instruments and formation of polyrhythmic and polyphonic bands of varying sizes and types (3).

Two important points emerge from an examination of these paired traits. First, the two groups have exchanged so many traits that it is clear that their musical styles are converging and will one day merge completely. Without going into details, one can now point to the blues, spirituals, ballads, jazz, and instrumental music which the two groups now practice in common (3). Second, it is nevertheless true that despite two hundred years of close collaboration, the white folk pattern in America still resembles the familiar folk-song style of Western Europe more than it does that of its Afro-American neighbors (4). In its turn, the Negro music of the United States still exhibits more traits in common with the musical dialects of the West Indies, South America, and West Africa than it does with those of backwoods white musicians in the nearby South (5). Thus each trait list becomes a yardstick by means of which one can define culture patterns that have moved between continents and through centuries of time.

Application of musical style analysis to the problems of one area thus opens the road toward the solution of a more important problem—the creation of a classification system for the traditional music of mankind. I am convinced that by linking music with its social and psychological setting in the way I have indicated, we will not only achieve a new understanding of the nature of folk music, but also that ethnomusicology can contribute to the understanding of culture. The body of this paper is a presentation, admittedly rough and partial, of the experiences and the thinking that have led to these conclusions. Complete exposition would require a large volume. Final proof, of course, demands a complex testing procedure, carried out by a number of specialists over a considerable period. All that I can say now is that the approach outlined in this paper has been tried out over a long period of time on a wide range of material and through varied field experiences. It has worked so well for me that I would like to share it with my fellow folklorists.

A CLASSIFICATION OF MUSICAL STYLES

As I have listened to the host of recordings available from many parts of the world, I have worked out a rough list of stylistic musical families. Because of the paucity of material from the Soviet Union, Eastern Asia and the Pacific, this list is incomplete, but it illustrates the world vision which the concept of musical style can afford. Each of the following descriptions is a sort of cartoon, in some cases incomplete and in every case subject to refinement, but corresponding, I believe, to a discoverable and operative aspect of reality. Each of these grand musical families has naturally many species and subspecies and local variations, produced by a variety of cultural cross-currents. With these cautionary remarks, here is a preliminary list of the main musical styles in the areas of the world from which records have been available to me.

I. American Indian: The tribal areas of North and South America, excluding the areas of high culture in the Andes where a totally different and highly cultivated system of music prevails (6). There seem to be occasional traces of this Andean music among some groups of jungle Indians (7). Otherwise, as Hornbostel and Sachs, among others, have observed (Sachs 1943: 23), one style of singing with a number of substyles seems to prevail among most of the Indian aboriginal groups of both North and South America. One remarkable feature of this whole area is that, considering the length of contact with Europeans, there has been so little exchange of musical materials between American Indians and colonial cultures in contrast to the lively cross-culturation of European with African and Polynesian music. The general rule in America has been that aboriginal singers hold to their tradition or else give it up entirely, accepting in its place, as is the case of several Mexican Indian groups, fragments of the colonists' folk music (8). In the other direction, the influence of Indian music on colonial folk song (again with the exception of Peru) (9) is so rare as to be noteworthy when it occurs. If one may be allowed to hazard a guess about so complex a question, this phenomenon is due not so much to purely musical differences between the two families, as to the fact that in function, in overall emotional content, the Indian and the Modern-European-Colonial styles stand poles apart.

Among American Indians, group performance in full-bodied, throaty unison is perhaps the dominant manner. Often leader and chorus alternate, and frequently a solo voice chants a long song, whose ritual or religious function is primary. The manner of Indian singing is strikingly muscular in character—a sound that reflects, often is a by-product of, and does not add to the weariness produced by long-continued physical exertion. Indians characteristically sing at full volume. Their singing tones are throaty, husky, sometimes grating, rich in nasal overtones, and produced at the normal speaking pitch (10). Some North American Indians punctuate their throaty chanting with high-pitched hunting yells, war cries, yelps, or other animal-like sounds, and it is out of this material that the electrifying Plains style of singing in a high-pitched, liquid, almost yodeling tone may have developed (11). The family resemblance between these two seemingly divergent ways of singing will become apparent if the reader will try singing, say, in the deep-voiced Iroquois manner for a time, feeling the air moving from a relaxed throat straight out between his lips. Then, by suddenly directing the same stream of air upward against the back of the hard palate, he will find he can produce the high clear yelling tone of the Plains.

Songs are often given in dreams, remain valuable individual property, and have a ritual, magical, or curative function. Singing often functions as a mnemonic aid in reciting long poems of religious or traditional material which must be repeated without the smallest error. Song also helps to induce a state of trance in which ancestral or animal spirits appear to use the shaman as their mouthpiece. But probably the greatest single function of song is for the dance and, perhaps largely for that reason, an enormous number of Indian songs are "all chorus," being composed of repetitions of easily vocalized and relaxing chains of nonsense syllables. The rhythmic accent is emphatic and regular, and tempo is maintained evenly. One tone per syllable is the general rule. Two types of melodic contour are frequent: tunes which move regularly around one level and within a small compass of notes, but are occasionally punctuated by high yells and big upward leaps; tunes which contain big upward skips followed by stepwise descending phrases moving slowly to the lowest singing pitch the singer can reach. Chordal singing and complex rhythms hardly occur and the most common instruments are rhythm-makers, such as the Asiatic hand-drum and various kinds of rattles (12).

The remarkable consistency of Indian singing style across two continents and its clear connection through Eskimo music with the music of Siberian peoples (Sachs, 1943) not only confirms the Paleo-Siberian origin of the American aborigines, but is another evidence of the extraordinary stability of musical styles through vast stretches of space and time.

II. Pygmoid: Small tribal groups in Central Africa, South-West Africa, Central India, Central Formosa and doubtless other areas still to be documented.

The communal style at its most extreme. Not only is singing conceived of as a group activity, but melodies are broken up into short phrases, each rendered by different members of the singing group. Melodies often take the form of rounds or canons. The vocal tone is often high, sweet, and clear, rather child-like, and the voices blend easily in unison and in rudimentary polyphony. The consistency of Pygmy vocalizing through space-time is dramatically shown in a disc prepared by Gilbert Rouget, which presents alternate and virtually indistinguishable bands of jungle Pygmy and desert Bushman singing (13).

III. African: The area includes the whole of Negro Africa, except for Pygmoid enclaves, those tribes converted to Mohammedanism or strongly affected by Arab culture (14), certain Nilo-Hamites to the North (15), and Ethiopia (16). It also extends to all areas in the New World where there are large groups of Negroes.

Music is communally produced, the group dividing responsibility for a number of melodic, harmonic, and rhythmic parts; these parts are exchanged with great facility. Dancing and singing in chorus. Polyphony and a flowering to polyrhythm, three to seven parts being quite common. A predominance of rhythmic and percussive instruments. The vocal style corresponds to the normal speaking voice of the singer, but there is a great deal of vocal play, intentionally humorous, aggressive (17) or dramatic. Singers leap into falsetto, insert bass parts, grunt, shout, yell. Voices blend easily. The body is always in motion; the music is danced. Facial expression is lively and animated.

Headed by talented improvisors and rhythmic artists, the African community becomes a singing, drumming, dancing throng. Their rhythmically-oriented music plays a part in every life activity—work, religion, dance, story-telling. Very often it frankly expresses orgiastic sexual pleasure and/or aggressive violence. A music of many moods, it shifts from humor to irony to joie de vivre.

The Reverend Williams, in Volume 1 of the *Journal of the African Music Society*, has set down a similar description of African musical style, showing how it differs from Arab music and pointing out that it remains essentially the same across the many language barriers of the Bantu world (19).

IV. Australian: The primitive tribes of the continent, with possible traces in New Guinea. The music is communally produced but tends to alternate between long arhythmic solos and unison choruses. The voice is rather harsh and strident and pitched fairly low. It remains within one vocal framework, and in group singing there is little vocal blend. A principal function of the music is to accompany elaborate ritual ballets; thus there is a remarkable control of tempos, with refined passages of acceleration and deceleration. Songs are often made up of passages of contrasting tempos. The instruments are rudimentary—rhythm sticks, a bull roarer, a hollowed stick into which the performer sings a bass figure. The prevailing mood of the music is serious, often tragic. Its principal function is the magical control of nature (19).

V. Melanesian: Parts of New Guinea and adjacent islands. I suspect that this area will turn out to be as complex as Europe, with primitive traces of Australian, Pygmoid, Eurasian and other as yet undefinable musical styles. However, along the northern coast of New Guinea and in adjacent islands, some seemingly constant traits may be noticed. A predominance of choral singing, accompanied by batteries of drums. Many bass voices, giving an organ-like sound to the huge choruses. Some tunes seem African in character, but the prevailing tone of the music is grave (20).

VI. Polynesian: Here too, few modern documents have been available to me. Apart from Micronesia, which has another character, the prevailing musical organization seems to be communal and there is an extraordinary control of tempos. The sense of Polynesian vocalizing—in their paddling songs, for example—is of a perfectly co-ordinated group, working together with great but relaxed energy. One principal function of the chorus is to accompany elaborate ballets in which the dancers perform, in perfect unison, highly refined and sometimes sensual movements. The singing is likewise incredibly precise, the great choruses pronouncing intricate chains of syllables in perfect unison and at extremely rapid tempos, so that the chorus resembles one great voice.

This primitive tendency has been continued in the modern Europeanized music of Polynesia, in which the Western system of harmony has been easily absorbed. The voices of the males are quite low-pitched, produced deep in the throat and chest, with relaxed yet dynamic energy. The singing tone is normally open and liquid. The prevailing mood of many songs is joyful and sensual, often dramatic. Orgiastic pleasure in sex and aggressive behavior is dramatized with little reticence; instruments are mainly rhythmic in character; there is much hand-clapped rhythm (21).

VII. Malayan: Inspection of numbers of recent recordings indicate that there may be a Malayan singing style which has spread across Indonesia and into the Philippines, which has deeply affected the music of Polynesia and Melanesia, and which is linked in ways as yet impossible to assess with the musical styles of Japan and China (22).

VIII. Eurasian: I believe that the area includes Ireland (23); parts of the British Isles and France (24); Spain south of the Pyrenees (25); Italy south of the Via Emilia (26); the Moslem areas of Yugoslavia and Albania (27); southern Greece (28); Turkey (29); Arab-Africa (30); the Near and Middle East (31); Pakistan (32); India (33) apart from tribal areas and the Tamil culture; Indo-China (34); Indonesia (35); China, Korea, and Japan (36), not including the Ainu. This musical style family includes the folk and cultivated music of the classical world and of the great empires of the past. There are many enclaves of tribal and primitive music on this vast Eurasian music continent which seem to be survivals of older style families.

The whole area is characterized by singing in solo, by unblended unison, by instruments used for accompanying songs or for dance tunes. The tone of these instruments very often corresponds to the voice quality, which is ordinarily high-pitched, often harsh and strident, delivered from a tight throat with great vocal tension, frequently with an effect of being pinched or strangulated. The expression of the singer's face is rigidly controlled or sad, often agonized. The singing tone—so frequently soprano or falsetto in character, even for male singers—is suitable for the presentation of long and highly decorated melodic line, where variation is achieved by the addition of rapid quavers, glottal stops, and the like.

The prevailing mood of the music is either tragic, melancholy, nostalgic, or sweetly sad, or else, in dance tunes, characterized by frenetic gaiety and a rather aggressive release of energy. Control and individualism are the key descriptive terms here. Cooperative music-making is achieved only by groups of adepts, and in some areas, such as China, was virtually nonexistent until recently. The whole area has a long history of slavery, serfdom, and exploitation by ruthless aristocracies. The position of women, though often idealized, is never equal, and, especially in the east, may be one of virtual slavery.

Seeger writes me that he is of the opinion that two, if not more, musical languages compose this grand musical family. It certainly appears that the music of eastern Asia was formed by influences that came into China from the North, and it seems very likely that this Proto-Mongoloid style has close affinities with the style which gave rise to American-Indian music in the Western hemisphere. Yet too few folk song recordings are available from China and from Eastern Siberia for more than a tentative opinion to be hazarded about the matter. In any case, it seems likely that the social forces that favored the dominance of strangulated solo singing were similar in the Far and the Near East.

IX. Old European: The area includes the Hebrides (37); Wales and the west and north of England (38); Scandinavia (39); Brittany, Pyrenean France (40); Spain north of the Pyrenees (41); northeastern Portugal, Switzerland, most of Austria, Germany, Italy north of the Apennines (42); Czechoslovakia, western Yugoslavia (43); northern Greece, parts of Bulgaria and Romania (44); Lithuania (45); White Russia, the Ukraine (46) and the Caucasus (47).

In this whole area, singing and dancing are basically choral and cooperative. The voice is produced from a relaxed throat and the facial expression is lively and animated, or at least relaxed. (Even the solo singers of Central Europe use a deeper pitch than Eurasian singers; their voices are richer in overtones, and their throats and facial expression less tense.) Old European tunes tend to be comparatively simple and unornamented. Blended unison is normal and many forms of polyphony exist. (Herzog 1949: 1032.) Some polyphonic types perhaps antedate the early composed tradition. Elsewhere the ready acceptance and adaptation of modern harmony show the aptitude of the peoples for polyphonic practice, and hint that older polyphonic styles may have been submerged. (Wales, Galicia, Genoa, Tyrol, and so on.)

The favored singing pitch is lower than in the Eurasian area; voices are generally rounder, richer in timbre, fuller; a liquid or yodeling tone is sometimes found, and bass and contralto voices, rarely used in musical Eurasia, are extremely common here. The mood of the music, while often affected by long contact with the Eurasian style and therefore tragic in tone, seldom expresses the degree of agony or frustration found in the folk music of that area. Often, in fact, it is joyous, tenderly sensuous, and noble.

The Old European area consists then of those regions of Europe sheltered in some degree by geography or circumstance from the successive waves of the Eurasian high culture and solo-song style, whether Persian, Roman Catholic, Arab, or Turk. In isolated high mountain valleys, the hilly centers of islands, in the lands to the Northwest, older and frequently communal social patterns persist alongside of what appears to be an old stratum of musical style. The position of women tends to be equal and opposite; courtship practices are less restrictive (bundling being common in Northern Europe), sexual contact and illegitimacy do not destroy the woman's position. A high value is put upon cooperative norms of every sort. Perhaps it is worth noting that the rise of industry, which depends on mutual trust, took place in the heartland of this group-oriented Old European style.

X. Modern European: Although this seems to be a hybrid style which grew up in the borderlands between Eurasian and Old European, it may deserve a separate description, if only for its great importance to contemporary folk song. The fact is that most of the folk singing which Western Europeans and Americans know belongs to the Modern European style. The area includes Lowland Scotland, Eastern and Southern England, Western and Central France, Central Spain (48), Central Italy, Hungary (49), Central Bulgaria, Romania, and Colonial America. Here people sing solo songs in harsh, hard voices, or combine in unblended unison on refrains. The whole area has a stronger interest in text than in tune, in sense than in emotional content. This is the land of the narrative ballad, the quatrain, the lightly ironic, lyrical love songs, which have come to characterize the folk songs of Europe. It is also the area which most strongly influenced the development of folk songs in the colonies of North and South America (50), perhaps because the witty, intellectualized Modern European ballads and songs could move into new cultures more readily than the vague and dreamy choral songs of Old Europe, or the highly charged, highly elaborate and melancholy music of the South.

Before I end this summary of folk music style, I must say a word about instruments. One primitive tendency is for the adoption of instruments which conform to the pattern of the vocal music. But instruments are often acquired or invented which are counterposed to the vocal style.

Rarely, however, do newly acquired instruments seem to alter these deeply rooted, traditional singing styles. The same instruments can and do function in a variety of ways in diverse cultures. The many-voiced bell and xylophone orchestra lives companionably with the monodic pinch-voiced style dominant in Indo-China and Indonesia, whereas the introduction of the xylophone into East Africa has vastly augmented pre-existing polyphonic tendencies there (51). Eurasian melodic instruments such as the violin or the lyre are mainly employed for percussive effects by members of the African style family. The bagpipe, with its drone system, often seems to stimulate experiments in vocal polyphony in areas where this tendency exists, such as littoral Yugoslavia (52) and in Slavic communities in Southern Italy (53); whereas in Spain (54) and the British Isles (55) it is thought of as another, and singularly accomplished, solo singer.

Instruments are part of the technology of music and can be diffused without profoundly altering the musical style of the areas they invade. The same may be said of melodies, poetic forms, systems of harmony, and rhythmic patterns. The Europeanized African has in recent years adopted all these elements from Europe but his music remains African in character, whereas the Moslemized African, whose family pattern has been profoundly reshaped by Arab influence, speaks a different musical language. He has become a high-voiced solo wailer, accompanied by virtuosos on the ancient bardic instruments of the Orient.

We come, then, to the several factors in musical style which seem most fundamental and by means of which the music of an area may be most readily classified and diagnosed.

(1) The degree in which song is a communal or individualistic product.
(2) The amount of blend in choral singing and the degree of chordal singing or lack of it.
(3) The quality of the voice and its mode of production.
(4) The position and use of the body by the singer, the muscular tension evidenced in the throat and the facial expression.
(5) The circumstantial and functional background of the music, both social and psychological.
(6) The prevailing mood of the music, evidenced by its melodic contour and the content of the verse.
(7) Of all the social and emotional factors involved, by far the most important in the areas in which I have worked, seem to be: the posi-

tion of women, the sexual code, the degree of permissiveness about sexual enjoyment, and the affectual relationship between parents and children.

These ideas were in process of development during my six months' field-recording survey of Spanish folk music in 1953, and were supplemented by observations as I made forty hours of tapes in all parts of that country. I went to Italy in 1955 to test this point of view against a fresh field experience, with the foreknowledge that several musical styles existed in this country. Fifty-five hours of field recordings and a year of varied field work have further refined the approach. And it is a summary of these experiences which, after this long but essential preamble, will be presented now.

MUSICAL STYLES IN SPAIN

Leaving aside Catalonia, which presents special problems, Spain may be divided into three main stylistic areas—the south, the center, and the north.

The South, including Andalucia, Murcia, Valencia and parts of Castile (56), is Eurasian, with strident high-pitched monody among the folk and a high, pure controlled tone among professionals (57), both delivered from a tense throat and with an expression of agony on the face. The melodies are long, highly decorated, and the mood varies from tragic to nostalgic; dances are solo or duo improvisations, tense, impassioned or frenetically gay. Both dance and song are, as in the Arab world, often performed by highly skilled folk professionals. Southern Spain formed a part of the Mediterranean world of high culture in classical times, and subsequently was thoroughly acculturated by the Arabs who brought fresh Oriental influences.

This is a land of great estates and of extremes of poverty and wealth. Labor was once performed by slaves, and today the country people who work on the land often live on the edge of starvation. Even today women are housebound, Arab style; courting couples may not be alone together except at the barred window; chaperones are strict, and marriages are arranged. Three main roads lie open to the Andalucian woman—marriage, prostitution, or old-maid dependency. Sexual pleasure is a male prerogative, and lovemaking is often forced on married women, wearied by child-bearing and fearful of pregnancy. Equal measures of physical punishment and passionate love are meted out to the children. The whole area is dominated by hunger and, beneath a surface gaiety, an underlying asceticism and melancholy and a mood of violence and sexual jealousy exist—all brilliantly expressed in a neo-Eurasian musical art, in which dance and song are inextricably linked. The instruments are the flute and tabor, the guitar, the Arab friction drum, castanets, and other rhythm-makers.

Central Spain, including Extremadura, parts of Castile, and Leon, is a Modern European region with Eurasian influences to the South, Old European traces to the North, and strong influences from the high culture of the Middle Ages (58). It is a monodic area with some unblended unison singing. The Castilian voice is lower-pitched and more open than the southern, but still is harsh, high-pitched, and strident, delivered from a tense throat, the body being rigidly held with the face a composed mask. The melodies are extended but not prolonged as in Andalucia and, compared to southern Spanish tunes, relatively undecorated. This is the ballad area par excellence of Europe, a culture where words have more importance than the melodic ornament. Work songs are similar to those of Southern Spain—long, high-pitched wails of despair. Instruments are the guitar, the *banduria*, played as rhythmic instruments, the flute and tabor, a simple oboe, castanets, a primitive violin, the Arab friction-drum, and various rhythm instruments. Dances are both duo and group in form.

This area, dominated by the Romans and conquered by the Arabs, is poor but there are many small holdings as well as large estates, and less misery than in the south. Women are still restricted to the house and jealously guarded. Contact between the sexes is difficult, but courtship customs are freer than in Andalucia, though marriages are still arranged between families. Children are given more independence and are not so often punished physically.

The North, including the provinces north of the Pyrenees as well as parts of Catalonia and Aragon, is Old European with Eurasian traces; the picture is further complicated by the Celtic ties of Galicia and by the mystery of the Basques. Although there are many types of solo songs— some, like the Asturianada, in flowery Eurasian style—the majority of songs and dances are choral. Voices are more open and more low-pitched than in Central Spain, with more liquid vocal quality and occasionally with ringing tones. Bass voices are fairly common (41).

There is less vocal tension. The singer's body is relaxed, the throat is not distended with strain and the facial expression is often composed and lively and, though not always animated, neither melancholy nor mask-like. The voices blend easily, and choral singing comes naturally to the people. I did not find any old polyphonic forms, but a bent toward polyphony is evidenced by the ease with which the northerners have adapted simple chordal ideas from Central Europe to the melodies of their regions. Melodies are brief and undecorated and most songs are short, except in the case of the Asturian ballads and the improvised satirical songs of the Basques. Often the singers pass from one tune to the other, weaving together long chains of tender, slightly ironic lyric songs—a trait of Udina in Italy and of Croatia. The mood of the songs is tender, gay, ironic, at times wholeheartedly joyous. The simple flute, the bagpipe, and the various forms of flat hand-drums are the commonest instruments.

This is an area of small holdings scattered in the mountains, of small villages of shepherds and independent proprietors, of factory towns and mines and strong unions. Lightly colonized by the Romans and hardly touched by the Arabs, this area was the base for the reconquest of Spain by the Christians. In the Middle Ages the pilgrim route linked this region with the rest of Europe. Yet beneath a Christian surface, there are many traces of a pagan past and a pre-Roman communal society, especially among the Basques. Women occupy a fairly independent position, courtship is a more relaxed affair, and there is freer contact between the sexes—as, for example, at the corn-shucking bees common to the Basque countryside. In spite of centuries of campaigning by the church, coastal Galicia has an illegitimacy rate of almost 40 percent, but the people themselves do not appear to be unduly disturbed by this. Children are treated with tenderness, and early acquire a sturdy independence.

When I left Spain, I had established in my own mind the possibility that a correlation exists between a musical style and certain social factors, most especially the position of women, the degree of permissiveness toward sexual love, and the treatment of children. I had also begun to see the bearing of local history on the problem, but this still seemed secondary to the more basic factors of social structure and sexual pattern. I then prepared to test these tentative conclusions in Italy. To say that the strident falsetto in Andalucia was Arab and the open voice of the North was Nordic was merely to beg the question—to put it comfortably in the distance. Why then do the Arabs sing in strident falsetto, the Nordics in a more open, deeper-voiced style? A more provocative question posed itself—why was one style acceptable and another unacceptable in a given area?

The main questions that I proposed for my Italian research were: (1)

What role did history play in the formation of musical style, and (2) what were the social and psychological mechanisms involved in implanting a musical style in all the individuals of a given region?

Italy proved to be an ideal laboratory for posing these questions and testing my hypotheses. Its equable climate, its fertility and beauty, had attracted invaders for thousands of years. Since the time of the Romans, however, no strong national culture had united Italy, and hundreds of cultural enclaves, some dating back to the dawn of European history, had been protected in the folds of her rough terrain. The early urbaniza-tion of Italy had worked for rather than against the preservation of a variety of folk patterns.

Since the high culture of the Italian city states of the Renaissance was based upon the culture of classical times, a high wall sprang up between the life of the townsfolk and that of the peasants, though each city was proud in a rather snobbish way of the peculiarities of its depend-ent villages. Thus the two-way exchange between city and country which gave unity to the emerging Spanish, French, and English national cul-tures, scarcely disturbed the ancient variety of Italy until modern times.

Italy proved to be a museum of music, as it was of classical art dur-ing the Renaissance. For example, the pagan practice of the sung funeral lamentation, which has virtually disappeared in the remainder of west-ern Europe, is still an everyday matter in most rural areas south of Rome. However, when the innumerable cultural pockets hidden in the folds of the Italian hills had been taken into account, the main contours of Italy's stylistic map proved to have the same north-south orientation as that of Spain.

The North (including the Alpine arc, the province of Genoa, the Valley of the Po, and the northern slopes of the Apennines) is Old European but far more markedly so than northern Spain, as it directly adjoins Central Europe and thus has been constantly reacculturated by invasions from the north. Dancing and singing is choral—so strongly so, in fact, that song is virtually impossible without a harmonizing group. Polyphony exists in a wide variety of forms, from the seven-part long-shoreman choruses of Genoa to the Slavic use of seconds and fourths to the East. Voices are open, clear, bell-like, and deep in pitch; in Genoa, again, basses are more common than tenors. Singers stand with arms round their cronies' shoulders, or, leaning across a wine-soaked table, blend their voices, smiling at one another benignly over the pleasures of drink, sweet chords, and the often bawdy or tenderly sexual verses of their songs. Most songs are short and lyrical in character, but even the ballads of Piedmont and Genoa are performed in chorus and with such a strong beat that it is plain they had once been danced as they were sung (57).

The open, comradely, tolerant spirit of the North is evident to any visitor who knows the whole of Italy. Where the people work in factories or in big estates, they sing together at work, organize powerful unions, and vote labor at the polls. The courtship patterns are closer kin to those of France, Switzerland, or Croatia than of Italy to the South. Contact between men and women is relaxed and friendly, and children, especially in the mountains, are treated with respect.

The Center. The Apennines, running in a southeasterly direction to the Adriatic South of the Po Delta, form the most dramatic stylistic borderline that it has been my fortune to encounter. I criss-crossed this hundred-mile-wide mountain barrier at a dozen points, and always found that I passed from one musical style area into another. As one musician, who lived in Northern Tuscany fifty miles south of choral Piedmont, remarked to me, "It is impossible to organize a chorus in my town. These people simply can't sing together."

Tuscany, Umbria, Lazio and parts of the provinces further South is Italy's Modern European area. Here, song is predominantly solo in performance, with occasional harsh and unblended unison choruses. Singers stand or sit stiffly erect, their throats showing the tension of this vocal delivery, their expression withdrawn, and their eyes often closed—in other words, following a familiar Modern European pattern. The singing voice is harsh or hard and clear, and notably higher in pitch than in the North. The function of the song is to mount the text, even more than in Central Spain, for Tuscan singers favor long, improvised, somewhat satirical verses (*stornelli* and *ottavi*) or present long, melodically dull folk operas (*maggi*). A generation ago, most marriages were arranged between the families of these small land-holders; girls were closely supervised until marriage, and illegitimacy was severely stigmatized. The texts of the countless *stornelli* consist of an allusive, ironic fencing with the opposite sex. One woman told me, "South of the Apennines, the men are wolves, and they wish only to eat you once" (60).

The South. The old kingdom of Naples, together with Sicily and Sardinia, is another Italy and is so regarded by many Italians of the North. From the point of view of musical style, it is indeed another world. The norm of Southern Italian singing is in solo, in a voice as pinched and strangulated and high-pitched as any in Europe. The singing expression is one of true agony, the throat is distended and flushed with strain, the brow knotted with a painful expression. Many tunes are long and highly ornamented in Oriental style, and in Lucania are often punctuated with shrieks, like the cries of the damned (61). The universal subject is love, the beauties of women, the torments of courtship; the commonest song-type is the serenade, of which there are two kinds—the serenade of compliments and the serenade of insults, if a suitor is refused. Laments for the dead are common to the whole area, and a singer from Lucania (which is the area of greatest isolation) moves from a lament to a lullaby to a love song (62) without change of emotional tone. Here, too, sexual jealousy reaches a peak unique in Southern Europe. The presumption is that a man and a woman left alone together for five minutes will have sexual contact, and thus the smallest violation of courtship taboos may stain a woman's reputation so that she will never find a husband. For a person sensitive to the treatment of children, travel in the South is a torment, so slapped and pushed and mistreated are the young people of this Arabicized world.

However, the poverty, isolation, and political retardation of Southern Italy have also permitted the survival of many cultural enclaves of varying musical style. Most of these cultural pockets, in which one can hear various types of polyphony, were formed when one or another group of invaders came into the area and took over a region or built their villages on hill tops. Thus we find chordal singing in the villages where Byzantine Greek is still spoken along the Eastern Coast of Puglia (63), and again in the Albanian-speaking villages of Abruzzi, Lucania, and Calabria (64). But there may be survivals of a more ancient level of Old European singing style in the strange, shrieked chords of Lucania and Calabria (65), and in the case of Sardinia, to which we will presently come.

In Italy, as in Spain, history and the social patterns seem to work together. For over two thousand years the South has been dominated by classical (Eastern) culture and exploited by imperialistic governments. The principal invaders, after the Romans, came from Eurasian musical areas—the Byzantine Greeks, the Saracens, the Normans, the Spaniards.

The center, between Rome and Florence, was formed by the Etruscans, an Oriental people of high culture who apparently brought the *saltarello* with them from the east. Later, the flowering of poetry in the Renaissance confirmed the folk of the center in their attachment to solo lyric poetry, to improvisation and to the primitive solo-decked Maytime operas of the high Renaissance.

In pre-Roman times, the North was the domain of the Ligurians, who today are the most accomplished polyphonic folk singers in Western Europe. Celts from the North poured into the Po Valley in the Roman era, and later invaders—the Longobards, the Goths, and the Slavs—all came from the heart-lands of the Old European song style. Moving across the North, from west to east, one passes from Liguria into French Piedmont, the ballad country of Italy, where ballads are invariably sung in chorus, into an area of Tyrolese and Austrian song, and finally into the eastern provinces where Slavic choral singing is found.

One of the most important discoveries of the trip showed a North-South line of Slavic influence which cut across these three Italian musical areas. In the mountains near the Austrian border are small enclaves of Slavic-speaking-and-singing people (66). The whole province of Friuli has a Slavic cast to its song (67). In La Marche, on the Adriatic coast facing Yugoslavia, the dominant type of work song is in two parts, harmonized in seconds and fourths and sung with an open, far-carrying tone in the Slavic manner favored in Croatia and the mountains of Bulgaria and Romania (68).

Anywhere in the mountains south of Rome one may come upon a community that sings part songs in a Slavic style (69). The province of Abruzzi, today an island of accomplished modern rural choruses in the Eurasian south, has a coastline closer to Yugoslavia than any other part of Italy, and its oldest choral songs, found on the coastal plain (rather than in the mountains which were once monodic) are Slavic in color (69). I believe it was by this avenue that the bagpipe and the custom of singing counter-melodically with the bagpipe entered Italy, for one finds this instrument and this practice all along the mountain routes of the shepherds from coastal Abruzzi into Calabria.

Many colonies of Albanians came to Italy as refugees from the Turks in the thirteenth century. In their villages, scattered through the hills of Abruzzi, Lucania, and Calabria, old Albanian dialects are still spoken, and singing is without exception in the choral, open-throated, Old European style. Some non-Albanian villages in the South have apparently adopted Albanian style, but it is interesting to note that here the harmony is shrieked in high-pitched, agonized voices, and that the mood is one of torment and frustration as compared to the Albanian. This may be a case of the formal elements of a musical style failing to carry with them their emotional content.

The folk-song map of the south is further complicated by the colonies of Byzantine Greeks in Puglia and Central Sicily, who practice an antique harmonic vocal style that they imported with their Greek Orthodoxy many centuries ago. However, as these villages have been absorbed into the southern pattern of sexual jealousy, the singing is harsh-voiced and strident and so is the harmonic blend.

Finally, I discovered in the mountains between Naples and Salerno some colonies of Saracen origin, people who had fled into the hills when their coastal cities were recaptured by the Christians, and who have preserved intact the music of their North African forebears (70). This is, I believe, the only occurrence of purely Arab music in Europe.

To return to the main theme, in every case which I had the opportunity to examine there is a positive correlation betwen the musical style and the sexual mores of the communities. The Slavic enclaves of the North are open-voiced and permissive, those of the center less markedly so, and finally, in the South, the Albanian and other Slavic communities stand like islands of feminine independence in the sea of southern jealousy and frustration, though the Eurasian social and musical patterns have altered the Albanian style considerably.

MUSICAL STYLE AND LIFE STYLE

There remains the question of the mechanism which links a musical style to the preference pattern of the individual, and to community mores. I found one answer in an examination of Italian lullabies, some two or three hundred of which are recorded. Southern Italian lullabies are agonized, sorrow-ridden wails, often hard to distinguish from funeral lamentations. Northern Italian mothers sing playful baby-bouncing songs, or wistfully tender sleep-songs. An apparent exception seems to emphasize the pattern: in the coastal areas round about Venice, there is a treasure of lullabies in the Southern Italian manner. The Venetian fisherfolk have harsh singing voices and are positively unable to sing polyphonically or to blend their voices. The existence of this Eurasian musical island in the North is explained by the isolated position of these people, who took refuge in their pile villages in the lagoons during the invasions from the North. Later Venice, as the Queen of the Mediterranean, faced East toward its Oriental trading empire (71).

The distribution of lullaby types in Spain conforms to this North-South pattern, but with a precision that would delight a linguist. From the Andalucian sleep-producing refrain vocable—a high-pitched, nasalized *ay-ay-ay* (72)—the refrain vowel gradually grows rounder as one moves toward the Old European area until, in the Basque country, the women signal their babies to sleep with a low-pitched, liquid *oo-oo-oo* (73).

The child in Southern Italy and Southern Spain has his first musical contacts with his mother and his other female relatives. Their voices, as they rock him to sleep or move about their housework, accompany his waking and sleeping hours. And what he hears is a high-pitched voice and a wailing melody, expressive of the tragedy of Southern Italian life, its poverty, and its frustrating sexual pattern. The lullabies call on the Saints to protect the little one, born into a harsh and menacing world, and they threaten the irritable child with the wolf who often comes to eat the lambs of the flock (74).

Lullabies for an Italian woman have direct sexual connotation. At first, unmarried girls flatly refused to perform them for me, overcome with embarrassment at having to sing them to a strange man. The reason for this is clear. The Catholic church virtually interdicts sexual relations except for the purpose of procreation, and since, at least in theory, no unmarried girl has sexual experience and no married woman permits intercourse without childbearing in mind, lullabies are intimately associated with lovemaking in the mind of the Italian peasant woman.

Now what is the quality of the sexual experience of the Southern Italian woman? In the first place, as a young girl, she has feared the father and brothers, who jealously protected her and would drive her from the house if they so much as suspected her of making love to a man. In her period of courtship, she feared all men. Carlo Levi says about the peasants of Lucania that they "consider love or sexual attraction so powerful a force in nature that no power on earth can resist it. If a man and a woman are alone in a sheltered spot, no power on earth can prevent their embrace; good intentions and chastity are of no avail. If by chance nothing comes of their propinquity, it is just as bad as if something had come of it, because the mere fact of being together implies love-making. . . . " (From the introduction of *Christ Stopped at Eboli*.)

The Southern Italian girl knows that there is no trick or deceit to which her hungry and predatory admirer will not descend for a sexual contact. She also knows that he will regard her as a whore if she yields to his sexual desires, and that her chances of marriage, her only career, may thus be forever closed.

In the minds of a Southern Italian there are two idealized feminine categories—the madonna, the virginal mother figure, and the prostitute. If he has any actual sexual experience in his youth, it is likely to be with a prostitute. He comes to the bed of his inexperienced madonna flushed with wine and the repressed passion of a long engagement, a feeling that is closely akin to anger. Little wonder that so many Southern Italian marriages are sexually infelicitous, and that the man goes back to his cards and to his prostitutes, after dutifully siring his children, leaving his nagging madonna to wail out her frustration in her lullabies and add her sorrowful feminine notes to the love songs she heard on moonlit nights. For now she is in prison. Even though unfulfilled sexually, worn out by hard work and childbearing, she will seldom attempt to escape her marriage. Divorce is forbidden and separation in this patriarchal community means condemnation to concubinage or slavery as a servant. Is it any wonder that the women of this land wail their children to sleep? The women bear the heaviest burden of pain in this Southern Italian world, bled white by the Romans and exploited since then by corrupt and rapacious feudal systems.

This is the social and psychological background of the singers who shape the musical preference pattern of the babies of Southern Italy. Their wailing voices blend with the child's first experiences of love and affection, the satisfaction of his need to be fed, cleaned, kept warm, and cuddled. When he grows up, he finds no reason to change his emotional perspective. The mother, who is pressed by church law into a succession of exhausting pregnancies, has a new baby in her arms and refuses the older sibling. When the child is obstreperous, he is severely punished or slapped and then may be covered with passionate caresses by a mother to whom he represents the whole of life's satisfactions. I have never seen children so harshly treated as in Southern Calabria and in Sicily, nor have I ever encountered such timorous little girls and such mischievous, maddening little boys.

Girls, from an early age, must stay at home to help their mothers. The idea of free play or long schooling for them is unthinkable. As soon as they begin to mature, they are housebound and guarded like so many potential criminals. The boys, on the other hand, have little or no organized sport, and spend their time standing in the streets and piazzas with the older boys, being cuffed and tormented, and in turn cuffing and tormenting the smaller ones. During adolescence they burn with frustrated desire, for contact is forbidden with the girls they yearn for. There are no dances, no parties, and unless a girl is engaged she cannot even go to the movies with her young man. Thus Southern Italy has become famous for the beautiful eyes of her women, eyes which can say everything in a glance. Thus your young Italian, summoned by the burning glances of the girls, stimulated by wine, by the sun, by a culture whose only folklore deals with love in the most passionate and romantic terms, is left to burn in the piazza. He becomes a silent hunter, waiting and hoping for the moment when he can catch a girl unaware, or briefly reach a haven in the arms of some complaisant married woman. In this culture, no man can really trust his friend, for to leave one's wife or fiancee alone with another man is far too risky.

Thus the whole society of Southern Italy comes to share in varying degrees the sorrows and frustrations of its housebound women. And there is almost literally nothing in the folk poetry of this area but yearning for unattainable love—love songs which the males sing in voices almost as high-pitched and falsetto as their mothers,' sending through the barred windows a vocal sign of their identification with the emotional problems of their imprisoned sweethearts.

But, you may ask, is high-pitched, strident singing necessarily a musical symbol of the burning pain of sexual starvation? It appears to me that this is so, for people sing in this fashion in all the areas in which women are secluded, owned, exploited, and thus never can trust or be trusted completely by their men.

However, when the relationship between the fundamental vocal means of expressing emotion (laughing, crying, and the like) are studied in relation to singing style, another great step forward will have been made in scientific musicology. In this particular case a few preliminary observations can be shared. When a human being, especially a female, is given over to agonized grief, she emits a series of high-pitched, long, sustained, wailing notes. Even grown men sound like little children when they howl in sorrow. Then the head is thrown back, the jaw thrust forward, the soft palate is pulled down and back, the throat is constricted so that a small column of air under high pressure shoots upward and vibrates the hard palate and the heavily charged sinus. An easy personal experiment will convince anyone that this is the best way to howl or wail. Then, if you open your eyes slightly (for they will automatically close if you are really howling), you will see the brows knotted, the face and neck flushed, the facial muscles knotted under the eyes, and the throat distended with the strain of producing this high-pitched wail.

This is quite an accurate picture of the Southern Italian or Andalucian folk singer. This is what the Southern Italian or Spanish child learns in the cradle and in the kitchen, and later uses for abstract expressive purposes, recalling feelings of infant love and security. The proof is that everyone in the culture sings or tries to sing in this way. Not only do mature women howl or wail when they sing, but so also do most of the men, especially the most highly esteemed singers. It is rare to find a low singing voice among Southern Italian men. Tenors with a falsetto quality are the rule. And this is the tale of Tunis, Egypt, Arabia, Persia, of the raga singers of India, and of all the lands where women are the chattel slaves of high culture.

I come now to a final example which sharpens this cartoon of Italian musical styles. In the central mountains of Sardinia there is a small area said never to have been conquered by the Romans. The population live a quasi-tribal life, pasturing their flocks on communal land, resisting the modern Italian government as they did Imperial Rome. In fact, they are celebrated brigands who make travel on the roads unsafe after dark, and frequently carry out raids on neighboring villages. Yet I was told that murders due to jealousy rarely occur among them. Women, as clan members, are not the slaves of their husbands, and infidelities and sexual irregularities are talked out between families.

Sard lullabies often run to the lilting rhythm of the *ballo londo* (75), the primitive Sardinian circle dance (76), and even in funeral lamentations, the voices of the mourning women are low-pitched and husky. The men, who practice the art of song to the exclusion of every other art and whose songs transmit the tribal lore, sing and dance together in a line with arms round each other's shoulders (77). Their voices are pitched so low that, in the Italian context, you think at once of Zulu singing style. All songs are choral and the choruses are composed of baritones and basses, sounding a lively polyphonic bass figure as their song-leader (sometimes a tenor) tells his story. Their harmonic system is unique in Italy and in Europe, and indeed seems to be the one genuine prehistoric chordal style that has survived intact in modern Europe.

Coastal Sards sing in modified Hispano-Arabic style, in high-pitched strident voices, mostly in solo (78), even though their accompaniment is the most elaborate polyphonic instrument produced in the Mediterranean—the Greek *aulos*, called in Sardinia the *launneddas*, which is in effect a triple clarinet (79).

The bass song style of Central Sardinia is linked, in my mind, with the polyphonic music of Liguria (80), and in both areas one finds a permissive attitude toward sex, more equality for women, tenderness for children, and many mementos of a primitive communal life. Indeed, I have come to feel that these areas belong to an Old European culture pushed back into the mountains and surrounded by the onrush of Oriental civilization which overwhelmed and shattered most of the older tribal societies, made chattels of the women, and brought in its train a folk-art of strident monody. The Catholic church, also Oriental in origin and in musical preferences, sustained this monodic pattern; indeed for centuries it resisted polyphonic influences from the North with all its strength. In the mountain Sard we have perhaps an indication of the kind of life and music that existed in Europe before high culture came from the East. The most recent and dramatic example of the disappearance of the Old European choral tradition was the clearing of the Scots highlands in the eighteenth century. The clan system was broken and the people shipped off to the Maritime Provinces of Canada. There in the Gaelic-speaking enclaves one hears the only non-Negro polyphonic singing on the Eastern seaboard (81).

I do not know how this system of stylistic analysis will work out in other parts of the world, especially in primitive cultures. It seems to me that it considerably clarifies the picture in the areas I know intimately—Britain, Italy, Spain, the West Indies, and the United States. It gives promising indications when applied in other areas. Perhaps sexual tensions may not prove to be a determinant for musical style in the music of many primitive peoples, but I feel that it is along the lines indicated in these pages that we will come upon the answers to many of the puzzles facing the new science of musical ethnology.

One of the most promising aspects of this approach is the possibility of introducing precise laboratory measurements into the study. The development of the melody-writing machine will soon make it easy to transcribe tunes and thus build up a picture of the melodic norms of any culture area. We have seen that the diagnostic factors in the musical style situation center around the way the voice is produced, its characteristic timbre and normal singing pitch. These elements may now be measured precisely and linked with studies of the psychological and emotional tension patterns of which vocal tension is the product. Thus, since voice production stands at the center of the problem—on the one hand limiting and coloring the formal musical product, and on the other sensitively reflecting the main emotional and social tensions of the society—an attack at this point could well produce decisive results.

What might be envisaged is a laboratory procedure with the following steps:

(1) A mechanical study of the physical characteristics of a series of singing styles and melodic contour patterns.
(2) A laboratory study of typical singers from each stylistic area, which would include measurement and description of the physiological traits basic to each style.
(3) Testing responses of members of musical culture groups to various aspects of their own and other musical styles.

SUMMARY AND CONCLUSIONS

Now to recapitulate the main points of this paper and to propose a conclusion.

1. Comparative musicology in studying folk and primitive music cannot depend upon our present system of musical notation, nor could such an approach possibly produce a picture of mankind's music, especially since, as we have shown, the formal aspects of music can be altered in culture contact without altering the fundamental color or intent of the song style. There is proposed a fresh concept—musical style—which includes these formal elements but sets them in their proper context of vocal technique, physical and emotional tensions, group participation, and social background.

2. Considered in this light, there appear to be ten or more musical style families in the world, whose number and precise description will be modified as more material comes in. Perhaps these categories may serve as a useful starting-point—Eurasian, Old European, Modern European, Pygmoid, African, Melanesian, Malayan, Polynesian, Australian, and American Indian. It seems quite clear that these ten styles have spread over large areas during extremely long periods of time, possibly with the diffusion of the modern races of mankind. They appear to change more slowly than any other human art.

3. The diagnostic elements in musical style appear now to be the degree and kind of group participation in music-making, the characteristic pitch and timbre of the voice and the vocal technique, the facial and bodily tensions, and the underlying emotions which determine these tensions. These emotions seem to arise from limited areas of social tension—almost like neuroses at the level of individual psychology. Thus the basic color of a music symbolizes a fundamental social-psychological pattern, common to a given culture.

4. In those societies considered, the sexual code, the position of women, and the treatment of children seem to be the social patterns

most clearly linked with musical style. Where women are made into chattels, as they have been during recent history in most areas of high culture, their feelings of melancholy and frustration have determined that the entire music of the various societies take on a nostalgic or agonized character, in singing style, melodic type, and emotional content. The women in these societies fix the early musical preferences of the young, so that when these children become adults they experience a pleasurable recall of childhood emotions associated with their mothers and their mothers' sad songs; thus a sorrowful music fills them with a feeling of security and they find it beautiful and pleasurable.

5. Since music has to do with such fundamental human values and such primordial human experiences, which do not alter until the entire underpinnings of a society are changed, we may now see clearly why musical style is so conservative and why musical patterns have seemed to externalize eternal verities. The Pythagoreans believed that the fundamental tonal patterns in music were a sign of man's relationship with the patterns of the physical universe—the music of the spheres. Now we see that musical styles may be symbols of basic human value systems which function at the unconscious level and evolve with glacial slowness because the basic social patterns which produce them also evolve slowly.

6. For us, these concepts open up several important possibilities:

(a) Using musical style analysis as a diagnostic instrument, we can begin the study of the emotional and esthetic history of the world's peoples.

(b) Using musical style as an analytic tool, we can perhaps reconstruct the emotional character of past societies.

(c) Musical style analysis may afford a fairly precise index of the deep-running emotional and esthetic factors which have been operative in the process of cultural evolution alongside economic and institutional factors.

(d) We can anchor the study of the arts of mankind in fundamental concepts of psychology and physiology, and perhaps discover a realistic basis for the protection of certain cultural values, about whose disappearance under the pressure of western technology we can now only express a sentimental concern.

(e) With musical style analysis as a predictive tool, we can start to make hypotheses and to test them upon the rapidly evolving music of our own times, and perhaps achieve a better evaluation of esthetic problems.

REFERENCES CITED

Metfessel, Milton
1928 *Phonophotography in Folk Music*. Chapel Hill, University of North Carolina Press.

Herzog, George
1949 "Song: Folk Song and the Music of Folk Song." In *Standard Dictionary of Folklore, Mythology and Legend*. Funk and Wagnalls.

Rouget, Gilbert
1954–55 *A propos de la forme dans les musiques de tradition orale*. Extrait de les Colloques de Wegmont, Vol I.

Sachs, Curt
1943 *The Rise of Music in the Ancient World*. W. W. Norton.

Seeger, Charles
1949 Oral tradition in music. In *Standard Dictionary of Folklore, Mythology and Legend*. Funk and Wagnalls.
1958 Singing style. *Western Folklore* XVII, no. 1, University of California Press.
1958–2 Prescriptive and descriptive music writing. *The Musical Quarterly*. XLIV: No. 2.

Traeger, George L.
1958 Paralanguage: A first approximation. *Studies in Linguistics 13*, Nos. 1–2, University of Buffalo.

RECORD BIBLIOGRAPHY

This list must deal selectively with the records from only two or three of the series which are available. Otherwise it would run to far too many items. First, here are the principal sources from which discs of field-recorded folk and primitive music are available.

The archive of American Folk Lore, Library of Congress, which will mail its catalogue of field recordings from North and South America on request.

The Columbia World Library of Folk and Primitive Music, edited by A. Lomax, with others, available from Columbia Records Inc., 779 7th Avenue, New York. 18 regional albums.

Folkways Records, 117 W. 46th Street, New York City, whose vast catalogue of excellent LPs includes material from most regions of the world.

The Department of Musicology, Musée de l'Homme, Place Trocadero, Paris, editor Gilbert Rouget, a small but extremely important catalogue of primitive music.

Westminster Records, Inc., 275 7th Avenue, NYC, with a growing catalogue of series of LPs which treat one region exhaustively.

The World Collection of Recorded Folk Music, UNESCO, Paris, editor C. Brailoieu, a small selection of otherwise unavailable recordings, arranged by type.

(1) Iviza, *Spain*, KL 216, Columbia . . . *Songs and Dances of Spain*, WF 12002 and WF 12019, Westminster.

(2) Good examples of white folk singing style may be found on: *Anglo-American Ballads*, L1; *Anglo-American Sea Chanties*, L2; *Anglo-American Songs and Ballads*, L21, L12, Library of Congress. . . . *The Ritchie Family of Kentucky*, FA 2316; *Pete Steele*, FS 3828; *Wolf River Songs*, FM 4001; *Folk Songs of Ontario*, FM 4005, Folkways.

(2a) *Sacred Harp Singing*, L11, Library of Congress.

(2b) Good examples of Negro folk singing may be found on: *Afro-American Spirituals, etc.*, L3; *Afro-American Blues and Game Songs*, L4; *Negro Religious Songs and Services*, L10; *Negro Work Songs and Calls*, L8, Library of Congress . . . *Negro Prison Songs*, TLP 1020, Tradition Records, Inc., NYC . . . *Negro Folk Music of Alabama*, FE 4471–75; *Country Dance* FA 2201, Folkways.

(3) Southern music at various stages of cross-culturation on: *Blues in the Mississippi Night*, United

Artists, 725 7th Ave., NYC . . . *Folk Music: USA*, FE 4530; *American Folk Music*, FP 251–3; *Jazz*, FJ 2801–11, Folkways . . . *Knee Deep in Bluegrass*, DL 8731, Decca Records . . . *Ray Charles at Newport*, Atlantic 1289.

(4) *Folk Music of Nova Scotia*, FM 4006; *Cajun Songs from Louisiana*, P 438; Folkways . . . *Venezuela*, KL 212, Columbia . . . *Bahaman Songs, etc.*, L 5, Library of Congress.

(5) *Afro-Bahian Music from Brazil*, Album 13; *Folk Music from Venezuela*, Album 15, Library of Congress . . . *Brazil No. 2—Bahia*, Musée de l'Homme . . . *Negro Folk Music of Africa and America*, FE 4500; *Music of the Bahamas*, FS 3844–5; *Cult Music of Cuba*, P 410; *Folk Music of Jamaica*, P 452; *Folk Music of Haiti*, FE 4407; *The Black Caribs of Honduras*, FE 4435, Folkways.

(6) *Traditional Music of Peru*, FE 4456, Folkways.

(7) *Venezuela*, Side I, Nos. 1, 7, 9, KL 212, Columbia . . . *Music of Matto Grosso*, P 446; *Indian Music of the Upper Amazon*, FE 4458, Folkways.

(8) *Folk Music of Mexico*, Album 19, Library of Congress . . . *Yaqui Dances*, FW 6957; *Music of the Indians of Mexico*, FW 8811; *Tarascan Music*, FW 8867; *Indian Music of Mexico*, FE 4413; *Folk Music of New Mexico*, P 426, Folkways.

(9) *Traditional Music of Peru*, FE 4456, Folkways . . . *Folk Music of Venezuela*, Album 15, Library of Congress.

(10) Examples of the Amerindian "norm" . . . *Canada*, KL 211, Columbia . . . *Eskimos of Hudson Bay*, P 444; songs in *Music of Mato Grosso*, FE 4446; *Songs from the Great Lakes Indians*, FM 4003; Apache, San Idelfonso, Zuni, Walapai material from *American Indians of the Southwest*, FE 4420; . . . *Songs from the Iroquois Longhouse*, Album 6, Library of Congress . . . *Venezuela*, Side I, Nos. 2, 3, 4, 5, 8, 10, KL 212, Columbia . . . *Bresil-I*, Musée de l'Homme.

(11) *Music of the Sioux and Navaho*, FE 4401; *Music of the Indians of the Southwest*, Taos and Navaho material, FE 4420, Folkways.

(12) Seventeen LPs dubbed from the field cylinders of F. Densmore taken in most Indian culture areas, are now available from the Library of Congress. Folkways lists additional records.

(13) *Musique de Boschman at Musique Pigmee*, LD-9, Musée de l'Homme; *Music of the Ituri Forest*, FE 4483; *Africa South of the Sahara*, Side I, Nos. 5 and 6, FE 4503 . . . *French Africa*, Side II, Nos. 34–38, KL 205, Columbia.

(14) *Musique Maure*, Musée de l'Homme . . . *French Africa*, Side I, Nos. 2–14, KL 205, Columbia . . . *Wolof Music of Senegal and Gambia*, FE 4462, Folkways.

(15) *Songs of the Watusi*, FE 4428; *Africa, South of the Sahara*, Side IV, Nos. 31 and 32, FE 4503, Folkways.

(16) *Folk Music of Ethiopia*, FE 4405; *Music of the Falashas*, FE 4442, Folkways.

(17) Notably in *Folk Music of Western Congo*, FE 4427, Folkways.

(18) A remarkable dramatization of intercourse and orgasm on *Guinée Française*, Side II, No. 13, MC 20, 097, Vogue, Paris, France. Three LPs give a summary picture of African Negro music: *French Africa* and *British Africa* on Columbia, and *Africa South of the Sahara* on Folkways . . . Hugh Tracy, director of the African Music Society, PO Box 138, Roodepoort, South Africa, has recorded over the whole area of British South and East Africa and has published a tremendous archive of records . . . Gilbert Rouget makes available a smaller but very good selection of pressings from the Musée de l'Homme. All in all, Africa is not only the richest but the best recorded continent, musically speaking. . . . Of special interest is *Folk Music of Liberia*, FE 4465, Folkways, in which the link between Pygmoid and Negro music becomes clearly evident.

(19) *Australia*, KL 208, Columbia . . . *Tribal Music of Australia*, FE 4439, Folkways.

(20) *New Guinea*, Side II, KL 208, Columbia . . . *Music of New Guinea* (Austral-Trust Territory, Inc. New Britain, New Ireland, Manus, Bougainville), Wattle Records Inc., 131 Cathedral Street, Sydney . . . *Indonesia*, Side I, Nos. 1, 2, 3, 4, 5, and 6, Vol. VII, Columbia.

(21) Most of the material I have heard was on private discs in London or Paris. A Polynesian specialist could certainly add more items to . . . *Maori Songs of New Zealand*, FE 4406; Tahiti, one item, in *Music of the World's Peoples*, No. 12, FE 4504; Samoa, one item, Side IV, FE 4505, Folkways. Europeanized Polynesian songs are available in any large record catalogue.

(22) *Indonesia*, KL 210, Columbia, strong Malay traces Nos. 1–5, Moluccan Music Nos. 7–14, Dyak, Nos. 15–18 Side I (See also Musée de l'Homme disc of Borneo Music), also Nos. 25 and 28 Side II from Bali, KL 210, Columbia . . . *Hanunoo Music from the Philippines*, FE 4460; *Temiar Dream Music of Malaya*, FE 4460; *Japanese Buddhist Rituals*, Side I, Nos. 1, 2, FE 4449; Veddic chant, No. 3, Side I, *Religious Music of India*, FE 4431.

(23) *Ireland*, KL 204, Columbia . . . *Songs of Aran*, P 1002, Folkways.

(24) *England*, KL 206; *France*, KL-207, Columbia.

(25) *Spain*, KL 213, Columbia.

(26) *Italy*, KL 5173–4, Columbia.

(27) *Yugoslavia*, Serbian bands, KL 213, Columbia . . . No. 28, *Music of the World's Peoples*, FE 4454, Folkways.

(28) *Folk Music of Greece*, FE 4454, Folkways.

(29) *Songs and Dances of Turkey*, FW 8801; *Folk and Traditional Music of Turkey*, FE 4404.

(30) *Musique Maure* (see 14) . . . *Folk Music of the Mediterranean*, FE 4501, Folkways.

(31) *Folk Music of Palestine*, FE 4408; *Kurdish Folk Songs and Dances*, FE 4469; *Music of South Arabia*, FE 4421; *Music of the Russian Middle East*, FE 4416; *Songs and Dances of Armenia*, FP 809, Folkways. *In Israel Today*, WF 12026–29; *Songs and Dances* (with material from Kazakistan, Uzbekistan, Khirgizia, and Moldavia), WF 12012, Westminster.

(32) *Folk Music of Pakistan*, FE 4425, Folkways.

(33) *India*, KL 215, Columbia . . . *Religious Music of India*, FE 4431; *Traditional Music of India* (remarkable examples of the female-male voice), FE 4422; *Music from South Asia* (the Indian subcontinent), FE 4447, Folkways.

(34) *Music of South East Asia*, FE 4423; *Burmese Folk and Traditional Music*, FE 4436, Folkways.

(35) *Indonesia*, KL 210, Columbia. *Music of Indonesia*, FE 4406, Folkways.

(36) *Japan, The Ryukyus, Korea and Formosa*, KL 214, Columbia. *Folk and Classical Music of Korea*, FE 4424; *Folk Music of Japan*, FE 4429, Folkways. No long playing records of Chinese folk music are available in the West, as far as I know, but one hears that field recording is being actively carried on there now.

(37) *Scotland*, KL 209, Columbia. *Songs and Pipes of the Hebrides*, FE 4430; *Songs from Cape Breton Island*, FE 4450, Folkways.

(38) *England*, KL 206, Columbia. In 1960–61 Westminster will publish a series of field recordings covering all regions of the British Isles.

(39) *Folk Music of Norway*, FM 4008, Folkways.

(40) *France*, KL 207, Columbia.

(41) *The Spanish Basques*, WF 12018; *Galicia*, WF 12020; *Aslurias and Santander*, WF 12021, Westminster.

(42) *North and Central Italy*, KL 5173, Columbia.

(43) *Jugoslavia*, Side I, KL 217, Columbia.

(44) *Bulgaria*, KL 5378, Columbia . . . *Romanian Songs and Dances*, FE 4387, Folkways.

(45) *Lithuanian Songs in the USA*, FM 4009; one Esthonian item, in Vol. IV, *Music of the World's Peoples*, FE 4507.

(46) *Music of the Ukraine*, FE 4443; No. 18, *Folk Music of the World's Peoples; Russian Folk Songs*, FW 6820, Folkways.

(47) *Folk Songs from Armenia*, WF 12013; *Folk Songs and Dances* including material from Georgia, WF 12012, Westminster. One Georgian item, *Folk Music of the World's Peoples*.

(48) *Castile*, WF 12022, *Leon and Extremadura*, WF 12023, Westminster. Examples of other regions in Modern European area to be found in LPs listed in 37–47.

(49) *Folk Songs of Hungary*, FW 6803, Folkways.

(50) For USA items see No. 2. Also, *Folk Music of French Canada*, FE 4482; *Spanish and Mexican Folk Music of New Mexico*, FE 4426; *Folk Music of New Mexico*, FE 4426; *Folk Music of Colombia*, FW 6804; *Folk Songs and Dances of Brazil*, FW 6953. *Folk Music of Puerto Rico*, Album 18, Library of Congress. *Venezuela*, KL 212, Columbia.

(51) *British East Africa*, KL 213, Columbia.

(52) *Jugoslavia*, KL-217, Columbia.

(53) *Southern Italy and the Islands*, KL 5174, Columbia.

(54) *Galicia*, WF 12020, Westminster.

(55) *Scotland*, KL 209, Columbia.

(56) *Spain*, KL 216, Columbia. *Cities of Andalucia*, WF 12001, *Jeres and Seville*, WF 12003; *Eastern Spain and Valencia*, WF 12019, Westminster.

(57) *Cante Flamenco*, WAP 301, Westminster.

(58) *Castile*, WF 12022, *Leon and Extremadura*, WF 12023, Westminster.

(59) *Northern and Central Italy*, Side I, KL 5173, Columbia.

(60) Side II, Nos. 18–25, ibid.

(61) *Southern Italy and the Islands*, Side I, No. 14, KL 5174, Columbia.

(62) Nos. 17–18, ibid.

(63) No. 12, ibid.

(64) Side II, Nos. 31–37, ibid.

(65) Side II, No. 22, KL 517.

(66) Side I, No. 12, KL S173.

(67) Side I, No. 11, ibid.

(68) Side II, No. 23, ibid.

(69) Side II, No. 27, 30, KL 5173; Side I, 6, KL 5174.

(70) Side I, Nos. 2, 3, KL 5174.

(71) Side I, 14–15, KL 5173.

(72) *Jeres and Seville*, Side I, Nos. 7, 11, WF 12003, Westminster.

(73) *The Spanish Basques*, Side II, No. 4. WF 12018, Westminster.

(74) Side I, No. 17, KL 5174, Columbia.

(75) Side II, No. 35, KL 5174.

(76) Nos. 34–39, ibid.

(77) Nos. 37, 38, ibid.

(78) No. 37, ibid.

(79) Nos. 33, 39, ibid.

(80) Side I, Nos. 1, 2, 3, KL 5174.

(81) *Songs from Cape Breton Island*, FE 4450, Folkways.

NOTE

  * Parenthetical numbers refer to notes indicating albums and other recorded music illustrative of the points made.

Chapter 19

Saga of a Folksong Hunter

To the musicologists of the twenty-first century our epoch may not be known by the name of a school of composers or of a musical style. It may well be called the period of the phonograph or the age of the golden ear, when, for a time, a passionate aural curiosity overshadowed the ability to create music. Tape decks and turntables spun out swing and symphony, pop and primitive with equal fidelity; and the hi-fi LP brought the music of the whole world to mankind's pad. It became more important to give all music a hearing than to get on with the somewhat stale tasks of the symphonic tradition. The naked Australian mooing into his *djedbangari* and Heifetz noodling away at his cat-gut were both brilliantly recorded. The human race listened, ruminating, not sure whether there should be a universal, cosmopolitan musical language, or whether we should go back to the old-fashioned ways of our ancestors, with a different music in every village. This, at least, is what happened to me.

In the summer of 1933, Thomas A. Edison's widow gave my father an old-fashioned Edison cylinder machine so that he might record Negro tunes for a forthcoming book of American ballads. For us, this instrument was a way of taking down tunes quickly and accurately; but to the singers themselves, the squeaky, scratchy voice that emerged from the speaking tube meant that they had made communicative contact with a bigger world than their own. A Tennessee convict did some fancy drumming on the top of a little lard pail. When he listened to his record, he sighed and said, "When that man in the White House hear how sweet I can drum, he sho' gonna send down here and turn me loose." Leadbelly, then serving life in the Louisiana pen, recorded a pardon-appeal ballad to Governor O. K. Allen, persuaded my father to take the disc to the Governor, and was, in fact, paroled within six months.

I remember one evening on a South Texas sharecropper plantation.

The fields were white with cotton, but the Negro families wore rags. In the evening they gathered at a little ramshackle church to sing for our machine. After a few spirituals, the crowd called for Blue—"Come on up and singum your song, Blue." Blue, a tall fellow in faded overalls, was pushed into the circle of lamplight and picked up the recording horn. "I won't sing my song but once," he said. "You've got to catch it the first time I sing it." We cranked up the spring motor, dropped the recording needle on the cylinder, and Blue began—

> Poor farmer, poor farmer,
> Poor farmer, they git all the farmer makes . . .

Somebody in the dark busted out giggling. Scared eyes turned toward the back of the hall where the white farm owner stood listening in the shadows. The sweat popped out on Blue's forehead as he sang on . . .

> His clothes is full of patches, his hat is full of holes,
> Stoopin' down, pickin' cotton, from off the bottom bolls,
> Poor farmer, poor farmer . . .

The song was a rhymed indictment of the sharecropping system, and poor Blue had feared we would censor it. He had also risked his skin to record it. But he was rewarded. When the ghostly voice of the Edison machine repeated his words, someone shouted, "That thing *sho'* talks sense. Blue, you done it this time!" Blue stomped on his ragged hat. The crowd burst into applause. When we thought to look around, the white manager had disappeared. But no one seemed concerned. The plantation folk had put their sentiments on record!

As Blue and his friends saw, the recording machine can be a voice for the voiceless, for the millions in the world who have no access to the main channels of communication, and whose cultures are being talked to death by all sorts of well-intentioned people—teachers, missionaries, etc.—and who are being shouted into silence by our commercially bought-and-paid for loudspeakers. It took me a long time to realize that the main point of my activity was to redress the balance a bit, to put sound technology at the disposal of the folk, to bring channels of communication to all sorts of artists and areas.

Meanwhile, I continued to work as a folklorist. That is—out of the ocean of oral tradition I gathered the songs and stories that I thought might be of some use or interest to my own group—the intellectuals of the middle class. I remember how my father and I used to talk, back in those far-off days twenty-five years ago, about how a great composer might use our stuff as the basis for an American opera. We were a bit vague about the matter because we were Texans and had never seen a live composer.

I kept on talking about that American-opera-based-on folk-themes, until one year the Columbia Broadcasting System commissioned a group of America's leading serious composers to write settings for the folk songs presented on my series for CBS's *School of the Air*. The formula was simple. First you had the charming folk tune, simply and crudely performed by myself or one of my friends. Then it was to be transmuted by the magic of symphonic technique into *big* music, just as it was supposed to have happened with Bach and Haydn and the boys. This was music education.

I recall the day I took all our best field recordings of "John Henry" to one of our top-ranking composers, a very bright and busy man who genuinely thought he liked folk songs. I played him all sorts of variants of "John Henry," exciting enough to make a modern folk fan climb the walls. But as soon as my singer would finish a stanza or so, the composer would say, "Fine—Now let's hear the next tune." It took him about a half-hour to learn all that "John Henry," our finest ballad, had to say to him, and I departed with my treasured records, not sure whether I was more impressed by his facility, or angry because he had never really listened to "John Henry."

When his piece was played on the air, I was unsure no longer. My composer friend had written the tunes down accurately, but his composition spoke for the Paris of Nadia Boulanger, and not for the wild land and the heart-torn people who had made the song. The spirit and the emotion of "John Henry" shone nowhere in this score because he had never heard, much less experienced them. And this same pattern held true for all the folk-symphonic suites for twenty boring weeks. The experiment, which must have cost CBS a small fortune, was a colossal failure, and had failed to produce a single bar of music worthy of association with the folk tradition. As the years have gone by, I have found less and less value in the symphonizing of folk song. Each tradition has its own place in the scheme of mankind's needs, but their forced marriage produces puny offspring. Perhaps our American folk operas will come from the sources we least expect, maybe from some college kid who has learned to play the five-string banjo and guitar, folk-style, or from some yet unknown hillbilly genius who develops a genuine American folk-style orchestra.

In the early days, when we were taking notes with our recording machine for that imaginary American opera or for our own books, we normally recorded only a stanza or two of a song. The Edison recorder of that first summer was succeeded by a portable disc machine that embossed a sound track on a well-greased aluminum platter; but the surface scratch was thunderous, and besides, we were too hard-pressed for money to be prodigal with discs. Now, the recollection of all the full-bodied performances we cut short still gives me twinges of conscience. Even more painful is the thought that many of the finest things we gathered for the Library of Congress are on those cursed aluminum records; they will probably outlast the century, complete with acoustic properties that render them unendurable to all but the hardiest ears.

This barbaric practice of recording sample tunes did not continue for long, for our work had found a home in the Archive of American Folk Song, established in the Library of Congress by the late Herbert Putnam, then Librarian, and there were funds for plenty of discs. By then, we had also come to realize that the practice among the folk of varying the tune from stanza to stanza of a long song was an art both ancient in tradition and subtle in execution—one which deserved to be documented in full. So it was that we began to record the songs in their entirety.

Learning that the Russians were writing full-scale life histories of their major ballad singers, I then began to take down lengthy musical biographies of the most interesting people who came my way. Thus, Leadbelly's life and repertoire became a book—the first folksinger biography in English, and unhappily out of print a year after it was published. Jelly Roll Morton, Woody Guthrie, Aunt Molly Jackson, Big Bill Broonzy and a dozen lesser-known singers all set down their lives and philosophies for the Congressional Library microphones. In that way I learned that folk song in a context of folk talk made a lot more sense than in a concert hall.

By 1942 the Archive of American Folk Song had become the leading institution of its kind in the world, with several thousand songs on record from all over the United States and parts of Latin America. With Harold Spivacke, Chief of the Music Division, I planned a systematic regional survey of American folk music. We were lending equipment and some financial aid to the best regional collectors. We had our own sound laboratory, had published a series of discs with full notes and texts which was greeted with respect and admiration by museums and played on radio networks the world over—though little in the United States. By teaching our best discoveries to talented balladeers like Burl Ives, Josh White and Pete Seeger, many hitherto forgotten songs began to achieve national circulation. Even music educators began to give serious thought to the idea of using American folk songs as an aid toward the musical development of American children—properly arranged with piano accompaniment and censored, of course.

Then came the day when a grass-roots Congressman, casually inspecting the Congressional Library's Appropriation Bill, noted an item of $15,000 for further building up the collection for the Archive of American Folk Song. This gentleman thereupon built up a head of steam and proceeded to deliver an impassioned speech, demanding to know by what right his constituents' money was being spent "by that long-haired radical poet, Archibald MacLeish, running up and down our country, collecting itinerant songs."

A shocked House committee rose to this national emergency. It not only cut the appropriation for the Archive out of the bill, but along with it a million dollars earmarked for the increase of the entire Library. Our national Library would have to get along without the purchase of books, technical journals and manuscripts for a year—but at least that poet would also have to stop doing whatever he was doing with those "itinerant songs."

I was hardly the most popular man in the Library of Congress during the ensuing week. My name had not been mentioned in Committee, but the blame for what happened fell on me—for my noisy round objects had never fitted into the quiet rectangular world of my librarian colleagues. For a few days I walked down those marble corridors in a pool of silence. Then logs were rolled and the million dollars for the Library were restored, apparently, though, with the understanding that the folk song Archive should get none of it—ever. To the best of my knowledge, no further government funds since that day have been appropriated for the pursuit of "itinerant" songs. Although the Archive has continued to grow, thanks to gifts and exchanges, it has ceased to be the active center for systematic collecting that we so desperately need in this unknown folksy nation of ours.

To the best of my knowledge, I say, because when it became plain that the Archive was no longer to be a center for field trips, I sadly shook the marble dust of the Library off my shoes, and have paid only occasional visits there since. However, once the field recording habit takes hold of you, it is hard to break. One remembers those times when the moment in a field recording situation is just right. There arises an intimacy close to love. The performer gives you his strongest and deepest feeling, and, if he is a folk singer, this emotion can reveal the character of his whole community. A practiced folk song collector can bring about communication on this level wherever he chooses to set up his machine. Ask him how he does this, and he can no more tell you than a minister can tell you how to preach a great sermon. It takes practice and it takes a deep need on the part of the field collector—which the singer can sense and want to fulfill.

I swore I would never touch another recording machine after I left the Library of Congress; but then, somehow, I found myself the owner of the first good portable tape machine to become available after World War Two. Gone the needle rasp of the aluminum disc; gone the worry with the chip and delicate surface of the acetates. Here was a quiet sound track with better fidelity than I had imagined ever possible; and a machine that virtually ran itself, so that I could give my full attention to the musicians.

I rushed the machine and myself back to the Parchman (Mississippi) Penitentiary where my father and I had found the finest, wildest and most complex folk singing in the South. The great blizzard of 1947 struck during the recording sessions, and the convicts stood in the wood yard in six inches of snow, while their axe blades glittered blue in the wintry light and they bawled out their ironic complaint to Rosie, the feminine deity of the Mississippi Pen—

> Ain't but the one thing I done wrong,
> I stayed in Mississippi just a day too long.
> Come and get me, Rosie, an' take me home,
> These life-time devils, they won't leave me alone.

Although my primitive tape recorder disintegrated after that first trip, it sang the songs of my convict friends so faithfully that it married me to tape recording. I was then innocent of the nervous torments of tape splicing and of the years I was to spend in airless dubbing studios in the endless pursuit of higher and higher "fi" for my folk musicians. The development of the long-playing record—a near perfect means for publishing a folk song collection—provided a further incentive; for one LP encompasses as much folk music as a normal printed monograph and presents the vital reality of an exotic song style as written musical notation never can. At a summer conference dealing with the problems of international folklore, held in 1949 [1950], I proposed to my technically innocent colleagues that we set up a committee to publish the best of all our folk song findings as a series of LPs that would map the whole world of folk music. Exactly one person—and he was a close friend of mine—voted in favor of my proposal.

The myopia of the academics was still a favorite topic of mine, when one morning, a few weeks later, I happened to meet Goddard Lieberson, President of Columbia Records, in a Broadway coffee shop. His reaction to my story was to agree on the spot that it would be an interesting idea to publish a World Library of Folk Music on LP—if I could assemble it for him at a modest cost. Out of my past there then arose a shade to lend a helping hand in my project.

The first song recorded for the Library of Congress, Leadbelly's "Goodnight Irene," had just become one of the big popular hits of the year; and it seemed to me, in all fairness, that my share of the royalties should be spent on more folk-song research. Thus, within ten days of my chat with Lieberson, I was sailing for Europe with a new Magnecord tape machine in my cabin and the folk music of the world as my destination. I loftily assured my friends at the dock that, by collaborating with the folk music experts of Europe and drawing upon their archives, the job would take me no more than a year. That was in October of 1950.

It was July, 1958, before I actually returned home, with twenty of the promised forty tapes complete. Seventeen LPs in all, each one capsuling the folk music of as many different areas and edited by the foremost expert in his particular field, were released on Columbia; and eleven LPs on the folk music of Spain were edited for and released by Westminster. "Irene" had long since ceased to pay my song-hunting bills. As a matter of fact, for several years I had supported my dream of an international "vox humana" by doing broadcasts on the British Broadcasting Corporation's *Third Programme*. I had also become a past master in wangling my recorder and accompanying bales of tapes through customs, as well as by a dyed-in-the-wool European tyrant in the dining room of a continental hotel.

There were several reasons why my efficient American planning of 1950 had gone awry. For one thing, only a few European archives of folk song recordings existed which were both broad enough in scope and sufficiently "hi-fi" to produce a good hour of tape that would acceptably represent an entire country. For another, not every scholar or archivist responded with pleasure to my offer to publish his work in fine style and with a good American royalty. There was the eminent musicologist who demanded all his royalties (whatever they were to be) in advance because he did not trust big American corporations (he was a violent anti-communist as well). Yet another was opposed to release his recordings prior to publication of his own musical analysis of them. Others, as curators of state museums, were tied down by red tape. In one instance, despite unanimous agreement in favor of my recording project, it took a year for the contract to be approved by the Department of Fine Arts and then a year more for the final selection of the tracks to be made. As for the folklorists of Soviet Russia, ten years of letter writing has yet to bring an answer to my invitation for them to contribute to the *"World Library"* project.

I simply could not afford to go everywhere myself. Much *"World Library"* material had to be gathered by correspondence—and that in a multitude of languages. So a huge file of letters accompanied me wherever I went, and inevitably there were a number of painful misunderstandings. One well-meaning gentleman hired a fine soprano to record his country's best folk songs. Another scholar, from the Antipodes and more anthropologist than musician, sent me beautiful tapes of hitherto unknown music—all recorded consistently at wrong speeds, but with no information to indicate the variations. The most painful incident, and one which still gives me nightmares, concerns a lady who, on the strength of my contract, made a six-month field trip and then sent me tapes of such poor technical quality that all the sound engineers in Paris were unable to put them right. I had no choice but to return the tapes, and the lady soon found herself with no choice but to leave her native land to escape her creditors.

Despite such problems, the job as a whole went smoothly, for the Library of Congress Archive records had preceded me and made friends for me everywhere. My European colleagues must have enjoyed leading their provincial American co-worker through land after unknown land of music, and though I had sworn to stay away from field recording and to act merely in the capacity of editor, the temptation posed by unexplored or inadequately recorded areas of folk music in the heart of the continent from which our civilization sprang was simply too much for me.

It so happened that mine was the first high-fidelity portable tape recorder to be made available in Europe for folk-song collecting. So I soon put it to work in the interest of the music that my new-found colleagues loved. The winter of 1950 I spent in Western Ireland, where the songs have such a jewelled beauty that one soon believes, along with the Irish themselves, that music is a gift of the fairies. The next summer, in Scotland, I recorded border ballads among the plowmen of Aberdeenshire, and later the pre-Christian choral songs of the Hebrides— some of them among the noblest folk tunes of Western Europe.

In the summer of 1953, I was informed by Columbia that publication of my series depended on my assembling a record of Spanish folk music; and so, swallowing my distaste for *El Caudillo* and his works, I betook myself to a folklore conference on the island of Mallorca with the aim of finding myself a Spanish editor. At that time, I did not know that my Dutch travelling companion was the son of the man who had headed the underground in Holland during the German occupation; but he was recognized at once by the professor who ran the conference. This man was a refugee Nazi, who had taken over the Berlin folk song archive after Hitler had removed its Jewish chief and who, after the war, had fled to Spain and was there placed in charge of folk music research at the Institute for Higher Studies in Madrid. When I told him about my project, he let me know that he personally would see to it that no Spanish musicologist would help me. He also suggested that I leave Spain.

I had not really intended to stay. I had only a few reels of tape on hand, and I had made no study of Spanish ethnology. This, however, was my first experience with a Nazi and, as I looked across the luncheon table at this authoritarian idiot, I promised myself that I would record the music of this benighted country if it took me the rest of my life. Down deep, I was also delighted at the prospect of adventure in a landscape that reminded me so much of my native Texas.

For a month or so I wandered erratically, sunstruck by the grave beauty of the land, faint and sick at the sight of this noble people, ground down by poverty and a police state. I saw that in Spain, folklore was not mere fantasy and entertainment. Each Spanish village was a self-contained cultural system with tradition penetrating every aspect of life; and it was this system of traditional, often pagan mores, that had been the spiritual armor of the Spanish people against the many forms of tyranny imposed upon them through the centuries. It was in their inherited folklore that the peasants, the fishermen, the muleteers and the shepherds I met, found their models for that noble behavior and that sense of the beautiful which made them such satisfactory friends.

It was never hard to find the best singers in Spain, because everyone in their neighborhood knew them and understood how and why they were the finest stylists in their particular idiom. Nor, except in the hungry South, did people ask for money in exchange for their ballads. I was their guest, and more than that, a kindred spirit who appreciated the things they found beautiful. Thus, a folklorist in Spain finds more than song; he makes life-long friendships and renews his belief in mankind.

The Spain that was richest in both music and fine people was not the hot-blooded gypsy South with its *flamenco*, but the quiet, somber plains of the west, the highlands of Northern Castile, and the green tangle of the Pyrenees where Spain faces the Atlantic and the Bay of Biscay. I remember the night I spent in the straw hut of a shepherd on the moonlit plains of Extramadura. He played the one-string *vihuela*, the instrument of the medieval minstrels, and sang ballads of the wars of Charlemagne, while his two ancient cronies sighed over the woes of courtly lovers now five hundred years in the dust. I remember the head of the history department at the University of Oviedo, who, when he heard my story, cancelled all his engagements for a week so that he might guide me to the finest singers in his beloved mountain province. I remember a night in a Basque whaling port, when the fleet came in and the sailors found their women in a little bar, and, raising their glasses, began to sing in robust harmony that few trained choruses could match.

Seven months of wine-drenched adventure passed. The tires on my Citroën had worn so smooth that on one rainy winter day in Galicia I had nine punctures. The black-hatted and dreadful *Guardia Civil* had me on their lists—I will never know why, for they never arrested me. But apparently, they always knew where I was. No matter in what God-forsaken, unlikely spot in the mountains I would set up my gear, they would appear like so many black buzzards carrying with them the stink of fear—and then the musicians would lose heart. It was time to leave Spain. I had seventy-five hours of tapes with beautiful songs from every province, and, rising to my mind's eye, a new idea—a map of Spanish folk-song style—the old choral North, the solo-voiced and oriental South, and the hard-voiced modern center, land of the ballad and of the modern lyrics. Spain, in spite of my Nazi professor, was on tape.* I now looked forward to a stay in England which would give me a chance to air my Iberian musical treasures over the BBC.

In the days before the hostility of the tabloid press and the Conservative Party had combined to denature the BBC's *Third Programme*, it was probably the freest and most influential cultural forum in the Western world. If you had something interesting to say, if the music you had composed or discovered was fresh and original, you got a hearing on the "Third." Some of the best poets in England lived mainly on the income gotten from their *Third Programme* broadcasts, which was calculated on the princely basis of a guinea a line. Censorship was minimal—and if a literary work demanded it, all the four-letter anglo-saxon words were used. You could also be sure, if your talk was on the "Third," that it would be heard by intelligent people, seriously interested in your subject.

My broadcast audience in Britain was around a million, not large by American buckshot standards, but one really worth talking to. I could not discuss politics—my announced subject being Spanish folk music—but I was still so angry about the misery and the political oppression I had seen in Spain that my feelings came through between the lines and my listeners were—or so they wrote me—deeply moved. At any rate, the Spanish broadcasts created a stir and the heads of the *Third Progamme* then commissioned me to go to Italy to make a similar survey of the folk music there.

That year was to be the happiest of my life. Most Italians, no matter who they are or how they live, are concerned about aesthetic matters. They may have only a rocky hillside and their bare hands to work with, but on that hillside they will build a house or a whole village whose lines superbly fit its setting. So, too, a community may have a folk tradition confined to just one or two melodies, but there is passionate concern that these be sung in exactly the right way.

I remember one day when I set up the battered old Magnecord on a tuna fishing barge, fifteen miles out on the glassy, blue Mediterranean. No tuna had come into the underwater trap for months, and the fishermen had not been paid for almost a year. Yet, they bawled out their capstan shanties as if they were actually hauling in a rich catch, and at a certain point slapped their bare feet on the deck, simulating exactly the dying convulsions of a dozen tuna. Then, on hearing the playback, they applauded their own performance like so many opera singers. Their shanties—the first, I believe, ever to be recorded *in situ*—dealt exclusively with two subjects: the pleasures of the bed which awaited them on shore, and the villainy of the tuna fishery owner, whom they referred to as the *pesce cane* (dog-fish or shark).

In the mountains above San Remo I recorded French medieval ballads, sung as I believe ballads originally were, in counterpoint and in a rhythm which showed that they were once choral dances. In a Genoese

waterfront bar I heard the longshoremen troll their five-part *trallaleros*—
in the most complex polyphonic choral folk style west of the Caucasus—
one completely scorned by the respectable citizens of the rich Italian
port. In Venice I found still in use the pile-driving chants that once
accompanied the work of the *battipali*, who long ago had sunk millions
of oak logs into the mud and thus laid the foundation of the most beautiful city in Europe. High in the Apennines I watched villagers perform a
three-hour folk opera based on Carolingian legends and called *maggi*
(May plays)—all this in a style that was fashionable in Florence before the
rise of opera there. These players sang in a kind of folk *bel canto* which led
me to suppose that the roots of this kind of vocalizing as we know it in
the opera house may well have had their origin somewhere in old
Tuscany. Along the Neapolitan coast I discovered communities whose
music was North African in feeling—a folk tradition dating back to the
Moorish domination of Naples in the ninth century. Then, a few miles
away in the hills, I heard a troupe of small town artisans, close kin to
Shakespeare's Snug and Bottom, wobble through a hilarious musical
lark straight out of the *commedia del'arte*.

The rugged and lovely Italian peninsula turned out, in fact, to be a
museum of musical antiquities, where day after day I turned up ancient
folk-song genres totally unknown to my colleagues in Rome. By chance I
happened to be the first person to record in the field over the whole
Italian countryside, and I began to understand how the men of the
Renaissance must have felt upon discovering the buried and hidden
treasure of classical Greek and Roman antiquity. In a sense, I was a kind
of musical Columbus in reverse. Nor had I arrived on the scene a
moment too soon.

Most Italian city musicians regard the songs of their country neighbors with an aversion every bit as strong as that which middle-class
American Negroes feel for the genuine folk songs of the Deep South.
These urban Italians want everything to be *"bella,"*—that is, pretty, or
prettified. Thus (in the fashion of most of our own American so-called
folk singers active in the entertainment field) the professional purveyors
of folk music in Italy leave out from their performances all that is angry,
disturbing or strange. And the Radio Italiana, faithful in its obligations
to Tin Pan Alley, plugs Neapolitan pop fare and American jazz day after
day on its best hours. It is only natural that village folk musicians, after
a certain amount of exposure to the TV screens and loudspeakers of RAI
should begin to lose confidence in their own tradition.

One hot day, in the office of the program director of Radio Roma, I lost my temper and accused him of being directly responsible for destroying the folk music of his own country, the richest heritage of its kind in Western Europe. At this really charming fellow I directed all the hopeless rage I felt at our so-called civilization—the hard sell that is wiping the world slate clean of all non-conformist culture patterns.

To my surprise, he took up my suggestion that a daily folk-song broadcast be scheduled for noon, when the shepherds and farmers of Italy are home and at leisure. I then wrote a romantic article for the radio daily, called "The Hills Are Listening", in which I envisioned my friends and neighbors taking new heart as they heard their own voices coming out of the loudspeakers. Then, months later, I learned to my embarrassment that my piece had finally seen publication in an obscure learned journal and that the broadcasts were put on late in the evening, well after working class Italy is in bed—and on Italy's "Third Program" to boot, which only a small minority of intellectuals ever listen to.

When are we going to realize that the world's richest resource is mankind itself, and that of all his creations, his culture is the most valuable? And by this I do not mean culture with a capital "C"—that body of art which the critics have selected out of the literate traditions of Western Europe—but rather the total accumulation of man's fantasy and wisdom, taking form as it does in images, tunes, rhythms, figures of speech, recipes, dances, religious beliefs and ways of making love that still persist in full vitality in the folk and primitive places of our planet. Every smallest branch of the human family at one time or another has carved its dreams out of the rock on which it has lived—true and sometimes pain-filled dreams, but still wholly appropriate to their particular bit of earth. Each of these ways of expressing emotion has been the handiwork of generations of unknown poets, musicians and human hearts. Now, we of the jets, the wireless and the atomblast are on the verge of sweeping completely off the globe what unspoiled folklore is left, at least wherever it cannot quickly conform to the success-motivated standards of our urban-conditioned consumer economy. What was once an ancient tropical garden of immense color and variety is in danger of being replaced by a comfortable but sterile and sleep-inducing system of cultural super-highways—with just one type of diet and one available kind of music.

It is only a few sentimental folklorists like myself who seem to be disturbed by this prospect today, but tomorrow, when it will be too late—

when the whole world is bored with automated mass-distributed video music, our descendants will despise us for having thrown away the best of our culture.

The small triumph referred to in the early part of this article—the growing recognition of the importance of folk and sometimes primitive music on long-playing records—is a good step in the right direction. But it is only a first step. It still remains for us to learn how we can put our magnificent mass communication technology at the service of each and every branch of the human family. If it continues to be aimed in only one direction—from our semi-literate western, urban society to all the "underdeveloped" billions who still speak and sing in their many special languages and dialects, the effect in the end can only mean a catastrophic cultural disaster for us all.

NOTE

* Besides Columbia, eleven discs from this trip were issued by Westminster.

Part III

The Folk Revival (1960s)

Introduction by Ronald D. Cohen

In early 1958, the Kingston Trio recorded "Tom Dooley," which appeared on their eponymous album in mid-summer and became a national hit by year's end. Following on the heels of the recent calypso craze, folk music had surprisingly become popular (and big business). In July, Alan Lomax permanently resettled in New York City, having spent a most productive sojourn in England and Europe. "Alan Lomax, considered by many America's foremost folklorist, has returned to the United States after nine years in England," Pete Seeger happily announced in *Sing Out!* in late 1958. "He left the U.S.A. as an 'enfant terrible' and he returns a legend. . . . I welcome back Alan Lomax, not just because he is an old friend, but also because, in my opinion, he is more responsible than any other single individual for the whole revival of interest in American folk music." After briefly recounting Lomax's manifold accomplishments over three decades, Seeger concluded: "Well, of course, the folksong revival did grow, and flourishes now like any happy weed, quite out of control of any person or party, right or left, purist or hybridist, romanticist or scientist. Alan Lomax probably looks about him a little aghast." In the next issue Israel "Izzy" Young also proffered his welcome: "Alan Lomax is busily creating work for American folklorists after spending eight years of collecting in Europe." In April 1958, *Newsweek* had already recognized Lomax's European accomplishments and soon reappearance "after seven years of tireless folk-song collecting across Europe. . . . In possibly a thousand villages he had become a familiar figure, swinging along lopsided with the weight of his tape recorder, laughing, scowling, cajoling, and bullying local singers to record in bars, on threshing floors, and even in sulphur mines."[1]

Lomax's photo appeared on the cover of the Summer 1959 *Sing Out!*, with the notice: "Folklorist, writer, folk-singer, impressario—Alan Lomax is one of the most interesting and provocative figures on the American folk song scene." The issue proved Seeger correct, as Lomax now established his position in the revival in his article, "The 'Folkniks'—and the Songs They Sing." He questioned the "so-called city-billies or folkniks" for mastering a traditional musical style without absorbing the music's emotional content. In reply, John Cohen, a member of the old-time revivalist New Lost City Ramblers, cautioned Lomax to take the "city folksingers" seriously: "The emotional content of folk songs is a different thing to different people—and it is hard to say that there is a single, correct way to emotional content." Lomax should stop preaching and listen, for "if folk music is valid and has force, the attitude of the folk singer towards his music will be communicated to and felt by those who hear it." If Lomax thought his return would only elicit accolades he would be sadly mistaken. In any case, he did not slow down in his zeal to shape and promote folk music in his native country.[2]

Lomax deftly made his presence felt on April 3, 1959, with "Folksong '59," a musical extravaganza at Carnegie Hall. Performers ran the gamut from Arkansas singer Jimmy Driftwood to the gospel groups the Selah Jubilee Singers and the Drexel Singers, blues performers Muddy Waters and Memphis Slim, the Stony Mountain Boys playing bluegrass, Pete and Mike Seeger, the Cadillacs, a rock-and-roll group, and Lomax himself doing prison work songs. "The time has come for Americans not to be ashamed of what we go for, musically, from primitive ballads to rock 'n' roll songs," Lomax declared, defending his eclectic, modern approach. John Wilson, in the *New York Times,* praised him for producing "an array of artists who gave a fascinating display of the source material that the juke boxes have diluted and distorted," and favorably compared the event to John Hammond's "Spirituals to Swing" concert twenty years earlier. Others expressed more skepticism. Aaron Rennert, in *Gardyloo,* generally admired the performers, but criticized the sound system, obvious lack of rehearsals, and jumbled program. Lomax made little attempt to explain the various styles, seemed "discourteous to both the performers and his audience," and some booed and hissed him, or even left the hall, when "he told them to lay down their prejudices and listen to rock 'n' roll." Izzy Young took a quite positive approach, recalling a few years later that Lomax "put on what is probably the turning point in American folk music . . . At that concert the point he was trying to make was that Negro and white music were mixing, and rock-and-roll was that thing."[3]

Perhaps the show's main contribution came in inaugurating bluegrass at Carnegie Hall, still a little-recognized style in the North. Lomax anointed bluegrass in the October 1959 *Esquire*, in his influential "Bluegrass Background: Folk Music with Overdrive." With no qualification or hesitation, he pronounced, "Out of the torrent of folk music that is the backbone of the record business today, the freshest sound comes from the so-called Bluegrass band—a sort of mountain Dixieland combo in which the five-string banjo, American's only indigenous folk instrument, carries the lead like a hot clarinet. . . . The result is folk music in overdrive with a silvery, rippling, pinging sound." Bill Monroe had recruited Earl Scruggs and Lester Flatt in 1945, launching bluegrass, according to Lomax, which drew on the rich, vibrant legacy of old time music. Short and to the point, the article stamped bluegrass with a patriotic pedigree, and Lomax's valuable seal of approval.[4]

To keep track of Lomax's activities and productions through 1959, surely a consequential year, is not easy. During the summer, in June, he gave a talk at the Second Annual Berkeley Folk Music Festival, appearing along with Jimmy Driftwood, Jesse Fuller, Sam Hinton, and Pete Seeger. He also spent two months traveling through the South on a recording trip, funded by Nesuhi and Ahmet Ertegun of Atlantic Records, ranging from Virginia and the Mississippi Delta to the Georgia Sea Islands. These recordings—including James Carter and the Prisoners performing "Po Lazarus" from Camp B at Mississippi State Penitentiary in Lambert, which appeared on the the soundtrack of the film *O Brother, Where Art Thou?*, earning the 2002 Grammy album of the year and the elderly Carter, found living in Chicago, a windfall in royalties—resulted in seven albums for Atlantic's Southern Folk Heritage series. Lomax would later write, with some hyperbole, that "after these stereo recordings appeared in 1961, there was no more talk about the dominance of Washington Square. In fact, many of the most devoted fans went into the field to do their own recordings." A further twelve volumes would be issued by Prestige/International the following year. (The *Southern Folk Heritage Series* and the "Southern Journey Series" were later reissued as Atlantic 7-82469 in a 4-CD box.) Also in 1959 Lomax published *The Rainbow Sign* (Duell, Sloan and Pearce), stories of two black figures in the South, one a minister and the other Vera Ward Hall ("Nora" in the book), and produced the record *Blues in the Mississippi Night* (United Artists), originally recorded in New York City in 1946. "To those who haven't already heard, Alan Lomax is back from Europe," Roger Abrahams wrote in *Caravan*, reviewing the book and record. "And in case any of you think he was idle

while he was over there, you have another think [sic] coming. To this
writer it would appear that Mr. Lomax stayed up nights thinking of ways
to sell folk-things to publishers, record companies etc., ergo to the public. This is a good thing whatever way you look at it."[5]

For the remainder of the new decade Lomax continued and
expanded the work he had done for almost thirty years, except now he
would no longer have a radio show and his field work ground to a halt.
During the summer of 1962 he revisited the West Indies, particularly
Trinidad and other small islands in the Lesser Antilles, where he recorded
and documented songs, dances, and games (later the basis for *Brown Girl
in the Ring*). A bit earlier he had recapped his previous two decades of field
work, in the May 1960 *Hi/Fi Stereo Review*, focusing on his European collecting. The previous month he apprised a *House Beautiful* audience with
his views of the current folk music scene, repeating his preference for the
authenticity of traditional performers and including a list of suitable
records and song books: "Under the smooth bland surface of the popularized folk songs lies a bubbling stew of work songs, country blues, field
hollers, hobo songs, prairie songs, spirituals, hoedowns, prison songs,
and a few unknown ingredients." Simultaneously, he published *The Folk
Songs of North America*, a masterful collection of 317 songs he had labored
over in England, the latest installment in the string of song books he had
published with his father since 1934 (followed by *The Penguin Book of
American Folk Songs* in 1964). Beginning with an informative introduction, he noted: "The first function of music, especially folk music, is to
produce a feeling of security for the listener by voicing the particular
quality of a land and the life of its people. . . . Folk song calls the native
back to his roots and prepares him emotionally to dance, worship, work,
fight, or make love in ways normal to his place." He placed the emphasis
on tradition, rather than innovation. In *Sing Out!*'s tenth anniversary
issue he encouraged folk enthusiasts to collect music from throughout
the country, continuing his work at the Library of Congress: "It remains
for the young professional of this generation to tell the whole story of
our folk culture. I can promise you that by collecting and mastering some
neglected corner of the vast world of folk song you will find the key to the
whole field." The recent issue by Westminster of eleven records drawn
from Lomax's collection of the *Songs and Dances of Spain* (with a separate
single disk coming out in the *Columbia World Library of Folk and Primitive
Music*) could serve as an example of what was possible in the modern
world, albeit from another country.[6]

Lomax also kept active in various organizations throughout the decade, asserting his authoritative voice when and where possible. In March 1963, during the winter meeting of the New York Folklore Society, he explained that folk music was officially popular during the New Deal because it gave a voice to "country people as opposed to city people, people living in far reaches in isolation in America, people living behind a foreign language barrier, people living behind a cultural barrier, people living in the Negro ghetto of that day, giving these people a sense that they, too, contributed very much to the building of America." His ingrained democratic impulses were particularly illustrated in his commitment to the Civil Rights movement, as it heated up through mid-decade.[7]

His support of the Civil Rights movement was total. "Certainly the conduct of the Southern Negro community in the past five years has been extraordinary," he wrote in *The Rainbow Sign* in 1959. "The success of the passive-resistance movement led by the Reverend Martin Luther King—the well-organized boycotts—the disciplined and dignified behavior of the Negro pupils who enrolled in white schools, are all testament to their new-found unity and confidence." The next year, in a letter to Guy Carawan included as part of the liner notes to the album *Freedom in the Air: A Documentary on Albany, Georgia 1961–1962*, released by the Student Non-Violent Coordinating Committee (SNCC), Lomax praised Carawan: "While I was squirreling round in the past, you were busy with the present, and how I envy you. It must be wonderful to be with those kids who are so courageously changing the South forever. I hope they feel proud of the cultural heritage of their forebears. It was a heritage of protest against oppression, of assertion against hopelessness, of joy in life against death."[8]

Lomax was not content to stay on the sidelines. Carawan, drawing on his musical preservation work on John's Island, South Carolina, and following a festival on the island the previous Christmas, along with civil rights workers Willie Peacock and Willie McGhee, helped organize a contentious musical workshop in May 1965, in Edwards, Mississippi. Including the Moving Star Hall Singers, the Georgia Sea Island Singers, Doc Reese, fife player Ed Young, as well as Lomax and folklorist Ralph Rinzler, the sessions introduced local organizers to traditional and contemporary folk music. Many of the young black activists found the older songs strange, smacking of slavery and oppression, and Lomax's remarks patronizing. Almost two dozen activists, including Carawan and Lomax,

next gathered in Knoxville, Tennessee, in October, to discuss the possibilities of a broader southern cultural movement. Lomax worked hard to
shape the discussions and wrote the final report. He stressed the value of
church music, particularly the spiritual tradition of the Holiness or
Sanctified Church; his hand can also be seen in the emphasis on the
value of collecting songs from prisoners, as well as railroad and levy
workers. Lomax continued to believe in the transforming power—political, social, spiritual—of cultural preservation and rejuvenation.

Lomax became involved in folk activities in numerous other public
ways. One mounting controversy in early 1963 was over the airing of the
ABC *Hootenanny* television show, which refused to allow Pete Seeger and
the Weavers to appear because of their radical backgrounds. Lomax
joined a group of protesters in late March and into April 1963, which formulated a boycott of the show by various performers, including Bob
Dylan, Peter, Paul and Mary, and Joan Baez. He kept in the forefront of
the increasingly popular folk revival in 1964 through participating in the
Newport Folk Festival, where he served on the Board of Directors for a
few years (and later as a member of the Newport Foundation), and introduced the opening roots session.

But in July 1965 his actions at the Newport festival led to some
heated moments. In his *New York Times* report, Robert Shelton focused
on the Friday blues stage, where "Alan Lomax, the folklorist, was an artic-
ulate, illuminating, fluent, but sometimes maddeningly pedantic host-
narrator. Likening the blues to the Italian stornella, the Spanish copla
and the Mexican corrida, Mr. Lomax described the Afro-American blues
and its variations as 'our most powerful, pervasive popular musical
form.'" Five former Texas prisoners, a quartet from the Mississippi Delta,
Mance Lipscomb, the Bill Monroe Band, and Willie Dixon demonstrated
blues variations; "[f]inally, after the narrator's challenge for them to
prove themselves capable of playing the blues, came the Paul Butterfield
Blues Band." Lomax left the stage and was immediately confronted by
the volatile Albert Grossman, Bob Dylan's manager, who had already
decided to manage the Paul Butterfield Blues Band and who felt that
Lomax had insulted the mostly white younger musicians from Chicago.
After a brief scuffle the two were separated. This was only a prelude to
the more controversial appearance by Dylan and members of the
Butterfield Band later in the festival.[9]

While Lomax was very involved in the moment, two of his earlier
efforts made their appearance late in the decade. First, his compilation

Hard Hitting Songs for Hard-Hit People, in conjunction with Woody Guthrie and Pete Seeger, was finally published by Oak Publications in 1967. Initiated in the early 1940s, the manuscript languished until finally reworked by Irwin Silber. Many of the songs came from Lomax's collecting for the Library of Congress, Silber noted, and various other sources, representing "the despair, the struggle, and the dreams of the working people of the United States in the Depression Years as expressed through the songs the people themselves made up and sang." Coincidentally, Guthrie died the same year after a lingering debility, and the next year Elektra Records released a three-record set of Lomax's 1940 Library of Congress interviews.[10]

Lomax had also begun to delve into a theoretical exploration of the world's music, soon named Cantometrics, which would absorb much of his creative life for the following three decades. His initial essay, "Folk Song Style," appeared in *The American Anthropologist* in December 1959. Drawing on his musical collecting, particularly in Spain and Italy, he called for a scientific approach to the world's music: "Using musical style analysis as a diagnostic instrument, we can begin the study of the emotional and esthetic history of the world's peoples. . . . We can anchor the study of the arts of mankind in fundamental concepts of psychology and physiology." The following year he received a grant from the American Council of Learned Societies to spend a year traveling the country, meeting with anthropologists, linguists, and others to begin mapping out his new musicological concepts. He first broached the idea in "Song Structure and Social Structure," appearing in *Ethnology* in 1962, followed by "The Good and the Beautiful in Folksong," published in the *Journal of American Folklore* (*JAF*) in 1967; the lengthy *Folk Song Style and Culture* was issued in 1968. He sketched his approach in the *JAF* article's opening passage: "Singing is an act of communication and therefore can be studied as behavior. Since a folksong is transmitted orally by all or most members of a culture, generation after generation, it represents an extremely high consensus about patterns of meaning and behavior of cultural rather than individual significance." He would get increasingly more theoretical and wide-ranging in his numerous writings in the future.[11]

During the sixties Lomax plunged into a plethora of folk music-related activities, drawing on and extending his work of the previous three decades. While he adhered to his reverence for traditional sounds and styles, he did not avoid making political commitments during this

volatile period, as he always remained committed to his belief in a people's culture and democratic values. In particular, his exploration and
appreciation of black music and culture never wavered, but also did not
take on the paternalistic cast of his father, John. Once again, Lomax
demonstrated his creative talents for organization, stimulation, and promotion, remaining in the forefront of the folk music revival as it accelerated into the decade.

NOTES

1. Israel Young, "Frets and Frails," *Sing Out!*, vol. 8, no. 4 (Spring 1959), 26; "Folk Song as It
Is," *Newsweek*, April 14, 1958, 80. For background information, E. David Gregory, "Lomax in
London: Alan Lomax, the BBC and the Folk-Song Revival in England, 1950–1958," *Folk Music
Journal*, vol. 8, no. 2 (2001), 136–169.

2. "On the Cover," *Sing Out!*, vol. 9, no. 1 (Summer 1959), 2; Alan Lomax, "The 'Folkniks'—
And the Songs They Sing," ibid., 30–31; John Cohen, "A Reply to Alan Lomax: In Defense of City
Folksingers," ibid., 33–34.

3. John S. Wilson, "Program Given by Alan Lomax," *New York Times*, April 4, 1959; Aaron
Rennert, "Folksong '59: A Review," *Gardyloo*, no. 2 (Mid-May 1959), 7; Richard Reuss Interview
with Israel G. Young, NYC, July 8, 1965 (in author's possession).

4. Alan Lomax, "Bluegrass Background: Folk Music with Overdrive," *Esquire*, vol. 52 (October
1959), 108.

5. Alan Lomax, Introduction to *Sounds of the South*, 1993; Roger D. Abrahams, "The Flesh, the
Devil, Alan Lomax and the Folk," *Caravan*, no. 18 (August–September 1959), 30.

6. Carroll Calkins with Alan Lomax, "Getting to Know Folk Music," *House Beautiful*, April
1960, 141; Lomax, *The Folk Songs of North America in the English Language* (New York: Doubleday
& Company, 1960), xv; Lomax, "Folk Song Traditions Are All Around Us," *Sing Out!*, vol. 11, no.
1 (March 1961), 18.

7. Ben Botkin, "The Folksong Revival: A Symposium," *New York Folklore Quarterly*, vol. 19
(June 1963), 121.

8. Alan Lomax, *The Rainbow Sign* (New York: Duell, Sloan and Pearce, 1959), 18; liner notes,
Lomax and Guy Carawan, producers, *Freedom in the Air: A Documentary on Albany, Georgia
1961–1962* (Student Non-Violent Coordinating Committee, SNCC-101).

9. Robert Shelton, "Folklorists Give Talks at Newport," *New York Times*, July 24, 1965.

10. Alan Lomax, Woody Guthrie, Pete Seeger, *Hard Hitting Songs for Hard-Hit People* (New York:
Oak Publications, 1967), 11.

11. Alan Lomax, "Folk Song Style," *The American Anthropologist*, vol. 61, no. 6 (December
1959), 950; Lomax, "The Good and the Beautiful in Folksong," *Journal of American Folklore*, vol.
80, no. 317 (July–September 1967), 213. See also, "The Adventure of Learning, 1960," ACLS
Newsletter, vol. 13, February 1962, 10–13.

Chapter 20

The "Folkniks"—and the Songs They Sing

The modern American folk-song revival began back in the thirties as a cultural movement, with overtones of social reform. In the last ten years our gigantic amusement industry, even though it is as yet only mildly interested in folk music, has turned this cultural movement into a small boom. As might have been expected, a throng of talented and ambitious city youngsters have taken over. These so-called city-billies or folkniks make most of the LPs and perform at most of the concerts. They have access to the impressarios and a-and-r men. They can quickly develop a local, then a national following among concert-goers and record buyers. And they translate folk music in ways that make it more understandable and acceptable to their market—an urban middle-class group, with a college background.

So far the folkniks have been mainly concerned with the formal aspects of folk song—the words, the tunes and the accompaniments. The tunes and the rhymes were easy to learn from books and records. The accompaniments presented much more of a challenge, the inventions of American folk guitar and banjo players for their instruments were both unconventional and complex, and require a considerable time for practice and study. However, since instrumental virtuosity has long been the hallmark of the talented musician in western culture, the challenge has been met by scores of ambitious and talented young people. It will soon be possible to say that folkniks play with as much brilliance and verve as the best country musicians.

The astonishing speed with which all this has been accomplished has had one unfortunate, though, I believe, only temporary result. Many city-billies, having quickly acquired the techniques of American folk song, believed that they had learned everything that there was to know and had become "folk singers" in the same sense as the talented country people who had transmitted or improved upon this art. This error arose, in most cases neither from malice nor snobbishness.

The American city folk singer, because he got his songs from books or from other city singers, has generally not been aware of the *singing style* or the *emotional content* of these folk songs, as they exist in tradition.

There are many, many *singing styles* on the map of the ethnologist of music. Most of them are older than the art of *bel canto* (which with its variation is the approved singing style of western city folk)—and they are, one and all, as difficult to learn, as full of subtleties and complexities and, in their own context, as expressive as *bel canto* which, with its derivatives, we western urbanites call "good singing" or "the proper use of the voice." When songs are ripped out of their stylistic contexts and sung "well," they are, at best, changed. It would be an extreme form of cultural snobbery to assert, as some people do, that they have been "improved." In my view they have lost something, and that something is important.

To describe all that they have lost would require a long essay. There is time here to mention only two things. First, the songs are deprived of the means for growing in their own terms, musically speaking. Both Negro and white rural singers felt free to vary the tunes they inherited, but according to quite different techniques. These techniques of variation formed the basis of the cultural heritage of each folk singer. His stature as an artist rested largely on the skill, the taste, the discretion, and the flair with which he applied his inherited knowledge of variation to the tunes he performed. Now this is a skill which can be acquired like any other; some city singers have learned it. Notable in this respect is Seamus Ennis, the Dublin-born son of a government worker, who can create brilliant and beautiful variants of the songs he has learned in the field or compose new tunes in the same manner, as easily as Sidney Bechet can improvise a new break on the soprano sax. It would seem to me to be a requirement for a "folk singer" that he learn the art of variation of a particular style of folk song before he begins to create variants of his own. In the first place, his new revision will, almost certainly, be in bad taste, an unpleasant, half-baked article like a pop song rapped out on Bizet or Tschaikovsky. And in any case, his variant will be something different from and less than a folk song, since he is different from and, in this respect, less than an accomplished folk singer.

Even more important, perhaps, is the relation of singing style to emotional content. It takes a master to make really good music when Bach is translated into boogie-woogie. Of course, it can be done, but it is best done tongue-in-cheek or with a completely developed musical style at one's command. Thus when a good jazzman, symphonist, or gypsy snatches up a folk song and plays with it, the results may be interesting or, occasionally, important, but important as jazz, symphony or gypsy music, not as folk song. In these cases the tune acquires a different emotional content. But when a so-called folksinger, with no respect for or knowledge of the style or the original emotional content of the song, acquires the shell of the song merely and leaves its subtle vocal interior behind, there is a definite expressive loss.

Singing style is the means by which the singer expresses the subtle emotional nuances of the song. If it is a folk song, then these nuances stand for the way that a whole culture has felt about a particular subject. We have as yet no language for describing these matters. They cannot be written down in conventional musical notation. But they can be heard and felt in a recorded or live performance. By the same token they can be learned, if the singer is possessed of sufficient seriousness and sensitivity, but not nearly so easily as instrumental technique can be learned. In order to acquire a folk singing style, you have to experience the feelings that lie behind it, and learn to express them as the folk singers do. This takes time, but there is no question that it is worthwhile. Here the city singer of folk songs is playing his full and serious role—that is, to interpret for his city audience, the lives and feelings of the past or of a far-off society—to link them emotionally. If he does so, he will grow within the terms of a folk art. As an interpretive artist, he will become one link in a vital musical chain anchored in the hearts of humanity and of the past. Finally, if he is truly dedicated, he will find his own way to making his personal contributions, great or small, within the limits of the artistic tradition he has chosen as his life's work. I hasten to add that I am not talking here about the amateur who sings folk songs for fun, but only about the performer who takes himself seriously enough to make records or appear on the concert stage.

It seems to me that more and more of the young singers are finding their own way to standards such as those I have been attempting to set forth. That these talented and positively motivated young people have concentrated for a spate on learning lots of songs and acquiring a dazzling instrumental technique is a good and positive development. Now I notice that many of them feel bored or embarrassed by their own sound and some are tackling the next and much more serious problems of style and content.

Chapter 21

Leadbelly's Songs

Born in 1885 near Shreveport, Louisiana, he was christened Huddie Ledbetter. Later his buddies on southern workgangs gave him the nickname which stuck to him for the rest of his life: they called him Lead- or tough-belly, because he could set the pace for the cotton-picking gangs all day and make music for the barrel-house dances all night.

Leadbelly had the strength of a tiger and the heart of a champion. He was born a champion and died one, struck down by the same disease which paralyzed the great Lou Gehrig. When Leadbelly boasted that he was "king of the twelve-string guitar players of the world," he meant that he had bested every other twelve-string player he had ever met. Like any other master musician, he acquired and polished his technique by hours of daily practice. When his cue came, he sprang rather than walked on stage, his handsome face alight with passion, his whole being dedicated to the conquest of his audience. Professor George Lyman Kittredge, dean of American folklorists, heard him at Harvard in 1934, and whispered, "He's a demon, Lomax, a demon!"

In the Greek sense he was demonic, that is, a man inspired by music and rhythm. Pat Neff, the no-pardon Texas governor, heard him sing and broke all his campaign promises to set Leadbelly free. My father and I recorded him in the Louisiana pen in 1933 and we, too, became possessed by Leadbelly. We carried his pardon appeal record to the Governor of Louisiana, who promptly paroled him. Then we devoted ourselves to his career for twelve months. We were hunting ballads and had met a great folk artist.

His voice in those days was clear, sweet and far-carrying, like a powerful jazz trumpet. Under his magic fingers his battered, green twelve-string guitar "talked like a natural man." The twelve-string had come to him from Mexican street singers in Dallas, but the music Leadbelly created for it was a folk history of East Texas and backwoods-Louisiana slave dance tunes, children's games, songs, cotton-picking chants, field hollers, early ragtime, the western Negro ballads, the early blues. His was the flower of the Southwestern folksong tradition, refined and recreated by a true creative artist.

His first white audiences could not understand a syllable of his broad southern dialect, but he set them on fire with sheer power. When he learned to compromise with Northern ways and "bring his words out plain," the fire was dimmed a bit, but his folk poems seized the imaginations of his hearers and he became the central figure of the developing American folk song movement. Leadbelly was the performer everyone thought of when they wanted honesty, authenticity and power.

His scores of recordings inspired a whole generation of young people in England, where song was a dead art, to take up their guitars and sing again. English "skiffle" is, to a very large extent, a trans-Atlantic reflection of Leadbelly. His favorite songs—"Pick a Bale O' Cotton" and "Goodnight, Irene"—are sung all over the world in scores of languages.

The purpose of this collection is to bring all his songs before that world audience. Certainly, his legend will continue to grow—the legend of a man whose music melted prison bars—the legend of a musician, who, more than anyone else in this century, has brought honesty and passion back into the mainstream of popular song.

Chapter 22

Bluegrass Background:
Folk Music with Overdrive

While the aging voices along Tin Pan Alley grow every day more querulous, and jazzmen wander through the harmonic jungles of Schoenberg
and Stravinsky, grassroots guitar and banjo pickers are playing on the
heartstrings of America. Out of the torrent of folk music that is the backbone of the record business today, the freshest sound comes from the so-
called Bluegrass band—a sort of mountain Dixieland combo in which
the five-string banjo, America's only indigenous folk instrument, carries
the lead like a hot clarinet. The mandolin plays bursts reminiscent of jazz
trumpet choruses; a heavily bowed fiddle supplies trombone-like hoe-
down solos: while a framed guitar and slapped base make up the rhythm
section. Everything goes at top volume, with harmonized choruses
behind a lead singer who hollers in the high, lonesome style beloved in
the American backwoods. The result is folk music in overdrive with a silvery, rippling, pinging sound; the State Department should note that for
virtuosity, fire and speed our best Bluegrass bands can match any Slavic
folk orchestra.

Bluegrass style began in 1945 when Bill Monroe, of the Monroe
Brothers, recruited a quintet that included Earl Scruggs (who had per-
fected a three-finger banjo style now known as "picking scruggs") and
Lester Flatt (a Tennessee guitar picker and singer); Bill led the group with
mandolin and a countertenor voice that hits high notes with the impact
of a Louis Armstrong trumpet. Playing the old-time mountain tunes,
which most hillbilly pros had abandoned, he orchestrated them so brilliantly that the name of the outfit, "Bill Monroe and his Bluegrass Boys,"
became the permanent hallmark of this field. When Scruggs and Flatt
left to form a powerful group of their own. Don Reno joined Monroe,
learned Bluegrass, and departed to found his own fine orchestra, too.
Most of the Bluegrass outfits on Southern radio and TV today have

played with Monroe or one of his disciples—with the noteworthy exception of the Stanley Brothers, who play and sing in a more relaxed and gentle style.

Bluegrass is the first clear-cut orchestral style to appear in the British-American folk tradition in five hundred years: and entirely on its own it is turning back to the great heritage of older tunes that our ancestors brought into the mountains before the American Revolution. A century of isolation in the lonesome hollows of the Appalachians gave them time to combine strains from Scottish and English folk songs and to produce a vigorous pioneer music of their own. The hot Negro square-dance fiddle went early up the creek-bed roads into the hills; then in the mid-nineteenth century came the five-string banjo; early in the twentieth century the guitar was absorbed into the developing tradition. By the time folk-song collectors headed into the mountains looking for ancient ballads, they found a husky, hard-to-kill musical culture as well. Finally, railroads and highways snaked into the backwoods, and mountain folk moved out into urban, industrialized, shook-up America; they were the last among us to experience the breakdown of traditional family patterns, and there ensued an endless stream of sad songs, from "On Top of Old Smoky" to "The Birmingham Jail." Next in popularity were sacred songs and homiletic pieces warning listeners against drink and fast company; and in the late thirties, the favorite theme for displaced hillbillies was "No Letter Today."

Talented mountaineers who wanted to turn professional have had a guaranteed income since the day in 1923 when Ralph Peer skeptically waxed an Atlanta fiddler playing "The Old Hen Cackled and the Rooster's Going to Crow," and Victor sold half-a-million copies to the ready-made white rural audience. Recording companies sent off field crews and made stars of such singers as Jimmie Rodgers, Uncle Dave Macon, Gid Tanner, the Carter family and Roy Acuff.

Countless combinations of hillbillies have coalesced and dispersed before radio microphones since WSB in Atlanta began beaming out mountainy music on its opening day. *Grand Ole Opry* has been broadcasting from Nashville for thirty-three years; the WWVA Jamboree has gone on for twenty-seven. In the beginning, performers sang solo or with one accompanying instrument: but before microphones they felt the need of orchestras, which, while originally crude, developed with the uncritical encouragement of local audiences.

By now there has grown up a generation of hillbilly musicians who can play anything in any key, and their crowning accomplishment is Bluegrass. When the fresh sound of New Orleans Dixieland combos hit the cities some fifty years ago, it made a musical revolution first in America, then the world. Today we have a new kind of orchestra suitable for accompanying the frontier tunes with which America has fallen in love. And now anything can happen.

Chapter 23

Getting to Know Folk Music

Carroll Calkins with Alan Lomax

Folk songs and singing are more popular than ever before. But unless we learn to distinguish the real from commercial versions, we will never know the world of emotion and experience from which folk music comes.

This is the stuff of folk music. The farther it gets from such roots, the less impact it has.

Into the rising tide of interest in folk music I would like to toss a bottle with a note. The message is this: Let's not forget that there's more to this music than first meets the ear.

There are some fine performers singing and playing folk songs today. And some of these timeless songs are among the most popular in the land. Harry Belafonte, the Kingston Trio, The Tarriers, Eddy Arnold, Frankie Laine, and many other artists are bringing folk songs to a wider audience than they have ever had before. I suppose that on Belafonte's recent television program more people heard "John Henry" in three minutes than had heard it in the previous ten years. To anyone interested in folk music this should be all to the good. The more widely it is heard, the better—except for one important point.

The popularization of a folk song is, in effect, a translation from one language into another and, as usual, something is lost in the process. Most of us like the popularized versions because they are engaging tunes in the familiar musical language of the popular song. The tunes are melodic, the harmonies close, the beat jazzy and strong, and the musicians are polished performers—by our standards. But this is not the musical idiom in which these songs developed.

In its original form, American folk music speaks a language that offers far greater rewards than just pleasant listening. After you have heard your fill of the popular versions, you are ready for the next step—

the step toward the original source of our folk music. This is where the real payoff is, if you know how to listen for it.

Under the smooth bland surface of the popularized folk songs lies a bubbling stew of work songs, country blues, field hollers, hobo songs, prairie songs, spirituals, hoedowns, prison songs, and a few unknown ingredients. This is the varied voice of our people crying out because they have something personal to say. Originally the folk singer was more interested in telling a story, in venting his feelings through music, than in performing for someone else. He cried out in the only way he knew. It might be a cry of sadness or of joy, but it came from deep inside. In its several regions American folk music speaks in the musical tradition of the people; it is a common bond of group feeling.

The songs that best expressed the feelings of a people were repeated by their singers. Passed on by word of mouth, they were constantly altered by slips of memory and the vagaries of fancy. They became communal compositions, revealing intense personal feeling as well as the unconscious feelings of whole peoples. The cowboys sang about the cattle camps, hobos sang of life on the road. Some of the Southern mountaineers sang the British songs they learned from their ancestors.

These early songs had no promotion budget. There were no publicity departments pushing them. They lived only by virtue of their usefulness to the singer. If they touched something universally true in his culture and served as a means of communication between singer and audience, they were repeated. The songs we hear today are those that have weathered this democratic process.

To some of us outside the environment in which they developed, these songs are the voice of other worlds. As we learn to listen, we begin to understand something of the spirit of the time and place from which they came. To many of us, this music is a familiar part of our own family background.

When the popular performer of today sings a folk song, he holds up a mirror that reflects a good deal of our own familiar world. He shows us what he thinks we want to see. But the music of the grassroots folk singer is like a picture in a frame that shows the way it was, or is, in America for him and his people. These songs last because they say something that was important in the past and still has meaning.

When you first hear some of the country performers, you may be thrown off by the unusual sounds. As we said, they speak a different musical language. But the language is *theirs*, and these people are artists among their peers. Their performance is a direct reflection of the taste, standards, and opportunities of their culture. To brush them off as crude and repetitive is to close one's mind to a rich slice of life as it was—and is.

Part of the joy of listening to some of the great folk singers, such as Leadbelly, Woody Guthrie, Blind Lemon Jefferson, and Big Bill Broonzy, is the respect one develops for them just for being what they are. They were true to themselves and their rural environment just as Bobby Darin and Frank Sinatra are true to their urban environment.

Beyond respect for the performer, there's the opportunity for personal involvement in what we hear. This calls for attention and creative thinking on the listener's part. This involvement, this opportunity for mental participation by the audience, is a part of every art that survives.

Here's an example of how a folk song can give a listener a chance to use his imagination. The song is "Grizzly Bear" (on *Folksongs USA* by Folkways Records). It is sung, without accompaniment, by a group of Negro convicts in a Southern prison camp. They sing because crying won't help. The call and response pattern of the song welds them together in spirit. The words are ambiguous, but the meaning to the individuals gives them some relief in a miserable life. The grizzly bear, of which they sing, may be the jailer, the boss, the system that oppresses them. The song warns of the bear and ridicules him too. Sung as the guards stand by, it is a statement of bitter humor and the unquenchable spirit of man. The singing has guts because that's where it comes from. The listener who wonders about these men, why they sing as they do, and what they are really saying is in touch with something he will never get from performers who sing only what they think he wants to hear.

Another example: The music of the Southern mountains tells much about the way of life in that remote back country. When you hear the virtuosity of Earl Scruggs on the 5-string banjo, or the unique power and excitement of the Bluegrass bands (such as the Stoney Mountain Boys), or the sweet compelling voice of Jean Ritchie singing the songs of her mountain family, you realize how much this homemade music is a part of their life. It is the musical tradition of the pioneer society and it still endures right here in our own country.

In our lives we have television, record players, radio, tape recorders, and probably a piano and other instruments. And few of us have time really to use all these things. But in many cabins in the Southern hills the voices of the family and the banjo, fiddle, or guitar hanging on the wall are the instruments that give them the music they prefer to play. They are not conformists to the automatic machine-age culture.

There is always time for music, and these people are steeped in it from childhood. It's no wonder they play with spirit and authority. The creative listener will cherish a glimpse of this lonely, independent, intimate way of family life as well as enjoy the music that reveals it.

HOW CAN YOU TELL THEM APART?

There's no hard fast line between the "authentic" folk performance and the commercial one. Some performers do both. To the listener the dividing line doesn't matter. The important thing is to know that there is music with a level of interest beyond its sound. It is the same with folk music as with any true art. If the listener applies himself to understanding, his taste will develop and his increasing discrimination will be a continuing source of pleasure. He will find the authentic for himself. And he will find that our indigenous music is the equal of that of Scotland, the Balkans, or any other part of Europe.

American folk songs are, above all else, American. They are a mixture of English, Scottish, Irish, French, and African influences stirred together in a way that could happen only in this magnificently heterogeneous country. This music belongs only to us, because only in America are there so many different cultures mixed together. The songs are the oral history of our country. They reveal traditions and beliefs that we cannot discover in any other way. They are the honest voice of people saying, "This is what I think is important, this is my place in the world, this is how I feel about being here." These historical insights are not just interpretations by researchers; they are the words of those who were there. There's value in this far beyond the music. You may find out for yourself—if you listen with your heart.

SOME RECORDS THAT SHOW THE WAY

Because this is the music of the people, it comes from many places and differs as the people differ. Accurate classification is the scholar's task. But, to help a stranger find his way into the vast field of American folk music, the following list of records is divided into five groupings. Old English traditional, blues and work songs, industrial and occupational ballads, regional songs, collections on one record.

This listing is, admittedly, a small sample of the available records (all 12–inch LPs, except as noted). But each of these has that quality of emotion and personal involvement which is the heart and soul of folk music.

TRADITIONAL SONGS AND BALLADS

These are the songs from which much of our American folk music comes. They were originally news and gossip set to music. Today they are a delightful musical reminder of the past as well as comments on the eternal nature of man.

· *The Unquiet Grave*, American Tragic Ballads by Andrew Roman Sommers.
Folkways   FP 64

· *Jean Ritchie.*
Elektra   125

· *Classic Scots Ballads*. Ewan MacColl with Peggy Seeger.
Tradition   TLD 1015

· *The Real McCoy*, Irish Folk Songs by Sam Hinton.
Decca   DL 8579

BLUES AND WORK SONGS

This is Negro music, and no one else can sing it with the same authority. It is a direct reaction to the harsh experiences of their lives. But their unquenchable spirit and love of life is a part of even the saddest songs. This is a deeply touching form of musical communication. It is also the tap root of American jazz.

· *Take This Hammer*, Leadbelly (Huddie Ledbetter). (10-inch LP)
Folkways   2004

· *Lightnin' Hopkins*, Country Blues.
Tradition   TLP 1035

· *Blues in the Mississippi Night.*
United Artists   UAL 4027

· *The Country Blues.*
RBF Records   RF 1

· *Folk Songs of Sonny Terry and Brownie McGhee.*
Roulette   R 25074

· *Big Bill Broonzy*, The Blues.
Emarcy   MG 36137

· *Negro Prison Songs.*
Tradition   TLP 1020

· *Negro Prison Camp Work Songs.*
Folkways   P 475

REGIONAL FOLK MUSIC

These are songs that give you the flavor of the place where they were
(and often still are) a vital part of everyday life. Anyone can sing a mountain song or a ballad of the Dust Bowl, but only those who have a deep
feeling for the place of which they sing can really tell you the truth
about it.

· *Talking Dust Bowl*, Woody Guthrie. (10-inch LP)
Folkways   FA 2011

· *Smoky Mt. Ballads*, Bascom Lamar Lunsford. (10-inch LP)
Folkways   FP 40

· *Saturday Night and Sunday Too*, Jean Ritchie.
Riverside   RLP 12–620

· *Instrumental Music of the Southern Appalachians.*
Traditional   TLP 1007

· *Folk Songs from the Bluegrass*, The Stoney Mountain Boys.
United Artists   UAL 3049

· *Mountain Music Bluegrass Style.*
Folkways   FA 2318

· *Banjo Songs of the Southern Mountains.*
Riverside   RLP 12–610

INDUSTRIAL AND OCCUPATIONAL SONGS

The songs of cowboys, sailors, and railroad workers tell a lot about
the life they lead and the work they do. The union songs remind us that
the unions were created to fight oppression and that they have done
wonders in this direction. These songs, and the people who sing them on
these records, played an important part in the trade union movement.

· *900 Miles and Other Railroad Songs*, Cisco Houston. (10-inch LP)
Folkways   FA 2013

- *Cowboy Ballads*, Cisco Houston. (10-inch LP)
  Folkways   FA 2022

- *The Cowboy. His Songs, Ballads, and Brag Talk*, Harry Jackson.
  Folkways   FH 5723

- *Blow Boys Blow*. Songs of the Sea. Ewan MacColl, A. L. Lloyd.
  Tradition   TLP 1026

- *American Industrial Ballads*, Peter Seeger.
  Folkways   FH 5251

- *Talking Union and other Union Songs*. Peter Seeger and chorus.
  Folkways   FP 85–1

FOLK SONG COLLECTIONS

These records offer the best way to hear a variety of folk songs from different walks of life. They are a good introduction to the field. The first three include a variety of music and performers on each record. The last two are one-man shows with a variety of songs.

- *Folk Music USA*.
  Folkways   FE 4530

- *Folk Song Festival at Carnegie Hall*.
  United Artists   UAL 3050

- *Folk Festival at Newport (Vol. 3)*.
  Vanguard   URS 9064

- *Carl Sandburg, Flat Rock Ballads*.
  Columbia   ML 5339

- *The Wilderness Road and Jimmy Driftwood*.
  RCA Victor   LPM 1994

BOOKS FOR SINGERS

Here are four excellent books of folk songs and a magazine.

- *Fireside Book of Folk Songs*, edited by Margaret Bradford Boni and Norman Lloyd. Simon & Schuster, $5.

- *The American Songbag*, Carl Sandburg. Harcourt Brace and Company, $5.75.

· *Best Loved American Folk Songs*, John and Alan Lomax. Grosset and Dunlap, $4.95.

· *The People's Song Book*. Sing Out Inc., $1.75.

· *Sing Out!* The Folk Song Magazine. Sing Out Inc., 121 W. 47th St., New York City. Sold for 50 cents a copy, $2.50 a year.

Chapter 24

Folk Song Traditions Are All Around Us

In the last few years many young people have asked me, "How can I begin in the field of folk music?"—and I realize that this is a question which a very large number of college and high school students are asking themselves today.

Most of these people would like to follow in the footsteps of Peter Seeger and other successful folk song singers. Others would like to make a serious study of the field. One can suggest that the performers study authentic recordings, meanwhile learning instrumental technique from real experts like Frank Hamilton and Bess Hawes. For the latter, there are courses of study at Indiana University, Pennsylvania University, University of Southern California, and other places. Information about such courses can be obtained by writing to the Secretary of the American Folklore Society, University of Pennsylvania, Philadelphia, Pa.

In reality, however, the answer for both groups lies deeper than any course of instruction. It seems to me that in folklore, more than in any other of the arts, the performer or student must have a devotion to the material which is akin to love, and a very selfless love at that. Performers who basically exploit the songs they know merely for gain or for ego satisfaction somehow always miss the boat, no matter how talented they are. Even the last decade of the folk song revival is full of examples of performers who stop short of thoroughly learning one of the arts of folksong, and who become sterile. There are others one can think of who used this partial skill for a career and then became bored or lost their public. I think it would be safe to say that only those performers who have modestly and patiently identified themselves with some one or two authentic traditional styles have continued to grow. Here one would think of the Seegers, the New Lost City Ramblers, Ewan MacColl. This group appears to be growing now.

Almost the same thing could be said of the scholars in the field. Those to whom folk song has been largely a source for publication and thus academic advancement have gradually fallen out of tune with a field which, in truth, presents perhaps the most difficult and subtle problems of any branch of the humanities.

Devotion to folk song, whether in performance or study, demands one thing first. This is contact with folk song tradition itself. In a word, some sort of collecting experience. Folk song lives in a rather mysterious world close to the heart of the human community and it is only through an extended and serious contact with living folk tradition that it can be understood. A folk song expert without field experience is like a Marine botanist who never observed life under the surface of the sea.

Many of the enthusiasts of this generation are aware of this dilemma and they say, "But how, if I'm not born in a community where folk song is a part of everyday life, or I cannot afford to go to the Kentucky mountains, can I acquire this experience?" The answer is that folk song traditions are all around us. I've never been anywhere that I did not find new material and new traditions and unknown folk performers who desperately needed to be discovered and brought to an audience.

The truth is that the Southern mountains, though there is still much to be discovered there, have received a disproportionate amount of attention. The great and almost entirely unknown field in America is situated precisely in the areas where most of the young singer-students live. That is, in the big cities of the United States—in the folk song traditions of the many non-English speaking minorities in this country.

Every group of people who came to America did roughly the same thing as the Scotch-Irish who settled in the Appalachian highlands. They attempted to perpetuate the culture they had brought with them and at the same time they changed it to suit their new environment. We know something about the folk musics of the Spanish people of the Southwest, the French of Canada, the Germans of Pennsylvania, and the Yiddish group of New York, but in spite of many folk festivals and some work by scholars little is known about the musical traditions of millions of other Americans who come from Italian, Hungarian, Wend, Syrian and scores of other backgrounds. Because there is no real national support for folk song collecting and there seems to be no prospect of any the likelihood is that we will never know and enjoy this rich treasure of international song unless a group of devoted and tireless collectors tackle the job of studying it.

I will confess that I am writing this piece as a challenge to the audience of *Sing Out*, because in this audience there are certainly the people to do this important job. To you who simply enjoy singing folk songs for your own pleasure and for the pleasure of your friends I have no more to say than "Welcome aboard. Folk song is fun and it's fine that you're singing and listening and learning." But to the professional, or those who are thinking of being professional, I suggest that you have obligations and since the field is really so little known these are the obligations of pioneers. There's no trick today if you work hard at it, in following in the footsteps of Leadbelly, Guthrie and Jean Ritchie, so far as their public careers are concerned. But to match them in the seriousness and originality of their contribution to American life the young city professional should help to bring new material and authentic new style to light.

One of the best ways of doing this is in setting out to document, record and present an unknown aspect of our rich and complex tradition. Tony Schwartz, in his records on New York City, has shown us how much can be done by one person, but there are worlds beyond worlds to be discovered and understood. At the Library of Congress we only scratched the surface. It remains for the young professional of this generation to tell the whole story of our folk culture. I can promise you that by collecting and mastering some neglected corner of the vast world of folk song you will find the key to the whole field.

Chapter 25

The Good and the Beautiful in Folksong[1]

Singing is an act of communication and therefore can be studied as behavior. Since a folk song is transmitted orally by all or most members of a culture, generation after generation, it represents an extremely high consensus about patterns of meaning and behavior of cultural rather than individual significance. In this discussion of the good and the beautiful, the fit of song performance behavior and cultural norms will be examined transculturally, and the terms of the argument, therefore, must be extremely general. In order to begin on somewhat familiar ground, it will first be suggested that there is not only a *fit* between performance behavior and culture pattern, but between these two and the emotional set embedded in them.

I once asked Vera Hall, one of the best of Southern Negro singers—an Alabama washerwoman, gentle, liquid-voiced, and a song leader in the folk Baptist church—what the word "chariot" meant in the song, "Swing Low Sweet Chariot." " . . . Chayot, chayot," she shut her eyes and smiled, "Chaayot. It swing way down, swing way down low an' it pick you up an' it ca' you off way up yonder where evy'thing sweet—it a swee-eet chayot!" This is a statement about ecstasy and about nurturance. Vera said about her childhood lover: "When us was right small I used to let him sorta touch me. And maybe you think it wasn't sweet by us bein' small? I often remembers it now and think to myself that bein' married wasn' no sweeter than when I was a little girl down back of the barn with Dudley . . . " She spoke in similar terms about her husband: "I didn' know you could be married to a man and he be as good to you as your mother was. My mother was better to me than anyone in the world I *thought*. But after I got married I thought my husband was more better to me than my mama was . . . "

It was Vera who initiated and coaxed into being the many-threaded, unified sound of the Negro spiritual among her neighbors in church.

Their habitual performance model may be described as: choral, integrated, and multi-parted. Most components of this spiritual singing style reinforce its cohesive effect:

a) It is refrain-filled, so that a group can easily catch the words and join in.
b) Its melodies are brief and repetitious, so that the melodic material provides no obstacle to group participation.
c) It is rhythmically steady, with a strong beat pattern, so that anyone can get the swing and easily follow the meter.
d) It is mellow voiced—a psychological cue inviting and welcoming others.

Vera was the right leader for this groupy, cohesive, non-specific singing style; "Chariot," to Vera, was not *first* a label on a visual image and *then* a feeling; it was a feeling about being nurtured and loved and being unabashedly together with others, the very feeling that the integrated style model of the spiritual seems to produce among its participants.

The come-all-ye ballad—the most common form in the tradition of the Northeast—provides a contrastive American folksong model. When I asked a bluff old lumberjack why he liked one of his ballads, he bellowed, "That there song is as true as steel. Everything in there happened just like I said it." When I asked what made a good bunkhouse singer, he was equally emphatic. "Why, a feller that has loud, clear voice so you can *hear* him—a man that can speak his words out plain so you can understand *what* he's singing about—and a fellow that *remembers* all the words."

Such is a folk definition of the underpinnings of the come-all-ye style that has dominated ballad-making in Britain and America for the last three centuries. "The Jam on Gerry's Rocks" is an American classic in this vein, purporting to relate the who, what, where, and when of the fate of a young riverman who broke a log-jam on a river and was drowned in the rush of the logs. Although old-timers swore they knew where this happened, the most patient research by scholars has never located Gerry's Rocks. In this, as in the cases of other American come-all-ye's, a traditional theme or fantasy pattern is presented in a factual, reportorial style, as if it were literal truth.

A ballad-hunting friend of mine, after weeks of search, finally found the one man in the community who knew a long narrative song that recounted "The Wreck of the Lady L," or some similar matter. The man was induced to sing. He assumed a traditional singing posture—turning his face to the wall, clasping his hands on his lap—and began. After a few verses his wife ran in, beating a dishpan and screaming: "It's a lie, it's a lie, the whole damn thing's a rotten lie." It did no good for my scholar friend to point out that all the facts of the disaster had been reported in a newspaper. The lady was protesting another matter. In her coastal world, the men did most of the public singing. Their songs dwelt upon the dangers of a seamen's life, and their implicit statement was: "We men risk our lives for you in a cold, watery world, while you women sit home safe and warm." The wife with the dishpan wanted the visitor to know there was another side to this story.

The themes of parting and of masculine heroism so dominate the ballads of the eighteenth- and nineteenth-century expansionist English world as to form a single theme, a single dream. A young man leaves his safe home and his women, faces danger or discomfort alone and among strangers—a universal experience of the country boy in an expanding semi-industrialized world, as Erikson recognized.[2] These ballads were tales of separation anxiety—disguised as fact, but vengeful, too—and the Newfoundland housewife probably felt this in her own way. So did her husband who, like all his fellows, kept his eyes tight shut as he sang. If he had opened them or allowed expression to creep into his face, he might have burst into tears.

	N.W. Europe	U.S. & Canada	World
Sung in solo to a silent audience	65%	67	40
Text laden	55	81	39
Clearly enunciated	81	100	60
Simple strophe	66	78	28
Little ornamentation	28	16	43
In simple meter	70	67	41
Unaccompanied	88	41	42

n = 2527.

In the ballad, nothing should impede or hinder the progress of the tale. In the ballad-circle round the hearth, no one should interfere with the solo singer's temporary but exclusive dominance of the communication space. Interrupt such a singer and he may sulk and refuse to go on. This relation of singer to audience is the social aspect of a specialized performance type which shapes most of the song performance of Western Europe. The table above indicates the dominance of this type in Europe and North America and its relative infrequency in the rest of the world. The figures given are the mean cantometric scores for these traits for northwestern Europe, the United States and Canada, and the world.

The two models proposed, the Afro- and the Euro-American, are not new developments. Our computer similarity program shows them to be distant from each other, yet comparison of their profiles to those from all other world areas shows that the Afro-American is closest to the African and the Yankee is closest to the northwestern European profile. This suggests that these are colonial singing styles, extensions into the New World of well-established patterns of performance.

An inspection of this table shows that: (1) USA-C is very similar to northwestern Europe, less similar to Africa and East Asia, and not similar to Plains song style. (2) Afro-America is similar to Guinea Coast, less similar to the two European areas, and not similar to Plains or East Asia. East Asia has a weak similarity to Europe and not to the others; Plains only to itself, so far as the areas examined are concerned. These similarity statements are the product of the comparison of profiles.

	US	NWE	AA	GC	PI	EA
U.S.A., Canada	100	84	74	72	...	70
N.W. Europe	84	100	74	76	...	66
Afro-America	74	76	100	86	...	...
Guinea Coast	71	71	86	100	...	...
Plains Indians	...	...	...	...	100	...
East Asia	70	66	...	...	...	100

(Blanks are for similarities which rank below the first quartile.) Similarity table giving percent overall similarity between cantometric profiles for areas from Europe and Africa, with two other areas for contrast.

Several questions arise. Do these performance structures suitably represent contrastive life styles? If so, should the continuance of these contrastive matched pairs in the New World be described as adaptive or due merely to cultural lag? We are concerned here with perhaps the most important question that relates to the arts, to style. My thesis is that esthetic style—the structural aspect of the beautiful—has a positive and dynamic relationship to the socially normative—the structural aspect of the good. This proposition will first be tested by comparing descriptive profiles of West Europe and Africa in terms of song style and social layout.

The West European ballad style comes from a culture area of small families dwelling in single households, of individual ownership, of lone producers and free enterprisers, and of respect for the specialist. In this world of competition and of small group organization, marriage and, indeed, all joint enterprises are matters of contract in which each individual's contribution and share are spelled out. Here it is obligatory for the specialist in song or work to assume control of an operation and for group members to subordinate themselves to him out of respect for his special knowledge or skill.

In the ballad circle, one singer after another assumes control of the communication space for long periods, as does the Western political speaker, and presents a seemingly factual account of events, straightforwardly put, often quoting what the actors are purported to have said to each other. This prosy, factual solo style reinforces the social norms of a complex, highly segmented, essentially egalitarian society, where social bonds are so often matters of contract between two individuals. Both these patterns were highly adaptive on the American frontier, where single individuals or families moved into the wilderness ("I am a poor wayfaring stranger, looking down that lonesome road . . . ") and formed a network of log cabin homesteads and jerry-built communities where every man and every family could sink or swim on their own. The themes of the pioneer, solo, unaccompanied style were loneliness, sexual frustration, and masculine heroism—a suitable preparation for a life in which austerity, alienation, and competition were normal experience.

The integrated African style comes from an area in which a system of polygynous clan lineages, based on hoe agriculture and animal husbandry had exploded across an almost empty continent in a matter of centuries. Teams of blood brothers took land and cleared it, their sets of wives planting and harvesting temporary gardens and producing new crops of babies to supply the ever-expanding labor force. Fecundity of the ancestral blood line—which brought more land under cultivation, more hands for labor, power to the clan village, power to the clan alliance—was the good in these African cultures. Sexual proficiency was inculcated in song and dance, and sexually-oriented behavior heightened the excitation level of all activities, work included. Ritual and recreation involved groups of active and yet highly coordinated individuals. It is rare in African performance for one person to sing or dance alone for more than a few seconds. His individualized display is interrupted, supported, seconded by the group present. African performance style is sensual and multi-leveled, i.e., polyphonic and polyrhythmic. These factors of sensuality and integration were appropriate statements for a culture of clan lineages, armed only with hoes and adzes, where increase of production depended upon the involvement and the increase of the total available labor force (men and women) in disciplined and cooperative action.

This African pattern was a great success in the American tropical and subtropical slave plantation areas. It peopled the fertile lowlands. Polygyny and the mother-child family continued in slave quarter and slum as serial monogamy. Coordinated group activity, laced with rhythm and sensuality, won productive victories in the fields and souls for the only institution permitted the Negro, the church. The church reinforced a lesson more sternly taught by the ruthless white establishment, that passivity was the key to personal survival. When Martin Luther King and Bob Moses combined these themes (collective decision-making, bisexual mass meetings, rhythmic singing of passive resistance slogans) the Negro became politically effective for the first time in American history.

In a test on these two cases, song style seems to mirror and support adaptive pattern. As a first guess, then, one may view the function of song style as a reinforcement of those norms of social interaction which are adaptive. I shall define the good, in behavioral terms, as the structure of adaptive interaction norms. The beautiful, then, will be defined as the appropriate, matching communication structure which reinforces these adaptive norms. The good and the beautiful, in this view, are two sides of the same coin, both to be discovered in the structure of observed behavior in culture. This hypothesis must then be tested cross-culturally and within a scalar, evolutionary framework on a number of song structures. Esthetics will, in this approach, become a study of the suitable in its dynamic relationship to the development of man. The special province of folklore will then become social esthetics: only in traditional tales, songs, dance, and design patterns does there exist such dependable evidence of the activity of man in choosing symbolic systems suitable to his economic and social condition.

Irving Child's careful study of the reaction of two teams of experts (one American, one African) to a set of African masks shows that the perception of the more beautiful overleaps culture barriers.[3] I suspect that the art experts in the Yale study recognized the "more suitable" cross-culturally, without being able to specify how they did this. The source of difficulty in this, as in many Western esthetic studies, is that it relies on reports of reactions to visual symbols. We are thus four steps away from behavior in context. Once painting lived on the body, sculpture was something which was used and handled, architecture was the result of cooperative labor, and literature was recited or danced. In civilization, all these arts have become representational and a dirty problem for the behavioral sciences. On the contrary, song and dance are acts that may be recorded anywhere as performed, and then studied as events which structure the relations of human actors in cultural context. Such structures may be compared to more everyday behaviors. From the pairs of song performance and social interaction, a series of stable, symbolic functions can be established.

All communication rests upon the redundancy principle and may be rated by the degree of redundancy. Speech and song are produced by the same organs, conform to the same linguistic regularities (grammar, vocabulary, etc.) and use the same given communication modes—pitch, stress, duration, speed, timbre, segmentation, meter, melody, volume, register, social ordering, etc. All these features are treated far more repetitively and formally in song than in speech. Indeed, song, where redundancy appears at all or most levels simultaneously, may be both recognized and defined as the most redundant form of vocal communication.

The high redundancy level of song has many consequences. Song is essentially louder and more arresting than speech. It shouts across social space and across human time as well, since its formal patterns are both emphatic and easy to remember. In song, groups of people easily phonate together and in coordination—a very rare speech event which adds to the social weight of the statement. Song, like other forms of folklore, establishes and maintains group consensus about a multitude of human concerns across time.

This highly redundant form of phonation most often appears in ritual contexts—funerals and weddings, religious, initiation, and political ceremonies, and the like, where the continuity of a culture is reinforced or reinstated for the entire community—or in situations where formal interpersonal relations prevail, such as work, courtship, and dancing. Song thus seems to function principally as a way of organizing group behavior and group response in public situations. It seems to be a group, rather than a personalized, communication. The serenade alerts the neighbors to a young man's sexual interest in a young woman. The sung soliloquy, except in the case of very young children, always seems to be drawn from the public musical tradition. This private singing probably serves to alleviate the pain of isolation by reminding the singer of his most pleasant, or anxiety-filled, or everyday social relationships.

In terms of cantometric measurement, at least, sung performance varies less by function than by culture area. In simple culture one usually finds only one or two basic performance models which are employed again and again for many functional categories. These interaction models for the singing group seem to mirror the norms of interpersonal behavior that are basic in a culture region. Song transmits this normative information efficiently because of its multi-level redundancy and formality. Thus, three essential symbol functions reach their peak in song: speed, total recall, and summation. A familiar melody or fragment thereof heard out of context can recapture the whole of a culture pattern. Most of this information in song goes "on the air" from a good recording. Thus the potential of an archive of field recordings as a body of objective data about the social process is potentially unsurpassed. The problem of cantometric research was to begin to locate the channels in song recorded performance which transmitted information about social norms. Cantometric research began with some guesses about where indicators of cultural structure were located in song performance:

A. About social ordering—in the social organization of the performing group.
B. About information flow—in the information rate of the performance.
C. About important role models—in the vocal stance employed.

A rating sheet was designed by Victor Grauer and myself so that a trained observer might consistently record his judgment about many levels of the song performance. Consensus tests on this rating system indicate that agreement between judges on most parameters is 80 percent or better and that naive judgement may be trained to achieve this level of consensus on at least half the system in a matter of a few days.

It will be hoped that the reader will not form his judgment about the structure and methods of cantometrics from this extremely summary presentation. The cantometrics coding book and much other necessary methodological information will be presented in other publications. Here the intent is only to summarize the approach in order to indicate the order and nature of the findings that are potential in it. This is what was done:

1) A coding book[4] of rigorous definitions of the rating parameter was written and used to establish conformity between the two raters.
2) Ten or more songs recorded in the field, usually by anthropologists or ethnomusicologists, were rated for each of 233 cultures. These represented 56 major culture areas from the 6 main culture regions as defined by George P. Murdock's *Ethnographic Atlas*.[5] For all 233 cultures, we had rated information about subsistence type and social structure from the same source, so that cross-cultural correlations between song performance pattern and cultural structure were possible.
3) Both bodies of information were computerized and programs were designed for its study.

The programmer and IBM printer, in due course, presented this data in many forms convenient for study:

1) In rank order by trait, such that it could immediately be seen which regions areas, or cultures rated highest in regard to polyphony, strophic form, yodel, or any other of a large number of characteristics of song performance.
2) Computer maps of trait clusters such that a student can see the distribution of the song type he wishes to study on a world map.
3) Correlation programs such that the coincidence of any set of song traits (for example, highly ornamented, text heavy, melismatic, rubato) with any set of cultural attributes available in Murdock (for example, highly stratified, large cities, and exclusive inheritance) might be examined statistically.
4) Profiles of culture by song trait; for instance, characterization in terms of eighty Murdock ratings of all the societies in which polyphony is frequent. In this way, the investigator may see which features of social structure are connected with any given musical trait.
5) A similarity program which compares the level of similarity between two profiles of the order of complexity of those [these charts are not included].

The cantometric similarity program grouped the fifty-six areas into nine large, homogeneous, though interrelated, style regions that correspond to the main distributions of culture as ethnologists see the matter. For example, although real differences show up (as between Plains and Pueblo Indian style) all North Amerindian cultures and culture areas cluster together when compared to the rest of the world. As a region, North Amerindia shows closest similarity to South American Indian areas. Next in order, the styles of both South and North American relate to Siberian primitive song. This ordering corresponds to the known historical movement of peoples out of Siberia and into the Americas, millennia ago.

The similarity figures trace the well-known and recent tracks of migration from Western Europe into the New World and from West Africa into the same area. They reaffirm the existence and significance for history of the area of old, high imperial culture that girdles Asia from Japan around through southeast Asia, India, and across the Middle East and North Africa into the southern edge of Europe. More such examples would simply re-emphasize the point that song performance, as defined in cantometric terms, seems (1) to be a stable cultural element, (2) to vary by culture type, and (3) to change drastically only with major shifts of culture pattern.

The next step in our procedure was to see against what frames of social structure song style characterizers varied. After considerable testing, two related scales have turned out to be most useful: social complexity and economic type. The size of the sample enabled us to use the following set of main subsistence types, devised by Dr. Conrad Arensberg and myself:

1) Collectors—cultures that subsist mainly by gathering food
2) Game Producers—cultures that mainly subsist by hunting and fishing
3) Incipient Agriculture—hoe or dibble agriculture, without domesticated animals
4) Cultivators—hoe agriculture with domestication
5) Pastoralists—specialized, nomadic animal husbandry
6) Horticulture—specialized agriculture, animal husbandry, specialized fishing
7) Plough agriculture—agriculture with the plough and fixed fields
8) Irrigation—agriculture with the plough, fixed fields, and large irrigation works

This scale of specialization and productive range proves to be a dependable scale of social complexity as well since, on the whole, the following factors increase along it: (1) Task complexity, (2) Specialization of labor, (3) Size and stability of settlement, (4) Social hierarchies—class and caste systems. As the productive system grows more specialized and complex, so, too, do other orders of social relations. Every human act and relationship must be more sharply defined. Song style seems to be a guide as to how specific a statement is appropriate at a given complexity level. From cantometric ratings it appears that there is a steady increase in the amount of new text (as against repetitions or use of nonsense) and in precision or clarity of enunciation of consonants, along this scale of subsistence type.

This joined set of factors we call the *explicit* or *specific* set. The main song style found in Western Europe—solo and specific—turns out to be a member of a much more general type, which is most common among complex producers and scarcely found at all among simple producers. Exclusive and explicit dominance of the communication space seems to be a generalized stylistic feature among complex producers.

Parameters relating to non-specificity decrease along this same scale even more sharply: repetition of text, slurred enunciation, and wide musical intervals.

Certain other parameters, unitary tonal blend of chorus, rhythmic coordination of the chorus, and polyphony—all factors relating to the cohesiveness of the group—reach their peak among the non-complex agriculturists, principally among the gardeners of Africa, Oceania, and the New World, as well as among some collectors.

The integrated song style we have called African then forms one aspect of larger singing style, most common among gardeners in Oceania *as well as* Africa.

Using cantometric measures, which relate to the way in which singers structure their performances, it is possible to locate all cultures on scales relating to degree and kind of complexity of statement and degree and kind of integration in presenting the statement. Many combinations of these modes are theoretically possible. A handful of performance models, however, account for most of the songs we have heard. Each one of them occurs most prominently at some level of complexity and production type and may be accounted for by reference to those social scales. In this paper, examples of six of these song style models will be presented, the suitability of each to its adaptive level will be suggested, and the statistical relationship of each of these states to a particular productive stage will be established. Since these six song styles delimit an evolutionary scale, it may then be proposed that, for each stage of human development, specialized communication styles emerge which are appropriate for the main adaptive behavior patterns found there. This will be the second of the tests of the notion that the good and the beautiful may be defined, in interaction terms, as a pair consisting of the adaptive and the suitable.

1) Style 1. Solo and non-specific—an unaccompanied, repetitive solo chant, with slurred enunciation, utilizing many wide intervals. This model, in which an individual expresses himself without reference to social structure or verbal signification, is found almost exclusively among hunters, fishers, primitive reindeer herders, and collectors, who live and work in very loosely-bonded and temporary bands and teams where, in fact, individuals spend a great deal of time alone in the wild. Chart 6 [not included] shows that this song style is strongly connected to simpler productive modes (chi square significance level for this relationship is .001) and that it virtually disappears in complex culture. The peaks noted at the pastoral (PC) level are due to the importance of this manner of lalling among the reindeer herders of Siberia. Among the Lapps of Norway, it is the exclusive mode of singing and is called "yoiking." Of course, we westerners lall to ourselves somewhat in this fashion, but not in public.

2) Style 2. Choral, acephalous, non-specific—a choral form of Style 1. Every member of the group phonates independently and somewhat out of synchrony with his fellows. The effect is like a mob scene, like birds singing in a bush or monkeys chattering in a tree. This may well be the earliest model for joint phonation. It is found principally among simple producers, especially collectors, who frequently live in acephalous bands or scattered habitations; tasks are simple, work teams are unstable. Altogether, social bonds are minimal. Again, this style is virtually non-existent among complex producers.

3) Style 3. Choral, acephalous, non-specific, and integrated. This structure is like Style 2 in all respects save one—integration. Here it belongs at the top of all world ranks—in tonal and rhythmic unity and in the variety of integrated levels present, for it is both polyrhythmic and polyphonic. It is the fashion of singing found

among the Pygmies and Bushmen of Africa and may be the first, as well as the most perfect, of integrated styles. Ethnologists who have lived with the African Hunters say that the main and almost only social bond is total sharing of all resources and intra-supportive behavior. There is no doubt about the fact that both in story and song they use the same communication model—a model so supportive, so tightly bonded, that leader and follower, call and response, are difficult to distinguish. The choral acephalous types (2 and 3) are generally sung in polyphonic counterpoint. In fact, counterpoint is more common in the songs of gatherers than at any other stage of human development prior to the age of Bach. Thus, counterpoint seems not to have been a late invention of high cultures, but one of the first musical discoveries.

4) Style 4. Unison, non-specific, poorly integrated. This style is most prevalent among hunters and fishers, and next most common among incipient agriculturalists (still dependent on extractive activities). Its non-specificity represents the common understanding of tasks and social relationships which unite the people of the simple tribal societies. Its individualized organization stands for the impermanent and individualized ordering of work teams and other social relations that generally prevail among hunters, fishers, and incipient producers. Furthermore, these are generally masculine societies where all ritual and all music-making is dominated by men, acting out an aggressive role—singing loudly, forcefully, and noisily. Loudness, forcefulness, and vocal harshness occur more frequently in male performances, transculturally, than in female singing. Performances of this type—small groups phonating non-specifically and noisily in poorly blended unison—are commonest among game producers (hunters and fishers). The chi square relation is .001.

Musical unison means that one path is being followed, one role enacted in a joint phonation. Polyphony, or singing in harmony, means that two or more independent parts or roles co-occur. It has been noted that independence of parts is at its maximum in the contrapuntal singing of the acephalous collectors, where parties of female gatherers perform the principal productive act. Unison, roughly organized, is the *only* musical mode used by hunters and fishers, where males fill the productive slots. Between the acephalous collectors and the tribal society with a chief (common among Amerindian hunters and fishers, for example), a step forward has been made in social unification, at the expense of one order of complexity—complementarity in relations between male and female. There are only two primal social roles—male and female—and two modes—the more and the less dominant. Unison (one role played at a time) is most often produced by choruses of males in societies where women take little part in musical or other public activities. Contrary to this, polyphony (more than one pitch level or role at a time) seems to stand for the existence of a complementary relationship between males and females. In fact, polyphony tends to be found far more frequently in societies in which women dominate the main productive activity than in those societies where the main subsistence task is largely or exclusively handled by men.

Polyparted singing, which gives the impression of openness and variety, then, is one indicator of a social situation in which women have important public roles on a par with those of men. This is not, of course, an exclusive correlation. Symbol function is such that two states may be signaled by one symbol or one state signaled by two symbols. In other words, I believe we shall certainly find other indicators of complementarity in song style and, at the same time, I know that the complementary relationship indicated by polyphony may occur in other areas of social life than that of work.

Another correlate, presumably another sign of complementarity, is provided by another cantometric indicator—vocal width or relaxation. Here we judged whether the singing voice seemed relaxed and wide-open or constricted and narrow. We tested the following hypothesis: that vocal constriction would be found where there were sanctions on feminine pre-marital sexual intercourse, and that vocal relaxation would be prominent where erotic behavior was relatively free of sanctions, an idea that had been discussed in earlier articles.[6] The results for 233 cultures show a highly positive relationship between vocal stance and the pre-marital sexual code.

Achieving a unified choral sound is the result of discipline, of subordination of all the levels of vocal calibration to one image, one goal. This degree of social and vocal empathy is reached in our society only after months and years of training in the great choirs. In other cultures it is the result of a different social experience and training than our own.

a)   For the limited sample shared with the Yale child training studies,[7] it is indicated that poor tonal blend is associated with youthful training for assertion and good tonal blend with training for compliance.

b) From the larger sample that shared with the Udy study[8] of the structure of work teams—good blend is found most frequently in those societies where large, stable, reciprocal work teams are most frequent.

c) Good tonal blend tends to be found most frequently in societies where large stable groups order the social experience so that the individual is in face to face contact throughout his life with the same people, that is, in villages and hamlets with clan organization.

In spite of the paucity of cross-cultural information available, then, tonal unity seems to be a measure of training for an experience of social stability and of intrapersonal unity. This conclusion is preparation for the fifth of our stylistic examples.

5) Style 5. Antiphonal, integrated, polyphonic, large choral performance. This song style is found right across the world in Polynesia, Melanesia, New Guinea, Tribal India, Central Europe and, most prominently, in Negro Africa. In the end this style area may turn out to be a relic of an ancient cultural distribution. In our present terms, it is the region where stability and complementarity most frequently co-occur. These conditions are, as has already been noted, concomitants of a certain level of production—gardening, with domestication. It is a matter of fact that such economies depend for their expanding growth upon a large, integrated, highly charged labor force, and thrive in cultures where large, stable social groups order the lives of everyone and establish a "groupy" interaction texture. The well-blended, unified, polyvoiced, antiphonal, sensually-charged song style symbolizes and reinforces this adaptive set. The strong tendency of the African and Oceanic gardeners to sing in well-blended, polyphonic choruses emerges dramatically. Both of these areas also rank high in world comparisons on: (a) stable villages, (b) large families, (c) clans, (d) lineages or ramages, (e) social importance and independence of women.

If there are few exclusive conditions for the behavioral scientist, there are even less for the student of communication styles. We deal here with pan-human possibilities. All can and do occur everywhere. Communication models, once found, are not discarded—they merely assume subordinate functions. New Yorkers amble into subways humming wordlessly to themselves like so many Lapps. New York children sing their games in poorly blended, acephalous repetitive unison because their group life, though based on shared experience, is temporary and egalitarian. However, the highly specialized, expressive styles developed by more complex societies occur very rarely in simpler societies.

6) Style 6. The elaborate, melodically complex, constricted, specific, exclusive style most common in the urban Far East—solo elaborate singing—is considered to be the peak of musical refinement through India, the Near and Middle East, and the southern Mediterranean. Thus, it is principally employed by irrigationists, plough agriculturists, and pastoral nomads. This was the style that appeared along with the birth of the art of music and poetry, when talented men in the temples of the gods and courts of the emperors devoted themselves to the development of music, poetry, and esthetic theory. David was such a man. He sang for King Saul and he sang for God, as do the cantors of our time. His passionate complexity produced awe in the listener; and it was intended to do so.

Save one, all of the main traits of this style have already been given explanatory hypotheses. Vocal constriction, like sanctions on sexual behavior, reach their peak in this bardic world. Specificity and melodic complexity combine to produce the longest and most complex song forms we know of, in societies where the economic network matches in size and reach, if not efficiency, that of modern industry. As Wittfogel,[9] among others, has shown us, these ancient irrigation empires rested upon an exclusive control of power by one man, the emperor, or his surrogates. In this world, a single bard, representing the center of power, might keep his (or her) head if he could entertain an uneasy caliph for 1001 nights of solo performance.

One distinctive factor in this style, hardly found to a comparable degree elsewhere, is *elaboration*. Elaboration in cantometric terms consists of two traits—melodic ornamentation and rhythmic freedom. They combine to produce songs of incredible delicacy and subtle delight, not by means of sheer innovation, but by the elaboration of melodic themes. In India, Andalucia, China, Japan, and the Moslem world, virtuosic use of ornament fills the hearer with an emotion that can best be described as rapture. The touchstone of such a performance is its finesse, also a hallmark of acceptable social behavior in a world of deferential etiquette.

Deferential etiquette—the means by which the lower class individual ensures his personal safety in relations with a superior—reaches its peak in hierarchic societies dependent on irrigation. Here, precisely, is where musical elaboration occurs along our productive scale, which has been slightly rearranged to show the importance of this trait in PC and IR.[10]

Though the *Ethnographic Atlas* provides no information on systems of etiquette, it does record the presence of complex class, caste, and hierarchical political systems which add to the layers of social stratification that confine the life of an individual. The juncture of all three of these systems increases the social distance between members of a society and presumably gives rise to deferential, elaborate behavior of all sorts. There is a very powerful relationship between the degree of level of social layering and the occurrence of elaboration in song style.

Some of the most distinctive performance patterns found along our productive scale have now been accounted for in terms of shifts of social norms that accompany an increase of productive range. So far as can be seen now, each socio-productive level is marked by a specialized approach to song performance. Each of these specializations is adaptive, each song type is suitable for the reinforcement of a behavioral syndrome adaptive at the socio-economic level of the culture in which it occurs. Other examples would afford no further theoretical contribution, even though the discussion of more style traits would more sharply define special cultural situations. The second phase of the test is now complete. The structure of performance style does indeed seem to symbolize and reinforce main adaptive modes cross-culturally. Without an evolutionary, as well as comparative, view of these matters, no rationale or explanation would have been possible. Productive esthetic analysis must then be a study of the dynamic relationship between the expressive and the adaptive modes in the human series.

It is a deeply moving experience to realize that every branch of the human family of which we have record has so nicely expressed itself and its situation. No matter how naked a people, no matter how hopeless or aimless or tormented it seems to be, its song style fits. Everywhere man the pattern maker and pattern perceiver has been at work, molding all behavior into forms appropriate to his situation. Thus, the principle of suitability, the esthetic factor, becomes the main stabilizer, if not the main dynamic factor, at work in human history.

It may be suggested with some justification that little or nothing has been said in usual terms about either the good (which I have called the adaptive) or the beautiful (which I have called the appropriate communication about the adaptive). The results of content analysis of song texts might seem closer to the mark because this data would be presented in terms of *verbalized* goals and values. In our specifying, legalistic West—since Socrates—the good and the beautiful have consisted of verbal definitions. In this paper, situations have been examined in which the good and the beautiful were acted and lived out and not verbalized, but the vital bond between the two seems no less strong for all that.

What, then, of the better or the more beautiful? Judgments about "the more beautiful" seem, in the Child study, to be independent of cultural barriers. Certainly no human need is more urgent than precisely to explain the nature of this perception if, indeed, all mankind can and does share it. If I am right, the first step is to recognize the relationship between the adaptive (the good) and the suitable (the beautiful) and to study this pairing as it occurs in behavior through human time. When the dynamic behavioral principles that link this pair in many human settings have been seen and understood, valid scientific statements about the nature of *the* good and *the* beautiful will be at hand. In other words, we will discern universal inter-pattern between the apt and the suitable in the varied matching of culture and art. The main value is already evident; the survival of humanity, itself.[11]

NOTES

1. This paper was an invited address before the Division of Psychology and the Arts of the American Psychological Association in New York City, September, 1966. The research was made possible by a grant from the National Institute of Mental Health, administered in the Department of Anthropology and the Bureau of Applied Social Research at Columbia University. The normative concepts were developed in collaboration with Dr. Conrad Arensberg; the system of musical analysis was the joint work of Victor Grauer and myself. [The original charts are here deleted—ed.]

2. Erik Erikson, *Childhood and Society* (New York, 1964, revised edition).

3. Irving Child and L. Siroto, "Bakwele and American Esthetic Evaluation Compared," *Ethnology*, IV (1965), 349-360.

4. In publication with a set of illustrative recordings.

5. G. P. Murdock, *Ethnographic Atlas*, in installments in *Ethnology*.

6. A. Lomax, "Song Structure and Social Structure," *Ethnology*, 1, 4 (1962), 425 451; A. Lomax, "Folk Song Style," *The American Anthropologist*. LXI, 6 (1959).

7. I. Child, Herbert Barry, III, and Margaret K. Bacon, "A Cross-cultural Survey of Some Sex Differences in Socialization," *The Journal of Abnormal and Social Psychology*, LV, 3 (1957), 332-337; "Relation of Child Training to Subsistence Economy," *American Anthropology*, LXI, 1 (1959), 51-63.

8. Stanley H. Udy, Jr. *Organization of Work* (New Haven, 1959).

9. The gamma is an index of order association. A high gamma, between .45 and 1.00, indicates that a high level of association exists between the two categorical variables.

10. Karl Wittfogel, *Oriental Despotism* (New Haven, Connecticut, 1957); Karl Wittfogel, "The Hydraulic Civilizations" in *Man's Role in Changing the Face of the Earth,* edited by Wm. L. Thomas, Jr. (Chicago, 1956).

11. The cultures in the cantometric sample that rank above the medians on both elaboration and rigidity are:

Turkmen	Viet Nam	Sakalava	Georgia, Caucasus	Hillbilly	Gondogram
Amami	Laos	Yoruba	Irish	Turkey	Egypt
Sherpa	Hakka	Bahima	Andalucia	Kunta	
Malaya	Bali	Tuareg	Naples	Kurd	
Korea	Hawaii	Ruanda	Sicily	Amhara	
Japan	Java	Southern U.S. Negro	Leon	Kerala	
Thailand	Bara	Tadjik	Nuoro	Village India	

12. Irving Child and L. Siroto, "Bakwele and American Esthetic Evaluation Compared."

* Stable defined as societies where lineages, ramages, or clans function in stable settlements (villages, hamlets, neighborhoods).

Part IV

Cantometrics and Cultural Equity: The Academic Years
Introduction by Gage Averill

There is a specter haunting this essay and this section of the volume: Alan Lomax's 1968 book *Folk Song Style and Culture*. Intended by Lomax and his team to consolidate their seven years of comparative research on music, dance/movement, and language, the book also presents many of the ambitious goals, theories, and cultural advocacy projects that Lomax embraced during the late 1950s and continued to promote in the decades to come. Why not, then, just read *Folk Song Style and Culture*? The book is certainly recommended as a companion to this section containing Lomax's selected shorter works, but the scholarly articles that appear herein add to our understanding of Alan Lomax's academic years, providing a better sense for the changes in Lomax's thought on comparative study and for the increasing scope of his comparative methodology.[1]

Lomax's scholarly pursuits grew naturally out of decades-old interests. As the essay by Andrew Kaye and Matthew Barton makes clear, Lomax had studied anthropology at Columbia in the late 1930s and sat in on classes at New York University with the leading German comparative musicologist, Curt Sachs. Lomax's writings had long before taken a turn away from simple description, cataloging, and classification and increasingly toward explanation and analysis.

In the years from 1958 until 1980, Lomax was principally concerned with adding to the scholarly knowledge of song and dance styles, and during this period he produced most of his scholarly work. For the purpose of this section, the start of Lomax's "academic years" coincides with his return to the United States from Europe. His fruitful period of academic research coincided with his association with Columbia University's Bureau of Applied Social Research, during which time his work was sustained by substantial grants from the Rockefeller Foundation, the National Institute of Health, the National Science

Foundation, the National Endowment for the Humanities, the Ford Foundation and others, and nurtured by close collegial relationships with researchers from many disciplines.[2]

Despite the fundraising successes, generous institutional support, and numerous publications of these years, and despite Lomax's steadfast conviction that this work was perhaps his most important legacy, his "metrics" have been highly controversial among scholars, but at the same time almost entirely overlooked outside of academia. Of the many obituaries and tributes that followed Alan Lomax's death in 2002, few even mentioned Cantometrics, the centerpiece of his academic project. This essay and this section of the volume constitute a brief reassessment of the academic years and of Lomax's scholarly contributions.

GENESIS OF THE ACADEMIC YEARS

Lomax's field trips to Spain and Italy between 1952–1955 convinced him that the sexual mores of the society (especially the severity with which premarital sexual contact was proscribed) influenced singing style. As discussed by Kaye and Barton, Lomax had published "Folk Song Style: Notes of a Systematic Approach to the Study of Folk Song," in the *Journal of the International Folk Music Council* in 1956. Invited by his friend, anthropologist Margaret Mead, Lomax presented his views on style and sexual repression at the 1958 meeting of the American Anthropological Association (AAA), a presentation that served as the basis for his expanded article in *American Anthropologist* of December 1959, "Folk Song Style: Musical Style and Social Context."

These articles constituted a remarkable critique of contemporaneous ethnomusicological praxis and a farsighted exploration of themes that would occupy his attention for decades. Although Lomax never mastered Western staff notation, by 1956 he was already aware of its limitations for musical scholarship; his Cantometrics coding charts were offered as an alternative "transcription" method. In his two manifestos published in the 1950s, he proposed that the essence of non-Western music and folk music "escaped through the lines and spaces" of staff notation and that comparative musicology had focused too strongly on these "distorted skeletons" of musical transcription/score and on "formal musical patterns torn out of their context," accounting for melody and harmony, but not for timbre, gesture, group interaction, and other characteristics of musical behavior that he considered fundamental (and resistant to change through acculturation).[3]

Lomax's concern for the treatment and status of women demonstrated a remarkable sensitivity to issues of gender in expressive culture for the 1950s. His core unit of analysis was musical style (patterns of musical behavior, including function, timbre, vocal technique, mannerisms of the singer, motor activity, social organization, emotional content), anticipating the attention to style among members of the "Birmingham School" of British cultural studies in later decades. Lomax anticipated the rising interest in issues of timbre, facial expression, gesture, and bodily movement that would later come to figure prominently in ethnomusicology, and he dismissed non-contextual studies of sound in favor of an emphasis on music behavior and performance. Lomax was, it is safe to say, more interdisciplinary than almost any ethnomusicologist writing today. Finally, as we'll see when we look at his "Appeal for Cultural Equity," Alan Lomax formulated what was then one of the most important critiques of musical globalization and the role of Western commercial media.

In his 1956 "Folk Song Style," Lomax was inspired by the problematic of acculturation, imagining that something of the cultural style matrix survives the adoption of a new cultural expression. What is it that survives, and what elements are consistent and stable? As the immutable part of a culture's performative repertory, "style" was that part of music that expressed the social or collective identity of its performers and listeners, what Lomax called the "security patterns of the community." Style could be read as an index of the "prevailing emotional temper of entire cultures." Even at this early date, Lomax had a general sense of the relevant world culture areas for his study, including Pygmoid (communal, voices "rather childlike"); African ("frankly orgiastic"); Eurasian (control & individuality); Amerindian (muscular, throaty); and so on. It is obvious that Lomax was not listening with completely unbiased ears, as these descriptions partake of a long history of European representations of these world areas. Lomax also had an instinctual feel for what would become his most powerful social correlations of musical style: sexual mores, the position of women, the treatment of children, and the degree of social cooperation. The 1959 version of "Folk Song Style" contains a full explanation of Lomax's thesis derived from his work in Spain and Italy that sexual repression correlates with tense vocal timbre.

Few have noted the role of what a later generation would call Orientalism in Lomax's early comparative work. Passages like the following, however, seem to harken to the "clash of civilizations," to wars with the Ottoman Empire and the Christian Crusades: "Old European culture [had been] pushed back into the mountains and *surrounded* by the *onrush of Oriental civilization* which overwhelmed and shattered most of the older tribal societies, made chattels of the women and brought in its train a folk-art of strident monody." Lomax clearly loved the old European choral forms, the relaxed singing style, the cooperative integrations of voices and instruments that suggested to him peasant egalitarianism. In North Italy, Lomax noted that men stand "with arms round their cronies' shoulders, or, leaning across a wine-soaked table, blend their voices, smiling at one another benignly over the pleasures of drink, sweet chords, and the often bawdy or tenderly sexual verses of their songs." Eurasian influences are described with metaphors of pain and violence. For example, the voice is "pinched and strangulated . . . The singing expression is one of true agony, the throat is distended and flushed with strain, the brow knitted with a painful expression . . . punctuated with shrieks, like the cries of the damned." Melodic ornaments "speak of tears, of fear, or trembling submission." He characterized the Old High Culture of Eurasia as elitist, soloistic, and virtually ornamented art: full of the wailing of women reduced to chattel with tense and strained voices—a description that suggests oppression and feudalism. Lomax cites Karl Wittfogel's 1957 book, *Oriental Despotism*, as a source for his view of Asian "Old High Culture."[4]

Africa, too, is integrated into this value-laden scheme. "In our [Euro-American] society only the children know how to organize and dramatize their feelings in the ancient, collective [pre-Eurasian] fashion. That the need for such song types still exists among adult Westerners is evidenced by the recent popularity of highly charged, choral-litany song patterns, rooted in erotic dance forms and created by Afro-Americans." In other words, Europe's musical origins, its musical childhood, is preserved in children's songs and rediscovered in African American music.

These two articles present Lomax's manifesto for the cross-cultural comparison of social structure and musical style, but they already hint ominously at the results of such a study. Moreover, they combine the best of Lomax's intuitive and grand theorizing with some of the tendencies that would undermine confidence in Cantometric's objectivity.

THE EVOLUTION OF LOMAXIAN "METRICS"

Phonotactics. The Lomax method for contrasting song, speech, and movement "performances" drew inspiration from work in other fields.

Linguist George Trager at the University of Buffalo had promoted a new field of study called metalinguistics (the systematic study of the relationship of language to other cultural systems) as early as 1949. Trager published on the importance of paralinguistics (the nonlexical parts of language: tone, stress, rhythm) in 1958. After Lomax invented a card system to keep track of vowel sounds in folk song, he showed his work to Dr. Trager, who was supportive of the effort. On a 1960–61 A.C.L.S. Fellowship, Lomax studied linguistics at Buffalo with Trager and became a student of Ray Birdwhistell, the founder of the study of kinesics (the communicative content of movement patterns). Birdwhistell's theories influenced the development of Lomax's Choreometrics, as Trager's did for Parlametrics.[5]

Convinced that his insights about correlations among song style, language style, and social structure would hold up to empirical scrutiny, Lomax applied for a grant from the Humanities Division of the Rockefeller Foundation to develop a method for describing, categorizing, and comparing recorded folk song performances. With the receipt of this grant, Lomax accepted an Associate Researcher position at Columbia University with the Bureau of Applied Social Research, and launched into work with Edith Crowell Trager on a study of language stylistics. Their manuscript would later be published in French as "Phonotactique du Chant Populaire." Lomax and Trager, in their investigation of what she was already calling "phonotactics," found preliminary evidence of an association between social tension and the frequent use of high, front vowels. Lomax then linked this preference for front vowel patterning to the tense monophonic solo singing of the Old Eurasian culture area. Here in germinal form is the link between Cantometrics and Parlametrics already established. Singing and speech, they argued, exhibit redundancies at the level of style, and these redundancies are intimately related to the emotional pattern of a culture and to key features of the social structure. Conversely, they argued, a group that exhibited a preference for low back vowels would be more likely to sing with blended choral polyphony and to have permissive sexual codes.[6]

Cantometrics. In 1960, on a trip to Wesleyan University to visit with an anthropologist of Native American music, David MacAllester, Lomax was introduced to MacAllester's first graduate student in ethnomusicology, Victor Grauer, who was then working on his Masters degree. They discussed Grauer's thesis on Hebrew chant and their shared interests in the relation between music, language, and gesture, and in comparative study. Lomax, searching for a musicologist collaborator, invited Grauer to test his theories on a sample of recorded music during the first phase of the Rockefeller grant in the summer of 1961. They assembled and reviewed 400 sets of recordings (soon expanded to 700) and tapes from 250 culture areas, testing and honing a crude rating scale for aspects of musical style. They sought to identify "gross traits" that didn't require a large sample ("more than two or three pieces" at first) and that didn't require skilled musicological coding. Lomax argued that because participants in folk culture had no specialized training, Cantometrics should be designed in populist fashion for a "normal listener anywhere" who would need only a cursory training to make proper coding decisions. Lomax defended the small samples by asserting that societies select at most about three musical styles, one of which is usually dominant. The rating that Grauer and Lomax designed had 37 rating scales on a data sheet (based on the limit of the size of the coding sheet), each parameter had between 3–13 points, limited to the 13 punches per column on an IBM card. All the sheets for a given culture were added up and compiled to provide a master profile. "Cantometrics" was originally defined as a "measure of song" but the term took on a new meaning later on, positing song "as a measure of society."[7]

Margaret Mead first suggested to Lomax that the product of the coding for each sample should be a graphic profile, in essence a series of bar charts representing each song's distinctive Cantometric ratings. Lomax's close friend at Columbia, anthropologist Conrad Arensberg, who served in a semi-honorary capacity as co-Director of the Cantometrics and Choreometrics Project, helped Lomax to clarify his hypotheses about choral and solo song performances, finding the interaction and integration of voices in ensemble performance to be an index of social cohesion and interaction. Their broad efforts to correlate cultural patterns with means of subsistence and political organization culminated in their jointly authored 1977 article, "A Worldwide Evolutionary Classification of Cultures by Subsistence Systems."[8]

In his article "Song Structure and Social Structure," published in January 1962 in the journal *Ethnology*, Alan Lomax outlined the Cantometrics project and provided early results from a few of its key case studies. Once again, Lomax offered a stinging rebuke of the state of ethnomusicology: "The suggestion of this paper is that ethnomusicology should turn aside, for a time, from the study of music in purely musical terms to a study of music in context, as a form of human behavior." Lomax's solution—to analyze decontextualized recordings—may strike some observers as less than sufficient to meet his own challenge. In seeking underlying emotional attitudes of cultures, Lomax responded to the kind of broad characterizations found in Margaret Mead and Gregory Bateson's *The Balinese Character.*[9]

In December of 1961, Lomax and his collaborators presented their preliminary findings to a joint meeting of the American Anthropological Association and the Society for Ethnomusicology. This presentation and the aforementioned 1962 article formed the basis for an application to the National Institute of Mental Health for a four-year grant under the name: "Folk Song as a Psycho–Social Indicator." The application proposed to extend phonotactics beyond its original Indo-European data set, develop content analyses of song texts, and to begin a pilot study of dance style. What especially interested the NIMH was Lomax's theory that a stronger sense of self, rooted in a more authentic cultural identity, could alleviate juvenile delinquency in minority populations and ethnic groups.

The NIMH grant started in February of 1962, and over the next summer, while Lomax was engaged in a field recording trip to the Eastern Caribbean, Grauer doubled the survey from 700 examples to over 1,400. Another year of work shifted the publication strategy toward collecting ten songs from every culture sampled (over 200 cultures). Lomax had his staff segregate the data that pertained to the list of cultures in George P. Murdock's *Ethnographic Atlas,* and the correlation of song, dance/movement, and language data with the Atlas's social and cultural profiles became a near-obsessive goal of the Lomax projects.

In 1965 Victor Grauer proposed a more elaborate coding process, less tailored to the appearance of the graphs and stressing a more logical, objective, and clearly definable coding system. Although this was eventually made compatible with the old system, Lomax decided it took too long to code a sample (one hour rather than one-half hour) and it was rejected. In the fall of 1965, Victor Grauer's article, "Some Song Style Clusters: A Preliminary Study," was published in *Ethnomusicology* (vol. 10, no. 3, 265–271). The article defined a new use for the Cantometrics material, in which a "cluster" of musical features could be developed which would serve as the basis for a search through all of the Cantometrics database of world music samples to identify matches.[10]

In the mid–1960s, Lomax and Grauer completed an ambitious multi-media package of recordings that they intended to publish by

Folkways Records, along with an accompanying book from Wesleyan University Press. The recordings were chosen to demonstrate the continuity of various Cantometric song style patterns around the globe. Completed around early 1966, the package lacked only an introduction by Lomax, who hoped to use an article that had been rejected by an anthropology journal. Unfortunately, the press balked at the length and the complexity of the introduction, and Lomax never completed the necessary revisions, and so the book and LP combination never appeared.[11]

Choreometrics. Around 1965, Lomax launched an ambitious project to develop a kinesics (dance and movement) "metric." Just as the phonograph and magnetic tape had facilitated the development of a collection of the world's music sufficient for Cantometric analysis, Lomax believed that ethnographic films constituted an emerging audiovisual database that could be analyzed for a comparative study of the world's dance and movement patterns, i.e. Choreometrics. Lomax contacted Irmgard Bartenieff, dancer, dance scholar, movement analyst, and physical therapist, who trained with Rudolf Laban. Laban's graphic notation for the encoding of movement, combined with Birdwhistell's kinesics, were major inspirations for Choreometrics. Bartenieff remained a consultant for some time, and her graduate assistant, Forrestine Paulay, joined Lomax as a principal collaborator on Choreometrics. As Bartenieff and Paulay viewed film records, they designed parameters reflecting aspects of visible movement that could be coded in the same way as Cantometrics. Their work was summarized in "Choreometrics: A Method for the Study of Cross-Cultural Patterns in Film," which appeared in a 1969 volume of *Research Film*. At the grossest level of comparison, Lomax, Bartenieff, and Paulay divided the world into "hippies" (who "dwell in the tropics") and "squares" ("who dominate the rest of the planet"), with the latter moving their trunks as a single unit while the former subdivide the trunk into articulatory components.[12]

Lomax pursued film archives and individual scholars for dance footage to use in the Choreometrics study. His 1973 article, "Cinema, Science and Cultural Revival," is couched in the rhetoric of urgent or salvage ethnography, promoting "urgent ethnographic film" in the service of a "total sound-film record of culture." Lomax championed the use of existing archives, encouraged rigor in shooting and preservation (even of outtakes) among ethnographic filmmakers, and demonstrated through his work the value of ethnographic film collections to post facto interpretive processes. He encouraged ethnographic filmmakers to:

1. Shoot to best preserve the data on film
2. Provide ample documentation
3. Properly store multiple copies of all footage for future use
4. Exchange films and make them widely available
5. Build up regional and global archives of film
6. Explore means to interpret the data in film (enter choreometrics)

Lomax's Choreometrics team produced three training films, *Dance and Human History*, *Step Style*, and *Palm Play*.[13]

Unlike the reception of Cantometrics, which at least provoked passionate responses on the parts of ethnomusicologists, Choreometrics found no comparable audience because the numbers of scholars pursuing comparative dance ethnology was so small. Thus its immediate academic impact was negligible.

The "coming out party" for the Cantometrics and Choreometrics Project took the shape of a day-long series of panels and presentations at the annual meeting of the American Association for the Advancement of Science, two days after Christmas in 1966. The event was a precursor to the publication of the volume *Folksong Style and Culture* in 1968.

Cultural equity. The more one looks at the work of Alan Lomax, the more one sees the disparate parts of his praxis—collecting, academic analysis, folklore revivalism, advocacy, and education—as a coherent whole. Lomax was always a proponent of empowering the "folk," those who lived at a distance from power and wealth, and he had an innate trust of the cultural integrity of folk cultures. Lomax saw his academic project as part of a larger project of community empowerment through what Lomax called "cultural equity." Two articles called "Appeal for Cultural Equity," the first in the *World of Music* in 1972 and a revised version in a 1977 volume of *Journal of Communications,* made the case for an environmentalist approach to cultural preservation. In these articles he elaborated on the phrase "cultural grey-out" that has entered into the scholarship on musical globalization.[14]

Lomax thoroughly embraced the rhetoric of the environmental movement in calling attention to the state of cultural diversity in the world. In the boldface précis of the article, he noted that Cantometrics "offers the world the basis for a global policy of cultural equity to halt *pollution of the symbolic environment*." He continued, "man's greatest achievement is in the sum of the lifestyles he has created to make this planet an agreeable and stimulating human habitat. Today, this cultural variety lies under the threat of extinction. A grey-out is in progress which, if it continues unchecked, will fill our human skies with the smog of the phoney and cut the families of men off from a vision of their own cultural constellations." Each human communicative system, Lomax argued, "is a treasure of unkown potential, a collective creation in which some branch of the human species invested its genius across the centuries."[15]

Lomax was also one of the first to introduce the concept of multi-culturalism: "We need now to plan a multi-culture, a world in which many civilizations, each with its own supporting systems of education and communication, can live." Noting that electronic communications are intrinsically multi-channeled and therefore capable of supporting diversity, Lomax articulated the egalitarian goal of giving "equal time" to every culture in broadcasting and education. He saved his strongest ire for "national" musics, which he found to be top-down impositions. "I think it may be stated flatly that most creative developments in art have been the product of small communities or small independent coteries within larger entities."[16]

Not surprisingly, Lomax championed Cantometrics as the means to describe the world's musical species and sub-species in order to provide a "rationale for their continued development." He even proposed a new bureaucratic position, a "cultural administrator—the defender of the principle of cultural equity."[17]

ACADEMIC RECEPTION

" I do not know if Cantometrics will survive the examination of my colleagues for a short or a long time." ("Song Structure and Social Structure," 431)

In his seminal book, *The Anthropology of Music*, Alan Merriam spoke positively of Lomax's attempts to bring precision to the discussion of vocal style, posture, and expression, but noted that "Lomax is also forced back upon a wide variety of adjectival [i.e. non-precise] terms."[18]

Although there were indeed some positive and mixed reviews in the reception of Cantometrics by ethnomusicologists, the prevailing tone was of dismissal. Certainly Lomax was hurt by the timing of his project, coming during an era in which ethnomusicologists had turned decisively away from comparative musicology toward a more Boasian intensive ethnographic approach. These critics saw Lomax's quest for universal, demonstrable correlations based on the comparison of abstracted trait lists to be quixotic, overly positivistic, and fundamentally at odds with the need for intensive study of cultures from an interpretive perspective. Steve Feld, in an article that examined the relevance of Cantometrics for his own research on the Kaluli, concluded that the important features of a culture, such as the metaphors musicians use to understand music, don't yield themselves to abstract trait lists: "It is my hope that a comparative sociomusicology will develop along these lines, elaborating not correlations of song structures and social structures, but coherences of sound structures as social structures."[19]

Another part of the problem for Lomax was that many ethnomusicologists were drawn to scholarship by their love of playing music, a passion that was then nurtured by Mantle Hood's apprenticeship models of fieldwork, but not addressed at all in Cantometrics. To the contrary, Norman Berkowitz's elaborate codings and data-crunching programs and Lomax's use of equations and statistical tables (as in the "proportion of Contoids to Vocoids, x sq./2df . . . 65.2 p<0.001) spoke a completely different language about music—an alienating language to most ethnomusicologists.

In addition, Lomax was not in an academic teaching position and wasn't a product of traditional academic channels. According to Victor Grauer: "Alan never wanted to become part of the academic world. He had offers of various professorships, but always turned them down. I think Cantometrics would have become much more widely accepted if Alan had a power base in the academic world and had produced graduate students to carry on his work." Although Lomax cited ethnomusicologists generously, many of his peers felt that the project was formulated, tested, and popularized in a hothouse atmosphere a few steps outside of the mainstream of the discipline. While some found his theories and evidence provocative on a global scale, few appreciated how they might bear on their work on a local scale. A few scholars, perhaps, were envious of the prodigious fundraising of Lomax and his team. The Cantometrics project was richly endowed by NGOs and philanthropic organizations for nearly nine years and had a supportive home in a major Ivy League university, all of which provided an institutional support and funding base unequalled in ethnomusicology.[20]

But the most damning criticisms were those that dealt with the quality of the science. In a 1972 review of *Folk Song Style and Culture*, Hewitt Pantaleoni accused Lomax of "bias in approach and sloppiness in method," and he cited the following problems among others:

the exclusion of data from China, without discussion

the exclusion of features that didn't yield desired results

the exclusive use of North American judges

the imprecision of the analytic categories and the rating scales

assumptions of European cultural superiority built into the study

the small sample of songs from any given culture, and the lack of a
   rationale for choice

the preponderance of field recordings by male researchers of male
   musicians[21]

Some criticisms have been raised concerning the coding sheets (which were arranged to produce the maximum visual contrast between "group" cultures and individualistic cultures), and the coding parameters (which were included or excluded based on their ability to produce high-contrast results). Victor Grauer had his own reservations about these procedures:

> What really became a problem was that Alan was so focused on getting the correlations with the Murdock data to come out "just right" that other very important, meaningful and less problematic aspects of the project were neglected. One of the really serious problems was his reluctance to make the system generally available until he got all his ducks neatly lined up in a row, which never happened. How can we blame ethnomusicologists for neglecting Cantometrics when, after all these years, the database itself remains unavailable? What's the point of doing a Cantometric analysis of one's own materials, when there's nothing there to plug it into.[22]

Many critics have pointed to the ambivalence in Lomax's work over whether musical correlations derive from historical diffusionism (the spread of cultural influences through war, migration, or expansion) versus those that derive from the system of subsistence, i.e., from an evolutionary "level." This contradiction is evident in Lomax's own statement that, "First, the geography of song styles traces the main paths of human migration and maps the known historical distributions of culture. Second, some traits of song performance show a powerful relationship to features of social structure that regulate interaction in all cultures." A Lomax associate, Edwin Erikson, made a convincing case for interpreting the data from a diffusionist standpoint.[23]

In a 1970 review essay in *Ethnomusicology*, James C. Downey raised a series of questions about the quality of the coding system: "Were the coders unconsciously influenced by the first items in a set?. . . . Were the coders influenced by geographical or cultural 'master profiles'?," raising questions about reliability, bias, and experimental control. In a companion piece in the same volume, Harold E. Driver was far more charitable, but still found some fault with the procedures by which the variables had been weighted to sharpen the differences among song culture areas. Driver noted that to fully understand the Lomax methodology, a reader would require "a good introductory course in statistics and another in cross-cultural methods. . . . a lengthier program in mathematics, computer operations, and the logic and philosophy of science."[24]

There was lingering concern over how neatly the principal conclusions of the Cantometrics coding reinforced Lomax's a priori beliefs about the relationship between music and social context (such as women's sexual freedom). As a result, some argued that the empirical apparatus of the project was weighted in favor of prior assumptions.

CONCLUSION

There is no doubt that the academic research and publications of Lomax and his team at Columbia constituted one of the most thoroughgoing, imaginative, and visionary projects in music research in the twentieth century. I have also argued that Lomax possessed a rigorous and insightful critique of 1950s-style ethnomusicological research, and that he proposed an innovative turn toward performance, embodiment, timbre, the centrality of gender, and style, and the use of ethnographic film, issues that were not fully embraced by the discipline in some cases for decades. However, the initial vision, too, was encumbered and deeply flawed by failure to critically challenge mechanistic cultural determinism, Eurocentric views of human cultural evolution, and Orientalist legacies. These flaws have ensured an unenthusiastic following for Cantometrics and its siblings. I don't need to point out that generations of ethnomusicology students have not been trained to code Cantometric profiles, despite the evident pedagogical benefits of training students to listen to and distinguish among the stylistic features represented.

Alan Lomax was more successful than any ethnomusicologist in obtaining grants, and he was also more successful in speaking to the world outside of academia (through books, films, radio, recordings, and talks). He may have taken some small comfort that, despite the many objections that scholars raised with his Cantometrics, Choreometrics, and Parlametrics projects, many of his central conclusions have been widely disseminated and can be considered a part of conventional wisdom on global musics. Although little research is currently taking place within the framework of Cantometrics or Choreometrics, it is likely that any future moves in the direction of global comparative study will have to engage seriously with the demonstrable successes of Lomax's metrics as well as learn from their shortcomings.

NOTES

1. Alan Lomax, *Folk Song Style and Culture* [with contributions by the Cantometrics Staff and with the editorial assistance of Edwin E. Erickson], (New Brunswick, NJ: Transaction Books, 1968).

2. Nevertheless, the period covered in this section was far from exclusively academic in focus for Lomax. The previous section of this volume concerned Lomax's continuing dialogue over these years with the folk revival that he had helped to inspire. In addition, Lomax also undertook one more extensive recording journey, this time to the Eastern Caribbean from April until August 1962. (Lomax believed that the collecting efforts on the part of himself and others had created the prerequisite sound archives upon which an ambitious comparative effort would have to rest.)

3. Lomax, "Folk Song Style: Notes of a Systematic Approach to the Study of Folk Song," *Journal of the International Folk Music Council*, vol. VIII, 1956, 48; Lomax, "Folk Song Style: Musical Style and Social Context," *American Anthropologist*, vol. 61, no. 6, December 1959, 928. These approaches anticipate the work of John Blacking and Alan Merriam later in the 1960s and 1970s.

4. Lomax, "Folk Song Style: Musical Style and Social Context," 942, 948; Lomax, "Song Structure and Social Structure," *Ethnology*, vol. 1, no. 4, January 1962, 443; Karl Wittfogel, *Oriental Despotism* (New Haven: Yale University Press, 1957).

5. See George Trager, "Paralanguage: A First Approximation," *Studies in Linguistics* 13, 1-12. Admittedly, the procession of linguistic-analytic methodologies—metalinguistics, paralinguistics, paralanguage, phonotactics, and parlametrics—is a bit confusing.

6. Alan Lomax (with Edith Crowell Trager) "Phonotactique de Chant Populaire," *L'Homme*, January-April 1964, 5-55. There is some confusion about when this work with Trager and Grauer first took place. Grauer recalls this as 1961, but Alan Merriam, who read the unpublished Lomax-Trager manuscript which mentions Lomax's collaboration with Grauer, provides a 1960 completion date for the manuscript.

7. Personal communication, Victor Grauer, 2002. I am indebted to Grauer for many of the details involving Grauer's work on the Cantometrics project.

8. Alan Lomax (with Conrad Arensberg), "A Worldwide Evolutionary Classification of Cultures by Subsistence Systems," *Current Anthropology*, vol. 18, 1977, 659-708. More than any other single document on which Lomax worked, this one is fully infused with the perspective that human societies have *evolved* from extractors (hunter-gatherers) to industrialists, and that the contemporary diversity of human production reflects human evolution at different stages, using "living cultures as illustrative of stages in human productive development." (660). This model is best represented in a table called "The Ascent of Man-Regional Episodes," on 672. In a "Coda" that laments the rapid extinction of many human cultures, the authors treat these as "subspeciation," conflating again, dangerously I think, the biological and the cultural.

9. Lomax, "Song Structure and Social Structure," 425; Margaret Mead and Gregory Bateson, *The Balinese Character* (New York: New York Academy of Sciences, 1942).

10. Victor Grauer, personal communication, 2002.

11. Victor Grauer, personal communication, 2002.

12. Lomax (with Irmgard Bartenieff and Forrestine Paulay), "Choreometrics: A Method for the Study of Cross-Cultural Pattern in Film," *Research Film*, vol. 6, no. 6, 1969, 512. Rudolf Laban is the innovator of the dance notation system known as Labanotation.

13. Lomax, "Cinema, Science, and Cultural Renewal," *Current Anthropology*, vol. 14, 1973, 475.

14. Lomax, Appeal for Cultural Equity," *World of Music*, vol. XIV, no. 2, 1972. The second version is included in this volume.

15. Lomax, "Appeal for Cultural Equity," *Journal of Communications*, vol. 27, Spring 1977, 125, 127.

16. Ibid., 128, 130.

17. Ibid., 131, 133.

18. Alan P. Merriam, *The Anthropology of Music* (Evanston: Northwestern University Press, 1964), 105-6.

19. Steve Feld, "Sound Structure as Social Structure," *Ethnomusicology*, vol. 28, no. 3, September 1984, 383–409.

20. Victor Grauer, personal communication, 2002.

21. Hewitt Pantaleoni, "Review of *Folk Song Style and Culture*," *Yearbook of the International Folk Music Council,* vol. 4, 1972, 158–161.

22. Victor Grauer, personal communication, 2002.

23. Lomax, *Folk Song Style and Culture*, 3–4.

24. James C. Downey, "Review Essay of *Folk Song Style and Culture*," *Ethnomusicology*, vol. 14, no. 1, 1970, 63–66; Harold E. Driver, "Review Essay of *Folk Song Style and Culture*," *Ethnomusicology*, vol. 14, no. 1, 1970, 57–62.

Chapter 26

Song Structure and Social Structure

Music-making is one of the most strictly patterned forms of human behavior. Its modes of communication are so limited that even a casual listener can distinguish quickly the best performers and identify the pieces in an idiom of whose technique and content he knows nothing. For many centuries and in many cultures, musical adepts have had at their disposal elaborate systems of notation and theory. The musicologists of our time have inherited this treasure of knowledge and have refined greatly their analytic tools. Thousands of volumes of accurately notated music exist, alongside of carefully wrought critical studies. Yet, it seems, none of us is much closer to understanding what music is and what it says than are the singers of primitive cultures. As one of America's leading musicologists remarked to me a year ago, "No one knows anything about melody." If melody, a possession of all human beings everywhere and at every stage of development, is a mystery, what of rhythm, harmony, and the superstructures erected with these three magic tools?

The suggestion of this paper is that ethnomusicology should turn aside, for a time, from the study of music in purely musical terms to a study of music in context, as a form of human behavior. In the first stages of such a study it is not necessary that all that is known and notatable about music be accounted for. It would be a positive step forward to delineate the varying shapes of musical behavior and to begin to frame this behavior in its precise cultural setting. It should then be possible to discern the bonds between musical patterns and the socio-psychological traits available to the other humanistic disciplines.

As a working hypothesis, I propose the common-sense notion that music somehow expresses emotion; therefore, when a distinctive and consistent musical style lives in a culture or runs through several cultures, one can posit the existence of a distinctive set of emotional needs or drives that are somehow satisfied or evoked by this music. If such a musical style occurs with only a limited pattern of variation in the similar cultural setting and over a long period of time, one may assume that a stable expressive and emotional pattern has existed in group A in area B through time T. Thus we might look forward to a scientific musicology that could speak with some precision about formative emotional attitudes pervading cultures and operating through history. In this first stage of investigation we need not be concerned about the way that musical symbolism works, but only with a method that would locate sets of musical phenomena cross-culturally.

Until recently, the musical habits of mankind were not well enough known to make such a cross-cultural study possible. In the past twenty years, however, excellent field recordings from a wide sample of primitive and folk cultures have been published. We need no longer depend upon notations of music from exotic sources. Unlike the musicologists of the past, we need no longer evaluate the varied music of the peoples of the world from a perspective of the fine-art music of Western Europe, for we now have adequate comparative data and can examine them at leisure on their own terms.

In the summer of 1961 a Rockefeller grant enabled me, with my musicologist assistant, Victor Grauer, to assemble and to review approximately 400 sets of recordings and tapes from about 250 culture areas. Each selection was played over ultra-high-fidelity equipment through a pair of matched speakers, one for each listener, and was rated in a comparable manner. In this preliminary survey we could not, of course, completely control the size or the authenticity of the sample from all areas. Normally each culture was represented by from six to twenty selections on an LP recording, edited by the field recordist. We believe that, on the whole, these editor-collectors, most of whom were anthropologists or ethnomusicologists, chose representative materials for these LPs. Elsewhere I had to trust my own judgment, gained in a lifetime of field work and editing field tapes. In any case, our analytic technique—which was designed to look at gross traits rather than the detail of music—obviates this difficulty to a considerable extent. The method shows up stylistic pattern so quickly and in such bold relief that, even when a very large sample was available, we found it unnecessary to analyze more than two or three pieces; additional data usually confirmed the first observations.

Furthermore, we found that our descriptive method took care of the normally troublesome distinctions between the more or less "authentic" or "genuine" songs in the sample. As long as the material was recorded on the spot from native informants, even strongly acculturated music from an area conformed in most respects to the profiles established for conservative and traditional songs. For example, we found that "folk," banjo-accompanied, American mountain ballads differed in only two or three particulars from contemporary hillbilly songs; both could be classified legitimately as adhering to the same performance style, at least in terms of our level of analysis. Many similar experiences made us confident that, even when the sample of data from an area is small and acculturated, our method always tells us something important about the structure of the musical performance in that culture.

CANTOMETRICS

This method is called *Cantometrics*. Cantometrics is a system for rating a song performance in a series of qualitative judgments; one day it may be a way of using song as an indicator of social and psychological pattern in a culture. Cantometrics takes into account the phenomena described by European music notation—melody, rhythm, harmony, interval size, etc.—but it looks beyond these European basics at many other factors present in and (as far as we could tell by intensive listening) generic to the song style of other areas. These factors include the size and social structure of the music-making group; the location and role of leadership in the music-making group; the type and the degree of integration in the music-making group; the type and the degree of melodic, rhythmic, and vocal embellishment in a sung performance; and the qualities of the singing voice normally effected by the chosen singers in a culture. Since these features of a performance are judged by our system in a summary fashion, we also looked at the purely musical traits at a similar level. For example, rhythm was rated, not in terms of the precise meter that occurred in a selection, but in terms of levels of increasing complexity—from the simple one-beat rhythm, often found among Amerindians, to the free, almost meterless rhythms common to much Oriental singing. In addition, however, we looked at the type of rhythmic organization of both the singing and instrumental groups, here again rating the sample in terms of increasing levels of integration, from simple unison to complex counterpoint. Thus our rating system, for rhythm, quickly summarizes in four judgments much of the information that would be obtainable from painstaking notation and analysis of hundreds of examples by normal methods of music notation.

Cantometrics does not depend, except at one or two levels, upon formal musical analysis, but is limited, I believe, to those features of a sung performance which are available and important to a "normal listener" anywhere. Using the cantometrics system, a trained observer can make the same series of defined observations about any song that he hears, whether recorded or "live." These judgments are recorded in a series of thirty-seven rating scales on a standard data sheet. Each one of these parameters or lines contains from three to thirteen points, each point being the locus of a proximate judgment in relation to the other points on the same line. The number of levels was limited to thirty-seven by the size of the coding sheet, and the number of points on any line was limited by the thirteen punches available in a column on an IBM card. No more points were included on any line than we felt could be handled by an attentive listener.

These thirty-seven lines, with 219 points, are set forth in a symbolic map on the right side of the coding sheet. The symbols, which are abbreviations for the distinctions made in each line, greatly facilitate learning and using the system. The listener records his judgments on the symbolic map and then transfers them to a number map on the left, which also serves as an IBM data sheet. Here the numbers are arranged and spaced so that they match the corresponding lines of symbols. With some practice, cantometrics enables a listener to describe a recorded song from anywhere in the world in a matter of minutes. The results of this notation may be compared and then averaged with material from the same culture, until, within a short working period, a master profile in numerical or linear form is ready for cross-cultural comparison.

THE CODING SHEET

The cantometric coding book now ready for publication runs to more than fifty pages and thus can be only summarized here. Therefore, in what follows, each rating scale, which is fully defined in the coding book, is explained in the briefest terms. An exception is Line 1, with which this article is particularly concerned. Unless otherwise stated, Point 1 in each line stands for the nonoccurrence of a trait, and the line itself, reading from left to right, is a scale from nonoccurrence to maximal occurrence of a trait. Figure 1 [not included] reproduces a sample cantometric coding sheet, coded for a lament recorded by Margaret Mead and Theodore Schwartz in Manus, New Guinea. A line-by-line explanation of the coding system follows.

(1) *Organization of the Vocal Group*, rated in terms of increasing group dominance and integration. This line asks the question: Is the performance a solo by a leader (L) with a passive audience (N) and the resultant situation that of the leader completely dominating the group (L over N), or is the group (N) in some way active in relation to the leader (L)? Point 2 indicates complete leader dominance (e.g., Orient, Western Europe). Points 3 and 4 represent other solo singing situations (e.g., Southern Spain). Points 5 and 6 denote simple unison singing in which leader and group sing the same material in the same way and in concert (e.g., Amerindian and many other primitive peoples). In 5 (L/N), the leader is dominant more than 50 percent of the time, whereas the reverse relationship prevails in 6 (N/L). Point 7 represents the situation in which both L and N are active in singing the same melodic material, but one part slightly trails the other and often adds small melodic or rhythmic variations (e.g., Oriental choruses, Watusi). Point 8 (L+N) is noted when L sings a phrase and then N separately repeats it. Point 9 (N+N) is indicated when N sings a phrase and another part of the chorus (N) repeats it. Points 10, 11, and 12 denote what we term interlocked relationships, i.e., when a part of a singing group overlaps another or performs a supportive function for the other (e.g., Negro Africa). L(N, in 10, indicates an interlocked relationship between L and N in which L is dominant; N(L, in 11, indicates a similar relationship with N dominant; N(N, in 12, denotes a similar relationship between two groups. Point 13 (W) indicates complete interlocking (e.g., Pygmy hocketing style, European contrapuntal choir).

(2) *Relation of Orchestra to Singers.* Point 1 denotes absence of orchestra or accompaniment. Point 2 indicates a simple accompanying relation by one to three instruments; Point 3, the same with a larger orchestra; Point 4, the same with a dominant big orchestra. Point 5 indicates a big orchestra alone. Points 8 and 9 denote the trailing relationship with a small and a big orchestra; Points 12 and 13, the interlocked relationship with a small and a large orchestra.

(3) *Organization of the Orchestra*, rated in terms of increasing group dominance from left to right, as in Line 1.

(4) *Type of Vocal Organization.* Point 1: no singer. Point 2: monophony. Point 3: unison singing. Point 4: heterophony. Point 5: polyphony, i.e., any consistent use of part singing, no matter how simple.

(5) *Tonal Blend: Voices.* This line rates voice blending in the chorus from none to homogeneous to well integrated.

(6) *Rhythmic Blend: Voice.* This line rates the rhythmic integration of the chorus in five degrees, from poorly to well integrated.

(7) *Type of Orchestral Organization.* Rated as in Line 4.

(8) *Tonal Blend: Orchestra.* Rated as in Line 5.

(9) *Rhythmic Blend: Orchestra.* Rated as in Line 6.

(10) *Words to Nonsense.* This line rates the relative importance of meaningful words as against nonsense syllables (including vocal segregates) in a sung text. Point 1: words important and dominant. Point 2: words less important. Point 3: words with some nonsense. Point 4: nonsense more important than words. Point 5: nonsense only.

(11) *Over-all Rhythm of the Vocal Part,* rated in increasing degrees of metrical complexity. Point 3: one-beat rhythm. Point 5 and 6: simple meters such as 2/4 or 3/4. Points 8 and 9: complex meters such as 7/8. Point 11: irregular meter. Point 13: no consistent meter.

(12) *Linking Rhythm of the Vocal Group,* rated in terms of increasingly complex integration. Point 3: unison. Point 5: heterophony. Point 7: accompanying rhythm. Point 9: polyrhythm. Point 11: polymeter. Point 13: rhythmic counterpoint.

(13) *Over-all Rhythm of the Orchestra.* Rated as in Line 11.

(14) *Linking Rhythm of the Orchestra.* Rated as in Line 12.

(15) *Melodic Shape.* Point 1: arched. Point 2: terraced. Point 3: undulating. Point 4: descending.

(16) *Melodic Form,* rated from through-composed (1), through five increasingly simple types of strophe (2 to 6) and five increasingly simple types of litany (7 to 12), to Point 13, which represents the special type of litany typical of much Pygmy singing.

(17) *Phrase Length.* The length of the basic musical ideas which make up a melody is rated in five points, from extremely long to extremely short phrases. Complex strophes are generally composed of long phrases, litanies of short phrases.

(18) *Number of Phrases in a Melody,* rated from left to right in eight degrees, from eight or more phrases to one or two in each melodic section.

(19) *Position of the Final,* rated in five degrees from left to right, from the final on the lowest note to the final on the highest note of the scale used in a given tune.

(20) *Over-all Range*, rated in five degrees, from a second to two octaves or more.

(21) *Average Width of Intervals*, rated in five degrees, from dominance of narrow intervals (microtones) to dominance of wide intervals (fourths and fifths).

(22) *Type of Polyphony*, rated in six degrees of increasing complexity from none to counterpoint.

(23) *Embellishment.* The degree of melodic ornamentation is rated in five degrees from left to right, from highly ornamented to virtual absence of ornament.

(24) *Tempo*, rated in six degrees, from very slow to very fast. Point 9, the center point (walking pace), has about sixteen beats per minute. Point 13 was not used.

(25) *Volume of Singing*, rated in five degrees, from very soft to very loud.

(26) *Rubato: Voice.* The degree of rubato (rhythmic freedom) which affects the overall vocal rhythm (Line 11) is rated in four degrees from left to right, from very great to none.

(27) *Rubato: Orchestra.* Rated as in Line 26.

(28) *Glissando* (voice gliding between notes), rated in four degrees from left to right, from maximum to none.

(29) *Melisma* (two or more notes per syllable), rated in three degrees, from great to none.

(30) *Tremulo* (voice quavering), rated in three degrees, from great to none.

(31) *Glottal Shake.* Rated as in Line 30.

(32) *Register(s)* most commonly used, rated in five levels, from very high to very low.

(33) *Vocal Width* normally used by the singer, rated in five degrees, from very narrow and squeezed to very open and relaxed (the yodel).

(34) *Nasality.* The amount of nasalization characteristic of a singer is rated in five degrees, from very great to none.

(35) *Raspiness* (any type of harsh, throaty voice quality), rated in five degrees, from very great to none.

(36) *Accent.* The forcefulness of the singing attack is rated in five degrees, from very forceful to very relaxed.

(37) *Consonant Enunciation.* The precision of enunciation of sung consonants is rated in five degrees, from very precise to very slurred.

This coding system has its crudities and its areas of vagueness. Even so, I have been able to teach it to other students of folk music and have discovered to my delight that they concurred in most of the judgments Victor Grauer and I had arrived at separately. I do not know whether cantometrics will survive the examination of my colleagues for a short or a long time, but I can commend it in several respects. It produces consistent profiles when applied to the music of large culture areas that both anthropology and musicology tell us share a common cultural history. These profiles enable us to recognize and describe song performance structures for the Amerindians of North America, for Negro Africa, for Western European folk song, for the folk song of Eastern and Central Europe, for Mediterranean and Middle Eastern folk song, for the music of the high culture of the Orient, for Polynesia, and for perhaps a dozen other musical culture areas. These structures shape the music of very large areas and may be presumed to have had such formative influence for centuries, perhaps for millennia. Regional and tribal variations of appropriate dimensions are also exhibited by the coding sheets, and it seems likely that Cantometrics can point up important differences as well as links between contiguous cultures. This paper, however, will concern itself only with contrasts between the profiles of large areas.

A final word of explanation is perhaps necessary for the way in which these large-area profiles were prepared. Normally the songs coded from any one area conformed to one, or at most three, profiles. Generally one of these was far more common than the rest. We presumed that this was the favorite mode of song performance in this area, and we brought all these matching profiles together into sets. Then we reviewed each number column and chose the most frequent number in each parameter. This list of numbers was then arranged on a master sheet, and a new profile was established, which became the master profile for the area. Random tests of this master profile indicated that it took care of the majority of song performances from its area. Deviations in subordinate profiles usually concerned minor matters which did not affect the overall impression of stylistic unity.

MUSICAL ACCULTURATION

The usefulness of Cantometrics is, perhaps, most quickly apparent in relation to the troubling problems of musical acculturation. The American folklore school, led by George Pullen Jackson (1943), studied the available musical scores and concluded that most so-called Negro melodies were variants of old European tunes. Africanists, such as Melville Herskovits (1941), pointed to the survival of African musical

habits and institutions in the New World. A comparison of the cantometric profiles of song performance from Negro Africa and from a wide
sampling of Afro-American groups provides the answer to this apparent
paradox (see Figure 2) [not included].

In most respects the African and Afro-American performance profiles are identical and form a unique pair in our world sample. The social
organization of the musical group, the degree of integration of the musical group, the layout of the rhythm, the levels of embellishment, and the
voice quality sets conform to the same ratings in both Negro Africa and
Negro communities in the New World. These paired profiles differ from
each other principally at the level where Jackson discovered Western
European influence, i.e., in Lines 16 and 17, which deal with melodic
form and phrase length. The African profile codes 10 (simple litany) on
Line 16 and 10 (short phrases) on Line 17. The Afro-American profile
codes 2 to 12 on Line 16, which means that American Negroes sing every
type of strophe as well as every type of litany; it also codes 7 and 10
(phrases of medium length as well as short phrases) on Line 17.

The cause for this shift of emphasis in the Afro-American profile
seems clear. Perhaps the most prominent and powerful trait of Western
European folk song is its attachment to the strophic melodic form, composed of phrases of medium length. It has exploited this trait pair (2 to
6 plus 7) to develop a body of melodies unmatched in the world for number and variety. It appears, then, that Negro singers, coming to the New
World, were impressed by the European strophic form and added it to
their musical resources, meanwhile keeping their own system more or
less intact in other respects. As melody makers, they retained their interest in the litany, short-phrase form but learned how to use and to create
melodies in the potent European style.

For another example of musical acculturation, we may look at modern Polynesian song. One of the most notable traits of old Polynesian
music is the choral performance in perfect tonal and rhythmic unison of
long and complex texts, where every syllable is clearly enunciated. In
some areas, a rudimentary form of polyphony occurs: one of the voice
parts rises in pitch and maintains this level while the chorus continues
to sing at the original pitch, thus creating a simple drone harmony.

Shortly after contact with European explorers and missionaries, this
older style was submerged by an acculturated choral style, which most
Polynesians mastered. They astonished, delighted, and sometimes horrified European observers by choral performances in perfectly blended

and often extremely banal Western European harmony. Indeed, a casually organized group of Polynesians could soon sing in the European harmonized style more skillfully than most Westerners. Recordings of these performances became popular hits in Europe and America, and today this Euro-Polynesian style is spreading into Indonesia, South Asia, and even aboriginal Australia.

The cantometric coding system provides a basis for understanding this historical development. In both Western Europe and Polynesia, text is of paramount importance. European singers, however, perform mostly in solo. Choral singing is rare in this area, and, when it occurs, it is badly integrated unison. In order to organize a polyphonic chorus, Western Europeans must be drilled to pronounce, attack, and accent each syllable together and in one manner. This ability to chant in perfect unison, which is a precondition for effective Western European harmonic singing, is a normal Polynesian culture trait. Ancient Polynesia had, as noted above, a leaning toward choral singing indicated by the presence of drone harmony, but it did not have a sophisticated harmonic system. Such a system was provided by the missionaries, eager for Polynesians to sing Christian hymns. European block harmony, when well executed, increases the tonal blend of a chorus to its maximum. Polynesians, concerned about voice blending, quickly adopted Western harmony as a part of their musical system and thus achieved maximal voice blending. In many other respects, however, the profiles of modern Polynesian song continue to conform to standards of the music of old Polynesia.

The stability of the profiles produced by the cantometric coding system is confirmed by a further discovery. I have said earlier that most folk and primitive cultures seem to erect their song structures on one or two or, at most, three models. Whatever the function of a song in a culture, it conforms to one of these models. Thus we have moved on beyond the crude analogies which functionalism has so far provided ethnomusicology—work songs, funeral laments, ballads, game songs, religious songs, love songs, and the like. On the whole, style, as a category, is superordinate over function, in song performance as in other patterns of culture. Therefore, the cantometric diagrams of song style, which represent the song-producing models in a culture, may stand for formative and emotional patterns that underlie whole sets of human institutions.

This extremely general statement must be qualified in one respect, but one that will be of special interest to ethnologists. Whenever a special profile is attached to a body of song with a special function, this exceptional phenomenon can often be explained by the survival, the adoption, or the recrudescence of an entire style in a culture for historical reasons. The Euro-Polynesian and Afro-American acculturated song styles are both pertinent instances of this process, but perhaps another, more general, example should be set forth.

In an earlier paper (Lomax 1960), it was suggested that an older choralizing, well-integrated singing style has survived in mountain areas, on islands, and, in general, on the fringes of Western Europe, largely submerged by the more modern and familiar solo-ballad style of folk song. Cantometric study has strongly confirmed and sharpened this hypothesis. We have found that, in those areas where people sing naturally in well blended choruses and sometimes in harmony, melodies tend to be in litany form, metrical pattern is more complex, melodic embellishment is less important, and voices are lower pitched, wider, more relaxed, less nasal, and raspy. In other words, the stylistic profile characteristic of this "Old European" area strongly resembles the model of simpler African song styles.

There are also choral-litany song types embedded in the repertoire of modern Western European folk song, notably the sea chanties of Britain, various types of work songs, children's game songs, and certain survivals of pagan ceremonial such as the Christmas and May carols of England. All of these song types integrate, strengthen, and direct group activity in various ways. With the exception of the children's games, however, all these functional song types seem to be survivals that are passing out along with the activities and the forms of social organization that supported them. In our society only the children know how to organize and dramatize their feelings in the ancient, collective fashion. That the need for such song types still exists among adult Westerners is evidenced by the recent popularity of highly charged, choral-litany song patterns, rooted in erotic dance forms and created by Afro-Americans. This summary exposition indicates how stylistic models maintain and renew themselves, by working hand-in-hand with history, to weaken or support functionally based song types.

Enough has been said to indicate the general nature and usefulness of the cantometric system. It looks at a level of musical activity which is highly patterned, resistant to change, and superordinate over function. The remainder of the paper will relate certain levels of song performance structure to social structure.

PYGMY-BUSHMAN VERSUS WESTERN EUROPEAN SONG STYLE

One of the universals of song performance seldom remarked upon by musicologists is the working organization of the musical group. There is a difference in kind between the main performance structure of Western European folk song, where a lone voice dominates a group of passive listeners (L over N), and the situation in which every member of a group participates, not only in the rhythm and the counter-point of a performance, but in recreating the melody, as in the Pygmy hocketing style (W). Figure 3 [not included] compares the master profiles of Pygmy-Bushman music and Western European folk song—and exhibits their contrasts. A comparison of the structure of interpersonal relationships and of role-taking in the two societies shows the same order of contrast, strongly hinting that musical structure mirrors social structure or that, perhaps, both structures are a reflection of deeper patterning motives of which we are only dimly aware.

The general shape of Pygmy music must first be summarized. Colin Turnbull, who has done field work among the forest-dwelling Pygmies, discovered that they had concealed the very existence of their musical system from surrounding tribes for centuries. He told me that solo song does not exist among the Pygmies except in the form of lullabies; that their choral songs may be begun by anyone, no matter what his talent; that leadership, during the course of a song performance, shifts from an accomplished to a less accomplished singer with no apparent lessening of support from the whole group; and that the chief delight of the singers is to listen to the effect of group-produced counterpoint as it echoes through the dark cathedral of the jungle. This situation we code 13 (W) on Line 1 and 13 also on Lines 4, 5, 6, 16, 17, 18, and 22. At the bottom of the code, where we deal with register, timbre, and other voice qualities, it turns out that the Pygmy voice is generally low, lacking in nasality and rasp, relaxed, and slurred—13 in Lines 32, 33, 34, 35 and 37. This group sings with yodeling tone, which, in the estimation of laryngologists, is produced by the voice in its most relaxed state. When a singer yodels, all of the vocal dimensions, from the chords through the resonating chambers, are at their widest and largest. This extraordinary degree of vocal relaxation, which occurs rarely in the world as an over-all vocal style, seems to be a psycho-physiological set, which symbolizes openness, nonrepressiveness, and an unconstricted approach to the communication of emotion.

Our coding studies show that a high degree of choral integration is always linked with a relaxed and open manner of vocalizing. This connection is strikingly dramatized by the Pygmy-Bushman style. These stone-age hunters normally express themselves in a complex, perfectly blended, contrapuntal singing at a level of integration that a Western choir can achieve only after extensive rehearsal. Indeed, the Pygmy-Bushman profile represents the most extreme case of total focus on choral integration in our world sample, and in this sense it is unique among folk cultures.

The vocal empathy of the Pygmies seems to be matched by the cooperative style of their culture. All that Turnbull has told us about the Pygmies in his remarkable book and his many papers (Turnbull 1957, 1959, 1960a, 1960b, 1961) confirms this point. Normally the group never goes hungry. Their environment furnishes them what they need for food and shelter. The men hunt in groups, and the women gather in groups. A precise system of dividing food assures every individual of his exact share. There are no specific penalties for even the greatest crimes, such as incest, murder, or theft, nor do judges or law enforcement exist. The community expresses its vociferous dislike of the criminal, and he may be belabored and driven out of the group for a time, but soon he will be pitied and welcomed back among his people.

A Pygmy baby lives, literally, on his mother's body, his head positioned so that he can always take her breast, her voice constantly soothing him with a liquid-voiced lullaby. Children grow up in their own play community relatively unhampered by their parents. When a girl begins to menstruate, the whole tribe joins in rejoicing that a new potential mother is among them. Her joyful maturation ceremony concludes with marriage. Pygmy men do not impose on their sons a painful puberty ceremony; in Pygmy terms, a boy becomes a man simply when he kills his first game. The Mbuti sometimes permit the Negro tribesmen with whom they live in symbiosis to put Pygmy adolescents through a rite of passage, but this is only one of many ways in which the Pygmies tactfully pretend to conform to the desires of their Negro neighbors in order to live at peace with them and to conceal the existence of their own forest culture. When the Negroes have gone back to their village, the Pygmy children are given the bull-roarer and the fetishes to play with, and the little hunters laugh together over the childish superstitions of their black masters. During the initiation ceremonies there is ritual whipping of the boys by the Negroes, but when this takes on a sadistic character the Pygmy fathers intervene.

The forest Pygmies do not share the magical beliefs of their Negro neighbors; indeed, the Pygmies look down on the Negroes because of their superstitious fears and their focus on evil. They have no myths and little formalized religious belief. Their only religious ceremonies occur in times of crisis, when they sing to wake the beneficent forest and to remind it to give them its usual protection. When the tribe gathers after the hunt, joy-filled dances and songs knit the group into a cohesive and fully expressive whole. In our code the Pygmy musical form emerges as a static expression of community joy sung in liquid, open-throated style.

I have dwelt upon this extreme, rare, and somehow utopian situation because it runs counter to most of the music we know and thus illuminates the rest of human musical activity in an extraordinary way. It points to the close bonds between forms of social and musical integration. The choruses of these hunting-gathering peoples sit in a circle, bodies touching, changing leaders, strongly group-dependent. Even their melodies are shared pleasures, just as are all tasks, all property, and all social responsibilities. The only parallel in our coding system is found at the peak of Western European contrapuntal writing, where again all the separate interests of a variegated musical community are subordinated to a desire to sing together with a united voice about universal human values.

Thus far we have assumed an identity between Bushman and Pygmy musical styles, and, indeed, this is what our profiles indicate. Perhaps no two peoples, so far separated in space (3,000 miles), living in such different environments (desert and jungle), and belonging to different racial and linguistic groups, share so many stylistic traits. Even after pointing out numerous musical idiosyncrasies, this cross-cultural mystery still disturbs the two researchers who have most closely examined it, Yvette Grimaud and Gilbert Rouget. Rouget (1956) speculates upon the possible influence of a common cultural heritage or similar environmental adaptation, then leaves the problem. It seems to me that he has neglected one important piece of evidence.

Solo songs are common among the Bushmen and rare, except in lullaby form, among the Pygmies. Otherwise, as far as cantometric analysis is concerned, the styles are, indeed, identical. Bushman males sing plaintive solo songs to the accompaniment of the mouth bow, which, like our blues, dwell upon loneliness and isolation. This sense of personal deprivation grows out of a special Bushman situation that does not exist among the Pygmies. Their harsh desert existence, beset by thirst and hunger, results in a scarcity of women. Thus, in order to have a mate, Bushman men often betroth themselves to infant girls. The result is long years of waiting for marriage and consummation, then a union with a capricious little girl who may be anxious to postpone the duties of a mother and a wife. Meantime the Bushman men, battling for their group's existence in a barren waste, suffer the deprivations common to lonely males everywhere, and they voice this emotion in their solo plaints (Marshall 1959).

In all other important respects Pygmy and Bushman social and musical structures are extremely close. Both groups share; both are acephalous. Their hocketing, polyphonic, polyrhythmic, maximally blended style seems to mirror this system of closely integrated relationships. The Bushman solo "blues," the only major deviation from this pattern, thus suggests the influence of environment on an otherwise consistent social and musical structure. It does not matter whether this Bushman solo song style has been borrowed from a neighboring group. A musical structure stands for a social adjustment, for the fulfillment of a commonly felt emotional need, whether borrowed or not. There is no better proof of this hypothesis than this one divergence of Pygmy and Bushman musical structures.

For further evidence of the link between song structure and social structure we may look at the other extreme of the coding system—a leader dominating a passive audience (L over N)—the principal pattern of Western Europe folk song. This profile shows only slight variation for most folk songs from Norway, Holland, the British Isles (apart from old Celtic areas of Wales, Cornwall, and the Hebrides), Western France, Central Spain, and colonial United States. Text is dominant and rhythm simple for three or four phrase strophes set in diatonic intervals, with an octave range and some degree of embellishment. Voices are from middle range to falsetto, with strong characterizers both of throat and nose and a clear enunciating pattern. The connection between voice type and the degree of integration in group song is reflected in unison singing with poor tonal blend and poor to moderate rhythmic coordination. We may think of the singing of a Rotarian meeting, a football crowd, a regiment on the march in World War II, or a pub group in Britain. Each of these situations is a gathering of extremely individualized specialists, each singing in his own normal tone of voice and uncompromisingly independent of others at the level of vocal empathy.

The familiar pattern in British and Kentucky ballad singing is for the singer to sit quietly with his hands passive in his lap as he sings; his eyes are closed, or he gazes unseeingly over the heads of his listeners. He tells his stories in simple strophes that permit a concentrated narrative pace and demand the full attention of his audience. Thus, during his song, the listeners must remain silent and physically passive. Any movement on their part would interfere with the story. Any distraction would break the ballad singer's spell. When the first singer has finished a number of such songs, another may take his place, and the same pattern is repeated.

The leading singer commands and dominates his listeners during his performance. His association with his audience is, in sociological terms, one of exclusive authority, a principal model for conduct in Western European culture (see Parsons, 1949: 43, 140–147, 178–179, 286–295). When a doctor or a lawyer takes over a case, his authority is absolute for the duration of the relationship. The same unspoken pact joins boss and worker, priest and penitent, officer and soldier, parent and child. Dominance-subordination, with a deep sense of moral obligation, is the fundamental form of role-taking in the Protestant West. Our cooperative enterprises are organized in terms of an assemblage of experts, each one temporarily subordinating his separate, specialized, and exclusive function to an agreed-upon goal. Workers on belt lines cooperate in this way to produce automobiles for Ford or bombers of Lockheed, just as instrumentalists combine to make the big symphonic sounds. Ultimately, this leader-follower pattern is rooted in the past, e.g., in the European concept of lifelong fealty to the king or the lord. Ignatius Loyola inculcated the same principle in his teaching of the Jesuits: "In the hands of my superior, I must be a soft wax, a thing . . . a corpse which has neither intelligence nor will."

This degree of compliance is precisely what the contemporary symphonic conductor demands and gets from his orchestra—and from his audience as well. In its role relationship the symphonic audience, quietly listening to a work of one of the masters spun out under the baton of the conductor (whose back is to his admirers), differs from the ballad audience only in its size. Even the most group-oriented and fully integrated Western music is produced by a collectivity, organized in a manner fundamentally different from that of the acephalous Pygmy chorus, where all parts are equal, where subordination does not exist, as it scarcely exists in the society itself.

A Western table of organization or a belt line or a symphony depends upon a series of clear and explicit commands, arranged in a clear pattern agreed upon in advance. Our Western European folk songs are arranged in the same fashion—a series of compact, clearly outlined strophes and stanzas, each of which bids the listener to view such-and-such an aspect of a sung tale in such-and-such an explicit fashion. While this series of explicit and well constructed packages of fantasy or fact are being delivered to the listeners, the leader-singer must not be interrupted. If he is, he will very likely refuse to sing any further. "If you know so much, sing it yourself," he will tell his rude listeners, much as a doctor might tell an anxious patient, "If you don't like my medical procedure, get another man."

According to Turnbull, a long Pygmy performance may, as a maximum, contain only enough text to make a normal four-line stanza. The rest of the phonating consists of hooted vocables or variations on one phrase of text. Tiring of this material, another singer is free to introduce another bit of text, which in its turn is torn apart into syllables and played with for a while in somewhat the manner of a child or a musing adult in our culture. Here language loses its cutting edge and becomes a toy in a delightful game with sounds. This contrast is noted in Line 10 of Figure 3 [not included], which deals with the relative importance of text as against nonsense syllables. Western Europe codes 1; Pygmies and Bushmen, 13.

THE BARDIC STYLE OF THE ORIENT

Having now described two styles which lie at the extremes of the cantometric system—one solo-unaccompanied and the other contrapuntal-hocketing—let us now consider three master codes that lie between these extremes and that show again how musical structures rise out of, or reveal, the general shape of their social contexts. First, there is the area which, for want of a better term, I call "bardic." Here solo performance is again dominant, but various levels of accompaniment support and reinforce the authority of the soloist-leader. Linking together several large subareas, this bardic style shapes most of the music of southern Europe and Moslem Africa, of the Near and Middle East, of the Far East, and indeed of most of Asia aside from certain tribal cultures.

A searching portrait of the societies which gave rise to the bardic tradition can be found in the analysis of the system of Oriental despotism by Karl Wittfogel (1957). Wittfogel argues that, wherever an agricultural system depends upon the construction and maintenance of a complex of great canals and dams, a despotic control of labor, land, political structure, justice, religion, and family life arises. All the great hydraulic empires—of Peru, of Mexico, of China, of Indonesia, of India, of Mesopotamia, of Egypt, of the Moslem world—conformed to the same over-all pattern. The center owned and controlled every person and all the means of production and power. Complete and blind obedience was the rule. The way to approach the throne was on the knees or the belly. Deviation was immediately and ruthlessly handled by capital punishment, imprisonment, confication, or torture. The ancient rulers of Mesopotamia asserted that they received their power from the god Enlil, who symbolized power and force. The ministry of justice in ancient China was known as the Ministry of Punishment. The Egyptian peasant who failed to deliver his quota of grain was beaten and thrown into a ditch. A court favorite could be executed or deprived of his perquisites at the whim of the emperor.

Wittfogel points out that this system results in a state of total loneliness for the top as well as the bottom of the society. The peasant or small official knows that no one will dare protect him if he disobeys; the king or the pharoah knows as well that he can trust no one with his confidence or, for that matter, with his life—neither his closest adviser nor the members of his family, and especially not his son and heir.

Depersonalized conformity to authoritarian tradition is the norm for such a society. Everywhere in the hydraulic world, song styles show an analogous set of traits. The singer learns to use his voice in a formalized way and then masters a complex set of rules for starting and improvising a theme, and he displays his talent by showing how far he can develop this theme without breaking the rules that apply. The growth of modal systems, with the elaborate set of beliefs and customs surrounding them, reminds one strongly of a society in which social stratification strictly limits the development and growth of each individual from birth to death. Above all there is one voice, expressive of doom and pain and anger, which speaks the varied moods of the center of power. It is a testimony to the noble spirit of the poets and musicians of the past that within this structure they created universes of plastic and plangent beauty.

The Oriental bard is a highly idiosyncratic solo singer, a master of subtly designed verse and of complex, shifting, and sometimes meterless rhythm. He performs highly complex strophes composed of many long phrases, with maximal ornamentation, vocal rubato, melisma, and tremulo, in a voice that is usually high or falsetto, narrow and squeezed—with maximal nasality, raspy, and often characterized by forcefully precise articulation. In places where a primitive type of feudalism still prevails, as in Mauretania and Afghanistan, bards are generally attached to a big or powerful chief and their duty is to celebrate the magnificence of their lords before their world. The bardic voice quality is generally tense, high, thin, feminine, and placatory. Sometimes it is harsh, guttural, and forceful, symbolizing ruthless power and unchecked anger. Its marked nasality, tremulo, and throbbing glottal shake and its quivering melodic ornaments speak of tears, of fear, of trembling submission. These vocal mannerisms are the norm among Eastern mystics, muzzein, and cantors—the bards of God—as well as among the epic singers and the composers of praise songs for the king.

King David, like the great singers of early high culture, probably sang in the bardic manner. This inference is strong, since the style still survives in the whole Orient today, reaching its apogee in the court music of Japan, Java, India, and Ethiopia. A profusion of musical flowers, representing a sort of conspicuous consumption of music, is everywhere pleasing to the ears of kings, and thus to the almighty, whatever his name or names. In the same way, the lover in the bardic area abases himself before his mistress, showering her with flowery compliments, telling her with trembling voice and lavishly ornamented melody that he is utterly her slave.

Thus the Oriental bard was a specialist and virtuoso of a high order. He was the product of long and rigorous training. He conformed to rigid and explicitly stated esthetic theories. In fact, it was in the bardic world that the fine arts of music and poetry arose, alongside of highly developed metrical and melodic systems. Here, too, instruments were refined and developed and complex orchestras established.

In his paeans of praise of the king or of God, the bard spoke for or about the all-powerful center, and it was important that these praise songs be as grand and impressive as possible. He extended this manner to all his productions. Normally he sang at length—in long phrases, long and complex strophes, often in through-composed style, characteristically in song or verse forms that lasted for hours and ran to thousands of lines. He also used his voice in a depersonalized manner, appropriate to the voice of the king, of the god, or of one of his ministers or supplicants. Generally the bard was unsupported by other voices; in an absolutely despotic situation, only one voice should be heard—the voice of the despot or his surrogate.

Thus group singing in the bardic area is at a minimum. Normally, when it occurs, it is unison with poor rhythmic or tonal blend, or it is heterophonic. One thinks here of the choirs of Ethiopia or Korea or the heterophonic style of the Watusi or the enforced unison of the royal choirs of Dahomey. Yet the bard, like the king, needs support. He finds it in an elaborate accompanying style. The court orchestras of the Orient are generally large and play together heterophonically, that is, each instrument speaks the same melody but in its own variant, with many voices independently following the same line. Always, however, a high-pitched nasalized singer or an instrument with a similar timbre leads and dominates the orchestra.

AN AMERINDIAN PATTERN

When Europeans first encountered Amerindian tribes, they could not understand how Indian society worked at all, for there were apparently no permanent authoritarian leaders. Walter Miller (1957) shows that American Indians and feudal Europeans followed two completely opposed concepts of authority. Europeans swore allegiance for life and carried out the commands of the representative of their king. Indians took orders from no one and bore allegiance to no one except on a temporary basis of personal choice. An Indian war party might be organized by a war chief if he were persuasive enough, but the braves who set out with him would desert if the enterprise encountered difficulties. A sizeable percentage of such enterprises ended in failure, and the participants straggled back to the village with no loss of face.

Among the Fox Indians, whom Miller particularly studied, each person had his own supernatural protector, whom he venerated when fortune smiled upon him but reviled in periods of bad luck. The permanent village chiefs had no direct authority; indeed, they were not much more than permanent presiding officers at a village council of equals. Individuals were trained from childhood to venture self-reliantly into the wilderness. Collective activity was at a minimum, and, when it occurred, it was unforced, each individual participating, not upon command, but because he knew from tradition what he should do and how and when he should do it. Just as the individual Indian might ask for and obtain power directly from a supernatural source, so he might acquire a medicine song from the spirit world that would give him the power to heal or to lead a war party.

The shape of the American Indian musical group conforms to the pattern of role-taking briefly sketched above. The solo singer uses a chesty voice, wide rather than narrow, yet with strong characterizers of nasal resonance and throaty burr and with forceful accent—a voice which is expressive of a full-blown and unrepressed masculinity or, perhaps better, of a strong bodily orientation. The major manner of Indian song performance, however, is that which we code as N/L—group superordinate over leader. The leader initiates the song but then is submerged in a chorus performing the same musical material in unison. This chorus links their bassy, resonant voices with moderate tonal blending (varying to well-integrated blend among the Iroquois and some Pueblo groups), but in precise rhythmic concert. Individual voices in these choruses can still be heard, and the effect is of a loosely knit but well coordinated group of individuals cooperating in relation to a common goal. Here, as with the Pygmies and in contrast with the West and the Orient, the importance of text is often minimized. Indian songs normally consist of a few phrases padded out by repetitions and vocal segregates, to form long strophes of complex structure, which the whole group knows how to perform.

Many Indian melodies may be described as through-composed, that is, basically open-ended, leaving the decision for extension and termination to a collective impulse. The strongest element in this situation is a dominant, one-beat rhythm that unites the group in a simple, highly physical re-enactment of their adventures on the hunt, on the war path, and in the supernatural world. Hardly anywhere in this system, except at this nonstratified rhythmic level, is the individual asked to conform either vocally or musically. The very style of conformity in group performances exhibits the principle of individualism.

The profile of Amerindian song remains remarkably constant throughout most of North America and many parts of South America. This consistency of style explains why Amerindian music has been so remarkably resistant to change and how it is possible for Indians to swap songs, as they frequently do, across linguistic and cultural barriers. Indeed, the solidity of this framework confirms a commonsense impression that there is an Amerindian music, distinct from other world musical systems and congruent with an over-all Amerindian culture pattern.

THE NEGRO AFRICAN PATTERN

We have designated the working structure of West African song style as L/N. African music might be called interlocked antiphony. A leader initiates and a group responds, litany phrase by litany phrase, but the group does more than respond and overlap with the leader's part, and the leader usually does more than overlap with the chorus. Very frequently both L and N support and comment on the other part with murmurs, bits of chords, or snatches of musical laughter and with a complex pattern of counterrhythms from hands, feet, and orchestra, not to mention kinesic comment from the dancers. In the solo line, itself, a playful lead voice shifts from open, ringing tones to strong nasalization to powerful rasp, from falsetto coo to bass grunt. Indeed, without such exhibitions of vocal display, an African song leader is soon replaced by another.

Yet, despite the shifting vocal timbre of the African singer, the choruses blend their voices in striking tonal effects. Visible speech analysis shows how this is possible. Although rasp and nasalization are present in the harmonic pattern of the solo voice, they are controlled and precisely placed instead of being pervasive characteristics, as is the case with the vocal characterizers that Western European bardic and Amerindian voices handle. Also, the harmonics are well and widely distributed—signs of the well-tuned voice.

A leader and a chorus part are normally implied in Negro African song, whether or not the performance is solo, for both elements are essential to African song structure. The song leader never performs for long without complex counterbalancing comment by the instrumental or vocal chorus. Furthermore, our research indicates that the length of the leader's part varies roughly with the importance of tribal chiefs over against the tribal council. In more or less acephalous African tribes, song leaders usually perform against a constant background of choral singing. Where chieftainship is paramount, vocal solos are longer and more prominent.

This hypothesis is strengthened by our coding of the ceremonial music of the Kingdom of Dahomey and the court songs of the Watusi of Ruanda-Urundi. In Dahomey, long solos are again important; no polyphony is permitted and highly embellished chromatic passages, rare in Negro Africa but common in Oriental song, become prominent. Among the royal Watusi, highly embellished heterophonic singing, meterless rhythm, long bardic performances, and other traits link Watusi style with that of the hydraulic empires. It would be improper not to observe that, in both these cases, song functions as a support to a powerful ruling hierachy rather than playing the role normal in most simpler African societies. Along the southern border of the Sahara, among peoples strongly influenced by the culture of Islam and in many tribes where powerful kingship systems dominate large nations, solo bardic singing of the type described previously is common. It is my conviction, however, based on examination of a number of cases, that bardic singing of a strongly Oriental type is not of significant importance except in those African societies where institutional patterns akin to despotic Oriental societies shape the whole social system.

This brief sketch of African song performance structure, as exhibited in the cantometric profile in Figure 2 [not included], matches in a remarkable way the gross structure of most African Negro societies (see Murdock, 1959). An African normally belongs to several interlocked groups—to a tribe, then perhaps to a series of segmentary patrilineal kin groups, to one or more cult groups, to a work organization, to an age group, to a political faction, and so on. Each of these groups may have a different head, and in each of them an individual may achieve a varying degree of prominence in accordance with his talents and his status. Although the society is stratified, it is quite possible for a witty man with a highly developed sense of political maneuver to rise to the top of one or several of the organizations of which he is a member. If he is an hysteric, he may become a religious leader and prophet. This provides an exact analogy to the emergence of a talented individual in the African musical group. African music is full of spaces. The loose structure of this musical situation gives the individual dancer, drummer, or singer the leeway to exhibit his personality in a moment of virtuosic display. He will then be replaced, but later on he may pre-empt longer and more elaborate solo passages, thus establishing himself as a recognized and talented musical leader.

Since music is keyed to group integration in a wide variety of African activities, a strong musical personality may be or become a religious or political leader. Yet the very structure of African melodies stands in the way of the L over N dominance pattern, for African melody is litany and responsorial, made up of more or less equal contributions from solo and chorus, with the chorus part dominant more often than not. Thus, in Negro Africa, musical performance structure and social structure mirror one another, reinforce one another, and establish the special quality of both African music and African society—whether in Africa or in African enclaves in the New World.

The strong rhythmic bias of African music also represents this many-goaled, many-headed, group-oriented culture. African rhythm is usually anchored in a strongly accented two or four beat rhythm, but around and through this positive, thrusting, rhythmic unity plays a variety of contrasting counterrhythms on numbers of instruments that give voice to the diverse groups and personalities bound together in tribal unity. At any moment, one of these tangential rhythms can seize the imagination of the group and become dominant, just as in a West African cult ceremony an individual may be mounted by his cult deity and rise from obscurity to total group dominance for a period.

Nor does the Negro group discourage women from taking leading roles in singing, as do many primitive peoples. Here Negro society reflects the comparative importance and independence of women, recognized in other spheres by their ownership of land, their control of marketing activities, and their part in religious ritual.

Perhaps, too, the prominence of polygyny in Negro Africa (cf. Murdock 1959) finds its expression in African musical structure. African education and custom place great emphasis on sexual matters—on fertility, on potency, and on erotic skill. This focus of interest supports the system of polygynous marriage, where a man must be able to satisfy several wives and a woman must compete for the favor of her husband with a number of co-wives. African dance prepares and trains both sexes for strenuous lovemaking, and the swinging, off-beat, rhythmically climactic rhythms of Africa motivate and support this frankly erotic dance style. Yet not all African dancing is a dramatization of courtship and lovemaking, just as not all group rhythmic activity in Africa is dancing in the strict sense. Collective rhythmic activity runs like a bright thread through the web of African life and is, indeed, one of its organizing principles. Work is done, journeys are made, law cases are argued, myths and legends are told, social comment is made, religious rites are conducted to rhythms which can be danced and sung by leader and chorus in accordance with the main structures of African music. The result is that the whole of African culture is infused with the pleasurably erotic, community-based pattern of African song and dance style. The attractiveness of African music for all the world today may, indeed, lie in the fact that it is so practical, that it operates successfully in more of life's activities than any other musical system.

It is my hope that the preceding thumb-nail sketches have indicated the usefulness of the cantometric approach for both ethnomusicology and anthropology. Several viable concepts seem to be indicated by the research at this stage. First, that, as long as music is considered cross-culturally as a whole and in behavioral terms, it is possible to locate structure comparable to known culture patterns. Second, that these esthetic structures remain relatively stable through time and space. Third, that these stable structures correspond to and represent patterns of interpersonal relationship which are fundamental in the various forms of social organization. Fourth, that analysis of cantometric structures may provide a precise and illuminating way of looking at the cultural process itself. Fifth, that, since the cantometric coding system deals with expressive material which all societies provide spontaneously and unselfconsciously, it may become a tool for characterizing and, in some sense, measuring group emotional patterns. Finally, the way may be open for us to make the all-important distinction, first discussed by Sapir (1922)— the intangible yet grave distinction that all human beings respond to— between spurious and genuine culture.

I should like to add one word about the troubling problem of esthetic level. The structures that appear in our coding system are basic to the acceptance of a musical performance in a cultural setting. Without the proper structure, a song is felt to be foreign, or unsuitable, or simply of no interest. The more closely a song conforms to the norm indicated by a given profile, the more acceptable and familiar it seems to be in its cultural setting, yet the beauty of a bit of music depends upon the way the performer and/or composer handle another and narrower level of patterns, which cantometrics is not equipped to examine.

This essay provides evidence that the principal messages of music concern a fairly limited and crude set of patterns; otherwise, they would not be so easily available to such a system. The art of music, however, lies in its capacity to repeat these main messages again and again in slightly disguised and subtly different ways. Here, at the level of musical conversation, we enter a limitless realm of nuance, where reinforcement never brings surfeit or fatigue, where the ear delights in playing with a scale of tiny differences, and the restatement of the familiar is not a command but an invitation to return home.

NOTE

1. The substance of this paper was read at the annual meeting of the Society of Ethnomusicology in Philadelphia, November 15, 1961. The research was sponsored by Columbia University and supported by the Rockefeller Foundation. Many of the ideas developed in the paper grew out of informal discussions with Professor Conrad Arensberg, under whose general direction the research was carried out.

BIBLIOGRAPHY

Bargara, D. A. 1960. *Psychiatric Aspects of Speech and Hearing.* Springfield.
Herskovits, M. J. 1941. *The Myth of the Negro Past.* New York.
Jackson, G. P. 1943. *White and Negro Spirituals.* New York.

Lomax, A. 1959. "Musical Style and Social Context." *American Anthropologist* 61: 927–954.

Marshall, E. 1959. *The Harmless People*. New York.

Miller, W. B. 1955. "Two Concepts of Authority." *American Anthropologist* 57: 271–289.

Moses, P. J. 1954. *The Voice of Neurosis*. San Francisco.

Murdock, G. P. 1959. *Africa: Its Peoples and Their Culture History*. New York.

Parsons, T. 1949. *Essays in Sociological Theory*. Glencoe.

Rouget, G. 1956 (?). *Music of the Bushmen Compared to That of the Babinga Pygmies*. Paris and Cambridge.

Sapir, E. 1922. "Culture, Genuine and Spurious." *American Journal of Sociology* 29: 410–430.

Turnbull, C. M. 1957. "Initiation Among the Bambuti Pygmies of the Central Ituri." *Journal of the Royal Anthropological Institute* 87: 191–216.

———. 1959. "Legends of the Bambuti." *Journal of the Royal Anthropological Institute* 89: 45–60.

———. 1960a. "Field Work Among the Bambuti Pygmies." *Man* 60: 36–40.

———. 1960b. "Some Recent Developments in the Sociology of the Bambuti Pygmies." *Transactions of the New York Academy of Sciences*, ser. 2, 22: 267–274.

———. 1961. *The Forest People*. New York.

Wittfogel, K. A. 1957. *Oriental Despotism*. New Haven.

RECORD BIBLIOGRAPHY

For an extensive list of selected records, see Lomax (1959). A wide range of material is available on Folkways Records and, in a more condensed form, on Columbia Records. A few representative long-playing records are cited below for each master profile.

AFRICA AND AMERICAN NEGRO

French Africa. Columbia Records KL 205.

British East Africa. Columbia Records SL 213.

Bulu Songs from the Cameroons. Folkways Records P 451.

The Topoke People of the Congo. Folkways Records FE 4503.

The Big Drum Dance of Carriacou. Folkways Records P 1011.

Folk Music of Jamaica. Folkways Records P 410.

Cult Music of Cuba. Folkways Records P 453.

Venezuela. Columbia Records KL 212.

Afro-Bahian Music from Brazil. Library of Congress Record 13.

The Roots of the Blues. Atlantic Records 1348.

Negro Prison Songs. Tradition Records 1020.

Afro-American Blues and Game Songs. Library of Congress Record 4.

Ray Charles at Newport. Atlantic Records 1289.

PYGMY AND BUSHMAN

The Pygmies of the Ituri Forest. Folkways Records FE 4457.

Music of the Bushman and Pygmy. Peabody Museum and Musée de l'Homme LD-9.

WESTERN EUROPEAN FOLK SONG

France. Columbia Records KL 207.

England. Columbia Records KL 206.

Ireland. Columbia Records KL 204.

Scotland. Columbia Records KL 209.

Folk Music of Norway. Folkway Records FM 4008.

Anglo-American Ballads. Library of Congress Record 1.

Wolf River Songs. Folkway Records FM 4005.
Pete Steele. Folkways Records FS 3828.

BARDIC

Wolof Music of Senegal. Folkways Records 4462.
Musique Maure. Musée de l'Homme Records.
Folk Music of Ethiopia. Folkways Records FE 4405.
Cante Flamenco. Westminster Records WAP 301.
Modern Greek Heroic Oral Poetry. Folkways Records 4468.
Arabic and Druse Music. Folkways Records P 480.
Music of the Russian Middle East. Folkways Records P 416.
Folk Music of the Mediterranean. Folkways Records P 501.
Folk Music of India. Folkways Records FE 4422.
Music of Indonesia. Folkways Records P 406.
Japan, the Ryukyus, Korea. Columbia Records KL 214.

AMERICAN INDIAN

Eskimos of Hudson Bay. Folkways Records P 444.
Canada. Columbia Records KL 211.
Songs from the Iroquois Longhouse. Library of Congress Record 6.
Music of the Sioux and Navajo. Folkways Records FE 4401.
Music of the Indians of the Southwest. Folkways Records FE 4420.

Chapter 27

Choreometrics: A Method for the Study of Cross-Cultural Pattern in Film

Alan Lomax, Irmgard Bartenieff, Forrestine Paulay

Although human beings always have been prime subjects for the cameraman, social scientists have, on the whole, been the last to recognize the research potential of films. Film can provide the data for a systematic world ethnography and for the systematic study of social interaction, but until recently it has been little used for these purposes. Excellent collections of films do exist, such as those in the Musée de l'Homme and in the Institut für den Wissenschaftlichen Film at Göttingen, but their function in science has been illustrative and supplementary rather than central and hypothesis-producing. Even the collection of film has been neglected by those whose studies it might best serve.

Margaret Mead, in her retiring address as president of the American Anthropological Association in 1960, urged her colleagues to make more use of available data recording and storing devices—the still camera, the tape-recording machine and, most especially, the movie camera. There were restless stirrings and angry murmurs throughout the hall, as these notebook-oriented scholars expressed their irritation at this revolutionary suggestion. Today, however, social scientists are beginning to see that the movie and the television camera are the best ways to gather their data. Psychologists, sociologists, anthropologists, musicologists are shooting tens of thousands of feet of film. The process of documentation is now beginning. What is often lacking, however, is a systematic and reasoned approach to some of the following questions:

1. How should films be shot and edited to serve the ends of social science? Agitated camera movements, frequent close-ups, editing for drama and excitement, and many other "artistic devices" sometimes render the best documentary films almost unuseable as data.

2.   How should films be documented, stored, and indexed so as to be
     of maximum usefulness to the whole scientific community? Very
     frequently there is no information provided about the culture, the
     location, and the group affiliation of the people who move through
     the film scenes. Detailed *dramatis personae* of the present is almost
     never given.

3.   How should films be edited and stored for maximum scientific
     use? It is shocking to learn that almost all footage, even that shot
     by trained social scientists, is cut to pieces in the process of making
     one single film. Practically no one keeps the original footage or
     even one print of their field film intact. Furthermore, it has been
     the habit of governments, archives, film companies, television cor-
     porations, and private individuals simply to burn footage when
     storage became inconvenient. Thus invaluable and never-to-be
     duplicated documents have been permanently lost. Some institu-
     tions are trying to deal with this problem, for instance the British
     Film Institute and the archive of the National Institute of Nervous
     Diseases in Washington. The technical questions concerning
     preservation are being worked out by photographic engineers, and
     it apparently will be possible to keep what film we have left and
     what film we now make as a future pool of information for science,
     provided central archives are now set up on the proper basis.

4.   How can films be organized and exchanged between scholars on a
     systematic basis? Here the pioneer worker, the *Encyclopaedia
     Cinematographica*, provides a model for services being planned in the
     many countries of the world.

5.   What kinds of information for social science can be systematically
     and reliably derived from film? In the final analysis this is the big
     issue. Film is now used as an illustrative supplement and a
     reminder in the work of the social scientist. In fact, a stretch of syn-
     chronized sound film is so rich with data that the problem is *not*
     how to find patterns in it, but how to pick a level of observation so
     that one question can be answered or one set of questions can be
     investigated at a time. This article is a brief account of one attempt
     to deal with this final point: How may film be used as data for
     cross-cultural studies in anthropology?

It is hoped that the European scholars who read this article will forgive
a somewhat provincial American for not knowing about the European

work in film analysis. Perhaps, even so, the mention of a few American studies would be of service to our European colleagues. Actually, G. Bateson and Margaret Mead made a pioneer beginning in their film and photographic studies that related Balinese character and dance to child rearing practices. (Bateson, Mead, *The Balinese Character*, New York Academy of Sciences, 1942.) This study led to an epoch-making conference in Palo Alto between linguists and students of body communication, where important problems in the field of non-verbal communication were threshed out. One unpublished study, resulting from this meeting, has shown that the whole course of a psychotherapy could be predicted from the microanalysis of the first five minutes of filmed interaction between patient and therapist. Dr. R. Birdwhistell, the acknowledged leader in this field, has developed the science of kinesics, including a notation system, which enables him to match and to check the linguist's micro-record of the vocal stream with an equally detailed and informative notation of the accompanying bodily movement. Birdwhistell shows that certain levels of movement shape a formal *"kinesic"* language. (R. L. Birdwhistell, *Kinesics and Context*, University of Pennsylvania Press, in press 1969/70.) Birdwhistell's students have continued to open up this field. P. Byers has developed a technique for the analysis of human interaction in series of still photographs. (Margaret Mead and P. Byers, *The Small Conference*, Mouton & Co., Paris, The Hague 1968.) A. Scheflen has demonstrated that the therapeutic process of psychoanalysis has a predictable structure as formal as that of a poem or a sonata. (A. E. Scheflen, *Stream and Structure of Communicational Behavior*, Eastern Pennsylvania Psychiatric Institute, Pennsylvania, 1965, revision in press 1969/70.) Scheflen is now applying this kinesics technique to the study of complete filmed records of several different family traditions in an urban setting. Here the camera turns for 48 hours without stopping in one family kitchen.

W. Condon uses the kinesics approach to study human interaction at the level of $\frac{1}{2}$ 5> and $\frac{1}{4}$ 0> of a second. Condon first makes a detailed phonetic record of the speaker in a scene. This micro-phonetic record becomes his base line. Condon then studies the speaker's bodily behavior phone by phone, frame by frame, using a stop motion projector. He has found that the body parts of every speaker move in rhythm to his own phonation and that all those within earshot synchronize their bodily movements in the most precise synchrony with those of the speaker. Condon has confirmed Birdwhistell's discovery that all communication is a function of social context. In order for one person to understand what another person says, he must be "in tune" with him. Condon finds that such intrapersonal synchrony is far more fine-grained than that of any *corps de ballet*. (W. S. Condon and W. D. Ogston, "Film Analysis of Normal and Pathological Behavior," *Journal of Neurological and Mental Diseases*, vol. 142, no. 2, p. 237.)

D. Carleton Gajdusek and R. Sorensen have established a large, systematically organized archive of ethnographic footage in the National Institute of Mental Diseases in Washington, to aid them in the study of hereditary nervous disorders. One outcome of this project is the work of P. Ekman and his colleagues in San Francisco, who have scanned film footage in a search of behavioral identifiers of physical and mental illness. In this study they are developing a rapid computer system for retrieval of organized data from vast film libraries. (P. Ekman and W. V. Friesen, "A Tool for the Analysis of Motion Picture Film or Videotape." *J. Am. Psychologist*, vol. 24, no. 3, May 1969, pp. 240–243.) These are a few of the noteworthy film analysis projects in process in the United States.

The remainder of this account concerns the Choreometrics Project at the Department of Anthropology of Columbia University. The first development, supported by a grant from the National Institute of Mental Health, was a technique for the cross-cultural analysis of song performance style from sound recordings. This holistic rating system, called Cantometrics, has been applied to the description of 4,000 songs from 300 plus cultures from every part of the world. The numerical information derived from these ratings, and analyzed with the help of computer programs, has had two main outcomes:

1. Song performance style proves to be an excellent indicator of culture type. Analysis of Cantometrics model performance profiles produces a satisfactory taxonomy of world cultures that traces the migration of humanity and the spread of culture throughout history.

2. Important elements of song structure, sufficient to characterize any style, symbolize basic elements of social structure such as social complexity, productive type, degree of stratification, degree of social solidarity, male and female interaction, and the like. In other words, when the rated information from Cantometrics is run against the rated measures of social anthropology, it is found that features of song style represent and reinforce the varied types of

social structure found in world cultures. These results are based on comparative analysis of high fidelity tape recordings in their cultural context. The data on culture came from sources such as G. P. Murdock, *Ethnographic Atlas*, University of Pittsburgh Press, 1967.

The success of the *Cantometrics* experiment in classifying song styles—perhaps the most elusive of mankind's creations—led to a similar attempt to classify dance and movement. This second technique is called *Choreometrics*—dance as a measure of society. Both methods depend upon direct observation of performance behavior on recordings or film. Both techniques are examples of the natural history method. In both, the measures used are features of behavior found to be prominent and diagnostic in the data itself. For first statement of results see A. Lomax, *Folk Song Style and Culture*, American Association for the Advancement of Science, Wash., D.C., Publication no. 88, 1968.

The first step in the cross-cultural study of movement style was to assemble a small collection of filmed dances from the main culture areas of mankind. The next was to find, through observation of this filmed data, a set of features that varied steadily and constantly cross-culturally and that parsimoniously described the observed contrasts. This rough taxonomic technique was then applied with more care to a larger set of examples, and crude statistical results were studied in order to find out which measures continued to be good classifiers and which were not. In this way, a descriptive rating system gradually developed out of the material itself and in such terms that others might repeat the observations.

After three years of analysis of film from several hundred cultures, the rating scales in *Choreometrics* began to represent a full world-wide range of features of a particular human behavior. For example, a parameter concerned with forcefulness contrasts the most lax movements we have found to the most vigorous we have seen in film, and includes as well the degrees that lie between these two extremes. The position that a particular dance occupies on a number of such rating scales forms a unique profile which can be logically compared to any other such profile. In practice, we find, within any one culture area, one small and distinctive set of movement profiles. When we move across these big cultural border lines, we find another such set which typifies the dances of the new territories.

In a sense, we are in the first stages of the creation of an ethology of human behavior similar in character to the study that K. Lorenz and others have made of the social behavior of animals. The difference is that we are looking at the different patterns of behavior that occur *in the varied culture types of the same species*. These differences are learned and culturally transmitted not biologically or genetically engendered. The contrastive patterns we find are traces of the varying ways in which human beings have organized productive and communication behavior in the world's culture regions.

These studies of song and dance have been sponsored by the Bureau of Social Research and the Department of Anthropology of Columbia University and carried out under the direction of C. Arensberg, the well-known anthropologist, and by A. Lomax, specialist in folksong. In the Choreometrics project, Lomax, a pupil of R. Birdwhistell (Kinesics), collaborated with Irmgard Bartenieff and Forrestine Paulay, leading specialists in movement notation. Thus, the Choreometrics system combines the points of view of the American Linguistic School and the Laban Effort/Shape theory in a context of classical ethnology.

Since anthropology provides the setting for the whole study, our concern has been with the differences produced by culture and by society rather than the differences between individuals or situations within these large contexts. Specifically, the aim is to define cultural style, a dynamic that is postulated to shape all types of communications within any culture, area, or tradition. A. Lomax predicted that dance styles would delineate the same style areas on the song style maps. In spite of the fact that independent methods were applied to the two media, the same large historical, geographic territories have been discovered by both.

In broad terms, *Cantometrics* and *Choreometrics* together affirm the existence of a few very large and very old style traditions:—1) the primitive Pacific, 2) black Africa with Melanesia and Polynesia, 3) high culture Eurasia, and 4) Europe. There also seems to be an Arctic style tradition that links northern Europe across Siberia to aboriginal North America. To the ethnographer with a world view, these big style territories represent the four great stages of human economic development—man the hunter in the Pacific, man the gardener in the tropical zone, man the irrigator and empire builder in Eurasia, and man the agriculturist and industrialist in Europe.

Another finding is that many features of song and dance vary in tight correlation with different kinds of productive activity. In film, we have been able to study the relation between workaday life and communication activity by describing and comparing work and dance of cultures in the same descriptive terms. Dance seems to be a heightened form of everyday activity in each culture. The people of a given cultural territory carry out all their activities within a single stylistic framework which identifies them as members of the same human community. Thus the intentionally coarse, highly consensible descriptive methods of *Cantometrics* and *Choreometrics* have registered the level of the human communications system where the main communication is one of identification. This is the level where the main communication is about culture pattern. The message here is, "'This is who we are. This is how we do things. *I* belong here!!'"

The study of the variation of song style parameters with measures of a social structure has shown that song performance always symbolizes the level of complexity of the productive system as well as the main interaction patterns that link the members of its work teams. A song team in a culture behaves like a work team there. Similar discoveries already emerge from the *Choreometric* study. For instance, frequency of hand and finger articulation in the filmed dances is a very accurate index of the complexity of its main productive operations. The degree and kind of synchrony found in a culture's dancing also will repeat the type of synchrony necessary to complete its community subsistence tasks. As a culture works, so it sings and dances. The dance, seen in this light, is a reinforcement of human adaptive patterns, and, as has already been noted, is a very good index of social evolution.

The Laban Effort/Shape system was the source of some of the measures used in the Choreometric system. Among the fifty features observed, two or three have emerged as the most potent classifiers and organizers in the Choreometrics rating system: 1) body attitude—the dynamic postural base line for all activity (lines 7–11, Dynamics Coding Sheet), 2) the parts, or zones, of the body most frequently articulated (lines 1 and 2, Dynamics Coding Sheet), 3) the geometry or dimensionality of the movement that results (lines 20–27, Dynamics Coding Sheet). These three easily observed features are sufficient to characterize the regional source of any stretch of filmed movement.

The single most potent observation to be made about movement cross culturally is whether the trunk is handled as one or as several units. Here the observer notes the degree to which the central portion of the body is maintained in a rigid or blocklike manner or whether, on the contrary, the pelvis, belly, chest, and shoulders are moved with separate and clear articulation. The human race can be divided into the "squares" and the "non-squares." The "non-squares," or "hippies," seem to dwell in the tropics all the way from Africa to Polynesia, and the "squares" dominate most of the rest of the planet. Within these grand regions there are zones in which the lower limbs are principally articulated—notably Europe, Africa, and Amerindia—and those where movements of the upper body and arms are more frequent—Asia and Oceania. Further classification emerges, if the geometry of the movement is divided into one-dimensional—linear, two-dimensional—curve, and three-dimensional—looping. All three types, of course, occur in all cultures. However, linear movement is far more frequent among simple producers, curved behavior among gardeners, and looping behavior in more complex economies such as irrigation. These three parameters produce the following very simple human geography.

This summary table [table not included] incorporates results that have emerged from careful statistical tests on the Choreometrics sample that now covers over 250 dances from 400 cultures, and includes at least some material from every section of the world.

Our method of studying film proceeds as follows:

Every film to be analyzed is first viewed, and a table of contents is established. We decide on the activity to be analyzed in greater detail: dance, work, or both. As a rule, two observers are engaged in the rating process. In our experience the codings produced by two observers, working and supporting each other, are in the long run more reliable and productive than that of a single rater. This probably is due to the enormous information load on film and to the disturbing experience of unfamiliar communications systems on the viewer.

The whole stretch of film is viewed two or three times and then the main features of its movement profile are recorded on the coding sheet in a first and preliminary representation of the overall character, as recalled in agreement by the two observers. The viewing team records its joint judgment as to the relative frequency or importance of a particular feature rather than an additive score of its actual occurrence. The system employs the normal 5 to 7 point rating scale, familiar to the psychologist, which registers strong tendencies rather than numerical frequencies. Since the observations are scalar and are made on a row of numbers, they may be transferred to computer cards and compared to other such scaled observations in digital and statistical operations. The results emerge as statements of the following kind: feature A is relatively more frequent in region A than in region B or than in the world . . . pattern A composed of features 1, 3, 5, 13 and 36 is unique to region A, whereas another cluster or combination is unique to region B. Cluster factor analysis, correlation analysis, and other techniques readily available to computer programmers, have marshalled tens of thousands of observations of dance style into a first taxonomy and typology of the dance. The rapid summaries and indices from the computer have made it possible to keep abreast of the volume of data produced by the observers and to revise and refine the coding system several times during the first three years of the world dance study.

Another piece of hardware at the other end of the operation has greatly facilitated the work. Stop-motion analyzers that can project the film frame by frame at speeds all the way from one to twelve frames per second make the analysis of zone and shape of movement far easier and more accurate. Normal speeds are used for dynamic judgments.

Inter-rater consensus is the baseline for the validation for both *Cantometrics* and *Choreometrics*. Twenty-four tapes of measures of vocal behavior have been tested by teams of naive judges with a proved average inter-judge consensus of 80–plus percent. These tapes are made up of examples of singing from every part of the world. The most important and new development in the *Choreometric* study is the compilation of similar consensus-training films of the 170–plus parameters that now compose the system. In these training devices, segments of film illustrating each point on a scale are arranged in order. Such films enable new judges to acquire in capsule form and in the space of a few minutes the experience that required years of work by the *Choreometric* team. The learner is taught, not by words, but in terms of contrasted visual experiences arranged in the order that best organizes the data. After he has studied teaching film and has shown some understanding of the features it describes, the beginner then tests his ability to make discriminating judgements on a collection of random examples from all over the world.

One aim of this method is to remove cultural bias from such studies as these. We feel that most cross-cultural analyses of communications have suffered from a strongly European bias. This data-based consensus approach is one way of dealing with this problem because of its own built-in objectivity. Here the observer—or rather the consensus of many observers—becomes the objective measuring device. We feel that this technique of measurement is more appropriate to the study of human behavior than any possible mechanical or electronic apparatus.

Finally, and in an overall sense, the aim of *Cantometrics* and of *Choreometrics* is to produce a straightforward and commonsense way in which all human beings can look at the expressive behavior that occurs in their own culture and to better understand the differences that they find in the expressive behavior of the members of other societies.

LIST OF ABBREVIATIONS TO THE CODING SHEET

Body Parts:

Tr: Trunk; Ch: Chest; Be: Belly; Pe: Pelvis; Sh: Shoulder; WL: Whole Leg; UL: Upper Leg; LL: Lower Leg; Fo: Foot; To: Toes; WA: Whole Arm; UA: Upper Arm; LA: Lower Arm; Ha: Hand; Flw: Fingers; He: Head; Fa: Face; Mo: Mouth; Ey: Eyes; Fid: Fingers individually

Type of Unit:

R: Torso rigidly held; M/a: Moderate Torso adjustments; V: Vertical with diagonal stress; I-: Sectional shifts of torso; U: Undulating; U/L: Upper, lower unit used separately; T: Upper-lower unit separate with twist

Stance:

N: Narrow; W: Wide; VW: Very wide

Relation to Vertical:

V: Vertical / Upright; C: Crouch (concave posture); /: Body pitched on a lateral incline; L: Bent at an angle; P: Prone

Maintenance of torso:

D: Sectional relationship to verticality maintained; C: Controlled smooth changes; A: Alternating between 2–3 Attitudes; H.: Punctuated, i.e. occasional dramatic change; H: Held throughout; P: Playful, irregular maintenance of posture; R: Radical changes

Others:

T-A: Trunk-Arm; T-L: Trunk-Leg; T-H: Trunk-Head; TAL: Trunk Arm Leg; BP: Body Part; Dim: Dimension to 3 dimensions; Tr: Traceforms from straight to loop-curve; Cir: Circuit (closed or open); Ch: Change (of direction): abrupt-smooth; Ra: Range (size of movement): small ↔ large

Chapter 28

Appeal for Cultural Equity

In our concern about the pollution of the biosphere we are overlooking what may be, in human terms, an even more serious problem. Man has a more indirect relation to nature than most other animals because his environmental tie is normally mediated by a cultural system. Since human adaptation has been largely cultural rather than biological, human sub-species are rather the product of shifts in learned culture patterns than in genetically inherited traits. It is the flexibility of these culture patterns—composed of technique, social organization, and communication—that has enabled the human species to flourish in every zone of the planet.

Man, the economist, has developed tools and techniques to exploit every environment. Man, the most sociable of animals, has proliferated endless schemes which nurture individuals from birth to old age. Man, the communicator, has improvised and elaborated system upon system of symboling to record, reinforce, and reify his inventions. Indeed, man's greatest achievement is in the sum of the lifestyles he has created to make this planet an agreeable and stimulating human habitat.

Today, this cultural variety lies under threat of extinction. A grey-out is in progress which, if it continues unchecked, will fill our human skies with the smog of the phoney and cut the families of men off from a vision of their own cultural constellations. A mismanaged, over-centralized electronic communication system is imposing a few standardized, mass-produced and cheapened cultures everywhere.

The danger inherent in the process is clear. Its folly, its unwanted waste is nowhere more evident than in the field of music. What is happening to the varied musics of mankind is symptomatic of the swift destruction of culture patterns all over the planet.

One can already sense the oppressive dullness and psychic distress of those areas where centralized music industries, exploiting the star system and controlling the communication system, put the local musician out of work and silence folk song, tribal ritual, local popular festivities and regional culture. It is ironic to note that during this century, when folklorists and musicologists were studying the varied traditions of the peoples of the earth, their rate of disappearance accelerated. This worries us all, but we have grown so accustomed to the dismal view of the carcasses of dead or dying cultures on the human landscape, that we have learned to dismiss this pollution of the human environment as inevitable, and even sensible, since it is wrongly assumed that the weak and unfit among musics and cultures are eliminated in this way. The same rationale holds that war is a necessary evil, since it disposes of weaker nations and surplus populations.

Not only is such a doctrine anti-human; it is very bad science. It is false Darwinism applied to culture—especially to its expressive systems, such as music, language, and art. Scientific study of cultures, notably of their languages and their musics, shows that all are equally expressive and equally communicative, even though they may symbolize technologies of different levels. In themselves these symbolic systems are equally valuable: first, because they enrich the lives of the culture or people who employ them and whose psychic balance is threatened when they are destroyed or impoverished; second, because each communicative system (whether verbal, visual, musical, or even culinary) holds important discoveries about the natural and human environment; and third, because each is a treasure of unknown potential, a collective creation in which some branch of the human species invested its genius across the centuries.

With the disappearance of each of these systems, the human species not only loses a way of viewing, thinking, and feeling but also a way of adjusting to some zone on the planet which fits it and makes it livable; not only that, but we throw away a system of interaction, of fantasy and symbolizing which, in the future, the human race may sorely need. The only way to halt this degradation of man's culture is to commit ourselves to the principle of cultural equity, as we have committed ourselves to the principles of political, social, and economic justice.

Here I fancy few would disagree. Thomas Jefferson was certainly thinking of cultural equity when he wrote in the Declaration of Independence "that all men are created equal and endowed with the inalienable right to life, liberty, and the pursuit of happiness." A century and a half later, Lenin put laws protecting the autonomy of minority cultures into the Constitution of the USSR, as an important function of government. The result is that most of the non-European musics of the USSR seem to be in a flourishing state. In spite of this and other sincere efforts, however, the reduction in the world's total of musical languages and dialects continues at an accelerating and bewildering pace, and their eventual total disappearance is accepted as inevitable. In what follows I will point to ways in which we can oppose this gloomy course.

Let me deal first with the matter of inevitability. Most people believe that folk and tribal cultures thrive on isolation, and that when this isolation is invaded by modern communications and transport systems, these cultures inevitably disappear. This "ain't necessarily so."

Isolation can be as destructive of culture and musical development as it is of individual personality. We know of few primitive or folk cultures that have not been continuously in contact with a wide variety of other cultures. In fact, all local cultures are linked to their neighbors in large areal and regional sets. Moreover, those cultures in the past which grew at the crossroads of human migrations, or else at their terminal points, have usually been the richest. One thinks here for example of independent but cosmopolitan Athens, of the Central Valley of Mexico, of the Northwest coast of North America, the Indus Valley, the Sudan in Africa where black culture encountered Middle Eastern civilization across millenia—such a list would include most of the important generative culture centers of human history. I say then that cultures do not and never have flourished in isolation, but have flowered in sites that guaranteed their independence and at the same time permitted unforced acceptance of external influences.

During most of man's history contact between peoples did not usually mean that one culture swallowed up or destroyed another. Even in the days of classical empire, vassal states were generally permitted to continue in their own lifestyle, so long as they paid tribute to the imperial center. The total destruction of cultures is largely a modern phenomenon, the consequence of laissez-faire mercantilism, insatiably seeking to market all its products, to blanket the world not only with its manufacture, but with its religion, its literature and music, its educational and communication systems.

Non-European peoples have been made to feel that they have to buy "the whole package" if they are to keep face before the world. Westerners have imposed their lifestyle on their fellow humans in the name of spreading civilization or, more lately, as an essential concomitant of the benefits of industry. We must reject this cannibalistic view of civilization, just as we must now find ways of curbing a runaway industrial system which is polluting the whole planet. Indeed, industrial and cultural pollution are two aspects of the same negative tendency.

Recent events show that we need now to plan a multi-culture, a world in which many civilizations, each with its own supporting systems of education and communication, can live. Until ten years ago, most Americans believed that their taxes supported a genuinely democratic educational system. Then came the black attack on the school system on the grounds that a Euro-American establishment was "brainwashing" them. Their first experience with integration brought a sharp realization of how different their orally transmitted culture was from what their children were being taught in the schools. Blacks saw that their heritage was strongly African, with a selective acceptance of European elements. American intellectuals learned that the educational system, in which they had such a large economic stake, is a system of indoctrination in the cultural achievements and techniques of Europe and the United States.

The administration of music in America is a prime example of how one cultural heritage maintains a monopoly.

Ninety percent of the federal and local money spent on music goes to support one musical tradition—the symphonic, fine-art tradition. Public music education is still largely devoted to increasing skill in appreciation of this one music. Nowhere, for instance, does anyone teach the art of the Negro spiritual, America's deep song. When we "educate" a non-European, especially when we teach him Western music or art or dance, as if no other system existed or had such value, we are brainwashing him. The standard Western European system of music education, taken to other cultural settings, is a form of aesthetic imperialism that is as destructive of native musical autonomy as the takeover of political and economic power is destructive of native initiative.

Many intellectuals thus reject the melting-pot idea and are seeking ways out of the mess this brutal educational policy has created. What we must have is a flexible educational policy which allows the content of education, especially in the arts, to be adjusted to cultural borderlines. One question, to be presently discussed, is how to define these cultural borderlines and the differential structures they delimit. But first the effect of mass communication must be considered.

It is generally believed that modern communication systems must inevitably destroy all local cultures. This is because these systems have largely been used for the benefit of the center and not as two-way streets. Today, unchecked mass communication bullies and shouts humanity into silence and passivity. Artists everywhere are losing their local audiences, put out of countenance by the tireless electronic systems manipulated by the center.

The remedy lies in a policy of decentralization.

Electronic communication is intrinsically multi-channeled. A properly administered electronic system could carry every expressive dialect and language that we know of, so that each one might have a local system at its disposal for its own spokesmen. Thus, modern communication technology could become the prime force in man's struggle for cultural equity and against the pollution of the human environment.

All cultures need their share of the airtime electronic communication can afford. When country folk or tribal peoples hear or view their own traditions in the big media, projected with the authority generally reserved for the output of large urban centers, and when they hear their traditions taught to their own children, something magical occurs. They see that their expressive style is as good as that of others, and, if they have equal communicational facilities, they will continue it. On my last field trip to the West Indies, I took along two huge stereo loudspeakers and, in every village where I worked, I put on a thunderous three-dimensional concert of the music of the place that I had recorded. The audiences were simply transported with pleasure. In one island, the principal yearly people's festival, discontinued for a decade, was revived the next year in all its richness.

The flowering of black orchestral music in New Orleans came because the black musicians found steady, high-paying jobs and prestige in the amusement district and thus had time to reorchestrate African style and then record this local music for export to the whole world.

The origin of the so-called "Nashville sound" is another case in point. Nashville was once the sleepy capital of the state of Tennessee in the United States. In the 1920s a Nashville radio station began to broadcast the music of the nearby Appalachian mountains between advertising announcements. These particular local audiences bought products so enthusiastically that other Southern radio stations followed suit by employing local musicians. This provided the economic base for the development of a vigorous modern Southern rural musical tradition.

Today it has several indigenous forms of orchestration which match the storied folk orchestras of Spain and Central Europe in virtuosity. Nashville has become the music capital of the U.S. because the once scorned style it purveys—reedy-voiced solo ballads accompanied by string instruments—has always been a favored style of the majority of white working-class Americans. This extraordinary event was taking place while most American intellectuals were bewailing the demise of American folk music. The reason that this tradition survived was that talented local performers got time on the air to broadcast it to local and regional audiences.

Nashville and other such new folk culture capitals are, at present, exceptions and accidents, but it is our responsibility to create others. By giving every culture its equal time on the air and its equal local weight in the education systems, we can bring about similar results around the world. Instant communication systems and recording devices, in fact, make it possible for the oral traditions to reach their audience, to establish their libraries and museums, and to preserve and record their songs, tales, and dramas directly in sound and vision without writing and printing them in another medium. Over a loudspeaker the counterpoint of the Mbuti pygmies is just as effective as a choir singing Bach. Thus neither contact nor rapid communication need inevitably destroy local traditions. The question is one of decentralization. We must overcome our own cultural myopia and see to it that the unwritten, nonverbal traditions have the status and the space they deserve.

Another harmful idea from the recent European past which must be dealt with holds that there is something desirable about a national music—a music that corresponds to a political entity called a nation.

In fact, state-supported national musics have generally stifled musical creativity rather than fostered it. It is true that professional urban musicians have invented and elaborated a marching music, a salon music, a theatre music, and various popular song types which please the managing classes and keep the urban working class happy. Yet the price has been the death of the far more varied music-making of regional localities. Italy, a country I know well, has, in almost every valley, a local musical dialect of enormous interest, largely unknown to the rest of the country. These myriads of song traditions are being drowned by a well-intended national communications system which, in the name of national unity, broadcasts only the fine art and popular music of the large cities. Cut off from its roots, Italian pop music, of course, becomes every day more and more dependent on Tin Pan Alley.

These sturdy local musics of Italy, some centuries old, need their own local radio stations as well as financial support for their own artists—jobs in the schools as music teachers, for example. Each local music needs its own institutional support so that each one may continue to produce a music that can add richness to its life as well as to the national and world communities.

Nations do not generate music. They can only consume it. Indeed, our new system of national consumption of music via national communications systems is depriving the musical creator of the thing he needs most, next to money—a local, tribal or regional audience that he can sing directly for. I think it may be stated flatly that most creative developments in art have been the product of small communities or small independent coteries within large entities—like the Mighty Five in Russia, like the small Creole jazz combos of New Orleans.

Real musicians, real composers, need real people to listen to them, and this means people who understand and share the musical language that they are using. It seems reasonable, therefore, that if the human race is to have a rich and varied musical future, we must encourage the development of as many local musics as possible. This means money, time on the air, and time in the classroom.

Furthermore, we need a way of defining musical style territories and thus providing a clear, existential rationale for their continued development. The extant systems of music notations are unsuitable for these purposes because (a) they require long periods of training; (b) none seems to be successful in producing either a classification of world song or an explanation of the connections between song style and social style; and (c) these systems reflect the musical concerns of the culture from which they come, omitting qualities important in other musical languages. Western European notation is highly efficient for recording melodies that use Western European interval types and poly-voiced styles that employ a vertical concept of harmony. Where these are not the main material of a musical tradition, Western notation often distorts the music.

The problem calls for a culturally sensitive way of describing music.

During the past decade, a system of speedily analyzing and comparing musical performances cross-culturally has been developed in the anthropology department at Columbia University. The system is called Cantometrics, a word which means the measure of song or song as a measure. The measures comprising Cantometrics are those that were found, in actual practice, to sort out the main styles of the whole of human song. On each one raters can record their agreement as to whether a single trait of performance—noisy voice or forceful accent, for instance—is markedly and constantly present, moderately so, or little heard in a recording. The 37 rating scales of Cantometrics give a wholistic overview of song performance: (a) the social organization of the performing group, including solo or leader dominance; (b) its musical organization, scoring level of vocal blend and the prominence of unison or of multiparted tonal and rhythmic organization; (c) textual elaboration; (d) melodic elaboration in terms of length and number of segments and features of ornamentation; (e) dynamics; (f) voice qualities.

More than 4,000 recorded examples from 350 cultures from every culture area were judged in this way. The computer assembled profiles of style from these 350 outlines, compared them, and clustered them into families, thus mapping world culture areas. It appears that ten plus regional song traditions account for a majority of world song styles. These regional style traditions are linked by close ties of similarity into four supra-continental style horizons (see Table 1).

1. The *Circum-Pacific* stylistic horizon embraces the exotic singing of tribal Siberia, the extraordinarily homogenous musical tradition of the Indians of North America, the multi-modal styles of Central and South America, and the remarkable aboriginal musics of Australia and New Guinea. The discovery of a continuum of musical style around the whole Pacific alongside of a similarly unified dance tradition seems to represent a human distribution out of Siberia dating back fifteen millenia or more. Ethnomusicologists and other students of the arts should take heart from this finding for it means that expressive systems are not the inconsequential surface of culture, but its most solid and enduring spine.

2. The highly contrastive *Tropical* style horizon includes the Pygmies and Bushmen along with the whole of black Africa, the large Negro population in America, parts of tribal India and Polynesia. Here is another continuity of music and dance, a set of basic patterns spread across a gigantic theatre of human development. The prime characteristic is collectivity, enhanced by choral and orchestral polyrhythms and polyphonies that add excitement to group-oriented performances.

3. In the *Oceanic* region, Proto-Melanesian style is most strongly related to the primordial counterpoint of the African Gatherers, while that of the Malayo-Polynesian is allied to the *Tropical* family, and in its Malay aspect, strongly influenced by the musics of East Asia.

4. *Eurasian*. This zone is dominated by the solo accompanied bardic style which links the entire world of ancient civilization, in both its agricultural and pastoral branches, from the Fertile Crescent east to Japan and west to Morocco and Andalucia. Today, the performance style of Europe and America, one of its sub-provinces, threatens all the other stylistic traditions, by imposing its entire musical tradition (from solo song style and dance to the symphony) through the agency of centralized communications systems.

European music is organized around performance ideas which seem to date back to the roots of European history and are no more sophisticated than the basic patterns found in the *Circum-Pacific* and *Tropical* worlds. Europeans must ask themselves whether they can justify the imposition of the expressive performance style of their hunting ancestors upon the peoples of the rest of the globe. The fact that the music of Europe and America is backed up by industry, science, air power and the electronic communications systems does not, I assert, make its songs and dances more appropriate to the entire human future. In accordance with the principle of cultural equity, the other regions, the *Tropical*, the *Circum-Pacific*, and the *Oceanic* and neglected parts in the *Eurasian* area, should share between them about three-fourths of the total budget of money and time and care humanity has to give. All music, everywhere, needs time, money, and concern in order to live.

The solid knowledge that each of these great regional traditions has a different approach to expressive problems, and therefore different ways of growing, makes the first step of planning for the human cultural future easier.

When each of the giant style regions is subjected to multi-factor analysis on its own—that is, when the musical profiles of its representative cultures are compared—we find a set of about fifty cultural territories that match in an amazing way those already known to anthropologists and ethnographers. From this finding we can draw two important conclusions for the defense of mankind's musical heritage. First, it is now clear that culture and song styles change together, that expressive style is firmly rooted in a real culture developments, and that it can be thought of in relation to the general cultural questions of areas.

Second, this parsimonious classification of musical styles into areas makes planning for the cultural administrator—the defender of the principle of cultural equity—far easier. Each of these style areas has clear-cut geographical boundaries and thus a general environmental character and distinctive socioeconomic problems. The people within these areas can see themselves as carriers of a certain expressive tradition and, sensing their genuine kinship with other cultures of the territory, can begin to develop the base lines for the local civilizations that are needed to protect their often underprivileged and undervoiced cultures. These discoveries compensate somewhat for the recent tendency of folklorists and anthropologists to emphasize the distinctions between neighboring and similar tribes and localities to the extent that neither natives nor experts could develop practical cultural politics. Local or tribal folkstyles should receive money, time, and space, but as representatives of the large, manageable regional traditions.

The mapping of the generative loci of human song is made far more significant by the discovery that each one has nourished a performance style which matches its social structure.

Our survey had drawn on the codified information of ethnography about political and economic systems, social mores, and many other features of culture from a representative sample of our song cultures; thus we could study the ways that society and song varied together cross-culturally. Our finding, backed by strong statistical evidence, is that a framework of performance traits varies directly with a framework of social traits, as follows:

1. The information load of singing increases with socioeconomic complexity.
2. Complexity of ornament and orchestral organization increases with social stratification.
3. Choral vocal blend increases with community solidarity.
4. Vocal tension increases with the severity of the sexual mores.
5. Use of polyphony increases with male/female complementarity.

These five main hypotheses make it possible to predict the general character of song style from knowledge of the social structure and vice versa. Knowing that musical structure mirrors and symbolizes productivity, stratification, solidarity, sexual restraint, and sexual complementarity gives music a clear-cut function. It symbolizes the basic adaptive social plan of a society. Thus it operates as a feedback loop, reinforcing the sense of identity in members of a culture by presenting them, in abstract and formal terms, a sort of audible collage of their lifestyle. People are vociferous in defense of their musical preferences, probably because they hear in a song performance the pattern in terms of which they live and relate to others in their culture.

In studying several hundreds of these performance profiles from as many cultures, the workers on the Cantometrics project were struck by the purity and integrity of each of these style models, no matter how "civilized" or "savage" its source. Every branch of the human species, in adjusting to its environment and its technological framework, has created expressive systems which delicately reflect its tempo, its style of social interaction, its productive system and the moods which they produce.

The sources of agony and conflict, present in all cultures, are voiced in these musical systems and compensated for. Each one is a plan for collective action and for compensatory expressivity which has the character of an ideal solution to a special adaptive problem. Man's history can be seen, then, not as a succession of failures, of botched jobs, but as a series of acts of profound creativity, each one of which produces an idealized model for human interaction that is preserved in art. Moreover, this series of ideal models, portrayed in the musical style of the world's populations, points the way out of the dilemma with which false Darwinism threatens the future of culture.

Further evidence came from another phase of our study of expressive behavior. Here standard measures of social structures (such as population size, productivity, community type, family type, and the like) were brought together with the rubrics of our song performance study—the performance variables to stand for the structure of human communication webs. The combination of these seventy-one scales afforded a rich and well-rounded view of human behavior, because for the first time measures of *both* social structure and communication were employed in describing and comparing a world sample of societies.

Factor analysis of the data had two outcomes. The first was a set of culture regions that could be arranged in a stair-stepped evolutionary order—see the bottom row of Figure 1 [not included]. The second result was to group the seventy-one measures into fourteen homogenous structural factors, clustered into two polar sets—(1) differentiative and (2) integrative. Figure 1 shows how these two principal centroids in human behavior relate to cultural evolution. The evolutionary arrangement of the geographic factors along the horizontal axis provides a time scale from gathering to irrigation agriculture. The vertical axis allows us to measure the rise and fall of the two main socio-communication factors along this evolutionary scale.

Differentiation, the factor combining measures of productivity, articulation of information, stratification, embellishment and the like, rises steadily along the evolutionary scale. In fact, this seems to be the evolutionary vector in culture, though it isn't by any means the only component of social change. Fourteen other independent and semi-dependent factors have also been identified. However, the specially close relationship of the elements of social complexity expressed in this diagram testifies that economic productivity, administrative systems, and communicative systems have evolved together in increasing differentiation across all human time, with steadily progressive steps from the simple gatherers to our own industrial age.

Integration clusters the measures for level of social solidarity, the complexity of integration, the complementary relationship of men and women in social and productive activities and the variables that indicate tension between the sexes—along with performance variables that score level of concert, the degree of vocal tension, and the presence of complementary parts in music. This factor describes the bonds that link team members and the character of the teams and relationships which carry on the adaptive and productive work of society. Its core is male-female complementarity in work and in performance. Where such complementarity is high, as with Pygmies, for instance, polyphonizing is constant. Thus, integration is at its peak right at the beginning of the human series, where the collecting activity of women provided more than 50 percent of the food of the community. This relationship changed in full hunting and fishing societies where men took over the main subsistence tasks. Then the feminine contribution to public performances diminished and the integration variable fell to a low level. It rose again to a peak in the gardening societies of the tropics where a complementary work relationship usually was to be discovered alongside chorally-unified polyphony. The level of integration dropped in complex agricultures where, because of the importance of the plough and of large domesticated animals, males tended to dominate food producing, and, by consequence, societal activities. Thus, this indicator of the character and level of integration in work, song, and dance teams varies in an orderly way over against the measure of social progress.

Human evolution can thus be viewed in terms of (1) increasing levels of socio-technical complexity and (2) cyclic changes in community plans for integrating its sexual and productive teams. Each stage of human progress produces a fresh and unique relationship between the two central variables, differentiation and integration. Each new combination is a witness to the endless potential of cultural adaptation.

This range of models displays many solutions to the human dilemma, expressed in both communicative and societal terms. In them, we can discover a testimony to man's endless creativity and a rationale for the advocacy of planetary cultural and expressive equity. We are impelled to a defense of the musics of the world as socially valuable because:

1. They serve as the human baseline for receiving and reshaping new ideas and new technologies to the varied lifestyles and environmental adaptations of world culture;
2. They perpetuate values in human systems which are only indirectly connected with level of productivity, and they give women and men—old and young—a sense of worth;
3. They form a reservoir of well-tested lifestyles out of which the species can construct the varied and flexible multi-cultural civilizations of the future; since they are living symbol systems, they have growth potentials of their own. As such they are the testing grounds for the social and expressive outcomes of human progress.

Human adjustment to socioeconomic change is usually painfilled and unpredictable. There thus arise explosive and puzzling confrontations between artists and the polities they serve, which are detrimental to the development of both art and society. The recent history in both the socialist and capitalist worlds are witness to this. The serious artist, in order to deal with the feelings of this audience, must not only react to the technical and physical achievements of his society, but to the burdens each system places on its members, to the shifts and imbalances it produces in human relations, to its eccentricities and its sorrows. The artist, in spite of the wishes of the state, deals with the sometimes precarious balance between the differentiative and integrative, the masculine and feminine factors in cultures. In other words, it seems clear that a major function of all art is to act as a link between the politico-economy, the social relations that arise to support it, and the consequent emotional growth of culture.

Each stage of human culture is thus productive of a unique set of social and aesthetic solutions to man's problems of social adjustment.

Practical men, especially if they have an engineering degree, often regard these expressive systems as doomed and valueless. Yet, wherever the principle of cultural equity is applied so that these worrisome musical systems are given a chance to grow, they can rise again.

I cite a few examples known to me: the renascence of Romanian pan-pipe music when the new Socialist regime gave the last master of the pan-pipe a chair in music at the Romanian Academy of Music; the revival of the five-string banjo in my own country, when I induced a talented young man named Peter Seeger to take up its popularization as his life's work; the magnificent recrudescence of the many-faceted carnival in Trinidad as a result of the work of a devoted committee of folklorists backed by the Premier. These and many other instances that might be cited from America and elsewhere show that any of the folk traditions can revive and can nourish important values if given proper administrative care.

But, it is argued, as the world is industrialized, folk and tribal culture must go down the drain. This view holds that all cultures must be indus-trialized and that this means the end of cultural variety. Industry, how-ever, is not an absolute good. Recently we have learned that industry can destroy the natural environment if it is not regulated. Now everywhere man is moving to manage it and to keep his planet green and livable. We can and must control industry's threat to the human imagination and to the human variety. With the aid of atomic energy and computerization, productivity is increasing so rapidly that industry may not be needed in every country of the globe. There can be zones where people can lead other than industrialized lives and produce other goods. Moreover, man can dissociate the rational procedures of industry from the particular social and aesthetic patterns that accompanied its Western origin. Japan is such a case. There, industry has been altered to suit a cultural tradi-tion, rather than to obliterate it. Now that we have a grasp on mankind's cultural range and zones of culture, we can—following the Japanese precedent—adapt industrial progress to local and regional lifestyles rather than the other way around. Now that we understand the relation between technical advances and human relations and expressivity we can better plan a future in which artists and politicians can work together. In such a future, as the function of the artist becomes better understood, the principle of cultural equity will guarantee that culture and art can grow in many directions.

European-Americans are called "pigs" and "honkeys" by other groups, because they feel that Euro-Americans, in preempting most of the airtime and the classroom time for their own cultural concerns, have taken up an unfair share of the communication space. A more rational and equitable solution must be found. If we are to halt the progress of cultural pollution, planetary cultural equity must become a universal principle.

Table 1: Song Style Traditions

1. Circum-Pacific	*2. Tropical (African)*
Siberian	African Gatherer
North American Indian	Black African
Central and South American Indian	
3. Oceanic	*4. Eurasian*
Proto-Melanesian	Central Asian
Malayo-Polynesian	Old High Culture
European	

Chapter 29

Cinema, Science, and Cultural Renewal

On the occasion of the IXth International Congress of Anthropological and Ethnological Sciences, I address my colleagues in every corner of the globe with a call to action in the field of ethnographic film. Formulation, adoption, and support of a program of global film work cannot only affect the development of anthropology in the most positive ways, but also vastly benefit the human race.

One of the greatest opportunities and most urgent tasks of this century is to film the full range of human culture while we can. With the new portable sound equipment, the job would require no more than a generation of concerted international effort. Many good ethnographic films have been made, but the extant footage, important as it is, represents the whole of human culture in only a fragmentary way and was shot and edited according to such a variety of standards that much of it is virtually useless as scientific data. Moreover, because film is expensive to preserve, many old movies recording the habits of people now extinct have been lost, destroyed, or damaged, and this process continues unabated.

The uncontacted peoples of the world have acquired a definite value for the global entertainment industry, and there is a rush to film them for television. Many of these films are simply trash. Most are seriously flawed as scientific data and as honest documents, because their makers do not know where to look, do not understand what they are seeing, or see other cultures as acts in a freak show. This footage, made at such expense to our society and to the aborigines, is often culled for the most sentimental and dramatic scenes, and the slashed-up remainder is destroyed or filed in such disorder that it can never be used by anyone. The situation could be ameliorated if our profession took the lead in planning and in action. Indeed, the creation and archiving of a large corpus of substantial and honest ethnographic film is a major professional responsibility. Only anthropologists can fully appreciate the value of such film and the cultures it depicts. In the final analysis, only if anthropologists do the filming or collaborate in a professional and pragmatic way with the media specialists will the job of filming man's culture be properly and systematically done.

There is little time left. The overwhelming success of the urban-industrial system in controlling and exploiting the biosphere has temporarily blinded the majority of mankind to other values. The entertainment industry, operating a one-way communication system, now threatens to obliterate national cultures as it has long shamed into silence neighborhood, peasant, and primitive cultures. The planet is littered with dead and dying communities, and cultural pollution begins to appear as great a threat to man's future as is industry's damage to his earthly environment. Unless we take concerted action now, what remains of human cultural variety will vanish. We must be concerned not only as scientists, but also as *aficionados* of humanity, for the potential loss is not only to science. Much of the human race stands to lose its continuity, its dignity, and its very ancestors. Meanwhile, the principal creation of the human species—the sum total of the symbolic, expressive, and adaptive systems of culture—is disappearing. The filmed record of this culture is being destroyed at about the same rate.

The literature of anthropology is eloquent witness to the profession's concern with the disappearance of culture variety, but although ethnographic books and museums store knowledge for science and enrich the life of the urban elite, they seldom strengthen or even adequately represent folk and primitive culture. The new media—tape and color film synchronized with sound—produce virtually total documents of culture and, at the same time, can beneficially affect it. Electronic devices now have the potential to record, store, retrieve, and reproduce the whole of man's culture. Moreover, it is clear from recent studies of style and culture that the traditions of visible behavior are quite conservative and that extremely old human patterns are stressed in the nonverbal behavior of living cultures. A range of behavior representing at least a 25,000–year time-span is still available for study and filming. Enough film exists and enough film analysis has been done to demonstrate that no data is comparable to what we can have from a well-organized sound-film survey of our species. Good sound films are almost infinitely rich recordings of multilayered, clearly structured interaction patterns, communication patterns, and stylistic controls. But not only can ethnographic film be a fundamental research tool for the historian and social scientist in the future, it can also serve the following general humanistic ends:

1. A full and eloquent sound-film record will enable the whole human race to know itself in objective terms, and the use of this material will make for a communication system that represents all cultures and all histories, not merely those of urban Eurasia. The principle of cultural equity will come into function in this better-balanced communication system. Moreover, the study of the varied life-styles of the planet will bring to education the multicultural approach it now requires. As we move toward planetary self-knowledge, the educational needs of young people, as well as their egalitarian ideals, can be met by the universal vision and the comparative objectivity of sound film.
2. A total sound-film record of culture will be a resource for our less varied future. Body style, behavior pattern, group organization, mind and hand skills, which are communicated with difficulty through print, can all be represented and captured easily on film.
3. We do not know how much demoralization, the loss of culture, language, and tradition bring about, except that it is great and long-lasting. All strong cultures depend upon a mature and crystallized self-image. The prime function of modern education, communication, and entertainment systems is to reinforce the official cultures of big nations. The smaller economies and the nonliterate folk, in whom the human variety largely resides, struggle vainly to maintain a healthy self-awareness. They lack school systems, scholar historians, time on the air, and the funds to pay for any of these modern essentials for cultural self-development. Now and urgently they need technical help in preserving and adapting their extraverbal and oral traditions, for there is no time to reduce them all to print. Where print leaves out the nonverbal and is too slow for present purposes, the new media are immediate and total.

The urgent matter is feedback. The voices and images of the underprivileged are, unlike ours, seldom or never amplified and repeated by the big communication systems. Quite naturally, then, these people fall into despair. Their enforced silence convinces them that they have nothing to contribute. Broadcasting sound film, especially song, dance, drama, narrative, ritual, and the like, however, can put the human race on terms of parity, if all have access to the media, for all aesthetic systems carry their own message of perfection. The vitality of folkways, given a fair share of airtime, is evidenced by their comeback in India and the Balkans. We have seen in the United States how the expressive styles of Southern Appalachian and Southern Black communities have thrived and developed (even though subject to a corrupt commercial influence) simply because they have had communication space on records and radio. If we film now for feedback to the carriers of all human traditions, we will learn as we work how to foster all cultural and expressive models and we can postpone the otherwise inevitable worldwide grey-out of culture.

The problems are vast, but they demand our most earnest attention. Today the field of ethnographic film lacks clear objectives and standards and is not yet clearly linked to the general anthropological effort. One reason for this is that most anthropologists in most countries have been indifferent to the medium. Filmmakers have been left to their own devices, and therefore this field has become an opportunistic morass. Professional planning and agreement on a minimal, but effective, program are required. Preliminary suggestions are offered herewith.

A filmed ethnographic sample. Our first obligation is to document completely at least one representative culture from all the main branches of the human species. My recent factor analysis of Murdock's 200–province Standard Cultural Sample indicates that about 60 cultures would represent the full range of human social and expressive structures at a crude level. Within some such frame, work could begin on a Standard Filmed Sample in the following steps:

1. Determine those areas in the sampling frame where cultures have already been filmed in a more or less complete and thorough way—such as the !Kung Bushmen and the Netsilik Eskimo.
2. Compile a bibliography and institute a lending system for extant footage so that it can be studied and further filming can be truly complementary. A preliminary survey under way in my office, under the aegis of the Anthropological Film Research Institute, shows that at least some useful film has been shot in almost every one of Murdock's 200 provinces, though some regions (like Patagonia) have been neglected and there is much duplication of effort in others.
3. Agree upon the cultures needed to complete the World Sample, including, of course, communities in Euro-America.

4. Establish standards for filming that will make the same data useful to a wide range of scientific investigators as well as for cultural feedback.

5. Set up an international production committee to stimulate and guide this essentially multinational project. The functions of this committee will be diplomatic as well as creative-scientific, in that it will develop projects, bring anthropologists and filmmakers together as working teams, and advise interested financing institutions (television networks, foundations, governments) at the top level.

Urgent ethnographic film. Film and videotape provide the speediest and most effective medium for recording culture patterns which are in the process of rapid change or are threatened with extinction. The problem is *vast*; every nation is losing part of its cultural heritage, and the need is so urgent that this task cannot be, everywhere, subject to the same level of scientific control as the Standard Filmed Sample. However, planning is still essential.

1. Establish which cultures and communities ought to be filmed immediately, in relation to extant footage.

2. Establish, with the Committee for Urgent Anthropology, a Production Group for Urgent Ethnographic Filming with correspondents in every country.

3. Involve field anthropologists and the national bodies concerned with ethnography and folklore in the task.

4. Work with national and local television organizations.

5. Bring in the amateurs and the nonprofessionals and, through handbooks and training programs, help them improve their standards.

6. Use the footage at the local level for culture renewal and then make other films reflecting the wishes of the culture members; aim to establish local film archives and encourage local filmmakers.

7. Employ these films in the study of the kinesic styles and languages of mankind.

8. Above all, keep one complete copy of every important film, together with its field notes, in the national archives.

Film preservation and archives. The extant corpus of newsreel, documentary, travel, amateur, and ethnographic film, with all its defects, forms the richest body of behavioral data available to the social scientists, the historian, and the humanist. Yet this great data bank is not only virtually unused, but also poorly housed and cared for. Most new footage is burned or fed into shredders. Old footage is thrown out or allowed to decay. What remains is inadequately documented. If drastic measures are not soon adopted, most of this record will be lost.

There is nowhere an institute, so far as I am aware, even in plan, to embody the concept of an electronic storehouse of human behavior, where the data on the visible and audible behavior of the species would be instantly retrievable at a distance. Modern recording and storage techniques make such an archive feasible, and this is, of course, what we need. Meantime, while the business of taking film booms on an international basis, the business of taking care of it remains national, local, or nonexistent. The National Film Board in Canada, Gosfilmofund in Moscow, and others are limited to special functions. No organization that I know of has the funds to gather and take care of even an adequate sample of the important footage of which it is aware.

If film in general is inadequately archived, the situation of ethnographic footage is scandalous. Most filming is underfinanced, and budgets do not provide for the preservation of the original, or even a complete copy of the original, as a field record. The original is cut to pieces to make one film for the general audience. Offcuts are seldom rejoined or cataloged and often end up in the dustbin. This destructive process has been somewhat slowed by Gajdusek and Sorenson's pioneer activity at the Behavioral Film Archive of the National Institute of Nervous Diseases; total cold storage for originals, study copies complete with detailed captions for each scene, and accompanying soundtrack descriptions by the filmers are among the many standards set.

In fact, there are a great many film institutes and archives around the world doing parts of this big job. A survey must be made and liaison established among these enterprises. Here one can give only a few examples. At the Institute for Scientific Film in Göttingen, under the direction of Gotthard Wolf, a serious effort has been made to assemble, preserve, and distribute a world sample of comparable filmed behavior in the *Encyclopedia Cinematographica*. Serious ethnographic footage is bought and field trips are mounted and subsidized to make new films covering a small but well-distributed set of cultures. The footage acquired consists of long sequences in undisturbed medium or long shot. Masters are preserved, and from them topical films are edited, each dealing with a single activity and accompanied by a scholarly descriptive pamphlet. The range of subjects is limited to food production, handicrafts, ritual, and dance; these limitations, which may be considered somewhat old-fashioned, provide comparable data on several types of basic human activity from a broad spectrum of culture. So far as I know, the *Encyclopedia Cinematographica* is the only sizeable body of comparable human behavioral data on film. Wolf has endeavored to give scholars everywhere a common data bank by establishing branch collections in various countries from which copies of the films may be cheaply rented or purchased. The ethnographic film archives and surveys that are to come will find much to learn in the great film workshop of Göttingen. It is distressing to hear that the generous government support which has made this trail-blazing effort possible may now be reduced.

The Center for Ethnographic Film, headed by Jean Rouch, has edited the UNESCO bibliographies, kept alive the international film festivals and organizations, and trained and launched scores of filmmakers, but lacks the funds to gather and take proper care of all the films and footage known, even in Paris. The UNESCO film section plans to locate an international ethnographic film archive in the Rouch center, and this plan deserves all our support. However, the field must grow in a decentralized way through a chain of linked archives on all continents. For example, in Australia three agencies engage in ethnographic film production, the Commonwealth Film Unit, Australian Broadcasting Commission, and Australian Institute of Aboriginal Studies. Step by step, the remains of Australian Aboriginal life are being filmed in a thorough and perceptive fashion. Each sizeable culture should have such a coordinated activity to plan, supervise, edit, publish, distribute, and preserve ethnographic films. Plans are under way to establish such a center in the Smithsonian Institution in Washington, but progress is slow, again because of lack of funds.

Indeed, financial support for ethnographic film is shrinking rather than expanding in comparison to the growth of the rest of the visual media. There are a number of contributing factors. In the first place, the showing of shorts and documentaries in regular movie theatres has steadily diminished in most countries. The television industry more and more tends to create its own films and shows less interest in the productions of outsiders. Moreover, the exploitation of cinema as entertainment by the film and television industries has degraded the medium itself and reduced its credibility. The cinema has such a low status among the arts that the industry itself has failed to preserve the film documents in which its own achievements are best recorded. If it had not been for Henry Langlois, the great French film collector, we would not have copies of the great films of the last fifty years and the history of cinema would have been lost.

Because of the overemphasis on the entertainment potential of the visual media, the networks, especially in the U.S.A., do a needlessly superficial job when they produce ethnographic documentaries. The insulting and tiresome formula "white man venturing among dangerous savages" is still the spine of too many of these programs. Because a lot of money is often spent, the public gets the impression that a thorough and sincere job has been done. Meanwhile, the specialist and the native are bitterly disappointed. The public lack of interest in and understanding of non-Establishment cultural patterns and their avoidance of them are symptomatic of a general practice of Euro-American society, which has consistently failed to give other cultural systems a fair share of airtime and funds for education. Finally, the funding institutions, which once backed documentary and ethnographic filming, have been withdrawing their support because their investment seems to have produced no outstanding scientific or humanitarian results. This is in part due to the inherent difficulties in the development of a science of visible behavior. Growth in this field has been slow because of the fixation of humanists upon written documents. The camera reveals the Euro-Asian exploitation of the planet and the resultant human misery in a way that the scientific essay could always avoid.

In the development of a world plan for making, storing, studying, and using ethnographic film, it should become our business to change these attitudes, and an immediate initiative of research activity must be the first step. Universities or local enthusiasts can easily pay for storage of film until it can be archived electronically or otherwise. Stimulating examples of the use of this film as scientific evidence and for social benefit will encourage the owners of footage to take care of it. Meantime, the following program should be initiated:

1. Establish local archives in which important footage can be stored under controlled-temperature conditions, with provisions to protect printing originals and masters.
2. Require that all film budgets provide for keeping one or two complete prints of all footage and a complete shot list.

3. Appeal to all the government agencies that make film for their cooperation in preserving film and making it available to scholars in each country.
4. Examine and report on all national collections of ethnographic film.
5. Enlist the participation of the commercial film industry.
6. Set up a program of graduate degrees in film research.
7. Devise a computerizable system for film subject and sequence indexing.
8. Develop an international system of electronic storage and retrieval of sound film and videotape.

This must be an international enterprise. There is no one country that can house the film or finance its care. The job cannot be done without world cooperation.

Standards for filming. The demand of scientists for footage that meets all their research requirements can be a technique for postponement. Many of the cultures and behavioral patterns in the available footage can never be filmed again. Older, if sometimes less perfect, documents give our fledgling science the time-depth it needs, provided we are willing to learn, like historians, to evaluate the available evidence. There is ethnographic data of some sort in all more-or-less intact documentary footage. This is not to say that we should not have data standards and that they should not improve, but rather that we should learn to use what is already in the record.

Everyone who studies film as data has suggestions which would make film documentaries more useful to science. However, the field is so new that all opinions about it are likely to be naive. The following remarks about standards are therefore made with genuine diffidence by one who has had little practical experience in filming and whose work depends upon the skill, talent, courage, and generosity of the cameramen who have spent years in the field. I hope these professionals will not take offense.

The farther away the cameraman gets from urban centers and the mainstream, the more valuable his film becomes. Non-Western cultures are being destroyed so rapidly that this film may one day be the only witness to a way of life which has vanished. Not only should shooting be accurate and well-conceived, but it should be of top technical quality, not degrading its subjects with poor exposures or "shooting down." Moreover, the temptation to sensationalize can be at least tempered by taking care to show the everyday hand skills, hard work, and constant care for others on which all human societies depend. Margaret Mead challenged the American system of child-rearing by showing in her films that in many ways the child-rearing practices in non-Western societies are vastly more humane than our own.

We need to agree to film the same areas of activity in the same way across the whole human range so as to have a body of film for comparative use. If we had footage of the following scenes from a fair sample of world cultures, our science would be well on its way: the most important food-producing activity, one or several of the most important public assemblies, at least one long family sequence (cooking and eating), child care, dance and song, handicraft, and conversation.

At least part of the filming in the field should conform to standards such as the following:

1. Start with an overview of the whole context of the event.
2. Continue medium-long shots that loosely frame the whole event with minimum change of focus and angle.
3. Persist in a mode of shooting which keeps the main actors in the frame throughout long and significant stretches of action.
4. Avoid closeups of one person or of one person's face or of isolated body parts. These are of little use, since viewers cannot judge them in isolation from their context. In practice, when a cameraman continually zooms in or turns his lens away, it is because the action contains behavior too painful for him to continue watching.
5. Keep notes on the what, when, and where of every scene made at the time.
6. In the absence of sync sound, use wild-track recording of the audible texture of events, the ordinary everyday sounds of conversation, weeping, laughter, music, etc., to add another dimension to the document.
7. Above all, take long sequences; three minutes should be minimal.

Training films are needed to sensitize filmmakers (whether or not they are anthropologists) to the cultural variation of movement style. Even the anthropologist filmmaker may not realize that he is the prisoner of his own culture's standards and will impose these standards on the things he sees and films unless he consciously strives against this. It is important to shoot in terms of the style of the culture. Although we still have much to do to confirm our findings, we know that every culture area has a style of movement and of interacting that shapes all its behaviors. This pervasive pattern not only forms its dance, but can be perceived in speech, song, and art. Of course, every sensitive cameraman is, to one degree or another, aware of these patterns of posture and dynamics.

It is a common experience in screening film to see movements cut off in mid-phrase or interactions sliced in two as they are unfolding. The length and spatial dimensions of movement phrases and segments of interaction vary profoundly among cultures. West Europeans, for example, use linear, punchy, abrupt, moderately long phrases. These factors strongly affect the way they shoot and cut films. Cultures with a different sense of timing and phrasing are often visually chopped to pieces by Western filmmakers. I believe this is the principal source of the fatiguing effect of a great deal of documentary footage on the ordinary viewer. The perceptual apparatus simply cannot deal with so much broken, incomplete pattern. Western filmmakers can take great liberties with Western material because they know the fit of everything in the behavior of their fellows. Lacking that intimate acquaintance when they deal with unfamiliar kinesic and social systems, they are likely to miscut.

The filmmaker working in his own culture falls into its rhythms naturally. If, like Flaherty, he can afford the time to soak himself in a foreign culture before he begins to shoot, its patterns will insensibly affect all his work. But most filmmakers are short of time. In that case, sensitization training may be of help. The length of movement phrases can be observed and measured. The spatial geometry of the subjects can be sketched and become part of the design and framing plan. The placement of accents—whether they come at the beginning or the end of actions, whether they produce an effect of follow-through or sustained energy—gives human behaviors different rhythms, and these can profitably affect the pulse of the shooting. The most profound determinant of movement pattern is, of course, which parts of the body are most actively articulated or posed in action. Body set varies profoundly among cultures. Taking these differences into account and observing where action is initiated and how it moves from one part of the body to another—especially which body parts normally come into play in various kinds of actions and interactions—will keep the cameraman in touch with the very wellsprings of the behavior he is filming.

A film that achieved much of this was Balikci's excellent *Fishing on the Stone Weir*. The camera watched a group of Netsilik Eskimos building a fish dam across a swift northern river in the polar summer, then spearing and smoking a winter's store of salmon. There are no sounds except those of nature and of the Eskimos talking. No commentary is needed because the shots are so loose and so long and the cutting rhythm at first so slow that one has time to learn and fall into the rhythm of the Eskimos as they trudge across the immense tundra, find their camping place by the river, and lift boulders to make their dam. Eskimo movement is composed of powerful phrases tied together in long strings of effort. Unhurried pacing permits the viewer to perceive this and to be drawn insensibly into the action. By the time the swift fish-spearing sequences begin, one is vicariously participating in the life.

Anthropologists working as or with filmmakers can plan films that conform in this way to carefully observed movement style. On the Choreometrics Project we are beginning to produce a set of illustrative films which will orient filmmakers and their audiences to these problems and sensitize cameramen to the size and shape of movement forms, the main postural habits of people, and the general shape of the dynamic pattern which runs through all their activities. The design of films may then reflect more clearly the aesthetics of the cultures photographed.

Most films, like all art, function to reinforce some particular cultural tradition. This is why films tend to be culture-bound, and though this is appropriate for dramatic filming it is inappropriate for documentaries of other cultures. Our Western bias is, for example, shown in the great emphasis placed upon the purely visual, the rectangular framing, and the preference for swiftly paced narratives and plots concerned with the fate of individuals, particularly young people struggling to find love. Western bias has often caused filmmakers to focus on the lives of some handsome young couple who are the culture's closest equivalent to a Hollywood hero-ingenue pair. While the film unwinds a remake of the familiar American fairy tale, one sees the people who should have been stage-center sitting off to the side and regarding the proceedings sardonically. The results of the Adair-Worth experiment, which turned cameras over to volunteer Navahos, often seemed to reflect the embarrassment and lack of expertise of amateur filmmakers more than they did "the perceptual world" of the Navaho. Nevertheless, this was a ground-breaking experiment that pointed in the right direction. Recently young filmmakers have been turning over the direction and the sequencing of their films to native leaders, and this seems a worthwhile preliminary step toward films that represent the world view of other cultures.

Even so, most of the "best ethnographic" footage I have seen in the past five years of intensive search was shot by anthropologists or folklorists or under their guidance. More often in those films was the "moment right," the telling sequence left undisturbed, the general patterns clear, and the sentimental or snobbish note omitted. Unfortunately, most of this footage was technically or photographically inferior to the less meaningful product of the professionals. Our aim now must be to marry the finest camera work to the best in field technique to produce permanent documents worthy of their subjects. A useful guide in planning this work is the audience(s) aimed at, since film is first and foremost a medium of communication. There are at least five audiences for ethnographic footage, all with different needs: general, national, school, scientific, and local.

The general audience is the one too many ethnographic filmmakers try to capture, without having the necessary money or production know-how. Many try to follow Flaherty without realizing how hard his road was. The Hollywood success image is so strong that many specialized filmmakers feel their product is a failure if it fails to get television or general theatrical distribution. One tends to forget the enormous 16mm audiences of today, the huge 8mm and cartridge audiences just around the corner, and the scientific and humane uses which should be the central concerns of the anthropologist. Even so, the splendid success of some ethnographic films shows that they can win the great mass audience for the people and the ideas we cherish if ethnographers have the money, time, and the right collaboration.

The public has thus far shown great interest in the natural environment and the fate of threatened animal species, but little concern about the disappearance of cultures. One reason, I suspect, is that the members of our piratical Western culture do not like to look at the victims of colonialism. Another is that often anthropologists have not been able to make clear what their films had to say. If films about the animal world outsell our views of culture pattern, it may be because we do not motivate our audiences to look at or teach them to see what we see in our films. Every anthropologist wants to involve his audience with "his" people as he is involved. Whether he succeeds in enlisting their sympathies depends, largely, on how much detail he can bear to sacrifice to an overall theme which involves the viewer. Films, of whatever genre, that appeal to mass audiences usually deal with themes of survival—the struggle of the hero, the underdog triumphant, the woes of lovers. All the truly popular ethnographic films, from *Nanook* to *The Tribe That Hides from Man*, fit this pattern. The perfect structure of the culture, the fascinating aspects of some human institution, may interest the film ethnographer more than the sort of fundamental theme that could elicit strong emotion in Leipzig or Dallas. If the anthropologist chooses to neglect the universal theme for the characterization of some interesting pattern of behavior, he must bid farewell to the mass audience. He will do so without regret, knowing that every general-audience film demands of the specialist that he omit and cut short much that is germane to the culture. Besides, his footage, if well and honestly made, has many other uses.

Films for the national audience show the customs and problems of a tribal group or a cultural minority to the people of the surrounding nation. One of the most important informational functions of documentary film has been to dramatize and win national sympathy for the situation of oppressed or neglected groups so that the behavior, the needs, and the potential of the group become more generally understood. These regional documentaries, if tactfully handled, can contribute much to the resolution of the fears, tensions, and rivalries of multicultural nations. Moreover, they open the national communications system to contributions from a wider sector of the populace, thus giving minority groups a sense of dignity and of belonging. It can be argued that this use of documentary footage can be inopportune or even counterproductive, but in most cases this will depend upon how the footage is handled or the context in which it is presented.

The development of ethnographic film programs designed to raise information and lower conflict levels within a national audience provides an important theatre of action for the anthropologist. Ultimately the emphasis of these nationally oriented films must fall upon the interdependence of groups within an ecological or economic territory. Since this theme has inherent drama for the national audience, this kind of cinema can often present a richer, more detailed, and more leisurely account of lifeways and communication styles than films aimed at a general audience.

Schools and universities are at the moment the major audience and the main source of finance for ethnographic film-making. There seem to be hundreds of films designed to show students how the people of other cultures live. These films play useful roles in teaching geography, history, social science, musicology, anthropology, and other subjects. Their main classroom use has been to illustrate "better than words" what is contained in lectures and books and to add an element of excitement and reality to the subject. One gathers that films are employed only infrequently as data or as the basic text. There are at least four approaches to the use of film in teaching anthropology:

1. The one-subject film, dealing with one activity such as a handicraft or a social event. This is the most common "scientific" approach to ethnographic film-making. Critics object that often the activities are staged and removed from their normal context. Perhaps too much of such film-making has been done without developing a method of analysis along with experimentally tested hypotheses.
2. The cultural episode, developed by Tim Asch and John Marshall, gives the student an uninterpreted, holistic slice of life, the camera sympathetically following one event from beginning to end. In the best of these episodes, the watcher feels himself a participant of a quarrel, an arrest, a game, a flirtation, or a family meal. Such in-depth treatment of cultural motifs gives the feel of character and motivation. The skilled teacher may use these films as the starting point for the analysis of similar episodes in the student's own life.
3. The stylistic comparative film offers the student cultural perspective by applying the same measures to similar episodes and activities from several cultures.
4. The total film allows the student to experience and then study a whole way of life. This approach is exemplified in the important film essays, such as *Dead Birds* or *Miao Year*.

Overemphasis on the classroom aim of film can seriously flaw the ethnographic film effort. The cultural bias of the particular school audience aimed at can distort both filming and editing. Our films must be judged not by how effective they are for teaching American college students, but by how thoroughly and honestly they report and interpret culture. The problem is not how to teach anthropology, but how anthropology can use film to illumine the human destiny. Such teaching must develop a sound comparative approach, resting upon a serious analysis of the visible events in the footage. As things stand at present, teachers and students often have very little to talk about after a film viewing, because they have no method for working through the structure of visible events and relating this information to whatever else they know about the culture. If students are to be involved in genuine study of film, they must learn techniques of film analysis, and in this case they will use all or part of the unedited footage, in which the camera dwells at length and with a minimum of movement on the visible event.

The scientific audience is concerned with understanding the structures of human behavior in their visible manifestations. With the insights of kinesics (the science of body communication), the most prosaic footage of the most ordinary human event becomes endlessly fascinating. The public will find it so as well when they discover that sensitive filming and sophisticated viewing will bring enriched understanding of the big human problems—communication, personal development, mating, child-rearing, work, illness, and peace.

Few film professionals are yet trained in these new techniques for seeing the structure in behavior. This training can bring rigor into the human sciences and an undreamed-of sensitivity to ethnographic filmmaking. The savants in the field—scholars like Gregory Bateson, Margaret Mead, William Condon, Albert Schefflen, and especially Ray Birdwhistell—should be supported in setting up orientation and training programs. Several methods are at hand, each useful for working at a different depth in the visible stream. Among them are Condon's microanalysis of interpersonal synchrony, Birdwhistell's kinesics-linguistic approach, Schefflen's situational analysis, De Havernon's study of authority in relation to food distribution, and the choreometric technique for comparing movement style cross-culturally of Lomax, Paulay, and Bartenieff.

Each of these methods contributes to an emerging science of human ethology. An important step, still to be taken, is to develop the concepts and the methods in terms of which the social science filmmaker can record the gross visible patterns of familial, community, economic, and political systems at work. Basic to all this scientific work is the improvement of field filming. Dramatic editing, shifts of perspective, and all the tricks of montage simply destroy the value of the film document for the scientist. He requires the whole event, the full context, the whole body in action, the entire group—and, above all, long, continuous, undisturbed shots, so that the overlay of patterns in the interaction itself will have time to emerge. Schefflen, in his study of a psychotherapy hour, discovered in this hour a number of rigidly patterned cycles, ranging from two or three minutes to half an hour in length. It is not usually possible to afford such full field documents, but if the activity is worth filming at all it should be covered at some length. Here the interests of science and of the people in the film closely coincide.

The local audience must not be overlooked. Even the social scientist tends to forget that the principal social function of film is to reinforce the culture of which it is the product. Ethnographic footage is far more interesting to the subjects of the film than to anyone else. When their friends and their lifeways fill the screen, no scene can be too long or can be rescreened too often. For this audience, too, all the details are important, because the footage concerns life itself—survival itself. Thus the people who figure in the films should see the footage in toto and as often as they like, both in local screenings and over local television. As far as practical, plans should be made to place a copy of the film at or near the site permanently. The videotape, with its instant and endless replay, is already an important field tool. The ethnologist will benefit from these showings, for here he can discover how people see their own culture and what his mistakes and omissions have been. If proper filming has been done, the people will rediscover in the footage the worth, the dignity, and the beauty of their way of life. There can be no question of the beneficial effect of such feedback for folk cultures in the vicinity of powerful and highly organized communication systems. Good film seems to act as a healthy reinforcement of old cultural values, in much the same way as do the mass media of communication in Western society. For the underprivileged cultures, who lack their own media systems, ethnographic film can, temporarily, fill a void and repair the damage the stronger systems have wrought upon the weaker. A number of filmmakers who have tried feedback in the field testify that, if handled correctly, it does indeed serve to strengthen or renew culture pattern.

Adrian Gerbrands by chance screened a documentary on Eastern New Guinea mask-making for a native group in New Britain. The audience reacted powerfully during and after the screening. They, too, had once known how to make such masks and should, they felt, try their skill again, especially if their art too would be filmed. After Gerbrands had filmed the group's mask-making, a lone native approached him with the offer to perform a very important and defunct ceremony if he would film it. Naturally, again Gerbrands used his camera. On his next trip to New Britain, the other men in the village insisted on seeing the film and were so distressed at the poor quality of the filmed ceremony that they vowed forthwith to reenact the whole ceremony, masks, costumes, ballet, feasting, and all, but at a length suitable for filming. This event and its resultant film were such a success locally that the ceremony is now being celebrated every year just as in former times.

A young American film team established its rapport with an Eskimo community on Nelson Island, Alaska, by setting up its apparatus in the village school and inviting the community to come in and find out how the equipment worked. After a few days, everyone understood syncsound filming, and people later paid little attention to the rig as they were being filmed. Meantime, the filmmakers settled down to convince the leading males that they, and not the filmmakers, should decide what was to be filmed. This took about a month, after which the community leaders became the directors of the cinema. The resultant film, spoken entirely in Eskimo, is a display of Eskimo survival strategies, using snowmobiles, but concluding with a long, well-choreographed, traditional hunting dance. The Nelson Islanders feel this technically excellent and culturally focused movie is by far the best of the many films they have seen. They show it to every stranger, to all returning community members, and on all public occasions. It has become a focus for the continuing growth of Nelson Island culture.

Jean Rouch tells me that he has always shown his films in the West African bush and that the effect there has been good. I assume that others have had positive experiences with feedback. If this be so, it seems clear that anthropologists have in film not only a useful tool for applied anthropology, but a means to stimulate genuine regional and national cultural development among modernizing peoples everywhere. Our concern is not directly with the political economy so much as with the shape of the culture and the continuance of its forms and vital style through whatever economic and political changes this era may enforce. By filming now with the express purpose of renewing, in the carriers of all human traditions, a sense of their worth and cultural integrity, we will learn, as we work, how to foster all culture and all expressive models.

Today our aggressive, expanding urbanism, with its gifts of technology and medicine, treats less advanced societies as obstacles to be changed or gotten rid of. A sense of valuelessness and anomie pervades the world. The filmmaker, working with feedback, can defend the age-old rights of people to the earthly and spiritual terrain they occupy. His function, his reason for filming, is to raise morale. His films will be works of art and history around which nonindustrial cultures can regroup and rally. In this way ethnographic film-making can play a part in social and cultural therapy, by giving not only voice and image, but heart, to flagging cultures. Especially to cultures that lack a written tradition and the assurance it brings, ethnographic film can provide a sense of continuity and worth. The stability and mental balance of all societies rest upon these feelings, which it is the principal business of education and the arts to engender. In fostering this condition, anthropologists will be playing a crucial role in world development, a role that cannot lack for support since it will forward both the humanitarian and the scientific goals which are basic to the social sciences, especially to anthropology.

Part V

Final Writings

Introduction by Matthew Barton

The articles in this brief final section give only the barest hint of the range of Alan Lomax's activities in the period from 1978 to 1995, when he suffered the first of a series of strokes that forced him to retire. During this time he was active in both the academic and popular spheres as a researcher, writer, field recorder, filmmaker, television producer, lecturer, performer, and multimedia designer. He typically had several projects going at once, and worked full days until his forced retirement at the age of 80.

In 1978, Lomax went back to the Mississippi Delta with John Bishop and Worth Long. Together they made "The Land Where the Blues Began," a sixty-minute television program that aired on Mississippi Public Television in 1981. The trip to Mississippi also yielded additional material for Lomax's book *The Land Where the Blues Began*, which he had been working on in one form or another since the 1950s. Published in 1993 by Pantheon, it garnered the National Book Critics Award that year. The trip to Mississippi may have whetted Lomax's appetite for field work after a long hiatus, and from 1982 to 1985 he undertook a series of video field trips in other parts of the country, including the Louisiana Bayou, New Orleans, and Appalachia. These excursions served as the basis for the five-part PBS series *American Patchwork*.

In 1986, Lomax completed the fourth Choreometrics film, *The Longest Trail*. Like the earlier films—*Dance and Human History* (1976), *Step Style* (1980), and *Palm Play* (1980)—it was a cross-cultural study of dance and movement using the work of various ethnographic and documentary filmmakers to illustrate the findings of the Choreometrics study. While the others presented a worldwide range of traditional dance, this film was different in that its goal was to show the stylistic consistency and cultural continuity of American Indian dance from the Bering Straits all the way to Tierra del Fuego.

In that same year, a new edition of the 1938 book *Cowboy Songs* by John and Alan Lomax was released. For the occasion, Alan and Joshua Berrett wrote a new introduction that paid tribute both to the cowboys and John A. Lomax, the original ballad hunter. In July of 1986, an unlikely scene was played out at the White House. Alan Lomax, a man whose name appeared in *Red Channels*, and who saw many of his closest friends and colleagues persecuted during the McCarthy era, received the National Medal of the Arts from President Ronald Reagan.

Lomax disliked reminiscing for its own sake. However, when he saw a chance to set the record straight, he took it, and in several of the pieces in this section he takes a long look back at some of his best known and least known field work. In 1993, Atlantic Records reissued the *Southern Heritage* series that Lomax had produced from his 1959 southern field recordings. The series originally consisted of seven long-playing albums, which were now squeezed onto four CDs and packaged in an attractive box along with a booklet of notes by Lomax and music critic Robert Palmer. Here Lomax reiterates one of his most passionately held beliefs— that folk music does not need to be revived so much as it needs to be maintained. Lomax and Palmer were nominated for a Grammy award for their work.

Though recognized as a classic, Lomax's 1950 biography *Mr. Jelly Roll* had been in and out of print since its first publication. The success of the Broadway show *Jelly's Last Jam* helped spark interest in a new edition, published in 1993, for which Lomax wrote a fresh foreword. It is both a tribute to Jelly Roll Morton and a withering critique of the stage show, which Lomax saw as a woefully misguided distortion of Morton's personality and music.

Brown Girl in the Ring was not published until 1997, two years after Lomax's forced retirement. It was finished by his two collaborators, Tobagonian musicologist J. D. Elder and his sister, folklorist Bess Lomax Hawes. Lomax first worked with Elder in the Caribbean in 1962. Lomax always sought out children's game songs when he was in the field, and the Caribbean was brimming over with such songs. A songbook seemed an obvious idea, but it took many years to bring it about. The final result is both ambitious and accessible, including sheet music and instructions for fifty-eight Caribbean game songs recorded by Lomax and Elder in Trinidad, Tobago, Dominica, St. Lucia, Anguilla, Nevis, and Cariacou. An accompanying CD, including most of the original field recordings, was released simultaneously on Rounder Records as part of the Alan

Lomax Collection series. Lomax's foreword—the first time that he wrote extensively for publication about the 1962 Caribbean field trip—is included here. It was probably written in 1993 or 1994.

Most of his work from this period, whether in print, on film, or other media, is explicitly or implicitly informed by the findings and conclusions of the Cantometric and Choreometric projects. He cited them frequently when writing about his past field work, and they served as the basis for the consuming project of his last working years: the Global Jukebox.

Work on the the Global Jukebox began in 1988, with plans to use the latest computer and video technology to create a multimedia interactive database based on and powered by the Cantometric and Choreometric findings and data. In its simplest application, it is indeed a jukebox that enables people to hear music and see dance from all over the world simply by clicking on a map. But users are also able to survey worldwide relationships between dance, song, and social structure in a kind of digital exhibit created by their own interests and queries. Lomax saw it as the world's first "intelligent" museum and envisioned it as a powerful medium for scientific research on human expressive behavior, a truly democratic educational tool, and a means for promoting "cultural equity," that ideal which he first named in the early 1970s, but which he had nurtured in all of his work in folk music since the 1930s.

Although he lectured on the Global Jukebox and made many public demonstrations of its prototypes, Lomax never wrote anything about it for publication. The piece included here is excerpted from a 1993 grant proposal, and will, it is hoped, give some idea of what Lomax sought to accomplish. As of 2003, the Global Jukebox exists in the form of a prototype, and plans have been made for its completion.

Lomax was often vexed by journalists and others who asked only about his most famous informants—Jelly Roll Morton, Leadbelly, Woody Guthrie, Muddy Waters, et al. In later years, he occasionally got the chance to write about artists far less well known but no less worthy. In 1987, Barry Ancelet and Michael Doucet compiled a two-album set of recordings of Cajun and Creole music that Alan and John Lomax had made in Louisiana in 1934. Alan contributed an analytical essay to the liner notes, which was included in the Rounder CD reissue of this album.

In 1994, he contributed a short foreword to Katharine D. Newman's *Never Without a Song: The Years and Songs of Jennie Devlin, 1865–1952*. Lomax had recorded Jennie Devlin for the Library of Congress in Gloucester,

New Jersey, in 1938. She was a servant and housewife from Philadelphia who endured a life of Dickensian hardship with heroic dignity, learning and singing tragic and humorous songs all along the way. Newman, then known as Kay Dealy, befriended her in the 1930s, and brought her to Lomax's attention. In her introduction to the book, Newman recalls what Lomax said to her at the time: "It's Gran's story more than her songs. Write a book about her." The book that she eventually published in 1995 is a moving and trenchant account of Jennie Devlin's life, and also includes a fascinating description of the 1938 recording session with Lomax at Jennie's home.

The foreword that Lomax contributed to this book is among the last pieces that he completed for publication. In it, there are many classic Lomax themes: the literary allusions (to Dickens, Defoe, Pepys, and others), the cross-cultural comparisons (citing female singers of Haiti, the Georgia Sea Islands, Scotland, Virginia, and Kentucky), and the importance of oral history. But running through it all is a bigger theme. Although Jennie Devlin did not attain the fame that Leadbelly and Woody Guthrie did, she was still one of those people with "a lot to say and a lot to remember" who John and Alan Lomax celebrated in their introduction to *Our Singing Country* (1941). It was the Jennie Devlins— and hundreds, perhaps thousands of others—who first inspired the Lomaxes. And it was their stories and their spirit, not only their songs, which they hoped would inspire America to look to its own people for culture. As Alan Lomax put it in a 1940 radio script; "The essence of America lies not in the headlined heroes . . . but in the everyday folks who live and die unknown, yet leave their dreams as legacies."

By the end of his life on July 19, 2002, Lomax had sought out the essence and championed the legacies of many other countries and peoples, but this statement of purpose still rang true. As John Lomax wrote of cowboy songs in 1938: "As long as red blood runs, the rough words and the plaintive lonely notes found in some of the tunes will move the heart of man."

Chapter 30

The Global Jukebox

The Columbia University Cross-Cultural Survey of Expressive Style
(1962 to 1982) employed techniques from social anthropology, linguistics, and ethnomusicology to describe, map, classify, and interpret the
social and cultural history of the non-verbal and orally transmitted performance traditions of song, dance, and speech. The project began with
a grant from the Rockefeller Foundation in 1961 and received generous
support from the National Institute for Mental Health, the National
Endowment for the Humanities, the National Endowment for the Arts,
the Ford Foundation, and the Rock Foundation. Its scientific goal was to
devise ways of analyzing and comparing recorded and filmed performances cross-culturally. The humanistic goal was to slow the rapid shrinking of human cultural resources, brought about by the centralization of
communication and education. Links were discovered between the taxonomies of several modes of performance style and of social structure.
The combination of the song-style system and social structure measures
produced a family of culture areas that corresponded to the views of historians of culture.

The project discovered adjunct, parallel taxonomies of various
modes of performance and culture style, together with correlations
explaining their co-variance. Factor analysis showed that the main features of cultures give rise to a set of factors which resemble those discovered by the performance systems. The main structural features of
culture, which seem to be reflected in performance systems include climate, main subsistence focus, population size, centralization of government, level of social stratification, solidarity of social groups,
technology, child rearing, gender, family size and type, sexual division of
labor, and the severity of sexual sanctions. Geographic factor analysis
also produces a set of regional culture factors which resemble those

already found in the factor analyses of the several performance sets. The projects' findings were reported in a series of books, papers, television programs, films, and conference presentations.

GLOBAL JUKEBOX PROJECT

The complexity of the findings and the measurement systems demanded audio-visual illustrations and graphics. This problem has been largely overcome in the Global Jukebox Project, which is rich in maps and other graphics. The Global Jukebox Project began in 1988 with a small grant from the Rex Foundation and continued with generous support from the Apple Corporation, the MacArthur Fund, and the National Science Foundation. This funding supported the development of a prototype stand-alone interactive multimedia and statistical analysis system for the statistical and media resources sources developed by the Columbia University Cross-Cultural Survey of Expressive Style.

The development of a multimedia, cross-cultural database, funded by the NSF/AAT Grant, marks an advance both for science and in the use of computers in science education. This so-called Global Jukebox presents the first numerical models of the full range of global cultural variation in holistic form, suitable for experimental study. In doing so, it integrates systematic, multi-modal, cross-cultural descriptions of performance styles to the matching data on social structure. LINKAGE provides instant audio-visual illustrations of every finding at every juncture. The whole database allows the scientist, the layman, and the student to explore, experience, and manipulate the broad universe of culture and creativity in a systematic fashion, with audio-visual illustrations at every turn of the road.

The people of the whole earth perform in the Global Jukebox. Such vivid portrayal of the human cultural heritage puts the computer center stage in humanistic education. Its multicultural content reaches out to users of every cultural background, both in America and overseas. As networks go online, its tested analytic and taxonomic canons can bring this statistically organized view of culture pattern to a world audience and, at the same time, help to order and give significance to the oceans of audio-visual materials that will soon be available through online digital libraries.

The discovered correlations between the 300 variables in the systems of measurement help explain the variation of tradition in time and space. Moreover, as our study of modern urban material shows, they continue to account for change in contemporary culture. This web of hypotheses, together with its explication, remains to be integrated into the data-rich models of the Global Jukebox. The ongoing scientific development of this database will produce a more dynamic model of tradition, rich in explanatory power, and, with the aid of Artificial Intelligence, capable of discovering many new hypotheses.

The appealing content of the Global Jukebox, which includes contemporary pop song and dance, attracts students to serious study and to exploration of their surroundings. It also vividly illustrates the importance 1) of careful empirical observation and 2) of mathematical operations with data and of the testing of hypotheses—the baselines of science. Furthermore it opens up the whole human universe to the student, enlarging his sympathies and training him in systems of audio-visual learning with which he can make sense out of the overwhelming audiovisual surround of today. Such training refines the sensibilities essential to the makeup of scientists and humane citizens of the world. Recent findings by Gardener and others clearly indicate that a wide range of interests and accomplishments characterize breakthrough intellectuals such as Einstein and Russell. An even broader breadth of vision and skills are generated by work with the Global Jukebox, which trains its users to become experts in a wide range of the arts of humanity, to approach it with the use of mathematics and the scientific method as well as to understand and value their own cultural backgrounds.

The Global Jukebox, therefore, is not just an encyclopedia of music, dance, and culture, but a dynamic model of the cultural universe which the user may explore, manipulate, and expand. It instantly generates modal profiles and picks out their most significant traits in six communication systems—singing, dancing, speaking, orchestration, instrumentation, and culture pattern.

Chapter 31

Preface to the 1993 Edition of *Mr. Jelly Roll*

When Jelly Roll was a boy, his loving godmother sold his soul to the devil in return for a gift of boundless musical talent. For him, I believe, this bargain with Satan became quite real. In spite of his outcaste origins, he fulfilled all of his ambitions. He defeated all comers on the piano and at the pool table and, as the leading composer and conductor of early jazz, could afford to wear diamonds in his teeth and on his sock-supporters. When he lost all that he had gained, he attributed his misfortune to sinister unseen influences. And on his deathbed, so his mistress said, he was calling for holy oil to cheat the devil of his godmother's bargain.

His Faustian story parallels that of Robert Johnson, the great bluesman, in fact, of many believers in voodoo. Zora [Neale] Hurston, the great black folklorist, tells of the crossroads encounters of would-be bluesmen with a satanic figure who clipped their fingernails or brushed his demonic hands across their guitar strings to make them masters of their instruments. Peetie Wheatstraw, who called himself the Devil's Son-in-Law, was said to have acquired his gifts in that way. A quirky old Irish fiddler told me about an unfortunate fiddler that "didn't have but the one tune," till one of the little people took pity on him and ran her hand along his bow, and he became the best fiddler in all the country. In olden times remarkably talented people were believed to be God-inspired, whether by Apollo or some other deity. But in these ancient and widespread beliefs there is usually no retribution, as there is in the Christian world, no sense of deadly sin as there was in Jelly's Catholic heart.

Wherever he is now, whether in heaven or hell, Mister Jelly Roll is probably well pleased that the recognition he sought—and which many critics feel he richly deserves—is coming his way. The August *Smithsonian* has reissued his great Red Hot Peppers orchestral series with worshipful scholarly notes. He figured prominently in *Pretty Baby*, the best film about Storyville. Twyla Tharp has devised a delightful and frothy suite of dances, called *The Four Jellies*, to his music. Bob Green and others have edited fine editions of his piano scores and orchestrations. His music is now standard fare at jazz festivals the world over.

I know of at least two performers who tour America enacting *Mister Jelly Roll*, with words and music that recreate his memorable recital on the Library of Congress stage. Two musicals about him are concurrently running in New York. There will be more to come, doubtless—movies, television, better musicals (I hope), and, God help us, deconstruction—all the recognition that our ravenous culture denies to the geniuses it neglects and punishes when they are alive, and lavishes upon them when they are dead. It appears that Jelly Roll, the Dizzy Dean of jazz, may outlast both his critics and his contemporaries.

The Broadway musical of considerable flair, *Jelly's Last Jam*, treats the Faustian side of Jelly's life with great imagination. It also confronts his Creole color prejudice, which estranged him from some of his fellow musicians. However, quite unfairly, the script gives the impression that Jelly was unique in his feeling that blackness was a mark of social inferiority. This prejudice was not only normal to his Creole mulatto background, it has poisoned most Afro-American communities. Well-born mulattoes objected when their children wished to marry down the color line. This painful color-caste attitude, which divided New Orleans into hostile neighborhoods, was not only a source of conflict in Jelly's life but, as I discovered later, an issue in the lives of all the old-time jazzmen of the city. I applaud the writer of *Jam* for confronting this painful theme, but it is unjust for him to send Jelly off to hell as the singular carrier of this hateful prejudice.

Jam seems to go out of its way to misrepresent its anti-hero. It has him "jamming," a practice Jelly Roll loathed. "This is something I never allowed in my bands, because most guys when they improvise, they'll go wrong"—that is, they would depart from the classic canons of New Orleans music. Jelly himself is portrayed as a tap dancer or hoofer, a role that as a musician he looked down on. In spite of the warm and brilliant performance of Gregory Hines, it is taps on the floor rather than fingers on a keyboard that interpret the subtle ideas of this remarkable American pianist and composer. Moreover, the square rhythms traditional in East Coast tapping obscure the subtle Caribbean beat which throbs in Morton's music.

I was astounded to see that the Harlem team which created this musical hardly touched upon the rich New Orleans folk traditions that Jelly Roll celebrated in his music and in his reminiscences. There is no hint of the jazz parades, the Indian maskers with their collective improvisations of Afro-Caribbean music and dance, which are the wonders of American folklore. Instead, we are given second-rate blues and cootch songs, mounted on routine New York choreography and pit-band arrangements, which succeed in making this supposed testament to regional originality look and sound as much like a routine Broadway musical as possible.

Jelly Roll was the first jazz composer, the equal or, some feel, the superior of Ellington. His arrangements form part of the basic vocabulary of jazz, but most of his music still has not won public recognition. It could have brought a fresh sound to Broadway, yet his innovative compositions are neglected by the producers of *Jam*. New York and Harlem, as they so often have done in the past, substituted their supposedly sophisticated formulas for this unique and charming regional music. They might have had something better than *Porgy and Bess*. Instead they have another slick Harlem musical hit. What a shame, for Jelly's sake especially.

In the roar of dance halls, the rush of recording sessions, handling a clutch of temperamental musicians, Jelly felt he had never managed to have his compositions properly played. He came back to this again and again. I remained a bit skeptical until, some time after his death, I was fortunate enough to attend an all–Jelly Roll concert at Steinway Hall. That afternoon Bob Gibson, leading an orchestra of great jazzmen, who had rehearsed Jelly Roll's scores for several months, produced sheer magic. Here in Jelly's exquisite program music—"Milneburg Joys," "The Pearls," "Wolverine Blues," "Doctor Jazz," "Steamboat Stomp," "Black Bottom Stomp"—an American Vivaldi at last emerged. He had created what Copland and Gershwin had fallen short of: an easy-going, sophisticated American orchestral idiom that was a match for Twain and Sandburg. Almost all of this charming regional music was omitted from or submerged in the show-biz hubbub of a musical whose title might better be *Harlem's Last Treacle*.

The author of *Jam* condemns Jelly Roll to hell for his boastfulness, for his obviously exaggerated claim to have invented jazz. Hasn't this gentleman heard of jiving and shucking, of rapping and sounding, which are the currency of street and barroom talk? Here anything goes to make your point. When Jelly told his audience that he had invented jazz, he was speaking up for his hometown in New York's Harlem, which so often has taken all the credit for black cultural innovations. Jelly had squelched Handy for asserting that jazz was born in Memphis. And here in Harlem, where the carriers of the great tradition were few, where big bands with horn sections were replacing the lacy counterpoint of New Orleans, he was sticking up for his hometown. He was grieved and shocked when he saw his musical acquaintances jumping on the band-wagon, which he and his hometown friends had started to roll, without learning to speak the language of jazz in classic New Orleans style.

As is true of everyone with a cause, his forcefulness annoyed some folks and has continued to provide fuel for his critics. But even when his star was fading, most of his listeners agreed that he could back what he said with what he knew and what he could do. His listeners were aware that the main innovations in jazz had come from Middle America—rag-time from Missouri, the blues from the Delta south of Memphis, jazz from New Orleans and Chicago, boogie-woogie and swing from Kansas City. In fact, New York contributed little and late to jazz, although Van Vechten and other 1920s' critics created the impression that jazz was born in Harlem. The roots of Harlem's entertainment tradition were rather in the minstrel show, modernized for Broadway. I say this, not in criticism of the elegant artists of Harlem—Fats Waller, Rosamund Johnson, Cab Calloway, Duke Ellington, and all the great men of bop—but only to cavil at the inhospitable treatment that New York gave to the great music of New Orleans and its cantankerous proponent, Jelly Roll Morton. Harlem's indifference crushed Morton, and the author of this Harlem musical also has it in for him.

On PBS he posthumously berated Jelly Roll for not acknowledging his sources, as if this great original were somehow a plagiarist, a credit stealer, when in the heat of barroom arguments he claimed credit for "inventing" jazz. This was Jelly's way of saying, "Jazz is from my home-town. I was rocking the cradle of jazz before you guys were born." All Jelly couldn't say—the whole complex and orchidaceous story he had in his mind—came pouring out in the recordings he made at the Library of Congress. Far from stealing credit, here Jelly introduced a huge cast of New Orleans musicians who would otherwise have been forgotten, and then brilliantly played their music and superbly sang their songs so that they will always be remembered. In language as raunchy as the life in this city of pleasure, he portrayed its streets, bars, neighborhoods, customs, and celebrations, depicting the whole rich background out of which jazz grew. In two weeks he recited a masterful history of the origins of jazz, including all its best tunes and harmonies. Sources! It was Jelly who first took us to the wellsprings of America's most original music!

In the 1970s a television series brought me back to New Orleans to probe into the origins of jazz. Again the essential truth of Jelly Roll's story impressed me. He tells us "we had people there from every nation." Sure enough, the Preservation Hall old-timer's band, packing in the crowds in the French Quarter, was an intercultural melting pot, manned by Creoles with French, Spanish, and Anglo-American names, led by an ex-levee-camp worker from across the river, and managed by a tuba-playing German from Pennsylvania.

The jazz parades, which in Jelly's view had been the seedbed of the jazz band, are still very much alive. Even now they turn almost every weekend into a small Mardi Gras. The jazz funeral of a popular figure becomes a huge street ballet, lasting for several hours and involving a cast of hundreds or thousands of dancers, all doing their own thing. Some leap, some twist, some roll on the pavement, some dance on top of or slide about under cars, some jive on telephone poles, others caper on housetops. Often they surround the band, taking off from its beat and in turn shaping it. As one horn man told us, "We ain't got no soul—*they* [the dancing crowd] got the soul!"

By then I knew enough about world performance styles to realize that this concept and the parades themselves were very West African. For example, the orchestra—a brass-and-drum combo improvising collectively in hot rhythm, within a throng of dancers, each one taking in and feeding rhythmic cues to the musicians—is a uniquely African transformation of the European marching band. The movements of the "second line," with their foot-sliding steps, their co-acceleration in perfect synch, and their dramatic shifts in level, could be matched with shots from Africa. African elements were equally apparent in the activities of the black Indian tribes of Mardi Gras—their red-hot percussive rhythm bands, the dueling war-dances at rehearsals, the cylindrical costumes so like the bulbous raffia ancestor masks of West Africa.

"New Orleans," Jelly tells us, "has always been very organization-minded . . . " The unions and lodges, so important among the black Creoles, sponsored marching bands to bring out the black vote after the Civil War. In the bad old days of Reconstruction, when all black political activity was savagely repressed, the joyful sound of these bands was the only way that blacks could voice their democratic aspirations. Today lodges, clubs, and burial societies still flourish in New Orleans, providing a safety net of community help in black neighborhoods. On all sorts of special occasions these organizations—the Invincibles, the Big Jumpers, the Zulus, and scores more—take to the streets with their gorgeous uniforms and their irresistible street ballets, displaying an almost tribal unity and pride. As one of them told me at the end of a parade:

"We call our parades super-Sunday, that's the way we feel about it. You see all those people there that participate in your parade and you say to yourself, 'How in the world did we do it?' Well, we doin it . . . " Another man chimes in.

> "Finances are tight, people can't get jobs it's hard. So everybody need to come together. You want communication. You want happiness between the brothers and the sisters . . . "

And another voice:

> "You have your clothes made, you have your streamers made, you wants to have it all together when you hit the street, cos you gonna have a congregation of people lookin' at you. You want to look good and feel good and get out there and do some good . . . "

And more soberly:

> "The vast majority are poor people. Some of the kids want so bad to be part of it that the parents will spend their last dime so a son or a daughter can be involved. Some kids who may have got in a little trouble, you know, they know that if they get into much stuff they can't belong, so that kind of keeps them straight . . . "

These are neighborhood people talking about what the parades mean to them and to their organizations—unity, pride, and high morale. Clearly a vigorous black aesthetic is at work here. Such are the insights that Jelly's penetrating memoirs led us to.

While I was busy with other things, Rudi Blesh, the jazz pundit, without bothering to tell me about it, edited and issued most of my interview with Jelly Roll in a set of 12-inch record albums. Jelly, with his growling bedroom voice and mordant wit, became an international household god of jazz. The ethnomusicologist and ardent jazz fan Alan Merriam was, I believe, much influenced by this work. In his standard text on ethnomusicology, he recommends the in-depth interview of native musicians as the best way to understand exotic musical systems.

The Jelly Roll recordings defined the roots of jazz and led to the taping of every old-time jazz musician in the city and to the formation of the jazz archive now housed at Tulane. A more significant outcome was the establishment of recorded history as a literary and historical genre of its own. I had experimented with the idea of recorded folk history in my field work for the Library of Congress for some time before I met Jelly Roll. My notion was that the great talkers of America could, if lovingly transcribed, contribute enormous riches of prose style and varied points of views to literature. What they had to offer was not literal history, as so many oral historians have mistakenly thought, but the fruit of their life-long experience, the evocation of their periods, and their imagination and style—the things that every good writer brings us. I knew that Jelly Roll had given me, as Woody and Leadbelly had done earlier, the living *legend* of his existence. I spent five years adding the voices of other jazzmen to Jelly's account, and in polishing all this earthy spoken prose so that the reader could feel the presence of the speakers while turning the pages.

The present book, an almost best-seller in 1949 [1950], turned many people on to the idea of "oral history." Among these was Studs Terkel, who interviewed me on radio about the book when it appeared, and who has since used this "oral history" approach to create a fresh and democratic vision of American life. *Mister Jelly Roll* was, I believe, the first altogether recorded book. Since it appeared in 1949 [1950] there have been others that have kept to the mark—tapings of wise and witty talkers lovingly translated into print—such as *He Pointed Them North* by Teddy Blue and *All God's Dangers* by Theodore Rosengarten. Unfortunately, libraries are also stuffed with the boring "oral histories" of important figures and "typical" ordinary folks, with no fresh perspective to share and no style at all. In these cases a notebook serves posterity better than a tape machine.

Now it is almost time to let Jelly take over the mike.

Chapter 32

Sounds of the South

I had been recording in the field for twenty-five years—beginning with the Edison cylinder machine and every few years moving on to a better device—before stereo came along. After years of work in Europe during the '50s I returned to America to find the folk song revival, that I had earlier helped to launch, in full swing. Where Burl and Pete and Woody and Leadbelly and a few others had held sway, now there were hundreds of singers and scores of groups. Some of the young folkniks, who dominated the New York scene, asserted that there was more folk music in Washington Square on Sunday afternoon than there was in all rural America. Apparently, it made them feel like heroes to believe that they were keeping a dying tradition alive. The idea that these nice young people, who were only just beginning to learn how to play and sing in good style, might replace the glories of the real thing, frankly, horrified me. I resolved to prove them wrong. Thus in the summer of 1959, supported by Nesuhi and Ahmet Ertegun of Atlantic Records, I returned to my native South, where I had worked before, to record the singers of mountain, bayou, prison and cotton patch with state-of-the-art equipment.

In a two-month tour, which took me from Virginia through the Middle South to the Ozarks, into the Mississippi Delta and back to the Georgia Sea Islands, I found proof that the South still held a rich heritage of musical traditions, performed in a variety of fascinating and ripened styles. Ancient songs lived on and new songs were being composed. Three instruments, previously unrecorded, were discovered—the mouthbow, the cane fife and the primitive panpipe. After these stereo recordings appeared in 1961, there was no more talk about the dominance of Washington Square. In fact, many of the most devoted fans went into the field to do their own recordings.

The material for these four discs was culled out of eighty hours of field tapes. The set reflects, to some extent, what the Erteguns felt might best reach their pop audience. Yet some of the songways date back to ancient European or African origins. Others were created in the pioneer period. Still others were born yesterday. The whole collection is a testament to the creativity of the South, where country folk—people of African and British descent—continue to shape the deep songs of this country.

It is the merging of these two ancient and very different traditions that has shaped the varied Southern soundscape. There the originals in every community—largely innocent of formal musical education—could shamelessly follow their own inclinations. There the rich and contrasting musical cultures of Northwest Europe and West Africa have lived together for more than 300 years, with little interference from learned or official culture. Their illegitimate offspring—minstrel songs, the spiritual, ragtime, jazz, blues, bluegrass, cajun, country, gospel and rock—became regional, then national, and finally international idioms.

Western European melodic forms and instruments provided the base for these Southern styles, but it was the black African, highly rhythmic, collective and improvisatory approach to music-making that clearly sparked most new developments. The wonderful tunesmiths of Ireland and Scotland felt a very friendly rivalry with a people who could make every hour of the day into a rhythmic event—and then outdance Satan himself on Saturday night. The very horrors of slavery and peonage prevented us, until recently, from seeing that African performance traditions played an active, not a passive part in shaping the Southern musical outcome of this encounter.

Even though African Americans were deprived of their languages, their customs, their religions and their musical instruments, they were isolated in their own communities by race prejudice and there continued to perform like Africans. Their ancient non-verbal systems shaped a new speech, a new melodism, a new harmony, new dances, that became the very lifeblood of Southern culture. In all this they competed and collaborated with their fellow colonists from Europe, who, for their part, maintained and developed their own folk heritage while enjoying and drawing upon the heritage of their black neighbors.

I was fortunate to arrive with stereo in time to capture lively images of these tonal experiments. There were awesome ballad singers and people who made the banjo ring like sunrise—spirituals and shouts were still rocking the rural churches—the great North Alabama shape-note singers were lofting their reedy counterpoint every weekend—bluegrass was in full bloom—the axe gangs were still chanting in the river bottoms—Mississippi picnics boogied to hot fife-and-drum bands—an ancient who picked the mouth-bow for me said he had ridden with Jesse James—Fred McDowell, who was to teach the Rolling Stones, was accompanied by a lady on a comb wrapped in toilet paper.

For the first time I had plenty of great mikes, a mixer, and, best of all, stereo. Folk music which, in its natural setting, is meant to be heard in the round, comes into its own with multi-dimensionality, for more than concert music, designed to project from the stage into an auditorium. I felt wonderful, because for the first time the musicians—the critical musicians—were enthusiastic about their recordings. They beamed and wrung my hand. One old fellow, who had made a fortune selling mules, kept shoving twenty dollar bills in my pocket and thanking me for the way I'd recorded his Alabama friends.

These Sounds of the South, the outcome of two centuries of friendly musical exchange between blacks and whites, amount to something of a cultural triumph. I like to believe they stand for a hopeful future for all the fine and beautiful things that may emerge as we continue our difficult experiment in how to make this multicultural democracy actually work.

Chapter 33

Brown Girl in the Ring

> There's a brown girl in the ring,
> Tra la la la la,
> There's a brown girl in the ring,
> Tra la la la la la,
> There's a brown girl in the ring,
> Tra la la la la,
> For she looks like a sugar and a plum, plum, plum . . .

This was the refrain of the summer I spent in 1962 recording folk songs in many of the small islands of the West Indies as, one by one, they moved away from British control and into independence. The children sensed that something was in the air and—as only children can do—summed up the whole situation in a song. This was their topical song that summer, but they had many, many more—a potpourri of fragments from all their many-sourced island traditions.

My work centered on a skein of small islands (called by some the Lesser Antilles and by others the Windward and Leeward Islands) that together with Trinidad and Tobago form the southeastern edge of the Caribbean Sea. They were colonized and fought over first by Spaniards, then by Dutch, French, and English, but after the indigenous native populations had been cruelly annihilated, they were mainly populated by Ibo, Yoruba, Ashanti, and other peoples transported from West and Central Africa. This complex history can still be felt as one moves from French to English to Dutch to Spanish language zones; for no one who ever settled in these islands ever wanted to leave their fertile soils, nourishing warm climate, and lambent fish-filled seas.

In 1962, because I was to some extent an old West Indies hand, having done field work in Haiti, the Bahamas, and those southern United States that form the northern edge of the Caribbean, the Rockefeller

Foundation sent me to the Lesser Antilles with a fascinating goal in mind. At that time there was a possibility that these various island polities could be joined together with Jamaica to form a new democracy, the Federation of the West Indies. The enlightened presidents of both Jamaica and Trinidad were working hard to bring this idea to reality. My task as a folklorist was to look for the creative cultural commonalities among these many powers in support of their great dream of unity.

As in the past, I took a recording machine with me as my carte de visite and a way of documenting the things I found. Besides, I wanted to test the effect of playing back to the village singers the recordings I would make; I called the notion "cultural feedback." There were no pocket-portable speakers at that time, and I hauled onto the plane two huge loud-speakers that stood three feet high and required high-voltage power so as to display even adequately the stereo sound that I was testing out in my fieldwork.

My companions on the voyage were my then wife Toni, and later on, my daughter Anna. Wherever we recorded, we played back the music to its makers, filling mountain hamlets and village streets with the thunder of the speakers, while whole neighborhoods danced in delight. My Caribbean colleagues told me that in two or three places musical practices that were on the point of dying out were revived by that one act of sonorous support.

It was a mad voyage, planing and deplaning, hauling, heaving, unpacking, working always through the good offices of the University of the West Indies and its friends throughout the islands to establish quick and fruitful working relationships in all sorts of little villages that aren't on the big maps. Trinidad, Tobago, Martinique, Dominica, Guadeloupe, Anguilla, Nevis, Carriacou—this chain of magic places poured out their jeweled music to us in that long summer.

Back in Trinidad, the home port of the trip, I wrote my report for the Rockefeller Foundation, putting together the patterns that, as I saw them, provided a rich soil of unity for the future Federation. The most striking was this very unity. No matter what their language or dialect, the hundreds of Windward and Leeward Islanders we had met were stamped with a common Creole style. Whether their vocabularies are French-, Dutch-, or English-based, all are clearly related black transformations of West African linguistic structures.

What was true of speech was even more patently true of lifestyle and of music. In this world, music was based in rhythmic movement, whether dance, ritual, or work. At that time every task of life was still made easier and more effective by group work songs. Teams of sailors hauled the native-made sailboats into the water and raised their sails with chanteys. A group of singing Windward Islanders could put up a pleasant dwelling made of native wood and roofed with palm leaves in a day—a house that breathed cool air in the hottest weather, demanding no importations of cinder blocks or corrugated iron roofing.

Everywhere I found tidal pools and freshets of indigenous music and dance styles reflecting both the particular qualities of local life and the mainstream Creole performance style that plainly stemmed from West Africa. Africa was present in the polyrhythmic accompaniment of the music, whether played on sets of drums, created by hot multipart clapping, or sounded in the fife-and-drum bands of the northern islands or the stringed orchestras of central Trinidad and the classic jazz of Martinique.

Africa was present in the normal singing style, which was collective, the chorus overlapping its part with the leader so as to produce unexpected harmonies and hot licks, the melodies repetitious but each one forever setting some everyday phrase into a never-to-be-forgotten form. And each island had a treasure of such melodies, potentially unlimited because still growing. I believed that all of this music could become a national resource for a federated West Indies.

Among the richest veins were the children's songs encountered on every island. These songs were usually sung by clutches of young girls about to become young women, who sometimes allowed their young brothers to join in. The enunciation of these young singers who danced as they clapped and sang was hound's-tooth clean. In spite of the rapid pour of short notes and many syllables that characterized their peppery songs, every syllable was as clear as a drop of water on a palm leaf.

And as I listened, it seemed to me that these children had adopted the same performance strategy as the calypsonians of Trinidad, whose crystal enunciations reinforced their satirical pieces, which so often were aimed at bringing down their British lords and masters. And going back to my old song-game recordings in Britain, Bess Hawes and I found that the same emphasis upon crisp languaging was distinctively characteristic of British game songs. Nothing is so potent in Great Britain as a "good accent." It will open any door, as Shaw's *Pygmalion* shows us. The children of the West Indies had picked up this key for climbing the social ladder and were honing it to perfection as they sang.

And there is one other part of this pattern I wish especially to mention. I once asked a very old lady on the island of Carriacou what she felt when she sang the kissing games. She and her friends broke into squeals of old-lady laughter, and she actually ran off into the darkness, remembering perhaps what I take to be a main social purpose of these games for the girls—to teach them in a safe circle of play what they need to know for the passages of courtship soon to come.

All these things—including my still-to-be-published observations on the even more complex and numerous adult repertoires of the Lesser Antilles—went into report of the Rockefeller Foundation and were sent on to Federation movers and shakers. Struggles for power between the politicians of the islands sank the scheme for federation long ago, but its essential dream, which many shared, may still not be vain.

My own subsequent studies of world performance styles show that the West Indies, in spite of underlying linguistic differences, constitutes perhaps the most culturally unified area of its geographic extent in the world. This is because the major population of every island has the same experience—transportation from Africa, enslavement by Europeans, and the subsequent development of a renewed and rich Creole African culture based in their hardworking and fête-filled lives.

Another believer in this dream of a new and unified democratic empire where Creole cultures could flower and people could dance and sing together across language lines was my longtime comrade and colleague J. D. Elder. Dr. Elder heard I was coming to Port of Spain on the Rockefeller mission. He met me at the plane, took me in hand, and introduced me to the incredible culture of Trinidad in two magic weeks. We have been working together ever since.

Among Dr. Elder's achievements as primary-school teacher and community development officer in his young days was to encourage the growth of the steel bands of Trinidad as an outlet for the restless youths of Port of Spain. He also helped develop the Best Village Folklore competition and still later the Tobago Heritage Festival movement on his home island of Tobago. He spent four yeas in Nigeria as a research professor at the University of Ibadan and dean of the Faculty of Social Sciences and Law at the University of Maiduguri, Nigeria. Upon his return to the Caribbean, he served as minister of culture for Tobago and as consultant for culture to the Ministry of Youth, Sport, Culture, and Creative Arts for the Government of Trinidad and Tobago.

Dr. Elder has written widely on calypso, the steel band, the Yoruba

religion in the old and new worlds, and Caribbean folktales. But his seminal work, *Song Games of Trinidad and Tobago*, has become a classic in international children's literature. Excerpts from his account, printed here, of
growing up with singing games in his native island of Tobago take us
straight into the heart, the very process, of cultural growth. We collaborated on this memoir in an amusing way. First, J. D. wrote the story in his
fine Dickensian prose. We both felt it was a little stiff. Then he retold it
on tape. Next I cut the two versions together into a lengthy autobio-
graphical account, portions of which you may read in part five, "I Recall
. . . " His vivid memories, as well as the actual voices of the children and
adults who so generously recorded for this project some thirty years ago,
bring our book alive and refresh us all with yet another demonstration
of the unstoppable forces of human creativity.

Chapter 34

Introduction to Katharine D. Newman, *Never Without a Song: The Years and Songs of Jennie Devlin, 1865–1952*

In our day at last, we are hearing the woman's side of the human story told, not as in *Pamela* and *Moll Flanders* by men, but by women. The heroine of this singing biography—and she is heroic—takes us into the little-known world of the serving maids and working-class women of middle America early in this century. Jennie Devlin was everybody's slavey, and many were the slings and arrows of outrageous fortune that fell upon her. Her staying power reminds one of the indomitable protagonists of *Great Expectations* and of *Moll Flanders*. Indeed, the account of how this unwanted waif became a serving maid, survived her bitter destiny, found a mate, and managed to raise a family has a true Dickensian flavor.

Jennie differed from Pip and Molly in being a lover of ballads. Singing, she makes clear, kept her heart alive through all her troubles. For her the beloved old songs summed up the truth of existence. They broadened her view of human destiny, particularly that of other women, so that she felt less alone in her own sorrows. By immediately learning and keeping in memory every song that appealed to her, little Jennie Hess [Devlin] became a cultivated woman. Indeed, she was a folklorist, a historian of her period, storing up a treasure that all may now enjoy, thanks to the sensitive and devoted labors of Kay Newman, the author of this volume.

Samuel Pepys, the seventeenth-century diarist, early noted the importance of women in transmitting native musical traditions. In one entry Pepys unfavorably compares the performance of a fashionable opera singer to that of the English actress Mrs. Knipps. "She sings mighty well . . . just after the Italian manner, but yet do not please me like one of Mrs. Krupp's songs to a good English tune . . . [I] was in perfect pleasure to hear her little Scotch song, *Barbara Allen* . . . " This middle-class Londoner extolled the musical talents of the serving maids of his household. "After dinner, talking with my wife and making Mrs. Gosnell (the maid) sing . . . I am mightily pleased with her humor and her singing." And of another maid, Mary Mercer, he wrote, "It being a very fine moonshine, my wife and Mercer came into the garden and my business being done, we sang till about twelve at night, with mighty pleasure to ourselves and neighbors."

These merry, musical maidservants of the seventeenth century were the cultural forebears of Jennie Devlin, who sang all day long at her work and was "as good a whistler as ever puckered a lip." She and they belong to a feminine mainstream that has kept the oral traditions alive across the centuries. Indeed in my lifelong experience in recording folksongs, it is the women who most stand out as the great song rememberers.

In the Haitian *vaudou* temples, the female servitors, the *hounsi*, lead the songs that bring the gods to the dancing floor. I have spent days recording these exquisite tunesmiths, as I did later on taping the great Bessie Jones of the Georgia Sea Islands, who required two months to tape the hundreds of folk songs that she knew. In the far Hebrides I found that the ancient Gallic work song traditions belonged to the women—the songs for quieting and milking the cows on the shieling, and the rowdy songs for working up the tweed, essential to the safety of their fishermen husbands on the freezing waters of the western isles.

Two women of the Stewart clan of northern Scotland—Belle Stewart and the formidable Jeannie Robertson with her orientally ornamented style—stand out as the stars of contemporary British ballad singing. Majestic Texas Gladden, of the musical Smiths of the Blue Ridge, knew a fine version of every ballad I could think to ask her for and performed each one with the elegance of a ballet dancer. Way over in Arkansas, I met shy Mrs. Ollie Gilbert, and induced her to sing one ballad for me. Later collectors overcame her shyness and eventually Ollie poured out a river of more than one thousand folk songs. Jennie Devlin, as this collection illustrates, belongs in this select company, but there is more in her book than the songs.

It was a Kentucky woman, a true sister to Jennie, who taught us that traditional songs were not mere relics but had powerful emotional and social significance for the singers. Aunt Molly Jackson was possessed of great talent for song and a fearless intellect. Not only did she compose radical songs to help bring the union into the poverty-ridden coal camps of eastern Kentucky, but she remembered how many of her traditional songs had also functioned as means of feminine protest. According to Aunt

Molly, there was a song sung by poor young girls like herself to protest against their forced marriage to some rich but unattractive old man:

> Old man come courtin' me one day,
> But I wouldn't have him
> He come down the lane, walkin' on his cane,
> With his durned old beard a-fallin' . . .

Aunt Molly's comments on women's problems in the southern back-woods provided a far more meaningful setting for the songs than the usual scholarly notes, and I threaded them through *Our Singing Country* (1941) and subsequent Lomax publications. These oral head-notes provided so much insight on the folk process that, in spite of the limitations of disc recording, I began to use the extra space on the ends of discs to elicit salient comments from the singers. With great talkers like Aunt Molly, Woody Guthrie, Jelly Roll Morton—these interviews grew into singing biographies. Indeed, the publication of the recorded saga of Jelly Roll, the flamboyant New Orleans jazzman, established the fascination of the genre that came much later to be called "oral history."

It was at this point in the growth of field recording method that Katharine Newman wrote me at the Library of Congress about the extraordinary singer she had found in New Jersey. This was welcome news because we lacked material from the Middle Atlantic area for our survey of American folk song. When we met, Jennie Devlin and I took to each other at once, as the chapter "Somebody," in this volume, makes clear. She had a fine quiet way with ballads, a trait she shared with the singers I had recently been recording in New England. She sang solo and unaccompanied in the impersonal style of the balladeer, so focused on the importance of the text that she was surprised when I expressed interest in the tunes.

Because of her northeastern style I felt quite confident that she would give me the risqué songs that she knew. I had discovered that in working-class New England, women were not excluded from the circle when bawdy ballads were sung. So while the other ladies whispered together in an upstairs bedroom, Jennie unblushingly confided in me a few salty rhymes, such as

> Some for the girl that dresses neat,
> Some for the girl that kisses sweet,
> But I'm for the girl with the lily white thighs,
> With a hole in her belly like a dead hog's eye.

Jennie was, in most respects, a reticent northeasterner, and it took years of painstaking interview and careful digging before the present singer biography was achieved. It is a deeply moving story, with sensitive insights into the heart of a folk singer. This unwanted child whose mother had literally tried to throw her away loved to sing the ballad of the lady who was haunted by the ghosts of her neglected babies. Small wonder that James Bird, who was hung for a crime he did not commit, was her favorite ballad hero, raised as she was by a series of demanding foster parents.

Not only did those foster parents work her like an animal, but, because they did not want to lose this perfect servant to marriage, they warned her against men and refused to allow her to go out. The night she was married, she was forced to stay in her room and her new husband was shown the door. Most males in her folk songs were threatening figures, like the murderous Henry Green and the cruel House Carpenter. In this respect life fulfilled her fantasied expectations; she was abandoned, sometimes for years at a time, by her charming but wayward husband, and left to bring up three children with only the skills of a perfect housewife to fall back on. Nonetheless indomitable Jennie brought her family through and even cared for her husband in his declining years.

We must be grateful to Katharine Newman for weaving this poignant life history together, and to Jennie Devlin for teaching us how important song is in the lives of the women who do the work of the world.

Alan Lomax Bibliography

"'Sinful' Songs of the Southern Negro," *Southwest Review*, vol. XIX, no. 2, Winter 1934, 105–131.

(with John A. Lomax). *American Ballads and Folk Songs*. New York: The Macmillan Company, 1934.

(with John A. Lomax). *Negro Folk Songs as Sung by Lead Belly*. New York: The Macmillan Company, 1936.

(with John A. Lomax). *Cowboy Songs*. New York: The Macmillan Company, 1937.

"Haitian Journey—Search for Native Folklore," *Southwest Review*, XXIII, no. 2, January 1938, 125–147.

Review of Arthur Hudson, "Folk Songs of Mississippi and Their Background," *Journal of American Folklore*, 1938, 211–213.

"Music in Your Own Back Yard," *The American Girl*, October 1940, 5–7, 46, 49.

"Songs of the American Folk," *Modern Music*, vol. 18, Jan.–Feb. 1941, 137–139.

(with John A. Lomax). *Our Singing Country: A Second Volume of American Ballads & Folk Songs*. New York: The Macmillan Company, 1941.

"Of Men and Books," interview with Alan Lomax, *Northwestern University on the Air*, vol. 1, no. 18, January 31, 1942 (on CBS).

(with Sidney Robertson Cowell). *Americana Folk Song and Folk Lore: A Regional Bibliography*. New York: Hinds, Hayden & Eldredge, Inc., 1942.

Check-list of Recorded Songs in the English Language in the Archive of American Folk Song in July, 1940. Washington, DC: Music Division, Library of Congress, 1942. 3 vols.

Preface, *14 Traditional Spanish Songs from Texas*. Washington, DC: Music Division, Pan American Union, 1942, 1–2.

"Reels and Work Songs," in *75 Years of Freedom: Commemoration of the 75th Anniversary of the Proclamation of the 13th Amendment to the Constitution of the United States*. Washington, DC: Library of Congress, 1943, 27–36.

"Archive of American Folk Song," *Journal of American Folklore*, vol. 56, 1943, 59–61.

(with Svatava Jakobsonova). "Freedom Songs of the United Nations." Washington, DC: Office of War Information, 1943.

"Mister Ledford and the TVA," Erik Barnouw, ed., *Radio Drama in Action: Twenty-Five Plays of a Changing World*. New York: Rinehart & Co., 1945, 51– 58.

(with John A. Lomax). *Folk Songs: USA*. New York: Duell, Sloan and Pierce, 1946.

"The Best of the Ballads," *Vogue*, Dec. 1, 1946, 208, 291–296.

(with Benjamin A. Botkin). "Folklore, American," in *Ten Eventful Years. Encyclopedia Britannica*, 1947, 359–367.

"America Sings the Saga of America," *New York Times Magazine*, January 26, 1947, 16, 41–42.

"I Got the Blues," *Common Ground*, vol. 8, Summer 1948, 38–52.

Foreword, *The People's Song Book*. New York: Boni and Gaer, 1948.

"Tribal Voices in Many Tongues," *Saturday Review of Literature*, vol. 32, May 28, 1949, 43–44, 54–55.

Mister Jelly Roll. New York: Duell, Sloan and Pierce, 1950.

Foreword, Jean Ritchie, *A Garland of Mountain Song*. New York: Broadcast Music, Inc., 1953.

Harriet and Her Harmonium. London: Faber and Faber, 1955.

"Folk Song Style: Notes on a Systematic Approach to the Study of Folk Song," *Journal of the International Folk Music Council*, vol. VIII, 1956, 48–50.

(with Peggy Seeger). *American Folk Guitar: A Book of Instruction*. New York: Robbins Music Corporation, 1957.

"Skiffle: Why Is It So Popular?", *Melody Maker*, August 31, 1957, 3.

"Skiffle: Where Is It Going?", *Melody Maker*, September 7, 1957, 5.

Rainbow Sign. New York: Duell, Sloan and Pierce, 1959.

"The 'Folkniks'–and the Songs They Sing," *Sing Out!*, vol. 9, no. 1, Summer 1959, 30–31.

"Leadbelly's Songs," in John A. Lomax and Alan Lomax, eds., *The Leadbelly Legend: A Collection of WorldFamous Songs by Huddie Ledbetter*. rev. ed. New York: Folkways Music Publishers, 1965, 6. (Originally published 1959.)

"Bluegrass Background: Folk Music with Overdrive," *Esquire*, vol. 52, October 1959, 108.

"Folk Song Style: Musical Style and Social Context," *American Anthropologist*, vol. 61, no. 6, December 1959, 927–954.

"Saga of a Folksong Hunter," *HiFi/Stereo Review*, vol. 4, no. 5, May 1960, 40–46.

Carol Calkins with Alan Lomax, "Getting to Know Folk Music," *House Beautiful*, April 1960, 140–141, 204–207.

The Folk Songs of North America. Garden City, NY: Doubleday, 1960.

"Zora Neale Hurston—A Life of Negro Folklore," *Sing Out!*, vol. 10, no. 3, Oct.–Nov. 1960, 12–13.

"Folk Song Traditions Are All Around Us," *Sing Out!*, vol. 11, no. 1, February–March 1961, 17–18.

"Aunt Molly Jackson: An Appreciation," *Kentucky Folklore Record*, vol. VII, no. 4, October–December 1961, 131–132.

"The Adventure of Learning, 1960," ACLS *Newsletter*, vol. 13, February 1962, 10–13.

"Song Structure and Social Structure," *Ethnology*, vol. 1, no. 4, January 1962, 425–452.

(with Edith Crowell Trager). "Phonotactique de Chant Populaire," *L'Homme*, January–April 1964, 5–55.

Foreword, Jean Ritchies, *Folk Songs of the Southern Appalachains as Sung by Jean Ritchies*. New York: Oak Publications, 1965.

"The Good and the Beautiful in Folksong," *Journal of American Folklore*, July–September 1967, 213–235.

(with Woody Guthrie and Pete Seeger). *Hard-Hitting Songs for Hard-Hit People*. New York: Oak Publications, 1967.

"Special Features of Sung Communication," in *Essays on the Verbal and Visual Arts*, Proceedings of the 1966 Annual Spring Meeting, American Ethnological Society, University of Washington Press, 1967.

(with contributions by the Cantometrics Staff and with the editorial assistance of Edwin E. Erickson), *Folk Song Style and Culture*, New Brunswick, NJ: Transaction Books, 1968.

(with Irmgard Bartenieff and Forrestine Paulay). "Choreometrics: A Method for the Study of Cross-Cultural Pattern in Film," *Research Film*, vol. 6, no. 6, 1969, 505–517.

"Africanisms in New World Negro Music," *Research and Resources of Haiti: Papers of the Conference on Research and Resources of Haiti*. New York: Research Institute for the Study of Man, 1969, 118–154.

(with Raoul Abdul). *3000 Years of Black Poetry*. New York: Dodd, Mead and Company, 1969.

"The Homogeneity of African-Afro-American Musical Style," Norman E. Whitten, Jr. and John F. Szwed, eds., *Afro-American Anthropology: Contemporary Perspectives*. New York: Free Press, 1970, 181–201.

"Choreometrics and Ethnographic Filmmaking: Toward an Ethnographic Film Archive," *Filmmaker's Newsletter*, vol. 4, no. 4, February 1971.

"Appeal for Cultural Equity," *World of Music*, vol. XIV, no. 2, 1972.

"The Evolutionary Taxonomy of Culture," *Science*, vol. 177, July 21, 1972, 228–239.

"Brief Progress Report: Cantometrics-Choreometrics Project," *Yearbook of the International Folk Music Council*, vol. 4, 1972, 142–145.

"Cinema, Science, and Cultural Renewal," *Current Anthropology*, vol. 14, 1973, 474–480.

"Cross-Cultural Factors in Phonological Change," *Language in Society*, vol. 2, 1973, 161–175.

"Singing: Folk and Non-Western Singing," *Encyclopedia Britannica*, 15th ed., 1974, 790–794.

"Appeal for Cultural Equity," *Journal of Communication*, vol. 27, Spring 1977, 125–138.

"Cantometrics: An Approach to the Anthropology of Music," *Lifelong Learning*, vol. 46, April 11, 1977.

"A Stylistic Analysis of Speech," *Language in Society*, vol. 6, 1977, 15–36.

(with Conrad Arensberg). "A World Evolutionary Classification of Cultures by Subsistence Systems," *Current Anthropology*, vol. 18, 1977, 659–708.

Cantometrics: An Approach to the Anthropology of Music. Berkeley: University of California Media Extension Center, 1977. Audiocassettes and handbook.

"The Language of Song," in Stanley Diamond, ed., *Papers in Honor of Gene Weltfish*, Mouton, 1980.

"Folk Music in the Roosevelt Era," in *Folk Music in the Roosevelt White House: A Commemorative Program*. Washington, DC: Office of Folklife Programs, Smithsonian Institution, 1982, 14–17.

Notes to *Louisiana Cajun and Creole Music, 1934: The Lomax Recordings*. Swallow Records LP-8003-3.

Introduction (with Joshua Berrett), *John Lomax, Cowboy Songs and Other Frontier Ballads*. New York: Collier's, 1986, xi–xxxv.

Preface, *Mr. Jelly Roll*. New York: Pantheon, 1993, vii–xiv.

Land Where the Blues Began. New York: Pantheon, 1993.

Introduction to *Sounds of the South*, Atlantic Records, 782496-2, 1993.

Introduction to Katharine D. Newman, *Never without a Song: The Years and Songs of Jennie Devlin, 1865–1952*. Urbana: University of Illinois Press, 1995, xiii–xvi.

(with J. D. Elder and Bess Lomax Hawes). *Brown Girl in the Ring: An Anthology of Song Games from the Eastern Caribbean*. New York: Pantheon, 1997.

About the Contributors

Gage Averill is Chair of the Music Department at New York Univeristy. He is the co-editor of *Making and Selling Culture* (1996), as well as the author of *A Day for the Hunter, A Day for the Prey: Popular Music and Power in Haiti* (1997), and *Four Parts, No Waiting: A Social History of American Barbership Harmony* (2002). He is the editor of a book series for Routledge, *Perspectives on Global Pop*, and is currently working on the release of Alan and Elizabeth Lomax's 1936–37 Haitian recordings for Rounder Records.

Matthew Barton is a music writer, producer of education audio materials, and music consultant for film and television. His association with Alan Lomax began in 1984 and included work on the *American Patchwork*, Cantometric, and Choreometric projects. Since 1996, he has been the production coordinator of the Alan Lomax Collection series on Rounder Records, and is currently Archivist of the Alan Lomax Archives.

Ronald D. Cohen is Professor of History at Indiana University Northwest. He is the author of numerous books and articles, including *Rainbow Quest: The Folk Music Revival and American Society, 1940–1970* (2002), and is the co-producer of three CD compilations, including *Songs for Political Action; Goodnight, Irene: The Weavers, 1949–1953;* and *The Best of Broadside*. He is currently completing *Golden Threads: An Illustrated History of Folk Music in the U.S., 1900–1970*.

Ed Kahn (1938–2002), as a graduate student helped organize the John Edwards Memorial Foundation (JEMF) at UCLA in 1962, and in 1964 he began co-editing the *JEMF Newsletter*. He wrote the liner notes for a range of albums, including *Pete Steele: Banjo Tunes and Songs, The Blue Sky Boys,* and the reissue of *Smoky Mountain Ballads*. After a long hiatus, while writing for computer magazines, he returned to folk music in the late 1980s, contributing the liner notes for the Bear Family Darby and Tarlton CD box and two volumes of Arhoolie's *The Carter Family on Border Radio*.

Andrew L. Kaye completed his doctorate in ethnomusicology at Columbia University and is Assistant Professor of Music at Albright College in Reading, Pennsylvania, where he teaches courses in world music, electronic music, and cinema. His association with Alan Lomax began in 1983, when he was hired to assist in the preparation of the *American Patchwork* television series. In 1996, working with Matthew Barton, he co-edited Rounder Records' 13-volume *Southern Journey* series in the Alan Lomax Collection, as well as the collection's sample CD and booklet.

Sources and Permissions

All material in this book written by Alan Lomax is used with permission, with the exceptions indicated below. The original publication information for each piece follows.

I. 1934–1950: THE EARLY COLLECTING YEARS

1. "'Sinful' Songs of the Southern Negro," *Southwest Review*, vol. XIX, no. 2, Winter 1934, 105–131.

2. "Haitian Journey—Search for Native Folklore," *Southwest Review*, XXIII, no. 2, January 1938, 125–147.

3. "Music in Your Own Back Yard," *The American Girl*, October 1940, 5–7, 46, 49.

4. "Songs of the American Folk," *Modern Music*, vol. 18, Jan.–Feb. 1941, 137–139.

5. Preface, *Our Singing Country*. New York: The Macmillan Company, 1941, 9–16.

6. Preface, *14 Traditional Spanish Songs From Texas*. Washington, DC: Music Division, Pan American Union, 1942, 1–2.

7. "Reels and Work Songs," in *75 Years of Freedom: Commemoration of the 75th Anniversary of the Proclamation of the 13th Amendment to the Constitution of the United States* (Washington, DC: Library of Congress [1943], 27–36 (originally comments at a concert in Washington, DC, December 20, 1940).

8. "Mister Ledford and the TVA," Erik Barnouw, ed., *Radio Drama in Action: Twenty-Five Plays of a Changing World* (New York: Rinehart & Co., 1945), 51–58.

9. "America Sings the Saga of America," *New York Times Magazine*, January 26, 1947, 16, 41–42, copyright © 1947 by the New York Times Co. Reprinted by permission.

10. "Folk Music in the Roosevelt Era," in *Folk Music in the Roosevelt White House: A Commemorative Program*. Washington, DC: Office of Folklife Programs, Smithsonian Institution, 1982, 14–17.

II. THE 1950S: WORLD MUSIC

11. "Tribal Voices in Many Tongues," *Saturday Review of Literature*, vol. 32, May 28, 1949, 43–44, 54–55.

12. Opening remarks on "Making Folklore Available," Stith Thompson, ed., *Four Symposia on Folklore: Held at Midcentury International Folklore Conference. Indiana University, July 21–August 4, 1950*. Bloomington: Indiana University Press, 1953, 155–162.

13. Manuscript, *Galacia* (written ca. 1960), 10 pps.

14. Introduction to the Columbia World Library of Folk and Primitive Music. vols. xv and xvi: *Northern and Central Italy and Southern Italy and the Islands*. Columbia Records KL 5173 & 5174. With Diego Carpitella. ca. 1955.

15. The Folk Song of Italy (proposal), ca. 1955. 2 pps.

16. "Folk Song Style: Notes on a Systematic Approach to the Study of Folk Song," *Journal of the International Folk Music Council*, vol. VIII, 1956, 48–50.

17. "Skiffle: Why Is It So Popular?", *Melody Maker*, August 31, 1957, 3; combined with "Skiffle: Where Is It Going?", *Melody Maker*, September 7, 1957, 5.

18. "Folk Song Style: Musical Style and Social Context," *American Anthropologist*, vol. 61, no. 6, December 1959, 927–954.

19. "Saga of a Folksong Hunter," *HiFi/Stereo Review*, vol. 4, no. 5, May 1960, 40–46.

III. THE FOLK REVIVAL (1960s)

20. "The 'Folkniks'—and The Songs They Sing," *Sing Out!*, vol. 9, no. 1, Summer 1959, 30–31, copyright © *Sing Out!* Magazine.

21. "Leadbelly's Songs," in John A. Lomax and Alan Lomax, eds., *The Leadbelly Legend: A Collection of World Famous Songs by Huddie Ledbetter*. rev. ed. New York: Folkways Music Publishers, 1965, 6. (Originally published 1959.)

22. "Bluegrass Background: Folk Music with Overdrive," *Esquire*, vol. 52, October 1959, 108.

23. Carol Calkins with Alan Lomax, "Getting to Know Folk Music," *House Beautiful*, April 1960, 140–141, 204–207.

24. "Folk Song Traditions Are All Around Us," *Sing Out!*, vol. 11, no. 1, Feb.–March 1961, 17–18, copyright © *Sing Out!* Magazine.

25. "The Good and the Beautiful in Folksong," *Journal of American Folklore*, July–September 1967, 213–235.

IV. CANTOMETRICS AND CULTURAL EQUITY: THE ACADEMIC YEARS

26. "Song Structure and Social Structure," *Ethnology*, vol. 1, no. 4, January 1962, 425–452.

27. "Choreometrics: A Method for the Study of Cross-Cultural Pattern in Film," *Research Film*, vol. 6, no. 6, 1969, 505–517.

28. "Appeal for Cultural Equity," *Journal of Communication*, vol. 27, Spring 1977, 125–138.

29. "Cinema, Science, and Cultural Renewal," *Current Anthropology*, vol. 14, 1973, 474–480, by permission of the University of Chicago Press.

V. FINAL WRITINGS

30. Grant Proposal regarding the Global Jukebox, *ca.* 1992.

31. Preface to *Mr. Jelly Roll* (New York: Pantheon, 1993), vii–xiv.

32. Introduction to *Sounds of the South*, Atlantic series reissue, ca. 1993.

33. Foreword, *Brown Girl in the Ring* (New York: Pantheon, 1997), ix–xii.

34. Introduction to Katharine D. Newman, *Never Without a Song: The Years and Songs of Jennie Devlin, 1865–1952* (Urbana: University of Illinois Press, 1995), xiii–xvi.

Index

The text of this book was composed in Legacy Serif, with Akzidenz Grotesk and Trajan display faces. Book design by Dutton & Sherman Design. Printed and bound in the United States of America by Sheridan Books, Inc.

TRACK LIST—LOMAX ANTHOLOGY CD

NB: Tracks 1, 3, 6, and 7 are excerpts from a speech given by Alan Lomax on March 7, 1989, at the New York Public Library as part of the "Witnesses" program of the Celeste Bartos Forum. All other tracks recorded by Alan Lomax except as noted.

1) Comments on early days of collecting with his father, John Lomax.

2) Go Down Old Hannah
   Performed by Ernest Williams and group.
   Recorded by John and Alan Lomax at Central State Farm, Sugarland, Texas, in December 1933.
   From "Deep River of Song: Big Brazos" (Rounder 1826).
   Further comments on this song can be found on p. 24.

3) "Poor Farmer" (story and song)
   These events are more fully described by Lomax on pp. 10–11, 92–93, and 173–174.

4) Excerpt from "Mr. Ledford and the TVA" radio program. Recorded in the summer of 1941. The script for the full program can be found on pp. 79–85.

5) Excerpt from "Your Ballad Man" radio program. Recorded in New York City on January 12, 1948. This program is described on pp. 98–99.

6) Comments on Spanish singing style
   Lomax's detailed analysis of Spanish singing can be found on pp. 154–156.

7) Cantar de Vendimia (grape trampling song)
   Performed by a mixed chorus.
   Recorded in Ourense, Galicia, Spain, in November 1952.
   From "The Spanish Recordings: Galicia" (Rounder 1761).

8) Comments on the "Tralalero" singers of Genoa, Italy
   Lomax's detailed analysis of Italian singing style can be found pp. 156–161.

9) La Partenza
   Performed by an all-male chorus of approximately 25 members.
   Recorded at the Rirovo dei Facchini (Longshoremen's Inn), Genoa, Italy, on October 15, 1954.
   From "Italian Treasury: The Tralaleri of Genoa" (Rounder 1802).

10) "Sing Christmas," introduction
    Recorded in Birmingham, England, on December 25, 1957.
    From "Sing Christmas and the Turn of the Year" (Rounder 1850).
    A description of Lomax's BBC activities can be found on p. 102.

11) Mary & Martha Is Bound to Wear the Crown-O
    Performed by a group of women at La Resource, Carriacou, West Indies.
    Recorded on August 2, 1962.
    From "Caribbean Voyage: Brown Girl in the Ring" (Rounder 1716).
    These recordings sessions are described in detail on pp. 336–340.

Rounder Records proudly presents
The Alan Lomax Collection,
all remastered in 20-bit digital sound.

Order these and other volumes in *The Alan Lomax Collection* at www.rounder.com

Texas Gladden:
Ballad Legacy

Deep River of Song: Big Brazos,
Texas Prison Recordings 1933 & 1934

The Land Where the Blues Began

Italian Voyage:
Folk Music and Song of Italy

Caribbean Voyage:
Caribbean Sampler

Hobart Smith
Blue Ridge Legacy

Alan Lomax Collection Sampler

Fred McDowell
First Recordings

Available Everywhere • 1-800-ROUNDER • www.rounder.com